OIL
POWER

OIL POWER

Carl Solberg

 MASON / CHARTER

NEW YORK 1976

Printed in the United States of America

FIRST PRINTING

Library of Congress Cataloging in Publication Data
Solberg, Carl, 1915-
    Oil power.

    Bibliography: p.
    Includes index.
    1.   Petroleum industry and trade—United States—
History.   2.   United States—Politics and government
—20th century.   I.   Title.
HD9565.S6   338.2'7'2820973   75-29034
ISBN 0-88405-126-9

To T. S., D. S., S. S., and A. S.

Contents

Introduction

Writing a history of oil requires the nose of a detective, the ear of a lawyer, the eye of an accountant, the stomach of a statistician, and the patience of Job. I claim none of these virtues. I have discovered in my searches, however, about the oil industry's sponsoring of books. No sector of American society has been more guarded in its disclosures. Practically everything that has been published about oil over the years appears to have been subsidized, or in some way subject to approval. Symbolically, a library copy I used of the most authoritative history of the petroleum industry, an admirable work by Professor Harold Williamson and his colleagues at the Northwestern University School of Business, was stamped "Gift of the American Petroleum Institute."

My own book, though not stylistically polemical, carries messages. First, it bears witness to the universal truth set forth by double allegory in Balzac's great novel *The Skin of Chagrin.* Oil is America's skin of chagrin. In Balzac's story it was a remarkable jackass's hide owned by a young man. This magic piece of skin granted the young man's every wish—but shrank each time the wish was granted. In the end, Balzac's Faustian figure came to know, much as our nation, with its terrific natural bounty of oil, is now being rudely taught, that every individual excess exacts its price. After two centuries of untrammeled industrial growth, all wayfarers on earth are being instructed in this law. To our chagrin, its reality for America in the 1970s with respect to petroleum has become too evident for much comment.

Second, this book asserts the power of oil in America. It says that oil became king in its time in much the same way that cotton was king a century and a quarter ago, with an implication that the oil kingdom, like that of cotton before it, is riding for a fall.

By mid-twentieth century, oil came to permeate and influence our private lives, and dominated and shaped much of our public one. As much as anything, this was because oil served a fundamental American urge for movement, for acceleration, for speed. Oil is not simply power but flowing power, inimitably suited to the dynamism of a nation that from the frontier to the freeway has always been on the go. With our twentieth-century machines, oil enabled us to move around as never before—anytime, anywhere. Oil, both as gasoline in the tank and as fuel oil and gas piped to freestanding suburban houses, kept us shuttling like electrons around our metropolitan space.

Though already first in war and first in the car-loving hearts of our countrymen, oil did not supplant coal as our prime source of energy until after the second World War. Then, in that strange time of neither war nor peace, oil and gas lifted America through a tremendous trajectory of expansion to the peak of its power. In those years the major oil companies, which had grown to gigantic size by taking out the greater part of our domestic oil wealth, leaped for greater growth to producing oil overseas. We built an imperial system that tapped the fabulous fields of the Middle East for the reconstructed economies of America's European and Japanese clients.

The system was not only profitable, however; it was vulnerable. The postcolonial oil lands of the Middle East, where the United States had to compete with the Russians for influence, seized control of their oil at precisely the moment the United States, having run through its own most accessible deposits, needed to import oil from the Persian Gulf. The Arab oil countries, making war against Israel, embargoed oil to the United States for giving arms aid to the Israelis. Torn between national origins and multinational exigencies, the major oil companies obeyed orders to embargo oil to their own country and boost prices fivefold to all (making huge short-term profits in the interval before they were, in turn, expropriated). The effect was to raise world oil prices to undreamed of levels, precipitate our energy shortage, fuel the fires of inflation, tip international trade balances into worldwide recession, and drive everybody to seeking out substitutes for oil.

Thirdly and finally, this book says that oil probably has had its day. The calls to regulate or even nationalize the industry are reminiscent of British and French moves to take over coal in the

1930s and 1940s, when that industry failed to keep up with economic needs. The splurge, the unbridled quarter-century burst is over: oil has released its energy, and we face the necessity of finding other sources.

No work of American social, economic, or political history has fixed upon this particular conjuncture of oil and American destiny. But beyond the primal elements of great spaces demanding mobility and great resources inviting extravagance, evidences abound; and I have looked for them in the evolution of the Truman Doctrine, the Marshall Plan, détentism, and other international policies, as well as in the output-curbing arrangements, the suburban housing and high-way-building programs, the railroad-and-tramway scuttling, and other automobile-oriented domestic policies by which oil got into the very bloodstream of the nation.

I wish to thank Columbia University, where I was a Visiting Scholar in the Department of History, and the New York Public Library, where I worked in the Frederick Lewis Allen room, for sanctuary and succor. The book owes a signal debt to the encouragement and criticism of Professor Henry F. Graff, who read all early drafts. It could not have been completed without the assistance of Eugene Sheehy and his superb staff at Butler Library, Mrs. Wanda Randall of the Dulles Library in Princeton, and the dedicated professionals of the great institution at Forty-second Street.

The following made suggestions and comments or criticized parts of the manuscript: Fred Allvine, John Banwell, Per Dahl, Thomas B. Davis, Robert Engler, Edwin Herricks, Jacob Hurewitz, Kenneth Jackson, Alfred E. Kahn, Douglass North, Jim Parkinson, Richard W. Solberg, John Tompkins, and Sam Welles. Others who lent help were John Berry, Shelby Brewer, Roger Carlsmith, Barry Good, M. King Hubbert, Dhun Irani, Anne Michaels, Sheldon Novick, Edward Symonds, and Harry Turton. William H. Forbis read the entire manuscript. With heart and hand, Tom Lipscomb and Peg Parkinson aided, respectively, at the beginning and at the end.

PART ONE

Onstream

1

The Force that Makes America Go

An appraisal of the America of our times need not wait upon an historian of the twenty-first century to look back and note the primacy of oil. Oil has resettled our population, elected our presidents, swayed our foreign policy, and legislated our morality. Oil has not only fueled our wars—the two World Wars, Korea and Vietnam—but is equally the sinew of our might in peacetime: it takes oil to be a superpower.

Of the fossil fuels ripped from the earth by modern industrialism, oil from the first was thought to be a peculiarly American form of wealth. America produced the most and, with the growing use of the internal combustion engine, consumed the most. Once oil and gas had ousted coal as the principal source of energy, America was on its way to the zenith of its power. Even when oil was found in other countries, Americans exploited it—almost as if by birthright.

The primacy of oil is due in large measure to a very special quality: it flows. As an adjective, the term *fluid* is not broad enough to convey the dimensions of this extraordinary property. From the time of oil's discovery in Pennsylvania in 1859, experts have spoken of its fugaciousness, or fugacity. This flowing and fugitive quality of oil (there is something slippery and elusive about the stuff) has made its pursuit and capture underground the quintessential venture of risk-taking capitalism—and thus for better or worse fostered and prolonged in the United States the dynamic of free enterprise when other countries were turning to socialism.

The fact that oil flows also led, through control of its transportation, to the emergence first in the oil business of the form of the supercorporation, then known as the trust, on which all large-scale enterprise in this country has since been patterned. Oil, rewarding both risk and its avoidance, thus produced the prototypical modern business organization.

It is oil's fugacity that won it preeminence over coal as an energy source. Oil, once found, is not produced; it is liquidated. After the second World War, when John L. Lewis and his United Mineworkers cut coal supplies by striking every spring, oil, liquidated and processed with no such need for human labor, became the driving force for the nation's terrific postwar expansion. Between 1945 and 1960, the use of oil and gas doubled as they generated the power for such industries as steel, cement, metalworking, glass; their use doubled again in the next fifteen years as they took over the ultimate industrial workhorse task and heated the boilers for manufacturing electricity in the nation's power plants. It was during these years that oil and gas built a giant new petrochemical industry, which clothed the people and almost every artifact they bought in plastic. It was also then that oil led American enterprise overseas in the formation of the biggest of the nation-dwarfing multinational corporations. Energizing a worldwide trade boom, oil also provided its number one cargo.

Oil, the lifeblood of industry, does not course through pipelines and tankers only to refineries, power plants, and factories. It also flows through pipes and tank trucks to homes in every corner of the land to heat, to cool, to generate power for innumerable appliances. And, of course, it pours through filling station hoses into automobile gas tanks—130,751,000 of them in 1974. Thus oil sweeps us quite literally off our feet.

Without such a mobile fuel, the giant automotive industry could never have boasted that one in every six jobs in the nation is created by the demand for cars and the roads they run on. As Simeon Strunsky wrote long ago, the automobile "restates the national principle." [1] Surrogate for power, outlet for recreation, instrument of passion, embodiment of escape, sign of virility, and still, though many now deny it, our chief national status symbol, the automobile satisfies most of all the fundamental American urge to be on the go.

America has traditionally been a country on the move. But the oil-driven wheels of the twentieth century have set all Americans in practically continuous motion. Responsible for creating the suburbs, wrecking the railroads, and bankrupting mass transit, the automobile is now, for millions, the only means of getting around. In vast clouds of exhaust fumes and invisible particulates, which perceptibly raise temperatures every morning and evening in America cities, 85 percent of all jobholders drive their individual cars between their homes and places of work.

So vast and unceasing is America's automobility that even these diurnal flows are noticeable only for the tidal regularity of their occurrence. From morning to night, life in America is in good part life on wheels. Our motor vehicles carry us 1.3 trillion miles each year, burning up no less than 27 percent of all petroleum consumed in America and about 10 percent of all consumed in the world. And as our cars multiply—half of all suburban families now own two cars and 7.7 percent own three or more—we drive them more intensively. Between 1945 and 1970, the average mileage for American cars rose from 7,771 miles per year to 11,600. Gasoline consumption, speeded by 140 million oil-company credit cards, rose during the same years from 600 to 736 gallons per car per year. Yet almost half of all trips are of three miles or less. The average family thus makes 3.8 automobile trips every day, and members of the 50 percent of American households with incomes of $15,000 or over make an incredible 2,500 trips a year—or seven trips a day.[2]

For three decades, each year, rising along with the gross national product, population, and other vital statistics, automobility advanced three percent. Then, in October 1973, warning signals sounded. On the other side of the world, the Arab states warred on Israel, the United States sent emergency arms to Israel, and the Arabs clamped an embargo on oil shipments to the United States. The president of the United States went on the air to proclaim "the most acute shortage of energy since World War II,"[3] and private American life-styles were in for some altering.

Astonished, we learned that we would have to go on daylight saving time, turn down thermostats both at home and in the office, and cut down on our driving.

With only a thirty-day supply of fuel oil on hand and winter coming on, the government clapped on fuel allocations and directed refineries to turn their petroleum stocks into heating oil rather than gasoline.

Nixon asked that everybody reduce speed voluntarily to 50 miles an hour; few motorists appeared to have heard him—most drivers who throttled back to 50 were honked at and tailgated. When state legislatures enacted lower speed limits, it was a body blow to owner-drivers of heavy trailer trucks. Many filling stations had put up fuel prices as soon as the Arab embargo was announced; and so, squeezed between 75-cent gasoline and a 55-mph speed limit which cut the distance that could be covered in a day, the truckers were threatened with bankruptcy.

Drivers had their own informal communications network: the Citizens Band radio linked them rig to rig as they rolled along. The radios crackled, and within hours tractor-trailers parked across turnpikes and barricaded traffic in eight states. One jam, staged by 350 trucks, backed up traffic for miles on roads leading to the Delaware Memorial Bridge, midpoint on the main route between New York and Philadelphia and Washington. The longest turnpike tieup strangled traffic between Cleveland and Toledo for nearly 24 hours before state police and National Guard units hauled away the trucks and the governors of Ohio, Michigan, and Pennsylvania arranged to get them fuel without price-gouging at truck stops.

At the end of December, Washington ordered mandatory allocation, limiting gasoline at wholesale levels—in effect, rationing the public's supply by inconvenience.

Throughout the country, as gas stations prorated supplies and sold out within hours, pump fever ran high. Never before had Americans had to wait more than ten minutes to fill 'er up. Now they drove, anxious and apprehensive, constantly aware of the gasoline gauge—should they try to get through the day on an eighth of a tank and take their chances tomorrow or stop now, get in line for more than an hour, and hope to gain the confidence that a fuller tank could bring?

It brought out the worst in everybody. When a motorist in Pittsburgh topped off his tank with only eleven cents' worth of gasoline, the pump attendant spat in his face. Drivers in Bristol, Conn., and others in Neptune, N.J., sat stubbornly in lines that stretched across railroad tracks, compelling trains to brake to a halt. Lamented a Texaco dealer in Lexington, Mass., "They smashed the glass on the pumps and tried to start fights when we closed. We were all so busy at the pumps that somebody walked in and stole my adding machine and the leukemia-fund can." [4]

Though Washington assigned Internal Revenuers to see that price controls were observed, drivers complained of price-gouging. At best, many station managers and owners became unapproachable to strangers; they would wait only on longtime customers. Some issued window stickers to regulars; others sold by appointment only. For a full tank of gas or some other treatment at the pumps, money, whiskey, tobacco, and even sex were offered at Stamford, Conn.

Bottles and cartons of cigarettes piled up at Ben Servidio's Exxon station, though he neither smoke nor drank. At Long Ridge Chevron, a woman offered $100 for a guarantee of a full tank daily at 3:30 P.M. "I told her it was impossible to make that kind of a guarantee," said owner Nick Palazzo. "Every day people come in and say, 'Name your price,' but you expect a badge to come out of their pocket—that's why I didn't say anything," said Wayne Konitchek, an Exxon dealer. A Getty owner said he had received whiskey and cigarettes, five-dollar and ten-dollar tips, and once a salesman had given him a new shirt. "Even when we were totally out of gas they were still offering me things so I'd remember them," he said. One dealer told of a Virginia girl who asked for enough gasoline to start her homeward. "I can't give you gas. I wish I could help you," he said. The girl replied, "You help me and I'll help you." The dealer asked, "What do you mean by that? You mean that for two dollars, worth of gas you'd give me your body?" "For two-dollars worth of gas at this point, I would," she said. She got a fatherly talk and about four gallons.[5]

Faced not just with the gasoline shortage but with plummeting prices in the used-car market, owners of gas-sucking old Cadillacs, Chryslers, and Buicks torched their fading land-yachts at a record rate. In Boston, records showed 330 cases of automobile arson in December 1973, up from 149 the year before. Almost all of them were aging luxury models that carried high insurance premiums far out of line with the basement prices that such models brought during the gasoline shortage.

When a huge bear of a man warned a Springfield, Mass., dealer, "You are going to give me gas or I will kill you," the dealer squeezed his parched pumps to find some. In New York City motorists fought with fists and knives when one of them tried to switch the "End of the Line—No More Gas" sign from behind the car ahead of him to behind his own. Inevitably, what the Washington planners had resignedly expected took place one March night in New Orleans. A man walked into a station and, told he could get no gasoline, drew a gun and shot the attendant dead.

At the height of the crunch in February and March, the number of cars crossing the George Washington Bridge fell off by a fourth on Sundays, by 12 to 15 percent on Saturdays, and declined some 10 percent on weekdays.[6] Then in April the embargo was lifted, the price of gasoline also rose—and America's heartbeat soon pounded again at its old night-and-day pace. By the end of the year the nation's motorists wound up paying $13.2 billion in state road-use taxes—but for the first time since the second World War the systolic count did not rise in 1974.

If oil runs through the bloodstream of our daily lives, it also permeates America's public affairs. The political power packed by oil is commensurate with its economic and social importance. Oil is embedded in the power arrangements of all government and politics. It is an incalculable force in the formation of public opinion. In an age when not even federal regulation stands a chance of controlling megacorporations, oil is supervised only by the states. In a time when oil makes its biggest profits abroad, the State Department works hand in glove with the big oil interests. Sixty years after his grandfather monopolized the business, a Rockefeller is vice-president of the United States.

Washington knows no lobby as potent as oil's. An aide to an influential senator says he gets ten phone calls a day from oilmen. The lobbying can be as discreetly effective as an Exxon chairman's visit to help dissuade President Nixon from ending import quotas four years before the energy crunch compelled such action. Or it can be as extravagantly counterproductive as a Gulf Oil lobbyist's offer of a campaign contribution to Senator Francis Case of South Dakota, which led, through its disclosure on the floor of the Senate, to a veto of an industry-sponsored bill in the 1950s.

Oil's real power is applied from the inside, in Congress, in the White House, in the so-called independent agencies. Some of Washington's biggest wheels turn as if synchronized with oil interests. Oil won a famous victory when Warren Harding gained the presidency in 1920. President Nixon, who broke into national politics with the aid of a secret $18,000 fund supplied largely by oilmen, received $5 million in known oil company contributions to his 1972 reelection campaign. In Congress, two all-powerful Texans, Speaker Sam Rayburn and Senate Majority Leader Lyndon Johnson, looked after oil interests so effectively that lobbyists had little to do. When Johnson was elevated to the vice-presidency, Senator Robert S. Kerr, an oilman, took over as guardian wheeler-dealer. A multimillionaire, he said simply, "I represent oil." [7] The assertion is echoed in the 1970s by his successor, Senator Russell Long, a Lousiana oil millionaire with wide lease interests in his state. As chairman of the Senate Finance Committee, he handles all tax matters affecting oil.

Of all the special advantages ever wrung from government under the American system, the single most corrupting has been the oil depletion allowance. Obtained in the closing months of the first World War as a break to help small oil prospectors take big drilling gambles and thereby boost the supply of much needed petroleum, this huge loophole in the income tax laws brought oilmen to politics as bees to honey. Among them was Andrew Mellon of Gulf Oil, who took office as Harding's secretary of the treasury. Under Mellon, a treasury ruling extended the benefit not only to small wildcatters but to the biggest of the oil-producing companies.[8] Along with the Rockefeller and Mellon interests, a whole generation of superrich Texans later fought with all the tax millions thus gained to preserve this arrangement by which you, the reader, pay taxes—and big oil, year after year, paid nothing.

It remained for a Democratic administration in 1950 to put through a tax benefit that in effect levied upon other U.S. taxpayers the payment of huge sums that the oil companies were required to pay in foreign lands. Carefully unpublicized rulings suddenly and summarily redefined as "taxes" royalties that the companies had been paying to such governments as Saudi Arabia. Then, on the unassailable proposition that double taxation of earnings was inherently unfair, these companies were permitted to subtract such payments from their corporate returns to the U.S. Treasury. The device was justified as required in the interests of "national security" inasmuch as the United States was then locked in cold war with "international communism" and competing with the Russians for influence in the Middle East states where oil companies operated.[9] The terms were so favorable for the oil interests that American companies, major and independent alike, turned their backs on domestic exploration after 1950 to drill abroad—with the result that the petroleum resources of the United States have been so neglected and American dependence upon these overseas finds has so increased that the nation is in danger of being drawn into another Vietnam in the Middle East.

The big five are Exxon, Mobil, Texaco, Gulf, and Standard of California. Spurred by special tax benefits, these companies grew gigantic by taking out the best part of the nation's oil. Then for greater growth they leaped overseas—and built up an immensely profitable system, in alliance with Anglo-Dutch Shell and British Petroleum, of pumping Middle East oil for the booming markets of Europe and Japan.

This was the system described by the Federal Trade Commission in 1952 as "the international oil cartel." [10] By a long series of price-fixing and market-sharing deals, disciplining of mavericks and co-opting of troublemakers, these so-called Seven Sisters maintained "price stability" and suppressed crude-oil surpluses year after year. Liquidating oil finds under these arrangements was the key to their entire business. Unparalleled production, induced by the lush tax benefits bestowed on oil produced overseas, grew into by far the most profitable segment of the companies' foreign and domestic business—far more than pipelining and supertankering and certainly more than marketing gasoline from filling stations (an operation on which the majors often lost money).

The postcolonial lands of the Middle East, where Russian influence mounted steadily, demanded increasing control over their oil and its price. The big American companies, cushioned by tax concessions, went along with the host countries' demands. Even when the Persian Gulf countries began setting prices and output levels, the major companies kept on producing most of their oil in these states and handling the marketing of the oil for them—though the larger interests of the United States might better have been served by looking for new oil sources elsewhere and letting the host countries themselves face the vicissitudes of the world market.

The day came when, anticipating squeeze-out at last from production revenues, the big companies had to look to other segments of their business for future profits—and the easiest place to get them was at the marketing end by stiff rises at the filling station pumps.[11] With the help of the Arab-Israeli war and the paralysis of the Nixon administration, their rough stuff in the marketplace worked, first in Europe and then in the United States. After three months' "energy crisis," in the winter of 1973-4, gasoline and fuel oil prices rose from 25 to 40 percent. The major companies, with the avidity of corporate men for short-term profits, collected huge windfalls on eleventh hour sales cf their soon-to-be-nationalized oil production, racking up record earnings at the public's expense.

With the shift of control from the big companies to the weak and warring sheikhdoms of the Persian Gulf, the supply of the oil the world needs became unstable. The bulk of readily accessible oil left in the world lies beneath the most volatile frontiers on earth. The tinderbox of the world is now its treasure chest.

In modern times nations without a secure access to oil go to war for it—the Germans and the Japanese launched attacks on Russia and the United States in the second World War to get their hands on oil. In its cold war confrontations with the Communists thereafter, the United States made allies of both these nations by holding its nuclear umbrella over them and keeping them supplied with oil —Middle East oil. But in the 1970s the system has broken down. The survival of Western Europe and Japan, the viability of the world trading community, and the monetary stability of nations all hang on the continued supply of energy from Persian Gulf oil—and a handful of small desert principalities there do not hesitate to raise prices fivefold, cut production to make these prices stick, or impose oil embargoes in support of their local wars. It is geopolitics with a vengeance.

For thirty years the Middle East has been the scene of warfare and violence—between nationalist and colonialist, Arab and Jew, Moslem and Moslem. The chief business of the United Nations has often seemed to be separating the warring parties. After 1949, when the Russians achieved their A-bomb, the proximity of one superpower and the commercial presence of the other lent to these squabbles and tensions a terrifying potential for escalation. UN efforts grew steadily more ineffectual. Conflict after conflict sputtered on these dangerous sands, all raising the threat of what the peace-makers feared most: a reckless local scrap that might blaze into nuclear blowup.

Until the 1970s one thing kept this from happening: both the United States and the Soviet Union had great oil reserves of their own. Such a consideration constrained the Russians in the first Middle East showdown at the end of the second World War, when under American pressure they withdrew their troops from Iran in early 1946. Such a consideration enabled President Eisenhower to distance himself from his British and French allies when they sought by force to assure their oil supply by invading Suez in 1956. It remains a geopolitical fact of life, however, that as long as the Persian Gulf lies no farther from Russia than Mexico City from the United States, the Soviet Union cannot remain indifferent to events in the area. And now, ironically at the moment American companies have lost control, a change of greatest long-term significance occurs: the United States, having run through the most accessible of its own vast petroleum wealth, begins for the first time to have the most direct self-interest in importing oil from these weak states on Russia's southern border.

Late in 1973, when Egypt and Syria, equipped with large stocks of the most modern Soviet arms, attacked Israel, the United States had a brush with war in the Middle East and was greatly discomfited to discover its new dependence. So preoccupied was the nation at the time with its own festering political scandal at home that many people did not comprehend the danger. Indeed, when the Nixon administration let it be known that it had rattled its nukes, many insisted that President Nixon had exaggerated the situation to distract public opinion angered by his firing of Watergate Prosecutor Archibald Cox and the resignation of Attorney General Richardson that same weekend. But what happened was only a hint of harsher crises to come in the Middle East power vacuum.

Starting in 1970, the members of the Organization of Petroleum Exporting States had been pressing for higher revenues from their oil. At the same time, Arab nationalists, infuriated at United States support of Israel, kept sabotaging pipelines. Then in April 1973, when the United States abandoned its restrictive policy and began importing sizable quantities of Middle Eastern oil, Saudi Arabia informed American officials that output could not be expanded to meet American demand unless America withdrew its support for Israel.[12] Egyptian President Anwar Sadat had long been proclaiming that the Arab states would fight to get back land lost to Israel in the 1949, 1956, and 1967 wars. The Russians had been shipping tanks and planes to Egypt to enable them to do so.

On September 22, 1973, Sadat informed Leonid Brezhnev that the war would begin October 6, and the Soviet party boss apparently raised no objections. A steady intelligence flow informed Israeli and United States leaders of plans for an impeding Egyptian-Syrian attack. Early on the morning of October 6, when Ambassador to Israel Kenneth Keating cabled that war was about to break out, Secretary of State Kissinger was urging the Israelis, "Don't start the war. Don't preempt."[13] Under heaviest pressure from Washington, Premier Golda Meir reversed 25 years of Israeli strategy and accepted the first blows.

To the astonishment of United States and Israeli leaders, the Syrian and Egyptian attackers scored big gains. The Israelis lost men and equipment, and when they tried to strike back in the air, new Russian-supplied weapons shot down large numbers of their planes. In three days Israel lost 45 F-4s, more than a fifth of all the aircraft ever sent them by the United States. The Israelis appealed to the United States for more equipment.

Secretary Kissinger, anxious not to offend the Arabs or the Russians, nonetheless asked Secretary of Defense James Schlesinger and the Pentagon to arrange to send supplies to Israel. With Soviet Ambassador Anatoli Dobrynin, Kissinger took the line that Congress was clamoring for quick aid to Israel and that the Administration policy of détente with Russia might be a casualty unless the Soviets cooperated in restraining the advancing Arab armies and in backing a cease-fire in the Middle East.

The warning had no effect. On October 9, Washington got intelligence of an increase in the number of Soviet supply ships steaming toward Syrian and Egyptian ports. Next morning, American and Israeli intelligence picked up the first clear signals of a Soviet airlift into Damascus and Cairo. Israeli Ambassador Simcha Dinitz again pressed Kissinger for supplies.

The Americans delayed. Deputy Secretary of Defense William P. Clements, Jr., who has been described as "a wealthy Texas drilling contractor with close ties to the oil industry," [14] apparently persuaded Schlesinger that he needed more information about United States inventories before he could provide the Israelis with an exact time-table for deliveries. By that afternoon it became apparent from urgent CIA reports that the Russian airlift was becoming massive. Late that night, Kissinger learned that three Russian airborne divisions in Eastern Europe had been put on the alert, presumably for possible deployment to the Middle East.

Finally, after four days' delay, Washington ordered 10 C-130 transport planes, loaded with military supplies, to the Azores for a quick Israeli pickup and 20 C-130s to fly direct to Israel; and Dinitz cabled Mrs. Meir that a "massive American airlift" had begun.[15]

Reinvigorated, the Israelis pressed hard against Syria and established a bridgehead on the west bank of the Suez Canal. And then, as the Arab states embargoed oil shipments to the United States, the scramble for a cease-fire was on. At Brezhnev's invitation Kissinger flew to Moscow, and the basis for an agreement was worked out. But by the time Kissinger was back in Washington, after stopovers in Jerusalem and London, the Russians were complaining of Israeli cease-fire violations. The Israelis had completed their encirclement of Egyptian troops on one bank of the canal and reached the outskirts of the city of Suez on the other side. Kissinger knew that the Soviets could not allow a serious Egyptian defeat.

At three o'clock on the afternoon of October 24, President Sadat radioed for a joint United States-USSR task force to enforce the cease-fire. Some felt the Russians solicited the plea, which found no favor in Washington. At the time, Soviet land and naval forces, including seven landing ships, were milling around the eastern Mediterranean, and seven airborne divisions numbering 40,000 troops were on alert in Russia. At five that afternoon Kissinger and Dobrynin were harmoniously discussing ways and means. Three hours later, Dobrynin had a note from Brezhnev to Nixon, urging United States participation in the joint peace-keeping force. Kissinger talked on the telephone with Nixon and quickly handed Dobrynin a reply: a firm no. It would be disastrous, the message said, for the powers to get into the tense situation on the ground. At the UN, meanwhile, Soviet Delegate Jakob Malik was accusing the United States of helping Israel break the cease-fire. United States Delegate John Scali informed Kissinger of this.

At 9:25 that night Kissinger received a phone call from Dobrynin, relaying a "very urgent" message from Brezhnev. So "urgent" was the message, said Dobrynin, that he would read it. Slowly he dictated the message to Kissinger; a secretary, listening on an extension, took down the text in shorthand. The message began with an unusually cool salutation—just "Mr. President," and the tone was unmistakably tough. Brezhnev denounced Israel for "drastically" violating the cease-fire, and said, "We strongly urge that we both send forces to enforce the ceasefire." What followed was electrifying. "I will say it to you straight," the message came through to Kissinger, "that if you find it impossible to act together with us in this matter, we shall be faced with the necessity urgently to consider the question of taking appropriate steps unilaterally." [16]

Kissinger immediately called Nixon, who concurred with the suggestion of a firm political response backed by a military signal. At 11 P.M. Kissinger convened a National Security Council meeting in the White House basement. The principal actors were Kissinger and Schlesinger. William Colby, chief of the Central Intelligence Agency, was belatedly called in. Also present was Admiral Thomas Moorer, chairman of the Joint Chiefs of Staff. The council soon agreed to order "Defense Condition 3," the middle of five stages of military alert, rising from Defense Condition 5 to Defense Condition 1, which is war. The aircraft carrier *John F. Kennedy*, with dozens of A-4 attack jets, was dispatched toward the Mediterranean. More than fifty Strategic Air Command bombers were ordered from Guam to the United States. The 82nd Airborne Division at Fort Bragg, N.C., was alerted, along with the Panama Command, and told to be ready at 6 A.M. to travel. Finally the entire SAC, controlling nuclear strike forces, was put on worldwide alert.

Next day, some twelve hours after Brezhnev's "urgent" message, the Soviet Union altered its stand at the United Nations and lent support to the United States resolution to set up a United Nations emergency force for the Middle East that included neither Russians nor Americans. Though no sign appeared that the Russian airborne units had been returned to their normal status, this Soviet switch signaled an end to the danger of escalation and the United States called off its alert. Kissinger proceeded to negotiate the withdrawal of the Israelis from the west bank of the Suez Canal, and the crisis subsided for the time being.

Richard Nixon called it "the most difficult crisis we have had since the Cuban missile crisis of 1962." [17] A more precise comparison would be with the Suez crisis of 1956. In the climactic moments of that affair, President Eisenhower, on hearing reports that the Russians were moving "volunteers" into Syria and perhaps Egypt, ordered a SAC alert—but carefully refrained from publicizing it. This was presumably what Kissinger intended on the night of October 24, 1973, but Nixon, under heavy attack for the firing of Cox and the resignation of Richardson a few hours earlier, broadcast to the world next morning that he had ordered the alert.

The brush with the Russians, following the Arab oil embargo, was a belated warning to United States policymakers: the United States had better look to its energy supplies.

In former times the United States might have made up its extra requirements by importing oil from secure sources in the Western Hemisphere. (That had been the idea of Herbert Hoover, America's only technologist president, who used to make speeches about "Fortress America.") But over the years America, by the rapacity of its oil imperialism, alienated Mexico, which belongs to the same oil province as Texas and held considerable reserves left after throwing out the American companies in 1938. As for the rest of Latin America and Canada, the United States has drawn upon their oil resources to the point where they cannot produce much more than they do, which is far short of making up the deficit in our energy budget. Indonesia has come back on the world oil market in recent years; and Africa, from Nigeria to Libya, is also an exporter of considerable oil. In 1974, however, not all of these together could expand soon enough to make up the difference. Even the other nations atop the giant Persian Gulf pool cannot supply both their present markets and the added margin America needs. Only one place on earth seems to have the capacity to supply the United States as needed—Saudi Arabia.

Just where and what is Saudi Arabia? Think of the Middle East as the cradle of civilization. Think back five and six thousand years to Sumer and Babylon beside the Tigris and Euphrates in what is now Iraq, and to Memphis and Thebes by the Nile in what is still Egypt—and think of the tawny deserts and mountain crags that loomed between. Down in the two rich valleys grew not only crops, but cities of law and learning. The bare, sere uplands between was Arabia, from which hungry, hardened tribesmen swept down in wave after invading wave upon the settled agriculturists of Mesopotamia and Egypt. Three great religions were carried down to mankind from those commanding heights. The last of them, Islam, still looks back to Mecca in Saudi Arabia as the seat of divine revelation.

Yet, as a nation-state, Saudi Arabia has no past—it is as ephemeral as a Bedouin tenting site. It was put together less than fifty years ago by a picturesque desert chieftain who subdued rival camel-riding sheikhs at the moment their Ottoman Turk overlords in distant Constantinople vanished into the dustbin of history. Its economy is neolithic; its polity, of the stone age. It lacks natural borders. It has no considerable citizenry—five or perhaps seven million pastoralists (no census has ever been taken) in a territory the size of Texas and Alaska combined. But under this backward and otherwise barren land—or rather under that portion of it that borders on the Persian Gulf—lies perhaps half the world's remaining accessible oil.

The United States treats Saudi Arabia as a most favored nation. There the United States won the Open Door for its prospectors in the 1930s and, having found the prize, closed the door to all rivals. Ever since, through all the wars and uprisings of the stormy Middle East, the United States has stood by the Kingdom of Saudi Arabia. When its monarch was penniless, the United States advanced him money against the promise of oil. When the British lent aid to his enemies, the United States helped him drive them out. When some called Saudi Arabia the most primitive and repressive monarchy left on earth, President Roosevelt paid a visit to its ruler and arranged Saudi membership in the UN. When the UN then tried to stamp out human slavery in Saudi Arabia, the United States maneuvered to head off the condemning resolution.

The United States built a huge air base in Saudi Arabia. Washington helped the Arabian-American Oil Co., the United States' chosen instrument and sole exploiter of Saudi oil, stay on the good side of old King Ibn Saud. To uphold his style of rule, which needed revenue mainly for purses of gold napoleons to toss to his restive sheikhs, Americans helped ransack the world for such coins. When the old king's countless sons developed a taste for comforts in the desert, Americans built air-conditioned palaces and shipped in air-conditioned Cadillacs. Finally, when political leaders in other lands began demanding a higher share in revenue from their oil, the Americans responded by presenting such concessions to the Saudis—first 50 percent of the profits, then 70 percent, then 80 percent. The end result was that when, early in 1973, the Americans turned to Saudi Arabia for oil imports to meet their growing demand, the king declined to allow increased production unless the United States ceased to support Israel. And when the United States then lent aid to Israel, the Saudis embargoed oil shipments to the United States and afterward took control of Aramco.

In due course, Saudi oil began again to flow to the United States. The Saudis set the price (four times above what had prevailed before) and within months possessed the world's fourth largest monetary stocks—and stood to hold half the world's monetary reserves by 1980 if things kept on the same way. Meanwhile, the Saudis met periodically with other Arab members of the OPEC to decide whether enough "progress" had been made in meeting Arab political demands against Israel to justify refraining from more oil embargos.[18] In the circumstances, the United States had to choose, not between Israel and the Arabs, but between strategic dependency on Saudi Arabia's oil and a set of options consistent with America's position as a superpower.

In a sense, that choice has already been made. Although the Pentagon for decades looked upon Saudi oil as an ultimate strategic reserve, and although postembargo American imports from the Middle East soared above a million barrels a day, the prudential pullback in the Persian Gulf has already been signaled by the retreat of the American oil companies. At the height of its power, the United States could build a wall of alliances and bases around the Communist bloc that made feasible the extraction of oil in the Middle East. But in a world of nuclear standoff, the United States cannot ever become strategically dependent upon oil brought to the surface so close to the frontiers of the Soviet Union.

America must find its oil at home, where it always has; and if it costs more to go deeper and farther offshore, so be it. That is the price of power. This is not to say that the United States can abandon the Middle East, because the Middle East is still the source of oil for United States allies in Europe and Japan. In all likelihood, therefore, oil is going to continue to cost everybody much more. Whether pumped from the Gulf of Mexico or the Persian Gulf, whether drawn from the Western or Eastern Hemisphere, oil will no longer be the cheap source of energy it was when America was riding high. We can now begin to see the end of the rule of king oil.

PART TWO

Upstream

2

The Making of a Monopoly

Until little more than a hundred years ago, of course, there was no such thing as a petroleum industry. By contrast, coal, the original energy source of the industrial revolution, had been known and commercially used for eight hundred years. But to suppose that man knew nothing about oil because it was an untapped wonder to the early nineteenth century world would be culture-bound.

Actually, oil was used quite commonly in the ancient East. The Bible bears witness to the fact that the Babylonians employed it to stoke the fiery furnaces in which such captive Jews as Shadrach, Meshach, and Abednego, like any other offenders against the state, could be sent to suitably frightful doom. Among the Sumerians and Assyrians, as well as the Babylonians, the oily oozings of Mesopotamia were widely used in more everyday ways—to asphalt roads, harden walls, cement mosaics, and caulk ships. Bitumen was mixed into paints, medicines, fumigants, magic potions, and aphrodisiacs. It was part of the weaponry of conquest—blackening and toughening the bludgeons and dagger hafts with which the barbarians terrorized the early agriculturists of the Middle East.[1]

The Greeks, in turn, caulked their proud ships not with tar but with pitch from the cedars of Lebanon. When Jason and his Argonauts set sail across the Black Sea, they may have been looking for riches on the oil coasts of Batum; the legendary Golden Fleece may well have been sheepskin dipped in the tarpits of Baku—to be brought back to the sacrificial altars of Eleuthis.[2] But in the main, the Greeks were taken up with epic wars, political disputes, and philosophical speculations.

Had the practical Romans seen how the Babylonians used bitumen, they would probably have reared oleoducts across the Arabian
desert to pipe the stuff to the Mediterranean—and is there any doubt
they would have paved their roads with it? But all that Periclean and
Alexandrian Greece handed on to the Romans was a set of observa-
tions on the occurrence of natural gas, petroleum, and asphaltic rock
as a curiosity of nature. With the fall of Babylon, the technology of
the ancient oil industry was lost until, so to speak, only yesterday.

Two thousand years later, the most widely known use of oil in
America was medicinal. The Seneca Indians, finding the stuff floating
on top of springs, used to soak it up in a blanket dropped on the
surface of the water and then wring out the blanket over a container.
They rubbed sore joints with it and drank it as a purgative.

Early white settlers obtained brine from wells, exposed it to evapo-
ration, and then marketed it as salt. Some salt manufacturers in
Kentucky had to abandon their wells, however, when an oily substance oozed up along with the brine. Certain traders took over one
such fouled well, formed the American Medicinal Oil Company, and
bottled "American Oil" as a remedy for nearly everything. When
Samuel M. Kier, son of a salt manufacturer, had trouble with the oily
stuff mixing into his Pennsylvania wells, he considered shutting them
down. But after his wife got consumption and the doctor prescribed
American Oil, Kier noticed that the fluid he bought in bottles was like
that which was ruining his wells. When oil began to flow in quantity
from them in 1848, he went into the medical-oil trade.

Kier had a flair for graphic advertising. He put out leaflets of
testimonials proclaiming the wonderful virtue of "Petroleum, or Rock
Oil. A Natural Remedy. Procured from a well in Allegheny Co., Pa.
Four hundred feet below the Earths Surface." Rock oil, he wrote, had
"wonderful curative powers" for rheumatism, chronic cough, ague,
toothache, corns, neuralgia, piles, urinary disorders, and liver ailments.
One of his leaflets was printed like a state bank note featuring the
number 400 (the number of feet below the earth's surface from which
the marvelous mineral was drawn), signed by S. M. Kier and dated
"A.D. 1848 discovered in boring for salt water; A.D. 1849 wonderful
medical virtues discovered." [3] By A.D. 1858 he had sold nearly a
quarter of a million half-pints of his wonderful Rock Oil at one dollar
a bottle.

Meanwhile, the growth of cities in both Europe and America was
increasing the need for better illumination. In colonial America homes
had been lit with candles or with a lamp little different from those

used in ancient Rome—a dish of animal or fish or mineral oil, in which a twisted rag served as wick. Oil from the sperm whale made the best flame, but was expensive. Then in 1830 a New Yorker devised "camphene" by redistilling spirits of turpentine. It made a bright light, but gave off an offensive odor and was dangerously explosive besides.

The best hope of cheaper illumination in the early nineteenth century seemed to lie in gas manufactured from coal. The British started lighting London streets with such gas by the 1830s, but the expense of piping it to the consumer remained so high that until midcentury gaslight was feasible only for public places or for the rich.

In 1854, Abraham Gesner, a Canadian doctor, patented a process for distilling a tarlike mineral found in eastern Canada that produced illuminating gas and an oil, which he called kerosene (from *keros*, the Greek word for "wax," and *ene* because it resembled camphene). Though cheaper than camphene, Gesner's kerosene also had an unpleasant odor. Manufacturers in Boston, searching for better lubricants, turned to producing "coal oil." Distilled from coal tar, this new oil had good lubricating and burning properties and was minus any bad smell. By 1859, called by the same name of kerosene, it was beginning to spread in the American market. These pioneers also found that petroleum could be substituted for coal in the production of their coal oil. At the end of 1859 nearly two million coal-oil lamps had been sold, but America was far from having a lamp in every room.

In the summer of 1854, George H. Bissell, a Dartmouth alumnus visiting his alma mater, chanced to see a bottle of oil that had been brought there by a doctor who had taken it from an oil spring at Titusville, in western Pennsylvania. Bissell thought there might be wealth in the spring that had yielded the bottle's contents. He and a partner formed the Pennsylvania Rock Oil Company of New York, capitalized at a half million dollars, and bought the spring without having yet any precise idea of what they would do with its product. They besought Professor Benjamin Silliman, Jr., of Yale to analyze a sample of their rock oil to see what it might be good for. Silliman, after tests, reported that the oil had wonderful lubricating qualities and confirmed the claim of the Boston coal-oil manufacturers that it was "chemically identical with illuminating gas in liquid form." He went on to say:

> The lamp burning this fluid [distilled from the oil] gave as much light as any which they had seen . . . the oil spent more economically, and the uniformity of the light was

greater than in camphene, burning for 12 hours without a sensible diminution, and without smoke.[4]

But there was very little oil in the Pennsylvania spring—only that which seeped to the surface. The idea of drilling deep into the ground for the express purpose of finding oil that could then be pumped to the surface—such an idea, if it occurred to anyone, must have seemed too farfetched to justify any investment. It was later said that Bissell may first have thought of the idea of drilling after seeing Kier's ad for medicinal "rock oil," which featured the "400" feet below surface, at which it had been found. Or it could have occurred first to another of the Rock Oil Company's backers, to whom a friend said in 1858, "Pumping oil out of the earth as you pump water? Nonsense, you're crazy."

In any event, the investors in the Pennsylvania Rock Oil Company decided to send somebody to their Titusville property to see what could be done about exploiting the stuff seeping up there. They chose Edwin L. Drake, a vagrant with neither technical training nor mining experience and with no more than a grade school education. Why they picked him is a mystery. His chief qualification for the job appeared to be the railroad pass that he still held as a former New Haven railroad conductor and that got him to Titusville free of charge.

Arriving there in December 1857, Drake found "a population of about 125, no churches, two hotels." He went to the site at the head of Oil Creek, where the medicinal oil oozed up into a pool. He watched how laboriously it was collected by spreading a blanket and then squeezing the liquid into a container. His idea, to which he held stubbornly for the next two years, was to bore for it as wells were bored for salt water—and "that I should be the one to do it."[5]

Local opinion held that "the oil was the drippings of the coal imbedded in the contiguous hills." If so, the only way to collect it was by digging ditches. But Drake soon became obsessed by the notion of "drilling" for oil. He went to nearby salt wells to see how they were drilled and to find an experienced driller. The first man he signed on never showed up and later explained that since he believed Drake to be crazy, he "thought the easiest way to get rid of him was to make a contract and pretend that he meant to come." Persisting, Drake found William A. ("Uncle Billy") Smith, who was not only an experienced salt borer, but also a skilled blacksmith, who knew how to make drilling tools. Uncle Billy finally got started in July 1859, when Drake's employers were on the point of giving up and calling him back to New Haven. The usual way of salt boring was to dig a hole and wall it around with a wooden "crib" until reaching bedrock; then an ironpipe was drilled into the hole. But when Uncle Billy tried this at the Bissell well, water flooded the hole long before the bedrock was reached. So he tried a revolutionary idea: driving a pipe all the way down through topsoil and bedrock. After he reached bedrock at 32 feet, he went on drilling, making only three feet a day by the method then used of manually working a spring pole. By Saturday, August 27, 1859, Uncle Billy Smith's hole was 69½ feet deep and (as Drake always required) drilling stopped for the Sabbath. That Sunday Drake went over with Smith to check on the well's progress; to their surprise it was full of an oily substance. "Well," Uncle Billy told Drake, "there's your fortune." [6]

Though the oily substance in the hole quickly dispelled Drake's reputation for insanity, making money out of it was not quite so easy. The well did not flow, but had to be pumped. Not having planned where to put the stuff, Drake used whiskey barrels and washtubs. One day in October, Uncle Billy took a lamp to look down the hole, and the whole outfit went up in flames. But Drake rebuilt the derrick and pump, and fortune hunters from all over soon flocked around him. Neither Drake nor his backers got much out of their discovery. Leaving the oil country, Drake went to Wall Street, where he became a broker in oil stocks and lost everything. To save the "inventor" of the oil well from destitution, the Pennsylvania legislature granted him a pension of $1,500 a year, but in 1880 Drake died in obscurity.

The oil mania touched off a boom second only to the California gold rush. But this was mining with a difference. No other mineral was so liquid, so inflammable. Above all, no other was so fugacious, so apt to fly away and be lost, so likely to be here today and gone tomorrow. If an operator did not tap the oil beneath his land, it might flow off to wells on adjoining land. From the very earliest days the courts sanctioned this "right of capture"—and by their action immensely accelerated the headlong rush to exploitation. American law assigned all rights to subsoil wealth to whoever owned the surface (in countries with Roman-law traditions, subsoil rights are reserved to the state),[7] and the impoverished farmers of Pennsylvania's Oil Creek Valley fell over each other to cash in on the riches suddenly discovered under their scraggly acres. Operators offered them as much as a quarter to one half of the oil they might find (it was not until the 1870s that royalty payments stabilized at 12½ percent) and pledged to drill within six months.

Though Drake's well was shallow and had to be pumped, it was different elsewhere along the seven-mile length of Oil Creek. At the James Evans farm, as oil poured out of a new hole, a daughter called to a neighbor, "Dad's struck oil." [8] The phrase signaled the new idea of a pent-up fortune lying ready for the tapping. Farther along the creek, drills not only struck but sent mighty jets of black gold spouting through derrick tops—the first of America's "gushers." Wells were soon brought in less than 50 feet apart in places along Oil Creek, and then the oil flow flagged.

One of the forces that made oil development so volatile was the early habit of selling fractional shares in leases. Subleasing, as it was called, made fortunes for speculators who obtained leases and then subdivided them at huge profits among persons with limited resources who wanted a piece of the action. Subleasing transfused new funds into risky ventures and permitted expanded drilling. It sparked the ruinous urge to space wells only a few feet apart and, with the random leasing to parties willing to pay large bonuses, gave a big push to phony stock-company promotions.

If psychobiography were ever to train its analysis upon the lives of business leaders, it would seize upon the spring of 1849 as the time of shattering, identity-shaping experience in the life of John D. Rockefeller.

He was then a carefree, ten-year-old farm boy at Richford in upstate New York, the oldest of three sons in a family of Palatine German and New England Puritan descent. In that spring his father, a restless farmer-trader who absented himself for long periods as a roving "doctor," dispensing cancer cures and herbal remedies, got into trouble in the community. This free and easy man, who used to say, "I trade with the boys and I skin 'em and I just beat 'em every time. I want to make 'em sharp"—this "big, powerful man afraid of nothing" was indicted for rape on the complaint of a hired girl in the Rockefeller household.[9]

In the settled respectability of a largely Puritan village, this was an appalling charge. The family left town, first for Owego in central New York, then for Ohio. The mother held the family together. John D. Rockefeller grew up as if bent on making up for his father's disgrace. He attended high school in Cleveland, and at 15 went to work as a $3.50-a-week bookkeeper with no other thought than to make a fortune. Under his mother's rigorous influence, he attended the Baptist church, acquiring a lifelong devotion to piety, which included teaching Sunday school and attending prayer meetings. Within three years, solemn, self-disciplined John Rockefeller, having saved most of his pay while mastering the commission-produce trade, teamed with another clerk to start his own business. He was 20. The Civil War was just beginning. This single-minded young man thought only of trade. The war, in fact, boosted prices. The business prospered.

Ohio wheat, Michigan salt, Illinois pork—from buying and selling such commodities, young Rockefeller cleared $16,000 in the year of the Emancipation Proclamation. Already there was the most intense interest among Cleveland merchants in Drake's oil strike in the western Pennsylvania wilderness. Cleveland was scarcely 100 miles away from Titusville. Fantastic stories were told of fortunes made overnight. In 1862 one J. W. Sherman of Cleveland took a lease on the Foster farm along Oil Creek. Forced to stop drilling when his primitive rig failed to find oil in the first 50 feet, he traded a sixteenth share in his lease for an old horse. With that much horse power, his drill ground on for a few more weeks. Then he gave another sixteenth for a secondhand small steam engine that drove his drill down a few more feet. Lacking cash to buy coal, he traded still another sixteenth for $80 and a shotgun. On the verge of running out of sixteenth shares, he struck the fabulous Sherman well, which yielded an estimated $1.7 million.[10]

One Oil Creek family took off for New York after striking it rich. At the hotel the clerk looked at their rustic getup and told them no rooms were available. The family then said they would buy the hotel—and did, with bills peeled off on the spot.

But from $20 a barrel in 1859, the price of petroleum plunged to fifty cents in 1861. No one, it seemed, knew how to store the stuff. It came gushing from new wells, sometimes to be lost in rivers or destroyed in inextinguishable well fires. At best, it was hauled away by mud-slogging teamsters in wagonloads of leaky wooden barrels for buyers in distant Eastern cities. Only the accident of war lifted prices.

Looking ahead, young Rockefeller could see that in grain shipping and meat packing, cities farther west would beat out Cleveland every time. And too many manufacturing businesses demanded more capital than he could command. But this fiercely ambitious young enterpriser had been studying the oil trade, and in its competitive chaos he saw his chance. The first person to make oil kerosene in Cleveland was Samuel Andrews, a member of Rockefeller's church. When Andrews said he wanted to start a refinery, Rockefeller and his partner backed him. Never one to do things by halves, Rockefeller within the year sold out his commission business and concentrated on the oil.

Slender, blond, silk-hatted, every inch the well-styled merchant at 25, Rockefeller abhorred waste; it was said of him that he had the soul of an accountant. Refineries in those days were thrown up carelessly wherever oil could be collected and operated with little heed for orderly business practices. From some Cleveland plants, oil left over after the kerosene was piped off was often poured down the bank into the Cuyahoga River, and passing bargemen amused themselves setting fires on the harbor surface. To plug leaks, Rockefeller hired his own plumber. To provide barrels, he built his own barrel factory and was on hand at 6:30 A.M. to help pile hoops and wheel out shavings. He backed Andrews's efforts to increase the yield of kerosene. And in later years instead of throwing away the leftover oil, he pressed tirelessly to market the sludgy residue in by-products—in paraffin, in naphtha, in heavy oils for lubricating the multiplying machines of America.

But at first little enough of the refinery's output went to these products. The overwhelming demand was for the kerosene, which was then beginning to be used in lamps. Yet the typical refinery did well to distill as much as one barrel of kerosene out of every two 42-gallon barrels of crude oil received.

The process of refining was deceptively simple—not more than a few hundred dollars were required to set up the first makeshift stills that multiplied in northwest Pennsylvania, Cleveland, Pittsburgh, and a score of American cities. All that was needed was a big pot in which the lighter gases could be boiled out while the heavier oils settled to the bottom. A single cooking could accomplish this, and as a rule that was all the early refiner wanted. To get the maximum amount of kerosene out of the crude, however, took several recookings, and this was something that few could or would tarry to do.

All of the lighter gases that were drawn off after the single cooking were barreled as "kerosene." It contained within it volatile elements that by further careful processing could have been, and sometimes were separated out as camphene, or naphthene. The same was true of an extremely volatile component that was ultimately to transform the whole business of oil refining—gasoline.

It is not written of John D. Rockefeller that he surpassed all others at refining oil. Men like Samuel Downer and Joshua Merrill in Boston, who got off to an early start processing coal oil before Drake drilled his well, consistently brought more innovations into the industry than Rockefeller ever did. But the newer and more progressive manufacturing techniques that others introduced—the multiple stilling, the controlled cooking, the continuous processing—were soon taken up by Rockefeller as they demonstrated their cost-saving worth. Rockefeller's genius was displayed on other levels. He was endlessly attentive to detail. He watched his coopers wrap their barrels in 30-inch metal strips, then ordered them to snip off the three overlapping inches that they had always left beyond the bare circumference—and thenceforth saved 10 percent on his metal purchases. He sent the barrel factory this note: "Last month you reported on hand 1,119 bungs, 10,000 were sent you at the beginning of this month. You have used 9,527 this month. You report 11,012 on hand. What has become of the other bungs?" [11]

An early practitioner of the American mass-production doctrine of a product "no better than it needs to be," Rockefeller kept his plant costs low so that he could make a profit even when prices skidded, as they did in those years. His overriding aim was to build up output to high levels as swiftly as he could, and there was no time to play around with time-consuming research. The kerosene that Rockefeller marketed was volatile stuff, and he knew it. Time and again costly fires swept through his buildings despite all precautions. At no point in these early years did either Rockefeller or his competitors bother to boil out the explosive naphthene and gasoline before shipping their kerosene. Governments also were slow to adopt laws providing for any tests of safety. According to the census report of 1880, 17 of 38 states still had no regulations. In consequence, the kerosene marketed was apt to explode.

In 1871, Chicago had already suffered one costly fire, which almost got out of control when, on the night of September 10, fire broke out just west of the Calumet River about one and a half miles from the city center. Witnesses later said the fire was first spotted in a cowshed belonging to Timothy O'Leary; unassailable legend says that it was caused when a cow kicked over a kerosene lantern Mrs. O'Leary had left behind after milking.

By a series of mishaps the report of the fire was not relayed to the fire brigade stationed nearest to the scene. A stiff wind whipped the flames through the flimsy structures along the river's west bank. It showered sparks on the roofs of the crowded center of the city on the other bank. Hovels, mansions, offices, and large factories crumpled to cinders before their onslaught. By midnight the imposing and supposedly fireproof new City Hall was a seven-story ruin, its brick-walled interior gutted, its tall roofs tumbled in. Marshall Field and

Levi Leiter's, Carson Pirie and other great stores burned to the ground. Late on the second day, the Great Chicago Fire, most extensive in the history of the United States, finally burned itself out. At least 250 lives were counted lost, and as many more were unaccounted for. About a third of the habitations in the city of 300,000 were left standing. The mayor estimated damage at $200,000,000. Government officials and newspaper articles alike ascribed the outbreak to the kerosene lamp.[12] But nobody seems to have known or said that the kerosene in the lanterns of Chicago, and presumably Mrs. O'Leary's, was so combustible because refiners barreled and shipped it without first removing the volatile gasoline and naphthene components. Through the rest of the 1870s, from five to six thousand persons continued to lose their lives yearly in fires caused by lamp explosions.

As Rockefeller plunged into the oil trade, American business was entering upon the great boom that followed the Civil War. They were years of crass moneygrubbing, lavish display, debased business morality. Compared to such gaudily rampageous animals as Gould, Vanderbilt, Carnegie, and Morgan, the plain, pious, closemouthed Rockefeller seemed an unlikely figure to emerge as king of all the beasts of the American business jungle.

But powerful forces were on Rockefeller's side, elements of geography and technology that only gradually became manifest to others than himself. Farseeing, relentless, a genius at organization and the management of men, Rockefeller marshaled these forces to fashion America's first and greatest monopoly.

He was a soft-spoken, unsmiling man, somewhat sandy of complexion. Between high cheekbones were blue eyes that could blaze, though few, even in his family, were permitted to see this. His mouth was a thin slit. On rare occasions, especially when he brought off a big business deal, his face lit up, and he clapped his hands and was even seen to dance a little jig. He feared only God and thought of nothing but his business. His was the temper of a military chieftain, combining audacity with thoroughness and shrewd judgment. He seemed to take account of no one's feelings in his plans. He flew in the face not only of human liberties but of deep-rooted custom and common law. What he worked for was done in profound secrecy, but with unceasing will. His faith in his star matched that of a Napoleon. And the problems he had to overcome to gain mastery over a chaotic oil trade surpassed those of Andrew Carnegie, whose rise most nearly paralleled his. In his heavily capitalized industry, Carnegie never had to worry about fly-by-night operators, wildcat discoveries, or sudden gluts and famines in supplies.

Rockefeller was determined upon a swift and tremendous expansion. Though his was but one of thirty Cleveland refineries at the end of the Civil War, he already saw further than merely besting his rivals down the street. The oil trade he aimed at was not in the Cleveland area at all, but in the eastern United States and in Europe. As early as 1866, he dispatched his brother William to New York City to concentrate on building up the export trade. At the time, cities were competing for commerce, for railroads, for citizens. Railroads, it seemed, were the masters of the nation's emerging economy; they had corrupted Congress and the executive departments in the Grant administration. As Carnegie said later, "In those days railroad officials, free from restrictions could make and unmake manufacturing enterprises." [13]

The mainspring of industry, railroads were also the richest of corporations. They held 200 million acres of land. Along their exclusive rights of way, they could charge passengers and shippers whatever they pleased and could without notice or explanation change those rates whenever they wanted to. Big as they were, they were getting yet bigger. By the late 1860s, local monopolists with names like the New York & Harlem and the Baltimore & Annapolis were merging into monster transport networks like the New York Central and The Baltimore & Ohio systems. This transformation of the railroads from way-station monopolists into long-distance competitors was a fateful development for John D. Rockefeller—and indeed for the history of the American business corporation.

On November 3, 1863, the Atlantic and Great Western, a British-financed rail line, ran its first trains into Cleveland from the East— an event of pivotal importance for Rockefeller's future. From Meadville and Corry, in western Pennsylvania, the new line gave Cleveland a link with the Erie Railroad and thus direct communication with New York City. It meant that the little manufacturing city on Lake Erie gained direct access to the markets of the Atlantic seaboard and Europe. At the same time, the new line opened the first broad-gage rail connection between Cleveland and the oil regions of Pennsylvania, for the A. and G.W. had obtained a branch connection from Corry to the oil capital of Titusville the year before. In consequence, oil that had been arduously brought out overland and then shipped, when weather permitted, down the Allegheny River to Pittsburgh, now found a year-round outlet by rail. Most of the oil went to New York, where the main markets were. But from the first some of the new product found its way to Cleveland, where refineries like Rockefeller's Excelsior and Standard plants sprang up to process the stuff.

Soon, as Ida Tarbell wrote later, Rockefeller's competitors in Cleveland

> began to suspect something. John Rockefeller might get his oil cheaper now and then, they said, but he could not do it so often. He might make contracts for which they had neither the patience nor the stomach. He might have an unusual mechanical genius for his partner. But these things could not explain all. They believed they bought, on the whole, almost as cheaply as he, and they knew they made as good oil and with as great, or nearly as great, economy. He could sell at no better price than they. Where was his advantage? [14]

A century later, even Rockefeller's official biographer Allan Nevins did not doubt that the answer lay in special concessions obtained by Rockefeller on rail shipments of his oil. The railroads wanted the traffic of the cities they entered and eagerly grasped for transportable new products. At Cleveland, Rockefeller and his associates found they held an advantage. They could insist on shipping their barrels of kerosene at very cheap rates via the Great Lakes and the Erie or Welland canals. If the railroads wanted this business, they had to offer Rockefeller concessions, and they did. By 1867, the Atlantic and Great Western-Erie connection was not Cleveland's only link with the Pennsylvania oil regions and the East. Rockefeller had carefully cultivated ties with the new Lake Shore Railroad, whose president became an early director of Rockefeller's newly formed Standard Oil Company. The Lake Shore came under lease to Commodore Vanderbilt's New York Central and opened an extension to Franklin in the oil area of Pennsylvania. At this very time, Vanderbilt of the New York Central and Jay Gould of the Erie were locked in a titanic struggle for mastery of railborne trade, and both sides in the fight offered concessions to get Rockefeller's business. Moreover, as he saw from the first, the rich and stategically placed Pennsylvania Railroad, though slow in pushing branches north from Pittsburgh into the oil country, had an even bigger stake in the new commerce than its big northern rivals.

Though little evidence of Rockefeller's early secret concessions are to be found in Standard's archives, it is known that Rockefeller won a fifteen-cents-a-barrel rebate in 1867 for shipping oil over the New York Central-Lake Shore line. Beyond this, six contracts dating from 1868 were found by an historian permitted to go through the papers of a western Pennsylvania oil field lawyer. By their terms, one of his clients, contracting to deliver crude oil exclusively to the Atlantic and Great Western Railroad, agreed to remit $12 to Rockefeller and two other Cleveland refiners for every carload of bulk oil shipped by the Atlantic and Great Western-Erie system to the East coast.[15] These and other competitive advantages given Rockefeller by the Erie contracts were presumably conceded by the Atlantic and Great Western-Erie contracts because Standard Oil had won its rebate the year before for shipping oil over the rival New York Central-Lake Shore line.

Rockefeller began getting these rebates from the earliest years (and the 1868 contracts show that some of his rivals got them too). Such were the secret rate advantages Rockefeller wrung from the railroads that he could ship the crude oil from Pennsylvania west to Cleveland and then ship his refined products the 610 miles east to New York for less than the refineries in western Pennsylvania had to pay to ship the stuff only 500 miles to the same market. He set up warehousing facilities at the Erie terminal in New York harbor, and soon Standard Oil was filling orders for boatloads of bright blue barrels of refined oil for the markets of Europe. By 1870, Rockefeller's Standard plant was by far the biggest refinery in Cleveland, and also, had anyone troubled to notice, the biggest in America.

Rebating, once begun, built up a terrific armament. By 1870, Standard could propose to the railroads that in return for guaranteed, large shipments, it be granted a bargain-basement rate of $1.30 a barrel on refined stuff shipped to New York, and thirty-five cents a barrel on crude shipped from Pennsylvania to Cleveland. Since to the rail carrier the assurance of 60 carloads each and every day meant large economies in its freight operations, the road that got the business was in every way a consenting partner. In fact, when Rockefeller's Cleveland competitors got wind of the deal, the railroads did not bother to deny it. Instead, they said "that this concession was at all times open to any and all parties who would secure or guarantee a like amount of traffic."[16] But by then nobody but Rockefeller could generate such a volume of traffic.

Aged 30, Rockefeller had become one of Cleveland's leading personages. His company was earning close to 100 percent on capital —and he and his brother owned a half interest in the company. "It would seem," wrote Ida Tarbell, "as if the one man in the Cleveland oil trade in 1870 who ought to have been satisfied was Mr. Rockefeller."[17] Not so. Rockefeller's orderly mind looked upon the operations of the oil business with a distaste bordering on pain. The guerrilla fighting among drillers, the warfare among railroads, the dizzying ups and downs of supply and market prices outraged his sense of ledger-sheet logic.

He saw with perfect clarity that petroleum was destined to be the light of the world. His great idea, his unifying conception, was to seize upon the strategic position that refineries held astride this stream of oil to control and regularize its flow. The way to this achievement was not by yet more ruinous competition—but by what he called "cooperation."

The first instrument that came to hand for Rockefeller's drive toward combination was the infamous South Improvement Company. Midway in 1871, men associated with Rockefeller and the railroads obtained for a pittance the Pennsylvania charter of a defunct corpora-iton that had been authorized to do almost any kind of business under the sun. All who joined them had to sign a written pledge of secrecy. By terms of their scheme, the big railroads, led by the Pennsylvania, would form a pool to divide up the oil traffic among themselves. A handful of leading refiners, headed by Rockefeller, as officers and shareholders in the South Improvement Company, would act as "eveners" of the pool, allocating the oil traffic so that 45 percent went to the Pennsylvania and 27.5 percent each to the Erie and New York Central.

Of all the devices for the extinction of competitors, this was the cruelest and deadliest yet devised. Rockefeller and fellow insiders would get a rebate of 40 to 50 percent on all crude oil shipped to them and 25 to 50 percent on the refined oil they shipped out. This alone would have been enough to ruin competitors: refiners in northwest Pennsylvania—excluded from the ring—would have to pay twice as much as Standard, shipping from Cleveland. But there was an even more lethal proviso in this monstrous scheme: for their services as "eveners," Rockefeller and his fellow insiders would collect from the railroads a percentage of the freight charges the roads collected from rival refiners; in some cases, half of a competitor's payments would be handed over to the Rockefeller group. These levies were called drawbacks.

When the railroads' sky-high new rates were prematurely disclosed in Pennsylvania, producers exploded in wrath and fright. A meeting of 2,000 oil producers at the Titusville Opera House voted an immediate embargo of shipments to members of the South Improvement Company. It was effective. The railroads disowned the scheme, the Pennsylvania legislature revoked the company's charter, and a barefaced conspiracy to establish monopoly overnight was averted.

But in the hushed conferences that led up to the creation of this short-lived scheme, Rockefeller had pressed ahead on what he called "our plan." [18] To the main oil firms of Cleveland he had said, "You see, this scheme is bound to work. There is no chance for anyone outside it. But we are going to give everyone a chance to come in. You are to turn over your refinery to my appraisers, and I will give you Standard Oil stock or cash, as you prefer, for the value we put upon it. I advise you to take the stock. It will be for your good." [19]

Rockefeller's offers of purchase were usually made for one half to a third of the actual cost of the property. One by one, his strongest rivals caved in. In this way, one of Cleveland's leading capitalists, Colonel Oliver H. Payne, accepted Standard Oil Stock and was taken onto the board of directors. To those who resisted, Standard's men said, "If you don't sell your property to us, it will be valueless because we have the advantage with the railroads." [20] Finding that the railroads would give no relief, the uncle of Political Boss Mark Hanna was glad to sell out his refinery at 40 to 50 cents on the dollar. When one refiner made a speech against the plan, Rockefeller, who had been rocking in a rocking chair during the conferences, his hands over his face, suddenly stopped, lowered his hands, and looked straight at his enemy. His glance was fairly terrifying.

> You never saw such eyes. He took me all in, saw just how much fight he could expect from me, and then up went his hands, and back and forth went his chair.[21]

Thus, in the midst of the South Improvement Company debacle, Rockefeller devoured 22 Cleveland competitors and emerged with a capacity to refine half of all the oil then produced. And while members of the Petroleum Producers' Council cheered their victory over the "conspiracy," Rockefeller arranged anew the secret freight rebates that had occasioned the outcry over the South Improvement Company, obtaining a discount on refined oil shipped from Cleveland that gave him a 25 percent edge over his competitors.

Rockefeller's goal, of course, was to bring all of America's oil refiners under Standard domination. As in Cleveland, his first step was to pressure the biggest firms in each area to join and then, with these as a nucleus, use his "advantage with the railroads" to compel the surviving independents to sell or merge. He went about his arm-twisting in secrecy. Many of the conferences took place in Saratoga, New York, the "Mecca of schemers," [22] where far into the night he urged the strongest firms in the Eastern markets to cease competing with him. Look at what has been done in Cleveland, he would say. He told the chosen ones that the Standard combine would gradually take over refineries everywhere, become the only shippers, and dictate its own terms to the railroads. Wealth would come to *all* the participants. Those who were about to be absorbed were given a glimpse of the economies as well as the profits of Standard Oil. It is hard to say which were more persuasive—the figures that showed how much less than its competitors Standard paid to ship oil or those that showed how great were the profits of "cooperation." [23] New allies were urged not even to tell their wives of the arrangements. ("Silence is golden," was a Rockefeller motto.) They were told to conceal the gains they made. They were even told not to drive fast horses or put on style, which could suggest that there were unusual profits to be made in oil refining.

And so the largest companies in Pittsburgh, Philadelphia, and New York came into the fold. Under like terms of "absolute secrecy," [24] Rockefeller took over the largest West Virginia firm—important because it was in Baltimore & Ohio territory, and Standard wanted to contain the threat that B. & O. competition might upset the favorable rates won from the other big roads. Even more impressive was the victory Rockefeller gained in the oil regions of Pennsylvania as John D. Archbold of the Acme Refining Co., leader of the earlier opposition to the South Improvement Company, secretly allied his firm with Standard. Archbold took over as the combine's political paymaster and, when Rockefeller stepped down many years later, became his sucessor to the presidency of Standard Oil.

A long depression had settled upon the country in these years and Rockefeller, like Carnegie in steel, took advantage of it to build industrial dominance. Before the panic of 1873, the refiners resisted Rockefeller, but when hard times closed in they were willing either to join Standard or abdicate in its favor. The depression also came to Rockefeller's aid when the mighty Pennsylvania Railroad decided to enter the refining business through a pipeline subsidiary it had acquired. This might have been the most formidable challenge Rockefeller's monopoly had ever faced, but by then he had grown too big to bring down. His reply to the Pennsylvania's challenge was to pull all shipments off that line. Times were hard, general business was off, and the railroad ran into a costly strike in Pittsburgh. Tom Scott, the Pennsylvania's boss, had other things than oil to think about; Rockefeller thought about nothing else. As troubles piled up, the Pennsylvania missed a dividend. In such straits, Scott and his agents capitulated and sold out their subsidiary interests to Standard.

That put Rockefeller fairly into the pipeline business. In early years, when small "gathering" lines spread out to carry the crude oil from wells to shipping points on the railroads, Standard made no move to control them. Indeed, when the oil producers tried to extend pipelines beyond the oil regions, Rockefeller helped the railroads crush efforts to get a "free pipeline bill"—that is, a bill granting pipelines the right of eminent domain—through the Pennsylvania legislature. Only after laying down an 80-mile pipeline to the New York Central to fight off the Pennsylvania's threat and then acquiring the Pensylvania's holdings when the railroad threw in the towel, did Standard Oil emerge as a major pipeline operator.

Having gained this position, Rockefeller was enabled to bludgeon the last of his competitors into submission. This was the Tidewater Pipeline Company. In 1879, frustrated oil producers pushed this newly formed company's pipeline over the mountains to a link with other railroads connecting to New York City. It was a tremendous engineering feat and, since it promised economies in transport over shipment by railroad tank cars, an important technological advance. Standard reacted swiftly. On June 4, 1879, the *Oil, Paint and Drug Reporter* noted

> A meeting of the Trunk lines was held at Saratoga at which representatives of the Standard were present, and . . . the through rate on oil for the Standard was reduced from 85¢ to 20¢ and finally to 10¢ a barrel. Thus, to enable the Standard to wreck the new Pipe Line the railroads carried the oil at from a third to a fourth of the actual cost.[25]

Unsure that even such ferocious pressures would break the Tidewater thrust, Rockefeller rushed to buy out the remaining independent Eastern refineries that might takes its oil. Then, signaling his acknowledgment that the railroads had outlived their essentiality, he ordered construction of his own 300-mile trans-Appalachian pipeline from the oil regions to the coast through New York State. The trunk lines soon began to go back on their Saratoga giveaway to Rockefeller. But the rival that had revolutionized oil transport could not hold out against Standard's many-pronged onslaught. When the Tidewater's railroad ally, the Jersey

Central, set out to lay a spur to oil docks on the Jersey City water-front, Standard even sent forces to try to tear up the rails. Within two years, Tidewater Pipeline, on which the oil producers had pinned their last hopes of independence, accepted a loan from Standard and meekly received a quota of 11½ percent of all oil piped eastward. Standard's pipelines, of course, got the other 88½ percent.

By this time the Standard Oil Company had become the Standard Oil Trust. So vast and complicated had Rockefeller's operations grown that a new way had to be found to organize and manage the whole proliferating enterprise. Rockefeller's lawyer, S. C. T. Dodd, had reached into the dusty, littered attic of the law and fetched out the trust. People commonly thought of a trust as a property interest held and managed for widows and children. The Standard Oil Trust, created in 1882, was a device by which the 30 or 40 subordinate companies gave their voting stock to a central group of trustees in return for trust certificates bearing the right to receive interest payments but not to vote. The central group consisted of Rockefeller and seven associates. With these new powers, they set common price and market policies for the more than 30 companies.

The Standard was America's first Trust. Others followed within a decade: the Meatpacking Trust, the Flour-milling Trust, the Sugar Trust, the Timber Trust, the Tobacco Trust, the Cottonseed Oil Trust, the Whiskey Trust, the Salt Trust, the Linseed Oil Trust, the Lead Trust, the Leather Trust, the Cartage Trust—indeed, by 1890 the term *trust* was applied to every seeming monopoly.

But as a corporate device, it was soon abandoned. The trust ran afoul of the common law and of state statutes. The holding company took its place, a single firm that acquired all the stock of its subsidiaries. This was made possible by terms of a general incorporation law passed by the New Jersey legislature in 1889, which for the first time allowed one company to own the stock of others. The Standard Oil Company then became the Standard Oil Company of New Jersey, and a great wave of corporate mergers followed as American businessmen again emulated Rockefeller in combining to raise profits by limiting competition. (In New Deal days, there was considerable agitation to outlaw holding companies. In 1936, Congress, with the Public Utilities Holding Company Act, put an end to the use of this device to manipulate profits and dividends in the public-utility field. But holding companies in the rest of the corporate world went on to greater heights than ever. By the 1960s, when "conglomerates" came into wide vogue, entities like International Telephone and Telegraph not only combined disparate types of manufacturing enterprise, but bought up banks, airlines, and insurance companies as well.)

★

In the first 25 years after Drake drilled for oil in Pennsylvania, American manufacturers sold much the largest part of their refined product outside the country. "Rock oil" struck everybody as such a novel product that for a long time the United States held a virtual world monopoly on its output.

But Europe had its entrepreneurs too. In the 1870s, two brothers of the Swedish munitions maker Alfred Nobel began to develop the ancient oil deposits of the Russian Caucasus and to ship the refined product as far north as St. Petersburg and Stockholm. Then, when more Russian oil began moving to Black Sea ports in the 1880s, the Rothschild banking interests of Paris supplied capital in return for "refined oil for export." Soon the European challenge to Rockefeller was clear: the Nobels introduced an oceangoing tanker capable of transporting oil in bulk all the way from Batum to the market cities of Europe. Standard Oil had a bad scare; then it got out of the barrel-making business and built some bulk-carrying vessels for the Atlantic trade.

Ties of long standing existed between Standard and firms in London, Bremen, and Le Havre that sold the famous blue barrels of Standard's illuminating oil to jobbers for further distribution. But when the Nobels and Rothschilds formed their own marketing firms, so did Standard. The first of these was the Anglo-American Petroleum Company Ltd., which in 1888 began acquiring storage facilities in British ports, built bulk stations inland, and soon was pushing tank-wagon delivery even to retail customers. On the Continent, except that language and legal problems led Standard to work through existing companies, it was the same. "One group of businessmen after another is made superfluous and pushed aside," complained a Berlin newspaper.[26]

By the closing years of the century, Russia was producing more crude oil than the United States and supplying a third of the world market for kerosene. Well before this, Standard had entered into talks with the Nobels and Rothschilds for "a scheme for parceling out between them the whole of the refined oil markets of the world." [27] Only the czarist finance minister's refusal to agree that *all* Russian refiners must join kept this program from formal adoption. As it was, the Big Three entered into deals that divided world petroleum markets in patterns that still persist. Standard's share of the British kerosene market was two-thirds; on the Continent, it took over Rothschild and Nobel marketing facilities in Antwerp while contracting to buy and distribute their kerosene in western Europe. In eastern Europe, Russian petroleum predominated; in western Europe, Rockefeller's did.

The unique mobility of his product enabled Rockefeller to push it into almost every part of the world: "oil for the lamps of China" was a catch phrase when John Hay announced the Open Door policy. As early as 1884, a fifth of all American petroleum exports went to Asia. When the new firms of Samuel and Shell began developing rich fields in the Netherlands East Indies, the Rockefeller group formed a subsidiary in the Netherlands to buy up wells in Borneo.

In the United States, demand grew more slowly. Most customers for kerosene were in the eastern seaboard cities. Even when illuminating gas was freely available toward the end of the century, householders could light their lamps with Rockefeller's kerosene for $10 a year, whereas more well-to-do families had to pay $10 a month to have gas piped into their homes.

West of the Alleghenies, the expansion of the railroads influenced the distribution of Standard's products. Trainmen swung kerosene lanterns; farmers bore them to the barn for early morning chores. As kerosene and other products began to be shipped more and more in bulk rather than in barrels and cans, Standard Oil began setting up bulk stations in Chicago, Detroit, and other midwestern centers. The opening up of the Lima, Ohio, oilfield, first major field to be developed outside of Pennsylvania, led Rockefeller to lay pipelines from western Ohio and eastern Indiana to large new refineries in the Chicago area.

Soon, rather than leave its wares to a multitude of jobbers, Standard began acquiring financial interests in certain important wholesale houses. Through an alliance made in secret with a big Louisville firm, the combine extended its marketing influence into the South, until in 1885 it took over the operation. In another concealed arrangement, Standard took a 40 percent interest in the Waters Pierce Company of St. Louis and became a power almost everywhere in the Southwest. Lesser Standard Oil companies marketed Rockefeller's products in places like Iowa, Colorado, and South Dakota.

By the late 1880s, Rockefeller companies operated in every state. His agents were spread all over the country, 500 in the state of Indiana alone. By then the goal was a great marketing machine through which Standard's red and green horse-drawn tank wagons would deliver kerosene directly to stores in towns and villages throughout the country. No other trust, not the meat packers or flour millers or sugar refiners, put together such a comprehensive network. In marketing, as in manufacturing, Rockefeller brooked no resistance. If a dealer persisted in buying from competing agencies, Standard agents invoked the aid of the railroads. After their prodding, freight agents, filling out endless manifests and bills of lading in far-flung railroad depots, keeping in touch almost hourly by telegraph, became a system of intelligence for Rockefeller. One Standard message went out:

> Wilkerson and company received car of oil Monday 13th—70 barrels which we suspect slipped through at the usual fifth class rate—in fact we might say we know it did—paying only $4.50 freight from here. Charges $75.40. Please turn another screw.[28]

By the end of the century, when the Duryea brothers had begun manufacturing road vehicles propelled by the gasoline engine and Henry Ford, R. E. Olds, and others were building their first automobiles in Michigan, Rockefeller's network for the distribution of petroleum products was already nationwide.

How, granted his goals, could the methods of Rockefeller have been anything but political? In the nineteenth century Americans took it as received truth that their society vouchsafed freedom. It was a supreme right guaranteed by the United States Constitution, and the economic structure that underpinned America's political order was in perfect consonance with it. Men were free to hold and acquire property, and this they did as the country grew.

But the rise of the railroads and the technology of industry gave some men the power to subvert freedom to private ends on a scale that endangered the national polity. Under the powerful impact of these new economic forces, the indispensable balance of freedom and order broke down. Laissez-faire became the passport first for individuals and next for the corporations they formed to aggrandize beyond anything the Founding Fathers had foreseen.

By the last quarter of the nineteenth century, local America was at bay. A relatively few men and corporations had cornered most of the wealth. The new order that was taking shape bore small resemblance to that of the original Republic. Yet those amassing vast power and wealth insisted that the conduct of their business was an entirely private matter. Vanderbilt, unwilling to concede that his state-chartered railroad was a common carrier as well as a speculator's gold mine, said, "The public be damned." It is not recorded, though Rockefeller was given to much less picturesque language, that John D. said anything of the kind. But his actions bespoke the same conviction. Whatever else he foresaw in the grandiose expansion of his Standard Oil Company, Rockefeller never foresaw the central difficulty of the law and the public will. He refused—it is the only word for his attitude—to see that his aggrandizements created giant problems for local and national polity wherever the force of Standard Oil was felt. He could not bring himself to awareness, let alone admission, that his combine was "in politics." It came therefore as a continuous surprise to him that the impact of his industrial enterprise brought him into sharp conflict with public opinion.

What Rockefeller aspired to was nothing less than world conquest, and in pursuit of this goal he used methods of commercial warfare in its most scientifically developed degree. Though secret conspiracy was his most congenial weapon, and the one which served him best, open violence was occasionally used on his behalf, although no member of Standard's governing body was ever identified as having instigated it. Lying and perjury to escape the strong arm of the State were freely resorted to by his leading aides; bribery and corruption became their common instruments. Standard Oil bought its way not only into the private business of rivals marked down for absorption, but also into the establishments of customers whose business Standard's men desired to secure. Standard Oil not only debauched the press, but schemed to control the courts of justice and the legislature for its own ends. Never in history had the "holy hunger for gold" showed itself more cunning, farsighted, unscrupulous, dangerous—and insatiable.

The American order of 1789 had been undone by traducing of its ideals. Late in the nineteenth century, the State began hacking at the tentacles of Rockefeller's monster. The balance of freedom and order that monopoly had crushed must be put right again. It was an urgently political matter, but it was hard to get to grips with Standard Oil. Unlike the railroads, it did not depend on the state for franchises. Unlike other manufacturers of the day, it did not demand subsidies or tariff favors. Throughout its early rise, it wanted nothing from government so much as to be left alone. Its interventions in the political arena were largely to forestall possible action by the authorities to regulate or otherwise impede its voracious expansion. For a long time these battles were fought mainly on local and state levels, and there was no gainsaying the fierce energy with which Standard beat off all public challenges.

It helped that in the Gilded Age, America was a nation of speculators. Everybody, from the farmer who got 160 acres of land free from the government under the Homestead Act of 1862 to the robber baron whose railroad lobbied ten million acres free from Congress, hoped eagerly for an increase in values. If the little man complained of the speculative greed of the big corporation, it was often jealousy that animated him rather than any real difference about moneymaking goals. Neither looked upon soil, forests, or minerals as in any way limited, and neither dreamed of paying an increased cost for more prudent resource management. Only a small number grew rich from the rise in values, but few failed to grasp any opportunity if it came their way.

Americans, when they face problems, have never hesitated to turn to government for help in their solution. When people clamored for the opening of the West, land was granted to the railroads to induce them to lay tracks across the plains. Later, when the railroads appeared to charge higher rates to deliver manufactured goods to the western settlers than to carry away the settlers' produce, people agitated for intervention by the state to correct perceived injustice. And when Rockefeller joined with the railroads to gain rates that ruined rival refiners and placed the oil producers at his mercy, the people of the Pennsylvania oil regions were quick to demand redress through political action. Though the nation at large was a long time taking Rockefeller's measure, the producers of Pennsylvania knew his aim and style. (Despite his ruthlessness, however, he was so mild as to be mealymouthed. People were more than suspicious; they were resentful of this plutocrat's piety. Some castigated Rockefeller for giving "tainted" money to churches and colleges. He answered, aggrieved, "God gave me my money.") [29]

The first public demonstration against Rockefeller was almost too successful. The South Improvement Company scheme was sprung so suddenly, and the outcry against it was so violent, that when oil regions men rushed to Harrisburg, they had no trouble getting the corporation's charter revoked. But from that time on, they were all but helpless in getting the state to curb his control. Standard was soon well armed with lawyers, with lobbyists, and, for that matter, with legislators. In the years of Rockefeller expansion, as someone said, Standard Oil did everything to the Pennsylvania legislature except refine it. In the fight for a free pipeline, Standard lent money to the Pennsylvania Railroad "to enable them to thistle [pay] up matters in Harrisburg," [30] a Rockefeller aide wrote. Not only were the rank and filers bribed: a scrap of correspondence preserved in Standard's archives shows that the dominant figure in Pennsylvania politics was in Rockefeller's pay. During these same years, Boss Matthew Quay let it be known that he needed $15,000. Reporting that he had lent Quay part of the sum, a Standard lieutenant asked instructions about the rest. "I feel that Mr. Quay might be of great use to us in this state but he is fearfully expensive," he wrote Rockefeller.[31] Later, when Quay's election to the Senate was contested for fraud, officers of Standard Oil wrote key members of Congress, successfully urging that the charges be disregarded.

Eventually, Pennsylvania oil producers prodded the state auditor general to bill Standard Oil for taxes commensurate with the wealth it was taking out of the state. Standard's legal eagles swooped with 25 objections, which tied up courts for three years: in the end, judges upheld the plea that Standard was a "foreign" company in Pennsylvania—and cut the state's tax bill to Standard from $3.2 million to a total of $25,000 for the five years in question. The producers then appealed to the governor and other elected officials. A Titusville editor (his paper was later bought out by Standard Oil) cried that "four thousand men were ready to shoulder their muskets." [32] On their behalf the attorney general brought a civil action against the railroads and Standard for unlawfully combining to control the oil industry. The hearings dragged and the frustrated producers attacked on another front: in April 1879, a grand jury in Clarion County in northwest Pennsylvania brought in a criminal indictment against Rockefeller and eight other Standard officers under the ancient common-law prescript against "conspiracy in restraint of trade."

Rockefeller, by now a resident of New York rather than Ohio, pulled wires in both Albany and Harrisburg to make sure he would not be extradited. Chauncey Depew, the country's leading lawyer, saw New York Governor Robinson, then wired Rockefeller: "I have a letter promising all needed protection." [33] Lesser lawyers obtained assurances from Pennsylvania Governor Hoyt, who owed his election to Matt Quay. The four Rockefeller lieutenants resident in Pennsylvania were arrested and gave bail. But with a helping hand from Governor Hoyt, the Standard officials used one pending case for not testifying in the other; and action was stalled until the producers, succumbing as usual to the necessity of selling their oil, accepted a paper settlement.

In Albany, where Standard Oil had sent $10,000 to the president of the Erie Railroad for corridor "expenses," [34] the state legislature appointed a committee, headed by A. Barton Hepburn, a young lawyer, to investigate the railroads. Forced to look at the facts of rate-rigging chicanery, New Yorkers were shocked. Chauncey Depew, fronting for both Vanderbilt and Rockefeller, later said, "Every manufacturer in the state of New York live[s] by violence and exist[s] by discrimination—by secret rates and by deceiving their competitors and by evading all laws of trade." [35] Though Rockefeller was not compelled to testify, Standard Oil was shown to be the chief gainer by rate discrimination among the railroads. William H. Vanderbilt said on the stand, "Yes, they are very shrewd men. I don't believe that by any legislative enactment or anything else, through any of the states or all of the states, you can keep such men down. You can't do it. They will be on top all the time. You see if they are not." [36] For the first time, the huge size of Standard Oil was made known, even though Archbold, then still president of Acme Refining in Pennsylvania as well as a director of Standard Oil, said under oath, "I know of no interests outside Cleveland or New York in connection with the Standard Oil Co." [37]

Witnesses told how the New York Central gave rebates. To the question of whether the Erie granted Standard "a special rate," its freight agent conceded, "We do." [38] An independent refiner testified that several railroads refused to carry his oil at all and said, "I think that if the books of the Erie were examined, it would be found that only ten cars of crude petroleum [have] been shipped to New York by any shipper outside the Standard Oil Co. or their connections within over a year." Asked the committee counsel, "Do you mean to say that the whole shipment, practically, that comes to New York over the New York Central and over the Erie is for the Standard Oil Co. and its connections?" "I do," said the witness, and others backed up his story.[39]

The Standard men were both arrogant and evasive. Like Archbold, H. H. Rogers of Charles Pratt and Co. of New York declined even to admit his company's connections with Standard, though he too was a Standard director. He acknowledged, though, that nine-tenths of the country's refiners were "in harmony" with Standard Oil.[40] Then other witnesses furnished lists of the 30 or so companies —Pratt included—that Standard controlled. The hearings brought out Standard's role as "evener" long after the passing of the South Improvement Company, still allocating among the railroads their agreed share of the oil traffic, still receiving from them payments —drawbacks—for oil carried for Standard's competitors.

The committee report labeled Standard "a unique illustration" of what clout the rebates gave such a firm; an object lesson in "the colossal proportions to which monopoly can grow under the laws of our country."[41] It pointed out that after Standard got control of the refining industry, the railroads obtained much less revenue from the oil trade than they should have, forcing them to charge more for other products to make up the loss—a tax, in other words, upon everybody else for the Standard monopoly's enrichment.

If Standard's defensive spending was most evident in Penn-sylvania (where a former state Republican chairman later admitted buying men for Standard in order to block a bill limiting the com-pany's pipeline charges), its influence in its native Ohio was para-mount in both parties. Standard Oil's house Democrat was Treasurer Oliver Hazzard Payne, whose father was both representative and senator from Ohio in these years. Thus when in 1879 the Ohio legislature also opened an inquiry into railroad rates, Treasurer Payne moved behind the scenes to defend company interests. Distressed to find that the investigation had been shifted from the Committee on Railroads, where the company was not without well-wishers, to that on corporations ("a very unfriendly committee," Payne told Rockefeller), Democrat Payne maneuvered to put matters back where they stood before. "This puts the investigation in the hands of *friends,*—and will probably not hurt us very much," he wrote Rockefeller.[42]

Rockefeller avoided testifying, but Henry Flagler, his closest associate, took the stand. Afterwards he reported to Rockefeller he thought he had satisfied the committee that "whatever the railroads have done for others, our Co. has no contract providing for discrimina-tion or rebates" [43]—this only months after Flagler had asked the roads for a "private reduction" for Standard. At that very moment Standard was not only getting rebates but exacting drawbacks—on

30,000 barrels, for instance, shipped over a two-month period that year to a surviving independent in New York City.

As in Pennsylvania, the most powerful figure in Ohio politics was secretly in Standard's pay. This was Governor (later Senator) Joseph B. Foraker. Archbold, Rockefeller's political paymaster, sent Foraker repeated requests for favors—for the use of his influence against bills in the legislature, for the support of a certain candidate for the state supreme court, for opposition to an aspirant for the Ohio attorney generalship. Archbold also sent Foraker an attack on a "vicious" antitrust bill before Congress, and the senator duly cast his anti-antitrust vote. And Senator Foraker also arranged for a Standard loan to parties seeking to buy an influential newspaper in Columbus. The deal fell through, but since Rockefeller held substantial interests in two Cleveland newspapers and a third in Toledo, the company hardly lacked for friends in the Ohio press.[44]

Months after Rockefeller had snuffed out the chance that Speaker Garfield might encourage a congressional inquiry into railroad rebates as part of his 1880 presidential campaign, the Republican nominee was writing a lieutenant in Indiana to get the Standard Oil president to use his 500 agents there to help sway that state to his side. Later Rockefeller, in response to Mark Hanna's plea for "protection of our business interests," [45] sent a conspicuously small ($600) contribution to Senator John Sherman's reelection campaign. Hanna had reason to think Sherman, author of the Sherman Antitrust Act, was backing a young Ohio attorney general who had put through his own state's antitrust law. In the late 1880s this young man prosecuted and convicted Standard Oil of violating this law.

The young reformer was defeated for reelection, and Standard simply ignored Ohio's order for dissolution of the trust until it could reincorporate as a holding company in New Jersey and thus pull safely away from Ohio's annoying statute.

Ohio's law was but one of many local attempts to curb this formidable new power. People had thought it was the railroads, merging into vast systems, that were taking over the country. In a brilliant 1881 *Atlantic Monthly* article entitled "The Story of a Great Monopoly," a Chicago lawyer named Henry Demarest Lloyd set everybody straight.[46] Citing the five thick volumes of Hepburn hearings, he showed how Rockefeller's trust, taking every liberty in the land of the free, had exploited rail rivalry to build a far greater threat to free enterprise in America.

Lloyd may have been wide of the mark on some of his facts. But he was everlastingly right in asserting that the corporate pyramid Rockefeller had reared, so to speak, right under the public's nose was a far more important development in American economic life than the local monopolies and rate-making powers of the railroads. Rockefeller grasped that in business, competition becomes the enemy of rationality, and combination stamps out instability, which was his idea of competition. General Motors, IBM, and the rest of the hundred supercorporations that dominate modern life are but later likenesses of Standard Oil. Yet the impact of Lloyd's attack was also formidable and lasting. It stamped a stereotype of Standard Oil upon the American mind. Tiger, octopus, anaconda—these were the images of Rockefeller's monster that thenceforth, as other publicists rose to keep up the assault, filled the public eye.

Among the Populists of the West, angered by the railroads' high-handed ways with the farmers, determination mounted to condemn Rockefeller for getting bargain rates from the railroads while they, as they thought, were being robbed. Throughout America, and more particularly in New England, there were also people of means and education, some of them lawyers and teachers and clergy, many of them members of families who had owned the small industries and factories of their towns, who found themselves jostled and pushed aside by the new forces of big-business monopoly. Like the oil producers of Pennsylvania, they were defeated by the size and scale of the monopolists. As Lloyd pointed out, state legislatures, controlled by the corporations, would do nothing; inevitably, the aggrieved elements turned to the larger arena in Washington to obtain the justice they demanded.

By evasions; by delays; by legal dodges; by incessant vigilance in Harrisburg, Albany, Columbus, Annapolis, and Washington; by outright threats and bribery, Rockefeller held all those at bay who sought to break his hammerlock grip upon the nation's oil trade. In 1887, Congress finally enacted the Interstate Commerce law, but the commission thus established made no move to stop the railroads' practice of giving rebates to Standard Oil. In 1890, John Sherman and other Republican leaders decided to enact a law that would satisfy the rising public clamor against the trusts without upsetting the combinations too much. Sherman said, "You must heed this appeal, or be ready for the Socialist, the Communist, the nihilist." [47] Senator Orville Platt of Connecticut said, "The conduct of the Senate has not been in line with honest preparation of a bill to prohibit and punish trusts. It has been in the line of getting something with that title that we might go to the country with." [48]

Neither Presidents Cleveland nor McKinley, to whose campaign Standard Oil contributed $250,000, made a move to enforce the antitrust law. When in 1898 Congress named an Industrial Commission to report on its enforcement, members included Senator Boies Penrose of Pennsylvania, who had succeeded to Boss Quay's seat and "ties" with Standard Oil. Such were the terms of these ties that Penrose showed Archbold in advance the report being prepared by the commission. Archbold objected to parts of it; so Penrose and his fellow commission members rewrote the passages. When the report was finally passed back to Standard's secret political bureau, Archbold replied, "We think the report is so fair that we will not undertake to suggest any changes." [49]

Those were Standard's grandest years; between 1898 and 1904, industrial America formed 318 combinations like Rockefeller's. He himself, taking in $100 million a year in dividends alone, was on top of the wave. But anxiety over the incessant demands to dismantle Standard Oil led to a series of mysterious illnesses. All his hair fell out, including his eyebrows. A man who had always been at pains to look and dress just like another businessman, he found to his horror that his bald head gleamed like a knob of marble. He forbade pictures and, so far as possible, mention of his altered appearance. For a time he wore a skullcap; then he acquired a wardrobe of wigs, one for church, another for golf, a third for street wear. Later his hair grew back. He kept increasing his charities.

Then in 1901 two bullets in the brain of President McKinley put Theodore Roosevelt in the White House. Roosevelt, with a flair for the dramatic and a keen sense of changing grass-roots politics, reached out to those elements in the West and South that had led in criticism of the trusts and in demand for legislation to outlaw them. The enemies of Standard Oil were finally not to be denied. In due course, the Bureau of Corporations in the newly created Department of Commerce and Labor recommended prosecution of Standard Oil under the Sherman act. Roosevelt, denouncing "malefactors of great wealth," directed his Justice Department to go after both the railroads and Standard Oil.

In 1906, in the Northern Securities decision, the Supreme Court forbade the merger of three big western railroads. The Standard Oil case, however, was fought all the way through Roosevelt's administration and through Taft's as well. It was not until 1911 that the Supreme Court handed down its decision. It held that the object of the Standard Oil Company had been "to drive others from the field and exclude them from their right to trade," [50] and—all judges agreed—the company had violated the Sherman act. The court ordered the huge holding company dissolved forthwith.

3
Texas, the Tin Lizzy— and the Big Tax Dodge

If all that had ever come of it was Rockefeller's kerosene monopoly, the rise of Standard Oil would remain as remote from modern American life as, say, John Jacob Astor's conquest of the Western fur trade. Even after the Supreme Court handed down its breakup decree in 1911, to be sure, many a poor city household and practically all farms continued to be lit by Rockefeller's humble lamp. But by then, electricity was the light of the world. Kerosene was on its way out, and so was John D., though he survived in plutocratic retirement, handing out dimes and other benefactions, until his death, at 98, in 1937.

Ironically, oil's days of destiny arrived as the great man walked offstage. Even as the twentieth century began, new forces were gathering that were to turn oil from a source of flickering light into all civilization's wellspring of power. These forces brought out such vast quantities of oil as Rockefeller never dreamed of, required such huge amounts as he never thought to control, and channeled oil into public affairs in ways from which he always shrank.

Dynamic but amorphous, these new forces can be broadly identified as Texas, the automobile, and the depletion allowance. The first signified the outburst of supply; the second, the explosion of demand; the third, the new political centrality of oil. In the first two decades of this century these forces transformed oil's place in America, giving it economic prominence, social weight, and political clout without parallel. No longer just another commodity ladled from barrels at the back of small stores, oil poured forth to cover, in one way or another, almost all human activity.

Among most human beings, uncertainty is widespread as to precisely what power is. Everybody agrees that it exists, and the wisest add that it is slippery. Oil, certainly, is slippery; and in our time oil creates power. Often oil seems to *be* power—as in Texas.

Watered by the sacred blood of the Alamo and grafted onto the United States as an already full-grown republic, the great and mighty state of Texas is the one member of the federal union that most easily calls itself sovereign. Its realm, bounded only as everyone knows by the endless skies, is much the biggest of the contiguous forty-eight. Everything about Texas is superlative, from its ten-gallon hats to its tooled-leather boots, from the five-mile runways of the Fort Worth jetport to the 80,000-steer herds browsing the 960,000 acres of the King Ranch. In all of America its roads are the longest; its hamlets, the loneliest; its cities, the rawest; its ranches, the rangiest; its rivers, the broadest; their waters, the shallowest; and the frogs in them, the scrawniest—some of them four years old and haven't learned to swim.

Less than a century ago, the citizens of Texas were seething in frustration. After the ordeal of the Civil War's Reconstruction Era, Yankee capitalists like Jay Gould and Tom Scott had rammed railroads across their state and looted their public lands. When John H. Reagan, Texas's man in Jeff Davis's cabinet, returned from Boston imprisonment to his farm in east Texas, he heard the fury of the cotton farmers and cattle ranchers at these robber barons. Rallying to the National Grange, joining in Farmers Alliance lamplight meetings, and backing a fierce strike against the railroads,[1] Texas was a have-not state in the age of greed. Returned to Congress in 1878, John Reagan introduced the bill that a decade later put bit and bridle on the rampant railroads, the Interstate Commerce Act of 1887.

Out of the hardscrabble farmlands west of the Sabine there came a country boy whose father had soldiered with Houston and Bragg. James Henry Hogg was a Texan born. At the age of eighteen, already six feet two, Jim Hogg helped a sheriff bring in a gang of ruffians who had shot up the town of Quinland. A year later, he was plugged through the back and nearly killed by a member of the gang who recognized him leaving a country store. Hogg recovered, but could no longer do heavy farm work. He got a job as a printer's devil and then ran a newspaper. He read law and then stood for public prosecutor. "Enforce the law" was his booming call,[2] and the farmers elected him county and district attorney. As enforcer, Jim Hogg made arrests in person, "cleaned up" whole towns, and gave railroad officials a hard time. In 1886, Texas was in ferment. Strikers fought pitched battles against railroad police. Trains were derailed; property, destroyed. Riots red with blood finally brought out the militia; only by the power of the state was the strike ended. At a Democratic convention that protested "foreign domination" of the state's railroads,[3] Jim Hogg was nominated for attorney general.

Massive, pink-jowled, chin-whiskered, he took the platform amid a ten-minute din of hog calls. He began: "I am one of those unfortunate animals from the pine and persimmon valleys of East Texas that is not altogether a razorback, but I am glad to respond to your call."[4] His campaign, roared Hogg, pitted "the people against emboldened corporations brazenly and defiantly disregardful of the law."[5]

Elected attorney general, he brought suit against fraudulent insurance companies and forced the return to the state by railroads of almost two million acres of land. He compelled the railroads to bring their headquarters back to the state. Campaigning for reelection, he rolled up huge majorities. A magnetic personality, he was unrivalled as a stump speaker. He drew his support, he said, from "the wool hat boys from the forks of the creek," and shouted, "As long as there's buttermilk and cabbage, I'll survive."[6] Opposition newspapers complained that he was coarse, jeered at his campground and tent-meeting followers, his hog-calling and squirrel-shooting campaign antics, and made frequent mention of his curiously named daughter Ima.

The issues on which Jim Hogg roused Texas to revivalistic fever were economic—ideas that were later called Progressive. Nobody in those days supposed that there was oil under Texas, and Rockefeller's man Archbold was supposed to have roared with laughter and offered to drink all the oil that might ever be found west of the Mississippi. But as Hogg saw it, Rockefeller was in cahoots with the railroads. And so, as attorney general, he wrote an antitrust law for Texas so tough that it appeared almost impossible for Standard Oil to go on doing business in the state. At the same time, he took up the idea of a state railway commission to regulate freight rates—the same cause that his father's old friend Reagan was championing nationally.

In 1890, Hogg ran for governor. His backers strung a barbed wire fence round the Houston convention hall, and 300 sergeants at arms let no one in until his men had all the seats. A banner bearing a picture of a huge hog waved over the building. One slogan proclaimed: "We do business at the forks"; another: "Don't loosen the belly band." Hogg's chosen foe was the railroad "monopoly," and his proposal for a railroad commission, as a constitutional amendment, went on the ballot with him.

Triumphantly upheld by popular vote, Hogg got Reagan to resign from the Senate to lend his prestige as chairman to the state's Railroad Commission. Lobbyists delayed and softened the bill, however, until Hogg bellowed "By gatlins, I will take a hand myself," [7] and forced the legislators to meet day and night until he obtained such powers for the commission that it not only regulated railroads, but could later take over management of the state's oil production.

The Railroad Commission was a landmark achievement, the high point of Hogg's four years in office. Having fought for the two-term limit in the state's constitution, he retired from the governorship after his second term in 1895. But Jim Hogg's influence and example lingered well into the twentieth century and visibly affected the political style of such later Texans as Tom Connally, Sam Rayburn, and Lyndon Johnson.

Rockefeller's combine operated in Texas through the Waters Pierce company of St. Louis, which aggressively marketed Standard's refined products in the state with all the rebating, arm-twisting, and and price-cutting practices for which Standard was notorious elsewhere. When Hogg's attorney general sued under the state law to oust Waters Pierce from Texas as a Standard affiliate, the company successfully fought a delaying action until Hogg left office. But in 1900 the United States Supreme Court upheld Hogg's antitrust law.

Waters Pierce at once dissolved itself, proclaimed its independence from Standard Oil, and thereby obtained the right to stay in business in the state. Hogg turned up at a bar association meeting in Houston to growl that the company "was found criminally guilty, and it has never been whipped of its crime." [8] The state of Texas kept the heat on Standard Oil. A half dozen Waters Pierce men were haled into court, and one was convicted, for conspiring to restrain trade. Finally, after Hogg's death in 1906, the head of Waters Pierce admitted in court that his company was still Standard-controlled. In 1909, Standard Oil was finally banished from Texas.

Ironically, it was Hogg, the man largely responsible for his state's official hostility to Standard Oil, who led in the turn-of-the-century transformation by which oil made Texas into the land of wealth it has been ever since.

In 1900, the economy of the state was founded upon timber and sugar, cattle and cotton. In the late 1880s, prospectors had struck oil in commercial quantities in Kansas and then in Oklahoma and in 1890 at Corsicana, in the northeast corner of Texas. James A. Cullinan, who had worked for Standard at Oil City, built a refinery at Corsicana with the idea of selling the output to Standard. But the two Pennsylvanians who had found the oil, John H. Galey and Joseph Guffey of Pittsburgh, suspected there was more oil in Texas.

They talked with Pattillo Higgins, a brickyard operator, and Captain Anthony Lucas, an engineer, who had drilled a site near Beaumont on the Gulf, only to be halted by caving that snagged their drill 400 feet down. Galey and Guffey decided that instead of pounding their way down with the usual Pennsylvania-style cable tools, they should try the rotating, solid-pipe drills that had been used in boring artesian wells in the Dakotas. This cost more, and so for financial aid Guffey turned to his usual backers, the Mellon family, at their bank in Pittsburgh.

The site at which these new partners finally sank their new drill flanked a pond on whose surface boys had for years tossed matches "to see the lake catch fire." [9] Gas, it seemed, kept bubbling to the pond's surface as it seeped out of the tremendous geological dome just below. Higgins, in particular, had always insisted that oil collected under such salt domes and that it was only necessary to bore through their limestone roofs to bring it up. Actually, the hill atop the dome was little more than ten or twelve feet high, and it was a steep-sided prominence crowned by spindly pines a mile to the north that gave its name to the drilling site—Spindletop.

Drilling started late in 1900, and in short order the new, Mellon-financed rig penetrated the quicksand barrier. Soon Captain Lucas picked up a chunk of rock lying near the derrick and shouted, "You're into the limestone, you're cutting through the dome." [10] On January 10, 1901, the drill was down to 800 feet. Then things began to happen. As Al Hammill, one of the men who had brought the new gear from the north, told it:

We put the new bit on and had about 700 feet of the drill pipe back in the hole when the rotary mud began flowing up through the rotary table. It came so fast and with such force that Curt, who was on the doubleboards, was drenched with mud and had a hard time getting out of danger.

Soon the four-inch pipe started up through the derrick, knocking off the crown block. It shot up through the top of of the derrick breaking off in lengths of several joints at a time as it shot skyward. It all happened in much less time than it can be told.

After the water, mud and pipe were blown out, gas followed, but only for a short time. Then all became quiet.

We boys ventured back, after a wild scramble for safety, to find things in a terrible mess—at least six inches of mud on the derrick floor and damage to our equipment. We were disgusted. We started shoveling the mud away.

Then suddenly without any warning a lot of heavy mud shot out of the well with the report of a cannon! Gas followed for a short time. Then oil showed up. In [seconds] oil was going up through the top of the derrick. Rocks shot hundreds of feet in the air. In a very few minutes the oil was shooting at a steady flow at more than twice the height of the derrick.[11]

Never had such a mighty gusher been seen anywhere—the roar of the untamed geyser of oil caused some to flee the countryside. Many thought the earth would cave in. Tidings of the event flashed around the globe. To view "the greatest sight on earth," [12] thousands swarmed by special trains from Galveston and Houston. They felt the earth shake with the bellow of 40,000 barrels of oil a day roaring from where it had been pent up for eons. For nine days, the oil rained down on Spindletop and ran into hastily dug pools. Then, working in five-minute shifts, men with goggles over their eyes, gauze shields over their noses, and cotton plugs in their ears took turns pushing a monster, sand-filled iron cylinder on top of the gusher. It held. The roar ceased; the ground trembled, but did not give way. The Lucas gusher, as it was called, was capped.

Spindletop was the Klondike of oil. It started a rush to Texas that did not end for decades. It did more to stir up competition in the petroleum industry than all the Supreme Court's trust-busting orders put together. Overnight, oil drilling became the state's most spectacular activity, and by 1920 oil was the state's leading industry. Within a year no fewer than 491 oil companies were chartered in Texas. One

40-acre tract at Spindletop went to a group of speculators for $40,000.
They drilled a well and sold it for $1,250,000—but kept all the 40
acres except the spot on which the derrick stood. As far as 150 miles
away from Spindletop, land prices soared; and not only Beaumont
but Houston, 75 miles away, became oil-rush towns.

Lucas and his partners had hit pay dirt, but to make the most of
their great find they needed a lot more money. They turned again to
the Mellons of Pittsburgh. Andrew W. Mellon knew that John D.
Rockefeller faced legal handicaps in Texas and that Waters Pierce
was looked upon with disfavor there. The Pittsburgh banker saw his
chance. He bought out Lucas for $400,000 and then rounded up $4.5
million to bankroll initial development of the field: drilling more
wells, laying a 25-mile pipeline to tidewater Port Arthur, and con-
structing a big refinery there.

A week after Spindletop's discovery, a friend who had been there
met former Governor Hogg on an Austin street. "You can't afford to
pass it up," the friend said. A few weeks later the friend returned and
spotted a huge, familiar-looking figure sitting on a porch, surrounded
by a small crowd. It was Jim Hogg holding court and telling his
stories. "I've bought a few oil leases," he called out.[13]

He certainly had. Though the Spindletop field covered no more
than 250 acres in all, Joe Guffey had given the 24-acre Page lease
atop the Dome to the Hogg-Swayne Syndicate. This was an intriguing
transaction in more ways than one. Joining Hogg in the deal were
several of his Texas cronies, and together they had scraped up
$105,000 to pay for the lease. But because the old foe of corporations
could not abide the idea of heading a corporation, the group called
itself simply the Hogg-Swayne Syndicate. As for Joe Guffey, who became Mellon's front man in developing the field, he later explained,
"Northern men were not very well respected in Texas in those days.
Governor Hogg was a power down there, and I wanted him on our
side."[14] Though the Mellons later fired Guffey, took over the Spindletop development, and turned it into the multimillion-dollar Gulf Oil
Corporation, they never said a word against the deal Guffey struck
with Jim Hogg. And as for Hogg, it suited him fine that the capital
coming into Texas to develop its first great oil strike was not Standard
Oil's.

It soon appeared that Hogg and his friends, mostly lawyers and
all of them innocent of oil-trade experience, had got themselves in
deep. The five syndicate members had used all the credit they had to
raise cash for their initial plunge. Now Hogg decided that they

should sell off some of their holdings to get out of debt, and he went about it in a way that also left its stamp on the Texas style of oil exploitation.

The first two and a half acres the syndicate sold brought $200,000. After that they sold, so to speak, to all comers—plots of a quarter acre, a sixteenth acre, a thirty-second of an acre, "doormats" as they came to be called. The syndicate kept half its tract. But the rest soon bristled with derricks, 120 of them. (Before long, no fewer than 300 wells were drilled on Spindletop. It was Guffey's Hogg-Swayne deal that led to the overcrowding, to the disastrous fires, to the reckless waste, and, long before it should have happened, to the exhaustion of its wells.)

Hogg's syndicate brought in five more wells, bought land for a pumping station at Spindletop and a refinery at Port Arthur, and started building a pipeline. An experienced oilman was needed, and Texas happened to have one—Cullinan of Corsicana. A swap was made, and in return for $25,000 worth of stock in Cullinan's Texas Fuel Company, the syndicate made over part of its holdings. About the same time, the New York industrial firm of L. H. Lapham and Co., which had holdings in petroleum and lamp black, bought a like amount of stock from Cullinan. Within a year, infused with new capital provided by Lapham and a Chicago group of investors led by the redoubtable John W. ("Bet a Million") Gates, the Texas Fuel Company emerged as the Texas Company, second of the giant new oil companies to spring from Spindletop. In deference to Hogg, who died soon after at the age of 55, the Texas Company made a point of establishing its headquarters in the state. And though its charter did not then permit it to go into oil producing, Cullinan at once set up a subsidiary, called the Producers' Oil Company, to do just that.

And so began the historic changes that Spindletop and the twentieth century brought to the oil business. Cullinan and Hogg saw that Texas as a source of petroleum would alter the geographical pattern of the industry. It gave a chance to the small producers of oil—the kind of men who had always been exploited by Rockefeller in the oil regions of the East, those whose derricks had made a pincushion out of Spindletop.

In a sense, then, both Gulf Oil and the Texas Company started out as natural allies of the small producers. Both were known as "independents," and both saw in the possibilities of owning crude oil properties the basis to build and compete successfully with Standard. Rockefeller had never bothered much about the producing of crude oil. Dominating the refining, transporting, and marketing of the stuff, he was content to leave crude production to independent producers, from whom he bought at prices set by Standard's purchasing agents.

That was not how the Mellons saw things at all. But being canny entrepreneurs, they journeyed to New York to make sure before putting their millions into Texas that their estimate of the situation was accurate. They met Archbold and H. H. Rogers of Standard Oil at the Holland House Hotel, and were pleased at what they heard. Said Rogers, "We're out. After the way Mr. Rockefeller has been treated by the state of Texas, he'll never put another dime in Texas. . . . We wish you well." [15]

Andrew Mellon's nephew, W. L. Mellon, who in his twenties had dabbled in oil in Pennsylvania and built a pipeline from the Pittsburgh area to the East Coast before selling out at a nice profit to Standard Oil, now became president of Gulf. He said, "I concluded that the way to compete was to develop an integrated business which would first of all produce oil. Production, I saw, had to be the foundation of such a business. That was clearly the only way for a company which proposed to operate without a by-your-leave to anybody." [16]

The same thoughts seized the men at the Texas Company, and impending disaster compelled swift action. As suddenly as Spindletop erupted in 1901, it sputtered out two years later. The 350 wells on its 200 acres ceased to flow. Then salt water invaded the field. Spindletop was done for—until twenty years later, when other men drilled deeper and found new oil.

Gulf and Texas, as part of their thrust into the producing end of the business, had both been frantically buying up oil rights elsewhere. Both struck it rich at Sour Lake, only twenty miles from Spindletop. Cullinan paid $20,000 for an option on a million-dollar holding that included a resort hotel, where Texans came to take the cure in the lake's mysteriously bubbly waters. Driving a third hole just before his option was to expire, Cullinan drilled to within a few feet of the crucial sands. His strategy was to wait for a stormy night to check out the property in all possible secrecy. Amidst a crashing downpour he made his strike—then sent the crew away. By morning torrential rains had washed off all traces of the oil; even guests at the hotel had no idea that treasure had been found. Hogg and the lawyers closed the contract at a bargain $900,000, and Cullinan rushed to raise the cash from his northern backers. In 1904 the Texas Company struck oil at two more Spindletop-type salt domes and then hit the Jennings bonanza in Louisiana; Gulf's leasers were not far behind.

Pennsylvania oil was light-bodied, greenish in color, and relatively free from sulphur and had a paraffin base. The new Texas stuff was heavy, black, and loaded with sulfur and had an asphalt base. Oil men used the words *sweet* and *sour* to suggest the difference. But the difference was far wider than that, say, between sweet apple cider and vinegar. For the first years, the most widespread use of this sulfurous Texas crude oil was to burn it under the boilers of industrial plants, locomotives, and steamships. Texas oil was so heavy that many thought it could never be refined into the "sweet-burning" kerosene that was the mainstay of the oil trade.

Then drillers struck a really big oilfield in Oklahoma—the Glenn pool. Its oil was sweet as a spring, and both of the rising independents in Texas made the big decision—build pipelines from their Port Arthur refineries to the Glenn pool, 500 miles to the north. The Texas Company went farther and extended a line from the Glenn field to Fort Worth. In 1909, a new Texas attorney general sued Standard's Waters Pierce affiliate once again and this time obtained a fine of $1,900,000. Texas thus finally forced Standard Oil out of the state. Already Texas's biggest producer, the Texas Company, with its refineries at Port Arthur and Fort Worth, now also became the state's leading supplier.

Unlike the caterwauling derrick owners of the old oil regions of Pennsylvania, the independents of the booming southwestern frontier flourished in country where any sort of constraints on personal freedom were brushed aside. In the Southwest the independents were more numerous; the fields and the quantities of petroleum found were far larger. Texas offered opportunities for oil prospecting richer than anything yet seen. It was there that wildcatting came into its own and that small operators obtained wealth and influence beyond any place else. In a sense it all began at Spindletop when Jim Hogg sold his "doormat" plots; it has been said that the Hogg-Swayne Syndicate financed the Spindletop University of Roughnecks and Roustabouts. There hundreds of Texans got their chance to learn the oil business from the ground up. Howard Hughes, Sr., who founded a billion dollar oil-tool industry in Dallas, began by drilling on a limestone patch obtained from Jim Hogg. Sid Richardson, Clint Murchison, Haroldson L. Hunt—all were wildcat offspring of Spindletop.

In the early twentieth century, practically all the new oil found and the great bulk of the crude produced were brought to the surface by small independents, who then sold it to the nearest pipeline operator. Both Gulf and the Texas Company had access to vast new supplies, but neither could have kept going, much less kept expanding, had they not built their long and costly pipelines almost at once to tap the mid-continent field: an area of Oklahoma and Kansas 75 miles wide and 175 miles long, which eventually contained 150 separate pools producing oil from 30,000 wells. It would be too much to say that their pipelines put Gulf and Texas into significant competition with Standard Oil, which operated a big pipeline linking the mid-continent field to its refineries in the North and East. The new pipelines at first carried off only a modest share southward to the new refineries on the Gulf.

In the way the oil trade was organized at the start of the twentieth century, pipeline operation was just about the most crucial —and profitable—part of the business. By then pipelines had supplanted the railroads as the means of transporting crude oil to the point of manufacture. Pipelines had become the chief arteries of Rockefeller's economic empire, and it tells much about how Rockefeller fashioned his empire that oil companies to this day treat their pipeline networks as a branch of their refining operations.

Like most commodities, crude oil had first been traded on an open exchange, and this determined the price. But when Standard Oil's ascendancy became so complete that the trust was practically the sole buyer of crude oil, it announced back in 1886 that its purchasing agents would set the price. Within days the Oil Exchange at Oil City, Pa., was dead. Thenceforth Standard's agents set their various prices for various grades in various parts of the country. In practice these prices were made known to the producers at the time and place they delivered their crude oil to Standard's pipelines. Later, even where other outfits such as Gulf and the Texas Company operated pipelines, Standard Oil, as W. L. Mellon said, "made the price." [17]

Pipelines were subjected to endless investigation in the trust's last years. In 1906 these protests brought action. Congress voted that pipelines were common carriers, subject to Interstate Commerce Commission regulation in the same way as railroads. On the face of it, this meant that the man who brought oil out of the ground could ship his commodity in pipelines, as he could ship it on railroads, for subsequent sale in markets of his choosing. Nothing remotely like this happened. Instead, Standard Oil, with its penchant for disregarding the law, appealed against every sanction and delayed by every device its officers and lawyers could think of. It was not until 1914, three years after the dissolution of the trust itself, that the Supreme Court upheld the law and the ICC bestirred itself to see to its execution.

Meanwhile, as the mid-continent field grew to be the biggest in the land, nothing changed in the monopolistic structure of crude-oil sales. Pipelines dominated the picture. Although small refineries had sprung up in the new fields, the crude oil still flowed largely through Standard's pipelines to big plants it had built near the major urban markets and after 1907 through Gulf Oil's and Texas Company's four-inch pipes to Gulf Coast ports. There were two sorts of pipelines—the small gathering lines that pumped oil from wellheads in the various producing fields and the long trunk lines that carried the crude oil great distances across country to the big refineries. Standard controlled both types of operations. Pipelines were expensive to build—the big ones, according to a government report, cost $9,000 a mile—and no small operator was likely to take the field against Standard when it controlled all the refineries that could use the oil. Only major companies were involved. They decided when to build and when a newly discovered field had produced enough oil to justify linking it with their trunk lines. Then the pipeline arrived at the small operator's property. And then the man from Standard's pipeline company was likely to say, "You've certainly got a whole lot of oil here. Guess that's what has depressed the market lately. Sorry, we can't pay the $1.05 a barrel we said we thought we could." It was take it or leave it, and only the big company had storage facilities in which one could leave the stuff.

Just as the Supreme Court's dissolution decree of 1911 did not prevent the Standard "group" from carrying on much as before, so the Court's pipeline ruling in 1914 changed little in the monopolistic practices of crude-oil marketing. After yet more delays, Standard's biggest pipeline companies announced that they would accept consignments from other shippers, but the minimum shipment would be 100,000 barrels—far beyond the capacity of any small well owner. The disposition of Standard to act as if nothing had changed with the Supreme Court ruling led to adoption in 1913 of the Clayton Act, which was supposed to put some teeth in the Sherman Antitrust Act. Penalties were voted, and the old Bureau of Corporations, which had provided Theodore Roosevelt with ammunition for his suit against Standard Oil, was given independent and visible status as the Federal Trade Commission, charged with watching out for competition in the entire private sector of the economy. Along with the Federal Reserve Act to keep guard over the way bankers made use of the nation's credit supply, the Clayton Act was part of Woodrow Wilson's New Freedom program. And some of the first reports issued by the Federal Trade Commission, under Chairman Joseph E. Davies, bore down hard on oil industry pipeline abuses.

Thus in 1916 the FTC reported that five major pipelines tapped the big mid-continent field. Of these trunk lines, three belonged to the Standard group. The biggest extended from the rich Cushing pool in Oklahoma to Standard of Indiana's mammoth Whiting refinery near Chicago, a distance of 700 miles. A second connected Cushing with Baton Rouge, where the Standard group had built another big refining center. A third carried crude oil south to refineries of the Magnolia Petroleum Company in Oklahoma and Texas, once the marketing region allotted by Rockefeller to the notorious Waters Pierce Company. Magnolia was owned almost entirely by two men, John D. Archbold, president of Standard Oil of New Jersey, and H. G. Folger, president of Standard Oil of New York. Upon the liquidation of Waters Pierce, said the FTC, the two senior operating officers of the Standard group had bought up Magnolia, turning the stock and voting powers over to a trustee named by Texas authorities. Having thus complied with Jim Hogg's antitrust law, Rockefeller's successors integrated the small Texas enterprise into the Standard group as their personal possession—and established it as the combine's marketing outlet in that state and in Oklahoma.[18]

The other two pipelines, operating since 1907, belonged to Gulf Oil and the Texas Company and bound their big refineries at Port Arthur, 450 miles to the south, to the seemingly endless mid-continent crude supply. Building on their position out of reach in Texas of Standard's compelling refineries and pipelines, Gulf and Texaco (the name adopted in 1906) had helped themselves to their share of the mid-continent supply and, prudently aggressive, had begun to move into northern and western markets that were growing too huge for Standard alone to handle.

The net investment of the companies in these five lines in 1913, the FTC said, was $43 million. Once built, pipelines operated at extremely low cost—from three to five and a half cents a barrel in gathering lines and something like two and a half cents a barrel mile on the trunk lines. This was about half the cost of shipping by railroad tank car. In 1913 the five companies obtained a 41.5 percent return on net investment, which meant that the pipelines had paid for themselves in little more than two years.

Since the price paid to producers ran from 40 cents to $1.20 a barrel that year, pipeline rates were clearly a big factor in the price of crude. For crude oil delivered all the way to New York, pipeline charges amounted to from 58 to 175 percent of the price. Speaking

for small producers, Charles Wrightsman of Oklahoma told the House
Committee on Interstate Commerce in 1914:

> Now we have two independent lines in Oklahoma. One is
> the Texas Company, founded by Gates, and the other is
> Gulf, owned by the Mellons of Pittsburgh. These are two
> very remarkable institutions. Prairie Gas and Oil [Standard]
> has in every instance but one taken the initiative on increas-
> ing or decreasing the price, and within 24 hours these two
> so-called independents have followed suit.[19]

As for the small producers, Wrightsman said, "We never sell our
oil, we simply take what the pipes pinch off to us. They have
absolute domination of the market." [20]

Calling lower pipeline rates "a necessity," FTC Chairman Davies
urged that pipelines be divorced from the big refining and marketing
companies and operated as separate common carriers. The Standard
group's only gesture was to announce that the 700-mile Cushing-
Whiting line would accept outsiders' shipments providing they were
at least 100,000 barrels and were delivered at a few specified stations
along the line. Some of the other lines set their minimum shipments
at 25,000 barrels, but this quantity too was too big for small producers.
Thus the Standard group, reckoning that the dissolution of the trust
was concession enough, hung on to its high ground after the 1911
decree.

Monopoly gave way insensibly to oligopoly. By a gentlemen's
agreement, Gulf and Texas, too large and too invulnerably positioned
in anti-Rockefeller Texas to be elbowed out of the field, were
gradually allowed to share Standard's monopoly on condition that
the latter always lead in setting the price of oil. They deferred to the
chief, but insisted on their own portion of the loot.

So it was in California. There the new rival was the first major
foreign-owned concern to win a toehold in the American market.
The Anglo-Dutch Shell Oil Company had successfully challenged
Standard Oil's dominance in the world market and now, in the
wake of the Supreme Court decree, took occasion to challenge
Standard's preeminence in its home territory. The company began in
the fields of Borneo and Sumatra, developed in the first instance by
the Dutch, but marketed later with the aid of British capital and
expertise. Although Rockefeller's empire from the first was virtually
worldwide and up to the first World War included at least a third
of the British and even European markets, Asia was as remote from

Rockefeller's refineries in the world trade scene as Mellon's and Texaco's were inside the United States.

Under the vigorous leadership of Sir Henry Deterding, Royal Dutch Shell, as it came to be called, expanded from the Indies around the world. Under Deterding's "straight line" theory, the company shipped oil everywhere on a straight line from oil wells to the geographically nearest market.

Deterding was the single figure of the next generation of oilmen who at all rivaled Rockefeller in force and vision, and his ideas about oil were provocatively at variance with those of the founding father. Both built world trade empires. But Deterding rose to power after oil became a source not simply of illumination but of energy. Expanding his operations from the Indies to Rumania, from Trinidad to Mexico, from Burma to California, Deterding saw no limits to what could be done with oil. He was utterly impatient of Rockefeller's habit of waiting for the crude oil to be brought to him. He said:

> Oil is the most extraordinary article in the commercial world, and the only thing that hampers its sale is its production. In the case of oil, make the production come first, and the consumption will come. Only what you need is an enormously long, long purse to be able to snap your fingers at everybody and if people do not want to buy it today, to be able to say to them, "All right, I will spend a million sterling in making reserves, and then in the future you will have to pay so much more." [21]

Deterding, arriving on the scene just as the world was embarking on the first of two great wars fought with machines, was Napoleonic in his audacity and Cromwellian in his thoroughness. When his Royal Dutch producing properties joined forces with the Shell marketing organization, he put together a combination that seemed as imperially powerful and aggressive as ever the Standard Trust had been.

From Deterding's point of view, the West Coast was the point at which to invade America. California was a hotbed of politically active independents. It was even remoter from Rockefeller's headquarters than Spindletop; and the Standard Oil Company of California, as the one part of the trust that had its own oilfields, pipelines, refineries, and marketing facilities, was the successor company least amenable to tight managerial control from New York.

Entering in 1916 by shrewd purchases of operations around Los

Angeles, which included both producing and refining units, Deterding poured in capital to enlarge his beachhead. Shell, as the company was called in the United States, consolidated its holdings on the shore and then pushed inland. By the time the first World War ended, the golden Shell emblem on tanks and tank wagons was already a familiar California sight, and the company was extending its operations into the mountain states. Thus in the Far West as well as Southwest, monopoly recrystallized into oligopoly. And for neither the Standard group nor for Royal Dutch Shell was there anything new about this sort of coexistence. For years these two giants had already been sharing markets in Asia, Europe, and South America.

In 1895, the automobile was not even known by that name—the vehicle that the Duryea brothers built to win the big race through Chicago streets in 1895 was called a "motor wagon." [22] In 1900, the automobile industry scarcely existed, but by the time Standard Oil was broken up in 1911, automobile manufacturing was a close second in size to the oil business, and by 1920 it was far in the lead.

The automobile ran on gasoline, a product for which refineries had practically no market up to 1900. It cannot be said that any important leader of America's petroleum industry foresaw the mushrooming of the gasoline market in the next decade. To the very end of its days, the old Standard Oil Company was a kerosene company. Archbold's feet were planted in the past. Rockefeller, Flagler, Archbold, Rogers—the whole tiny group at the top of Standard—seemed more concerned with multiplying their own fortunes, largely in ventures outside their own company, in the years when the automobile was taking over the bicycle works and wagon factories of Detroit.

By 1911, almost unnoticed in the excitement over the dissolution of Standard Oil, gasoline sales in the United States topped those of kerosene. The output of automobiles rose swiftly up to and through the first World War, and led on to the boom of the 1920s.

The first problem was manufacturing enough gasoline to meet the new demand. In the old-fashioned process of refining crude petroleum, there was no way to extract more than about 18 percent of gasoline from crude oil. Unless someone could find a way to "crack" some of the heavier products given off in the distilling process, petroleum would simply not yield the quantities of gasoline being demanded as more and more cars poured out of Detroit.

At the big Standard refinery at Whiting, Indiana, Chief Chemist

William Burton judged that the likeliest source from which to extract more gasoline was gas oil. Gas oil, sold mainly to utilities for mixing with coal in manufactured gas, constituted no less than 39 percent of what emerged in the old distilling process. Burton began by breaking down gas oil in hot-tube and lead-bath experiments. Ordinarily, gas oil distilled out of the crude before cracking temperatures were reached. But Burton's idea was that if it could be held in a still by pressure until such temperatures were attained, it might give a high yield of gasoline. This was the cracking process.

Applying pressures to volatile hydrocarbons seemed risky, and when the main office heard about these doings, Burton was told to stop. He waited, then quietly resumed, and succeeded in building up pressures to 75 pounds, enough to keep most of the gas oil from distilling—and drew off quite a good grade of gasoline. At the same time, his staff found ways not only to get rid of the residual coke settling from the oil but to recycle some of the kerosene vapors back into the still, so that the yield of gasoline from crude oil rose toward 40 percent.

In 1911, Burton asked for $100,000 to construct six pressure stills at Whiting. The Standard board replied, "No, you'd blow the whole state of Indiana into Lake Michigan." [23] Then came the Supreme Court decree. In the resulting split-up, Burton was elected to the board of Standard Oil of Indiana. The new board gave the green light for a dozen Burton stills, and by 1913 Burton's cracking process was producing yields of gasoline twice as high as those obtained under the old-fashioned distilling method.

The new process gave Standard Oil of Indiana a terrific boost into the expanding new market for gasoline (Burton was soon rewarded with the company presidency). Only those licensed by Indiana Standard could use the process. In one respect, the new process set oil refining back to where it was when Rockefeller first went into business—the oil was processed in batches, which meant that the stills had to be closed down every 24 hours or so while the residual coke was cleaned out of the still. Texaco, gritting its teeth as it paid fees to Indiana Standard, eventually devised a continuous process of thermal cracking—and gasoline aplenty gushed out of the refineries for the automobiles of America. [24]

The second problem was getting the gasoline to the motorists. In the beginning, Standard insisted on selling gasoline the same way it sold its kerosene. This was through general merchants, hardware and grocery stores, and blacksmith shops. In these places, gasoline was kept in a barrel or drum at the rear of the merchant's store and dispensed in a one-gallon or five-gallon can to the motorist's car.

The system was so cumbersome that some early owners devised their own ways of storing fuel for their automobiles. Having converted their stables or sometimes built stately new structures on their estates to house their horseless carriages, wealthy owners installed underground tanks at a safe distance from them to which the oil company's tank wagons made periodic deliveries of the volatile stuff. But even in the first decade of the automobile, not all motorists were millionaires. Before long, structures for cars began to be built behind modest homes as well as mansions. Some of these new car owners installed tin tanks of their own in which to store gasoline and bought gasoline direct from an oil company.

In the cities, it was the well-to-do who bought cars, and more often than not, as with their horses and carriages, they employed others to drive them and look after them. Since it was next to impossible to keep these new vehicles on the urban owner's premises, very soon after the arrival of the motor car there arose a new kind of stable, which overnight gave its name to all edifices that housed and served motor cars. This was the garage.

The primary function of the first, early twentieth-century garages was to store automobiles, which no one would then have dreamed of leaving overnight on the street. Otherwise, these first commercial garages offered the services that an automobile owner was soon found to need. An important one was washing the vehicles: in the four-story, elevator-equipped People's Garage and Livery Company building in Chicago and in the equally splendid Bond Motor Company structure in downtown Kansas City, large spaces were reserved and four men kept busy at this task, which was mainly performed at night. Chauffeurs were significant personages at all such establishments; special quarters were reserved for them "in which games of chance [were] in progress at various hours during the days and nights." At the Foss-Hughes garage in Wilmington, the chauffeurs' room, on the second floor, was furnished with a pool table and piano.[25] According to a trade-paper report of 1912, New York City "chauffeurs who have stored at various garages" found rates running generally from $35 a month for limousines to $20 for small Ford and Hupp runabouts.[26]

All such garages made money selling gasoline. At the People's Garage in Chicago, no cars were accepted for storing unless their owners agreed to purchase their gasoline and oil from the garage. That was the early practice, although the same trade-paper report said that New York City garages sold it for twelve to twenty cents a gallon in 1912, but acknowledged that certain "shanties around the city" also dispensed gasoline at prices as low as twelve and a half cents per gallon. To stock and sell gasoline from indoor premises courted fire hazards, which brought high insurance rates and municipal ordinances. In consequence, such well-appointed places as Campbell's garage in San Diego, the Clinton garage in Brooklyn, and the Blue Ribbon garage in Bridgeport were all built with gasoline tanks installed underground outside and equipped with the latest thing in "long-distance, self-measuring pumps." By means of these pumps, hand-operated of course, the gasoline could be drawn into small, portable tanks inside the garage and then lugged or wheeled to the thirsty vehicle in its stall. Such a fancy establishment as the People's Garage and Livery Company, located on Chicago's "bon ton South Side," positioned its hoses in marble-tiled walls near the front office. Clerks could then keep a vigilant eye on sales and minimize the drawing of gasoline by "irresponsible parties." [27]

Since these garages were selling a lot of gasoline (the 540-gallon tank at the Britton garage in Hartford had to be filled daily), the owners usually placed their underground tanks beneath the front sidewalk, where tank wagons (still horse-drawn in 1912) could most easily replenish them. This feature was not without significance. As motorists began using their cars more, they became impatient of waiting for them to be filled from billycans at their stalls. They began wheeling their automobiles right up to the garage pumps for quicker replenishment. And as Henry Ford built more cars (his assembly line went into production in 1913), motorists who could not have afforded to store their cars there began driving into the garages and demanding to have their automobiles refueled. By 1914, Atwood's garage in Toledo kept one man attending to gasoline sales only. Since the garage had no fewer than five underground tanks and an elaborate pump and hose system, the attendant was able to pump fuel directly into cars that drove in, filled up, and drove right out.[28]

The fluidity of the petroleum industry's product was now for a time surpassed by the mobility of the wheeled vehicle it powered. In 1913, the S. F. Bowser Company of Fort Wayne offered a new, long-distance gasoline pump for garage installation. Dubbed the "Red Sentry," the device had a significant safety feature: enclosing the top of the pump was an iron door, which could be locked shut when the pump was not in use.[29]

Handy as this feature was in the hurly-burly of a busy garage, it was especially desirable, as advertisements for it pointed out, if the Red Sentry were put to "street use." A few months later Bowser announced that its "sidewalk pump" now came equipped with an electric light for night service—"conspicuous for a considerable distance and forming a good advertising medium for the garage in front of which it may be stationed." [30]

By now the automobile was creating difficulties for cities. In 1915, Mayor James Curley of Boston refused permits to place gasoline pumps on the city's sidewalks. But gasoline companies were beginning to push gasoline sales hard. In Springfield, Mass., the Standard Oil Company of New York, which handled almost all sales in New England as well as New York at the time, offered to install streetside gasoline pumps for a nominal lease of one or two dollars a year for dealers who would sell the company's products. By 1916 there were so many cars on Springfield streets that the town supervisors relented. A new ordinance allowed pumps to be installed where they did not "seriously interfere" with traffic and where "a neat appearing sign" was "attached to each pump stating the kind of gasoline sold from the pump." [31] In Seattle, merchants tried to vend gasoline to motorists from portable tanks on sidewalks in front of garages and stores, but this practice was ordered stopped by the authorities. In Cleveland, gasoline was sold at what seems to have been the first municipal garage (where in 1915, 2,262 drivers paid fifteen cents each for a day's parking).[32]

At about the same time that garages found their service facilities outgrowing their indoor space, the oil companies ran up against a similar problem at their bulk stations. Many of the people who were acquiring automobiles in the years before the first World War, irritated at the price charged for gasoline by local kerosene dealers but unwilling to keep a tank and pump at home, began to drive to oil-company bulk plants, where sometimes they were able to buy their gasoline at wholesale prices. To accommodate such motorists and to keep this growing traffic from interfering with the scheduled movements of their own tank wagons in and out of these bulk plants, oil companies began to rent adjacent premises for the retail sale of gasoline.

The question of what constitutes a service station, offering along with gasoline, facilities for such elementary services as changing oil, grease, and tires, makes it difficult to say exactly which was the first gasoline service station in the country. As early as 1907, the Automobile Gasoline Company opened a station in St. Louis; and the Oriental Oil Company, another independent, opened a drive-in filling station in Dallas in 1911.[33] The Gulf Oil Company claims to have opened the first drive-in station in Pittsburgh on December 1,

1913, and sold gasoline at the rate of 1,800 gallons a day there by the following spring.[34] The Atlantic Refining Company claims to have opened the first modern, company-operated, drive-in service station in the East in 1915—after the company had sent a committee to St. Louis to look over the independent Pierce Oil Company's service station there.[35]

The third force working to change the oil business after Rockefeller's time was the industry's evolving relationship to public policy. The 1911 Supreme Court decision was less than punitive in all its provisions. Although Standard's trust was broken up into some 27 separate companies, the very small group of officers who controlled them received proportionate shares of stock in all 27 companies. Archbold, Rogers, and others ran these companies as before, and Rockefeller continued to be the dominant shareholder. The Standard group, as they began to be called, intended to operate after the decree much as they had before—they controlled the great bulk of the nation's refineries and, still more important, its principal pipelines; and they dominated the marketing of products in just about every corner of the land, setting the local price of these products just as they always had.

But a rising population (up from 75 million in 1899 to 105 million in 1919), an expanding national income, widespread industrial adoption of oil as a source of energy, and the arrival of the automobile brought a sevenfold increase in demand for petroleum products— far more than any such tightly controlled, centrally managed organization as Standard could manage. Some of the oil was used to enrich gas produced from coal and pumped to homes and factories. Sulfur-heavy Texas and California oil, largely produced by independents, was used in rail and marine transportation. By 1914, all American battleships, cruisers, and destroyers burned oil under their boilers; fuel consumption of the U.S. Navy rose from 360,000 barrels in 1912 to almost six million barrels in 1919; and the California and Texas companies got a large part of this business.[36] In 1900, there were 3,723 automobiles in America; a decade later, 200,000; and by 1919, output topped a million and the nation used almost 75 million barrels of gasoline—nearly half of it produced by non-Standard companies.

Companies such as Gulf and Texaco, which did not share Standard's old aversion to government, won fat shares of the new navy fueling contracts and gained strong competitive positions in the new automobile fuel market as well. The Mellons and the men behind the Texas Company plunged right into the production of crude oil and operated as "integrated" companies engaged in every phase of the business from well to consumer. Rockefeller had never cared a dime for the oil producers of his day. These rising competitors of Standard tended to think, with the other oil producers of California, Texas, and Oklahoma, that government should act in aid of their activities.

By the early years of the twentieth century, the element of conservation had entered into the picture. The age of greed that had opened after the Civil War had passed its peak. The nation's frontier had reached the Pacific. The sense of unlimited riches was shaken. A great many people in the eastern United States, and President Theodore Roosevelt was one of them, thought that the natural resources of the nation, above all those remaining in the public lands of the undeveloped West, ought not to be profligately wasted. The issue was dramatized in the fight, in which Roosevelt and later Taft joined, to save the remaining forests from unlimited logging. But it was fought perhaps more effectively on the question of oil deposits, because there the national security was involved. On the grounds that the United States might need reserves of oil for waging future wars, President Taft in 1909 issued an executive order setting aside the Elk Hills tract of public-domain oil land in California, and in 1914 President Wilson yielded to the pleas of Secretary of the Navy Josephus Daniels and added the Buena Vista tract in California and the Teapot Dome reservoir in Wyoming as underground reserves of petroleum for the navy.

These considerations of national security came to the fore at a time when the whole world seemed to be making vast new demands for America's oil. Soon after war broke out in 1914, it became evident that this greatest of all wars was also to be the first fought with machines—machines that ran on oil. Everybody knew the story of how Marshal Joffre, in the war's crucial first weeks, won the Battle of the Marne by rushing reinforcements to the front in taxicabs commandeered from Paris streets. Equally well known was the deal by which First Lord of the Admiralty Winston Churchill, forehandedly putting government funds in an Iranian oil concession, got fuel by which the Royal Navy's dreadnoughts held the seas. And when the United States entered the war in 1917, Marshal Foch at once made it known that without oil from America his armies must collapse.

In the next eighteen months, the United States organized a supply effort that brought the Germans to their knees. At the head of the powerful War Industries Board, Bernard Baruch led it. Business carried it out. And none took more vigorous part than the oil industry. On the initiative of Baruch, the Wilson administration formed a Petroleum War Service Committee. Baruch appointed A. C. Bedford, president of Standard Oil of New Jersey, its chairman.[37] Mark Requa, a California oil engineer who had been assisting Herbert Hoover in the Food Administration, moved in as director of the government's oil policies.[38]

Bedford, unlike his predecessor Archbold, saw positive advantages in taking an active role in public policy, especially in time of war. In short order, he and his committee of fellow oil-company presidents proposed that supplies be pooled and efforts coordinated to produce all possible oil. Oil Administrator Requa took it from there. Overnight, the industry, with President Wilson's support, was doing what the Sherman Antitrust Act forbade. Six years after the dissolution of Standard Oil's trust, its chief executive was in Washington helping direct industry's cooperation with government. Such cooperation was directed toward the war effort—but it could also advance such industry ambitions as stabilization of production and prices. It could even promote conservation, when to conserve meant the orderly development of a new oil field instead of the extravagantly hasty exploitation typical of unbridled competition. Finally, government cooperation might be quite helpful in the process on which Bedford and other chiefs of Standard successor companies were now embarked—extending their operations into the exploration and production of crude oil and otherwise turning their outfits into "integrated" companies capable of holding their own against Gulf, Texaco, and Shell.

As soon as Bedford and other Standard chieftains took this new tack, not only the rising majors of California and the Southwest found new reasons to work more closely with the Standard group. So did the smaller independents, certain of whose political demands, sidetracked in the past, began to be taken with utmost seriousness in Washington as Bedford and his committee lined up behind them.

Such was the case with the perennial demand of small independent prospectors and well owners for preferential treatment on their individual and corporate income taxes. These people kept asserting that in their business, in contrast with others, their capital (in the form of underground oil deposits) was constantly being used up. Since these assets, once gone, were gone forever, it was only fair that in computing taxes, allowance should be made for their depletion.

In 1913, five years after enactment of the income tax, Congress voted to provide such a depletion allowance. Oil and mining interests were granted the right to deduct five percent of the gross value of their oil and gas production in computing their taxes. The Revenue Act of 1916 then removed this depletion allowance and replaced it with a "reasonable" allowance for depletion. But to the great disappointment of the independent producers, Congress at the same time specified that such allowance must not exceed the cost of discovering the oil on which the calculation was to be based.[39]

So matters stood when the Wilson administration, still at peace with Germany, sought a second term in office. And had the Revenue Act of 1916 remained in force, the petroleum producers of America, big and little, would have enjoyed no great advantage under the tax laws. The determination of what oil wells were worth would have remained tied to the cost of getting the well into production. Under such rules, the oil prospector would have been assured against ending up in the red because of the tax he had to pay—but that was about the limit of his benefit.

Nothing better showed the industry's new tilt toward "cooperation" in Washington and toward crude-oil production in the field than what happened next. As part of the war effort, Congress had worked up a vast program of war taxes and excess profits taxes. Obviously, American industry was in for some hefty payments to the federal treasury. And as the bill passed the House, the petroleum industry stood to pay at the stiff new rates too—with only the nominal benefits for depletion conferred by the Revenue Act of 1916. A treasury official testified that the average manufacturing firm would have to pay excess profits taxes at the rate of 20 percent, petroleum companies at 13 percent.[40]

Alone, the small producers would have been swamped under patriotic tides. But the producing element of the oil business had always been strong in California, which had provided the Wilson administration with its new oil administrator, Requa. The independents also counted in their ranks such rich and influential new oil moguls as Harry C. Sinclair (Sinclair Oil) of Kansas, Henry L. Doherty of Oklahoma (Cities Service), and Edward L. Doheny (Pan American Petroleum), the king of the Los Angeles oil fields and number one contributor to the 1916 Democratic National Committee campaign chest. At the time, the big new oil companies of Texas were still counted as independents, and they too favored a bigger tax break for those who searched for and opened up new wells.

Impressive as these reinforcements were, what counted still more in the new lineup was the shift of the Standard Oil group, which had read the writing on the wall and followed Gulf, Texaco, and Shell into the crude-oil producing business. The biggest of these companies, Bedford's Jersey Standard, had just got into crude production in a big way by purchasing Humble Oil and Refining Company, the biggest producer in Texas. So Bedford joined with the other oil company presidents on his committee in urging that if America were to have enough oil to win the war, Congress must create greater inducements to produce the stuff.

The oil kings centered their effort in the Senate, where the war tax bill had arrived in the hands of the Finance Committee. It proved utterly receptive to their pleas. Bedford, Sinclair, Doheny, and other oilmen worked mainly in the wings. Their spokesman on the witness stand was J. Harry Covington, counsel for the Petroleum War Service Committee's panel on taxation. Judge Covington, as he was called, was a former member of Congress and Judge of the Supreme Court of West Virginia. He was also the founder and head of the potent Washington law firm of Covington and Burling, in which Dean Acheson, Abe Fortas, and Paul Porter were later partners. Courtly and dignified, Covington bore down in his testimony on the "very substantial shortage" of gasoline for war purposes. He made this pitch:

> Unless there is a fair encouragement of new development, an opportunity for exploration for the wildcatter, this country unquestionably faces a genuine and critical shortage of crude oil in a time of [war].[41]

On behalf of the independent producers of Oklahoma and Kansas, Judge John J. Shea then asked the senators to think about the plight of the indispensably venturesome wildcatter who risked everything to find new oil against great odds, only to be taxed at the same rate as any sure-thing manufacturer. Chairman Simmons, wondering aloud why the House had let the 1916 proviso stand, exclaimed, "It must have been an oversight." [42]

Senior Republican member of the committee was Boies Penrose of Pennsylvania. This was the same Penrose who twenty years before had secretly passed the draft of a government committee report to Standard Oil President Archbold and then incorporated Archbold's "suggestions" in the document. The senator from Pennsylvania was also mindful of his state's coalfields. Should not coal mining be treated in the same way as oil drilling? Senator Thomas Gore, Democrat from Oklahoma, set him straight:

> There is this distinction—if a big concern owns oil leases adjacent to a small concern, and the big concern puts down wells near their line, the small concern has to put down its own wells or else the neighbor will take their substance. That differentiates it from coal or gold mines.[43]

The burden of the testimony was that it was the little man, the chance-taking wildcatter, who would be protected against the giant oil company and induced to find the new oil America needed to bring the war to a triumphant conclusion. And the overriding reason for singling out the oilmen for special treatment when everybody else in the country was being asked to pay sky-high war and excess profits taxes was that oil was in short supply and ways must be found to get what the armies needed in Europe.

> *Administrator Requa:* Forty percent of the oil is exhausted.
> *Senator Thomas (Colorado):* We need oil now worse than we've ever needed it. We need every available source of supply to the end that the war may be vigorously prosecuted. We want oil now.
> *Senator Lodge (Mass.):* Is it not better to increase production than to cut down consumption . . . tending to paralyze the business of the country?
> *Requa:* The United States imported 30 million barrels from Mexico last year.
> *Senator Penrose:* Is not the fact that we are dependent on a foreign nation for a very large percentage of our consumption a reason for providing in this revenue bill some means of stimulating the American field as much as possible during this war period?
> *Requa:* I think it is necessary.[44]

These exchanges took place October 11, 1918, when headlines proclaimed the retreat and impending defeat of Germany's armies, and the armistice was only weeks away. But the senators called on Requa to submit an amendment embodying their desire to help shorten the war by offering tax inducements for increased production of oil. The key passage in the resulting amendment, cleared with Bedford, Sinclair, and other National Petroleum War Service Committee members, was this:

> Where the fair market value of the property . . . is materially disproportionate to the cost, the depletion allowance shall be based upon the fair market value at date of discovery or at the election of the taxpayer at the conclusion of that year or any subsequent year.[45]

The senators wasted no time debating the revised measure.

> *Penrose:* Let us adopt what the experts agree on.
> *Requa:* The amendments as they now stand have the endorsement of the industry.
> *Thomas:* That simplifies it very much.
> *Penrose:* Are the amendments satisfactory to the producers whom Judge Shea represented?
> *Gore:* Except as to one point—the House allowed ten percent expressly for the hazard of the industry based on the value of the oil underground. Judge Shea does not think it ought to be stricken out.
> *Penrose:* If we put that in, the whole thing would be fixed up to suit them, wouldn't it?
> *Chairman Simmons:* Senator Penrose, you know we are not here fixing a bill up to suit the industry.
> *Penrose:* I know that, but we are here to fix up a bill to get the maximum production of oil.[46]

As adopted in the final Revenue Act of 1918, the Senate amendment transformed the depletion allowance into a major instrument of government policy. At the same time, it drove a huge wedge—it was far too big to be described as a loophole—into the system of a graduated income tax for any and all Americans. For by explicit act of Congress, oil producers from that point onward could base the "reasonable allowance" for their depletion either upon the cost of discovering their oil, as formerly, or upon a "fair market value" of the well after it had begun producing the oil. Of course, they chose the latter, which was likely to be a hundred or even a thousand times greater. Thereafter (until Congress fixed the rate at 27½ percent in 1926 to spare the treasury the headache of adjudicating every single claim) the allowance varied widely, but averaged for most oil companies between 28 and 31 percent of gross income.[47]

Rockefeller's Standard Trust would have had little enough to claim under such a law. But now all that was changing, and the great man's successors were falling over themselves to get into crude oil production. And all those companies that had already expanded into the exploration and production end of the business benefited mightily by the new definition of the depletion allowance. The Gulf Oil Corporation received such huge tax rebates in 1921, as Andrew Mellon took over as secretary of the treasury, that a congressional committee subsequently ordered a searching inquiry and reported "gross unfairness." [48]

The depletion allowance, which was to receive such widespread and prolonged publicity later, attracted virtually no notice at the time of its adoption. *The New York Times* carried only the briefest mention. On October 19, 1918, in the last paragraph of a brief story on page 18, it noted that Oil Administrator Requa had appeared before the Senate committee. It reported that Requa "presented his views on taxation of oil and mines," was "in favor of a liberal policy toward oil development," and had submitted "amendments which the committee will consider carefully." [49] Exhaustive analyses of the Revenue Act of 1918, which subsequently appeared in the press, detailed the long lists of new taxes levied in the war emergency—and totally left out any mention of the giveaway depletion allowance for the oil industry.

The military victory it was supposed to insure had already been won before the depletion allowance was enacted. But its impact was felt at once, and for years thereafter. In effect, the depletion allowance opened the doors of the treasury to all who could bring in new oil. It enormously accelerated the drive to hunt for oil fields across the nation and unquestionably gave wildcatters a big break. A very few of the luckiest and toughest and shrewdest of Texas and California independents managed with the help of the depletion allowance not only to keep what they struck, but, as in the case of the Murchisons and Richardsons, the Gettys and H. L. Hunts, to parlay their new wealth into big-time oil operations; some of the bigger independents, like Sun, Phillips, and Skelly, were helped by the big tax break to grow into major oil companies. The depletion allowance also speeded the transformation of the successor Standard corporations into "integrated" companies. Soon not only Standard of New Jersey and Standard of New York, but also Standard of Indiana and the Atlantic Refining Company, the trust's big marketer in Pennsylvania and Delaware, began acquiring large crude oil supplies for their refining operations. The immediate result of this surge was the abrupt cessation of industry cries about an oil shortage. After the dire forecasts that the country might run out of the stuff, the 1920s brought wave after wave of major oil finds in Texas, Oklahoma, California, Wyoming.

But perhaps the war's chief consequence for the oil industry was the establishment of close ties with the government. The day when the oil trust kept as far away from government as possible was long gone. The day of punitive antitrust sanctions against the oil empire seemed to have vanished too. By the end of the war, a trade journal reported "sentiment in the oil country favoring the idea of continuing the functions of the National (Petroleum War Service) committee." [50] The same machinery that had coordinated wartime production, said Chairman Bedford, could now carry out the task of "stabilizing" the industry. In the fall of 1918, leaders of the industry met at Atlantic City and formed the American Petroleum Institute, with Bedford as first president. Oil was not only organizing to participate vigorously in public policy-making. Under the pressures of the new depletion-allowance incentive, oil was openly intervening in politics in a campaign to throw open the Western public lands to prospectors and oil-company concessions.

4
Teapot Dome

Mrs. Hannah Nixon, mother of Richard Nixon, once told how her teen-aged son was lying in front of the fireplace of their California home in 1924 with newspapers spread out, reading about the Teapot Dome scandal and the stories of corruption in the handling of the government's oil reserves. Suddenly he said, "Mother, I would like to become a lawyer—an honest lawyer, who can't be bought by crooks." [1]

In 1950, when Congressman Richard Nixon was running for re-election in California, newspapers headlined charges that oilmen had put together a large fund to help his campaign. "Another Teapot Dome!" exclaimed a horrified Hannah Nixon.[2]

The scandal of the Teapot Dome oil leases was the most flagrant in United States history until Watergate and provoked further disclosures that saddled the Harding administration with the sorry name of the most corrupt ever to hold office, with the possible exception of the nineteenth-century regime of Ulysses S. Grant. By the time the Watergate scandal burst into the open and exposed evidence of widespread malfeasance throughout the highest reaches of the Nixon Administration, the president's mother was dead. Still, it seemed hardly possible that her son did not at some point in the hectic and drawn-out crisis think of the stories he once read so indignantly on the floor of the little bungalow in Whittier. For the vast majority of the 47 million who had just overwhelmingly voted President Nixon back to office, Teapot Dome was little more than a vaguely unsavory name out of the history books. Yet as congressional investigators grilled cabinet officials, public confidence in the president sagged, and the very business of government slowed for a time almost to a halt, comparisons between 1923 and 1973 were inevitably invited.

In both the Teapot Dome affair and the Watergate incident, explicitly unlawful acts were proved, in the one case the taking of a bribe and in the other a burglary. In both cases, the unmasking of these felonies led to the disclosure of others, uncovering evidence that seemed to point to widespread corruption among those holding high office. In the oil scandals, as in the midnight break-ins of a half century later, national security was invoked as justifying cause for the secrecy in which they were enshrouded. In both cases, at least two cabinet members were in due course indicted and brought to trial. In both cases, the president appointed special prosecutors to try them. In both cases, the prestige and moral reputation of the presidency itself were placed in balance. In 1923, as in 1973, the executive branch of government was ranged against the legislative branch, although here, as in other respects, there were significant differences. In the Teapot Dome affair it was not the Congress, as such, controlled as it was by the same party as the executive, but rather a single, relentlessly determined member of the Senate minority who provoked the confrontation; in the Watergate scandal it took intervention by the judicial arm of government, a United States district judge's courageous probing, to impel a Democratic Congress toward showdown with a Republican chief executive.

This was, in fact, the first of the big differences between the scandals of 1923 and 1973—that for all the inquisitorial sharpness of Democratic Senator Tom Walsh, the Republican party in his time never ceased to control both the executive and the Congress, an advantage that Nixon was unable to attain even when in winning reelection he carried 49 states. The second difference, even more important, was that the Teapot Dome oil steal was pulled off during the administration of one president, but only disclosed during the presidency of another. In 1973, Nixon had to bear the brunt of his own people's doings. By 1923, when the Teapot Dome scandal finally burst out into public view, Harding was dead and Coolidge, a Republican, elected along with him, to be sure, but a new president all the same, was running the government and preparing to stand for reelection the next year.

Making all due allowances for such differences and similarities, the real issue in both Teapot Dome and Watergate was political power. In 1973, the Nixon administration made no bones about this. Failure to match the Republican performance of the 1920s and take control of the legislative as well as the executive branch in the 1972 landslide doubtless compelled such candor. It also led White House spokesmen to condone the felonies its servants had committed with the specious excuse that the burglaries were never committed to steal money or goods, but only to "obtain information."

Thanks to the Republican command over both arms of government, the conspiratorial motivations have long remained somewhat more submerged in the tawdry Teapot Dome affair. After all, Harding's interior secretary was caught and sent to prison for accepting money from oilmen, thus becoming the first corrupt cabinet member in United States history to receive something like his just reward. But the detection and punishment of such a sensational and still unique example of venality, as well as the even ranker flagrancies subsequently uncovered in the Harding administration, have tended to obscure the real nature of the struggle waged during the Teapot Dome affair to win and keep power in Washington. Of this struggle one historian of the era has written: "The slanting of government during the 1920s to support whatever stand the dominant business interests wanted was far more scandalous than the merely political depravity for which the Harding regime was noted." [3]

In the center of the conflict, in Teapot Dome as in Watergate, were the large campaign contributions made by business interests. In the Watergate episode, such contributions, first "laundered" by being passed through Mexican banks, financed the crime. In the Teapot Dome scandal what appear to have been the crucial contributions came from an oilman, a partner in the crime. In both cases, all those involved sought to prevent disclosure of the contributions, partly because wealth in a democracy wants to keep its influence invisible, but also because donors and recipients alike feared that disclosure might jeopardize the election outcome both sought. Seen in the context of Watergate and in the perspective of a political evolution that campaign contributions raised to the appalling level of $107 million in the presidential election of 1972,[4] the Teapot Dome story stands out after fifty years as one of the most instructive in the history of oil and polity in America.

★

Oil had a room in an office building [at Chicago] and presumed to summon potential presidential and vice-presidential candidates to that room, where men good-naturedly discussed our foreign relations with Mexico in the oral examination which was given to those whom oil was about to bless with its support. . . . Oil controlled the Republican convention of 1920. It worked through the Senate cabal, led by the irrecon-

cilables—who were so busy hating Wilson that they became
easy victims of the greed of oil.[5]

—William Allen White

The 1920 Republican convention at Chicago stands out in the
annals of American politics as the one at which the nomination and
the presidency were dealt to Senator Warren G. Harding of Ohio in
a smoke-filled room. The Grand Old Party, reaching for power across
the broken body of Woodrow Wilson and his tottering administration,
found itself deadlocked. On the one side were the progressive elements of the party, the so-called Bull Moosers, who had split away in
1912 to follow their hero, the late Theodore Roosevelt. Back now in
the ranks, they were lined up behind the candidacy of General
Leonard Wood, foremost of the Rough Riders of '98 and friend and
heir of the great Teddy. Arrayed on the other side were the regulars,
who placed organization before ideas and never forgot the disloyalty
of the splitters, which had let the Democrats into office back in 1912.
The regulars had formed around Governor Frank O. Lowden of
Illinois. It was soon evident that neither commanded a majority.

Early in the convention, Wood coolly rejected the Pennsylvania
delegation's demand for three cabinet places as the price of its crucial
support. Then, when the Oklahoma national committeeman, the multimillionaire oil wildcatter Jake Hamon, walked into Wood's headquarters with word that he could deliver 52 delegates from the Southwest in return for naming the next secretary of the interior and minister
to Mexico, the general lost his temper for the first time—it should be
explained that he was a surgeon general—and shouted, "I am an
American soldier. I'll be damned if I betray my country. Get the hell
out of here." [6] Thus the stage was set, after deadlocked balloting, for
the scene the wily, walleyed politico Harry M. Daugherty had fore-
told some months before:

At the proper time, after the Republican National Convention
meets, some 15 men bleary-eyed with loss of sleep and per-
spiring profusely with the excessive heat, will sit down in
seclusion around a big table. I will be there, and will present
the name of Warren G. Harding to them; and before we get
through they will put him over.[7]

Except that Daugherty was absent, everything in the smoke-
filled room 404 at the Blackstone Hotel went just as he had said it
would. Senator Henry Cabot Lodge began by announcing that it was

"impossible and undesirable" to nominate either front-runner, and after hours of drifting talk, hallway huddles, and phone calls from bathrooms, "the availability of Senator Harding," as Pennsylvania Boss Joe Grundy explained later, seemed "so outstanding as to justify nominating him next day." [8]

Though collusion between oil interests and politicians who made possible the first convention swing to Harding has never been proved, it was amid such scenes that the man was chosen who was president during the daring oil lease steals of the early 1920s. Amiable, hearty, trusting, Harding was out of his depth in the job. He appointed his old Senate seatmate, Albert B. Fall of New Mexico, secretary of the interior, with responsibility for conserving the nation's natural resources. He made Daugherty, the backroom political operative, attorney general, charged with enforcing the new Prohibition laws. Other old cronies became veterans administrator and alien property custodian, and still others, flocking in from Ohio, found places in the Justice Department and White House, where they joined in almost nightly poker sessions with the president. In Washington the "normalcy" that Harding had called for after the big war and Wilson's bid for world leadership now translated as "revelry."

After two years in office and before the public had got wind of the goings-on around him, Harding died of a heart attack in San Francisco on a transcontinental trip. Great was the grief of a nation that knew only that it had lost its leader in his silver-haired prime, and at a mass memorial in New York, Bishop William T. Manning mourned the "honest humanity" of a president who had "died in the service of his country." [9] But there is reason to believe that Harding by 1923 was a man dissolving in dismay at his inability to cope and in fright at discovering that his friends were betraying him. After his death, details began to seep out. Somehow Harding had learned that Charlie Forbes, his veterans administrator, had been stealing millions. Summoning his old pal to the White House, the president was throttling him against the wall and shouting, "You yellow rat! You double-crossing bastard!" when a visitor arrived unannounced for an appointment.[10] Later it became known that Jesse Smith, the Ohio political fixer and intimate of Henry Daugherty, whose 1923 suicide was ascribed to ill health, had killed himself after Harding found out that Smith took thousands in rake-offs and kickbacks and ordered Daugherty to get rid of their old poker-session companion. Only decades later did Herbert Hoover, Harding's secretary of commerce, disclose that a few days before he died the president summoned him to ask, without explanation, "If you knew of a great scandal in our administration, would you for the good of the country and the party expose it publicly or would you bury it?" [11]

★

Though "a thousand little stories," as William Allen White said,[12] were circulating in Washington about strange doings in the Harding administration by 1923, the shock of the president's death, the grief that followed, and the necessity of getting used to Calvin Coolidge as the new president distracted public attention for yet more months. It was not until early 1924 that the first of the frauds exploded into the open.

Albert B. Fall, a self-made lawyer and the first senator from the frontier state of New Mexico, seemed as much the embodiment of Manifest Destiny's westward thrust as Sam Houston of Texas before him. He had been cattle herder, chuck wagon cook, mucker, and hard-rock miner before he won political leadership of the desert beyond El Paso by winging the county's deputy sheriff in a shoot-out on Las Cruces's main street. The Rio Grande was scarcely a border in his rising career of involvement in Mexican mining and oil politics. After the Mexican revolution broke out and Fall moved to Washington, he spoke so forcefully against it in the Senate Foreign Relations Committee that his friend Harding wanted—at a time when foreign affairs were largely hemispheric affairs—to make him secretary of state.[13]

Had history sent the American Expeditionary Force to Mexico instead of Europe in 1917, the notion might not have been so far-fetched. On the day Harding gave the job to Charles Evans Hughes, Hughes told him in a visitor's presence that Fall—"in my opinion the ablest international lawyer in the country"—was the better man.[14] As things turned out, Fall's filibustering temper and contractual dexterity were directed to the Department of the Interior, whose main business was managing the public lands and natural resources of the West.

If Fall thought the United States ought to annex northern Mexico, his views about the public lands of the West were even more flamboyant. To this steely-eyed frontier statesman, who had been known to carry his six-shooter on the Senate floor, the public lands were wide open spaces and should be open to all comers, no questions asked. In Al Fall's eyes, conservationists who wanted to restrict the access of enterprising Americans to the water, minerals, and woodlands of the West were effete Eastern bleeding hearts who knew nothing of the untrammeled freedom by which a continent had been won. If Theodore Roosevelt and some of his friends had made the preserving of what was left of the forests and wild mountains a burning twentieth-century issue, Al Fall wanted no part of it. He grumbled when Taft took the conservationist step of withdrawing a huge tract of public land at Elk Hills in the midst of California's most promising oil field and designating it as an underground reserve to be held as a sort of insurance policy for possible emergency needs of the United States Navy. As a senator, Fall was hostile when Wilson by executive order withdrew two more tracts for the navy—at Buena Vista in California and at Teapot Dome, an oddly jutting sandstone formation amid the sagebrush flats of central Wyoming.

Every inch the man of the old West that he looked with his mustache and goatee, gambler's string tie and black, broad-brimmed stetson hat, Fall quickly set about reversing the restrictive public lands policy of Roosevelt, Taft, and Wilson. He urged "liberalizing" the laws and opening up Alaska so that "the boys back from the war can do what their forefathers did in 1849 in California." He also let it be known that he wanted the national forests transferred from the Agriculture Department to his and their 220,000,000 acres turned over to private operators. The United States Forest Service was the conservationists' most dearly prized achievement, and with Secretary of Agriculture Henry C. Wallace on their side they managed to stop the grab. But in 1921, Fall talked President Harding and Secretary of the Navy Edwin Denby, a millionaire car dealer from Michigan, into transferring the three naval oil reserves to the Interior Department's control. Soon after, on April 7, Fall secretly leased Teapot Dome to the Mammoth Oil Company, owned by Harry F. Sinclair. The following December he leased Elk Hills, again secretly, to the Pan American Petroleum Co., owned by Edward F. Doheny.

News of the leases leaked out at once. Even before the first one was signed, President Walter Teagle of the Standard Oil Company of New Jersey rushed to inform his friend Albert Lasker, chairman of the Shipping Board. Years later, Lasker recalled this statement:

> I understand the Interior department is just about to close a contract to lease Teapot Dome, and all through the industry it smells. I'm not interested in Teapot Dome. It has *no* interest whatsoever for Standard Oil of New Jersey. But I *do* feel you should tell the President that it *smells*—that he *must* not permit it to go through.[15]

That night, said Lasker, he spoke to the president. Harding replied, "This isn't the first time this rumor has come to me, but if Albert

Fall isn't an honest man, I'm not fit to be president of the United States." [16] In answer to a Senate inquiry, Fall declared that he had leased Teapot Dome to Sinclair in the interest of national preparedness and was about to authorize Doheny to carry out limited drilling at Elk Hills lest oil under these lands be drawn off by neighboring wells. Harding backed him up.

The Senate ordered an investigation and, at the request of colleagues who believed that the chairman and other members of the Lands and Surveys Committee were unfriendly to its purposes, Senator Thomas J. Walsh, Democrat of Montana, took the lead. Walsh was no conservationist, but among senators, Western and Eastern, he stood out for his respect for law as law. Working slowly through the mass of documents sent over by the Interior Department, Walsh gradually swung round to the view that the oil leases were contrary to public interest and that bribery and fraud might well have been committed.

Like Fall, Walsh was a self-made lawyer of the West, but a very different sort of frontiersman. Having made a name handling injury suits against mines and railroads in the Montana mining capital of Helena, he reached what he later recognized as the great turning point in his life when he turned down an invitation to move to Butte and become counsel to the Anaconda Copper Mining Company, the dominant economic force in the state. He thus established himself as a man who could not be bought; and six years later, just elected to the Senate over Anaconda opposition, he joined the ranks of Senate progressives. Thin, pale, unsmiling, Tom Walsh brought to his inquisitorial task a clear mind, relentless purpose, and high-collared rectitude. [17]

Harding was dead and Fall had been out of office for nearly a year when hearings finally got under way. Fluent, forceful, hard-nosed, Fall brushed aside Walsh's queries; and neither Sinclair nor Doheny, with their ranks of lawyers, had much to tell. But a man from Albuquerque testified that Fall, broke by his own account when he took office, appeared to have come upon sudden prosperity in late 1921. The secretary had spruced up his property with costly improvements, paid up eight years' tax arrears, and bought an adjoining ranch, "one of the best small ranches in New Mexico." [18] As Walsh continued to probe, puzzled over where Fall got the money, senior Republicans urged Fall to give an explanation and so end the investigation.

Walsh suspected that Fall's angel must have been Sinclair, a Kansas druggist's son who had parlayed an early lease in the mid-continent oil field into one of the biggest independent oil businesses of his day. Sinclair had visited the Fall ranch at the end of 1921. And when Fall left office in 1923, it was to accompany Sinclair on a trip to try to snag a Siberian oil concession from the Russians. Precisely because of these ties, Fall came under the most intense pressure from another quarter at this time to produce an answer to the question that would throw Walsh off the scent. Will Hays, who had resigned as Harding's postmaster general in 1923 to become czar of the motion picture industry, had great concern about Fall's financial dealings with Sinclair, and with reason. As chairman of the Republican National Committee in the victorious 1920 campaign, Hays had incurred a big deficit and was still trying, two and three years later, to pay off the $1,200,000 debt so as to put the Republicans in a strong position for the 1924 race. The largest contribution he had obtained was $160,000, from oilman Sinclair, whom he had once represented as a lawyer. Practically all of this sum had been tendered covertly in the form of Liberty bonds, and Sinclair had handed it over to Hays at about the same time that Walsh began uncovering damaging details about Fall's finances. What worried Hays was that Walsh might unearth Sinclair payments to Fall and then find out that Sinclair had been making secret contributions to the Republican campaign chest at the same time. The prospect of such a tie's being exposed and heralded in headlines across the land was enough to give any campaign chairman nightmares.[19]

Under such pressures, the former secretary of the interior began to lose his nerve. He drank heavily. He sent his son-in-law to ask Price McKinney, a Cleveland mining and steel magnate with whom he had traveled in 1921, if he would say he lent Fall the money to fix up the ranch. McKinney refused. Fall then went to New York, where he conferred with Doheny and Sinclair, and to Washington. After that he went to Atlantic City and entered a hospital. When the committee again sent for him, his doctor wired that he was too "run-down" to appear. Then his wife telephoned Evalyn Walsh McLean, wife of the owner of the *Washington Post*. Could Mrs. McLean send her husband to Fall at once on "a matter of life and death"? [20]

Edward B. McLean was the playboy son of an Ohio utility magnate who had inherited all kinds of property, including the *Post*, and was constantly in the headlines with his wife, an heiress in her own right, as the most glamorous hosts and companions in the social hijinks of Harding and his Ohio cronies. Postponing a trip to Palm Beach, Ned McLean rushed in his private railroad car to Atlantic City. He found Fall in his hotel room wrapped in a dark red dressing gown, trembling and "in terrible condition." Fall said he was in trouble and asked McLean if he would tell Walsh's committee that he had lent him $100,000. "It has nothing to do with Harry Sinclair or Teapot Dome," Fall assured McLean, who obligingly agreed to say he had lent the money and wrote out a dummy check to that effect.[21]

The day after Christmas, Fall was back in Washington. Former party chairman Hays waited upon him that night at his quarters in the Wardman Park Hotel. In the presence of Hays, Sinclair, and Sinclair's lawyer, Fall dictated a long letter to the Senate committee that was calculated to end the 15 months of investigation. Fall later called it "the one big mistake in my life." [22] In this letter he explained that he got the money from

> a friend of mine here [in Washington] who had spoken to me about acquiring a ranch in New Mexico and particularly about the raising of thoroughbred horses in that state. I placed before him . . . immediate purchase of real estate and cattle of the estate [at] $91,500. . . . It was . . . agreed that he would loan me $100,000, and I have my note for that amount. . . . The gentleman from whom I obtained and who furnished me the cash was the Hon. Edward B. McLean of Washington, D.C.[23]

With this letter in hand, Chairman Irving I. Lenroot said briskly, "We want to close these hearings as soon as possible." [24] Walsh, who had tracked down all clues and was about to call it quits, still had doubts. A. Mitchell Palmer, a former Democratic attorney general retained at this point by McLean to speed a favorable outcome, weighed in with a wire affirming that his client said, "In 1921 I loaned Fall $100,000 on personal note" and adding that McLean was "resting" in Palm Beach with no plans for getting back to Washington in time for talks with the committee.[25] Walsh growled, "The committee will want to hear some details in the framing of an ex parte affidavit." [26] On New Year's eve he got the committee to send him to Florida as a subcommittee of one to question McLean under oath about the loan story.

That did it. Up to this time the fun-loving McLean had been willing to go along in a trumped-up story to help Fall and others past a tight spot. Wealth, glamour, and some of the power and perquisites of the executive branch operated to favor such a maneuver. Harding, Coolidge, and half the Cabinet golfed at Friendship, Ned's fancy Washington estate; and Bascom Slemp, the president's secretary, was at that moment his Palm Beach guest. Sporting the badge of a

Justice Department agent was only one of McLean's government privileges. But when he heard that Walsh was pushing south to Florida, obviously prepared to demand straight answers under threat of jail for contempt of Congress, he panicked.[27] He wired Fall to join him and, using his copy of the Justice Department codebook, kept his private line to Washington (manned at the other end by a White House operator) crackling with such cryptic messages as:

JAGUAR BAPTISMAL STOWARD BEADLE HUFF PULSATOR COMMENAL
FITFUL LAMBERT CONATION FECUND HYBRIDZES.[28]

This said that Walsh ("Jaguar") "leaves Coast Line ten twenty-five tonight instead of Seaboard. Lambert on same train." Lambert was Ned's lawyer and stood guard at his elbow as the questioning began:

Walsh: Mr. McLean, did you loan $100,000 to Mr. Fall?

McLean: I did, sir, in checks.

Walsh: Whose checks?

McLean: My own checks.

Walsh: Drawn on what banks?

McLean: Drawn, to the best of my recollection, on the Federal, the Commercial, and there might have been a smaller one drawn on one other, third bank which was a small account.

Walsh: Have you got the checks?

McLean: I do not think so. I am not positive.

Walsh: Were they returned? What became of them?

McLean: Senator Fall returned them to me.

Walsh: When?

McLean: In the last part of December, 1921, sir. The last week, I am not positive as to date.

Walsh: They never did go through a bank?

McLean: No sir.

Walsh: So that, as far as you are concerned, you did not give him any cash?

McLean: Cash? No, sir.[29]

It was such a lame story McLean now told that Walsh did not even bother to pursue the details. He brought the cross-examination to a close:

Walsh: When did you see Senator Fall last?

McLean: Fifteen minutes ago.

Walsh: Have you and he conferred in this matter?

> *McLean:* This morning, sir. . . . I conferred this morning with Fall and my attorney Mr. Wilton J. Lambert. Mr. Fall suggested I make the statement which I have just made. . . .[30]

The confrontation in Florida had established that Fall had lied in trying to explain away the $100,000 or more he had received to buy the ranch in 1921, and now the fat was in the fire. Three days later, as Walsh finished reporting to the committee on his trip, there was a sudden stir in the caucus room. A door opened, and into the crowded room filed America's most famous political family. First came two tall sons of former President Theodore Roosevelt and their wives. Then came their sister Alice with her husband, Nicholas Longworth, majority leader of the House of Representatives. Alice was stunningly arrayed all in red, a reporter noted, but her face was "dead-white." [31] The head of the clan, Assistant Secretary of the Navy Theodore Roosevelt, Jr., was also pale as he stepped forward to announce that his younger brother, Archibald, for whom he had got a vice-president's job in the Sinclair organization a few years before, had resigned and wanted to testify before the committee.

Shored up by the presence of the clan behind him, young Archie Roosevelt disclosed that his boss had just taken off abruptly for Europe. Troubled already about the company's Teapot Dome lease, Archie said that he had asked Gustav D. Wahlberg, Sinclair's secretary, why the hasty departure and been told that it was probably "on account of the turn in the investigation occasioned by McLean's testimony in Florida." Roosevelt then said he asked Wahlberg point-blank whether he thought Sinclair had bribed Fall. Wahlberg had hesitated—"That is a nasty word," Roosevelt apologized—and then said that he thought "somebody might have lent Mr. Fall money." [32] Wahlberg, called before the committee, admitted that he had said as much, but denied that he had told Archie he held $68,000 in canceled checks that had gone to Fall. Before he left the stand, Wahlberg also mumbled something about some Liberty loan bonds that Sinclair had loaned to a "Mr. Hayes."

Though Walsh's cross-examination of playboy McLean in Florida cracked the Teapot Dome case, it was Roosevelt's "lurid story," rambling, confused, and never corroborated on the point of the $68,000 in checks, that turned the inquiry overnight into a national sensation. Up to now it had been a tedious, slogging investigation full of baffling technicalities about "defensive" drilling, underground pressures, and above-ground storage tanks that the public found hard to follow. Suddenly, it was a scandal of personality and corruption, of piratical oil multimillionaires offering bribes to members of the president's cabinet. Newspapers splashed headlines, and readers woke up and licked their lips. In Mexico the long revolution ended; in Russia Lenin died that week; in Britain Labour for the first time prepared to take power; but for the moment America was oblivious to all else, "wading shoulder deep in oil," the *New Republic* said. "In the hotels, in the streets, at the dinner tables, the sole subject is oil. Congress has abandoned all other business. . . ." [33]

The tremors from McLean's testimony that sent Sinclair flying had also been felt in California, where Edward L. Doheny, taking alarm, boarded a train for the East—to testify before the committee at his own request. Fall, who met Doheny in New Orleans, later claimed it was Doheny who had suggested McLean be persuaded to say he had lent Fall the money. At all events, Doheny now saw no choice but to speak. An old-time Irish mine prospector who had struck it rich and become one of the wealthiest men in the West, he was a small man who parted his sandy hair in the middle; he testified in an inoffensive, high-pitched voice. But his squeak was a bombshell: "I wish to inform the committee that on 30 November, 1921, I loaned Albert B. Fall $100,000 upon his promissory note to enable him to purchase a ranch in New Mexico." [34]

As Doheny now told it,[35] the transaction had nothing to do with the Elk Hills lease, though Walsh, recovering from his astonishment, drew from the wealthy oilman the statement that he hoped to make $100 million for his private pocket by tapping the public land. It was just a matter of friendship, said Doheny. "I had known Fall for some thirty years or more. We both worked in the same mining district in New Mexico." He had been very fortunate, whereas Fall had never had such prospecting luck. Besides, Fall had suffered loss in recent years by the death of his son and daughter. At this point, Doheny found it hard to go on talking. Then, regaining control of himself, he said that he was rich. He was not only rich; he had cash. He could produce a million tomorrow. For almost any affectionately remembered old prospector he might have had a hundred thousand to spare. "The amount I was loaning was a bagatelle to me—no more than $25 or $50 would be to the average individual." So it was that when Fall told him he needed $100,000 to close the ranch deal, Doheny had said, of course, he could have the money. Then in November, right after the lease was put through, handing over Elk Hills to Doheny's company, Fall raised the subject again.

Walsh: How did this happen?

Doheny: By phone.

Walsh: Where?

Doheny: He was in Washington and I was in New York. He called and said: 'I am ready for that loan now,' if I was still prepared to make it as I had said earlier I would.

Walsh: When?

Doheny: Oh, probably three or four weeks before.

Walsh: How was the loan paid?

Doheny: I sent it in cash.

Walsh: How did you transport the cash?

Doheny: In a satchel.

Walsh: Who was your messenger?

Doheny: My son.

Walsh: How did you get the cash?

Doheny: I got it by cashing a check—from Blair and Co.'s bank in New York.

Walsh: Could you let us see the check?[36]

After Doheny's sensational disclosure, it was time for Fall to appear. He was a pitiful figure to behold, this lord of the Southwest frontier who had shot down opposing politicos, lectured the Senate Foreign Relations Committee on Mexico, and bent a president and a fellow cabinet member to his purposes. It was an old man in a wrinkled and baggy blue serge suit who now shambled down the crowded caucus room aisle, leaning on the cane he had once swung so jauntily. His cheeks were sunken, his mouth seemed to droop with his mustache, and his arrogant eyes were cast down. His lawyer attended him like a nurse. He did not look at his former colleagues as, in a flat but still clear voice, he read a prepared statement. After denying the committee's technical authority to carry on its investigation, he ended with a phrase never before heard from the lips of a member of the president's cabinet, "I decline . . . to answer any questions, on the ground that it may tend to incriminate me." [37] Then, his eyes still fixed on the ground, he took his lawyer's arm and moved slowly toward the door, the silence of the room broken only by his shuffling feet and tapping cane.

"This is the worst scandal in the Government in many decades, a smelly mess," wrote the famous *Baltimore Sun* pundit, Frank Kent.[38] In less than a year the nation would go to the polls again to elect a president, and the Democrats saw their chance. They could gun down the Republican administration on the corruption issue and regain the White House. Senator Thad Carraway of Arkansas rose in the Senate to compare the infamy of Albert Fall with that of Benedict Arnold.[39] Democratic National Committee Chairman Cordell Hull thundered that the Republicans were dominated "by a crowd of ruthless reactionaries—scandal, scandal, scandal." [40] In gleeful anticipation, the Democratic campaign committee of Clackamus County, Oregon, placed an order for 24,000 aluminum teapots.[41]

On the administration side, not a word was said for Fall. Instead, on the very day that Doheny divulged that it was he who lent Fall the money to buy the ranch, the White House announced that the president had decided to appoint two special prosecutors, one Republican and one Democrat, to start possible criminal action on the oil-lease matter. Silas Strawn, a Chicago lawyer, and Thomas W. Gregory, attorney general in the Wilson Cabinet, were the two names put forward for this assignment. "What luck for Calvin Ccolidge that Fall got out of the cabinet before he became president," wrote Frank Kent.[42]

While moving thus to establish that President Coolidge was free from the taint of oil and ready to bring down the law on those who had brought it into government, the Republicans next set out to show that the Democrats, far from being incorruptible lily-whites who abhorred and condemned the blackening influence of oil, were actually soaked in the stuff. Senator Lenroot, chairman of the Teapot Dome Committee, knew that Doheny, for all his old prospector camaraderie with Al Fall, was a prominent Democrat, the largest contributor to the Democratic party in both 1912 and 1916 campaigns. Accordingly, Doheny was invited back to the stand, and this time the Republicans asked the questions.

Was it not true, Lenroot asked, that Doheny had a number of Democrats on his payroll? Precisely because eager Democrats had exploited his testimony as evidence of a corrupt transaction, the multimillionaire oilman took the stand in a defiant mood. The meekness of his earlier appearance had vanished. His eyes snapped, and his voice shrilled as he reeled off names in answer to Lenroot's questions. Watching from the press seats, Mark Sullivan wrote that he "called the roll like an ostentatious king giving an inventory of his possessions, like a parvenu art collector calling the roll of his Rembrandts and Van Dycks." [43] Doheny said that no fewer than four members of Wilson's cabinet worked or had worked for him and he did not mince words about it. "I hired them for their influence." [44] The first mentioned was Gregory—the very Democrat Coolidge had just proposed to prosecute the oil lease cases. Then there were ex-Secretary of War Lindley K. Garrison and ex-Secretary of the Interior Franklin K. Lane, who was now a $50,000-a-year executive of Pan American Petroleum. Finally, Doheny announced that he had paid $250,000 for legal services to former Secretary of the Treasury William G. McAdoo.

This was the most devastating disclosure of all. McAdoo, the son-in-law of former President Wilson, was far and away the leading candidate for the Democratic presidential nomination in the 1924 elections. McAdoo himself might protest that his fees—actually $150,000—had been legitimately earned in pressing Mexican claims that had nothing whatever to do with the oil reserves. From Los Angeles he wired the committee, asking to be heard in his own defense. But the damage had been done: at the very moment the Democratic party was spitting on its hands before swinging the oil-corruption haymaker that would knock out the Republicans and gain the White House, their best candidate was disclosed to have taken money from the man they charged with corrupting Fall. The very next day President Wilson died after long illness in Washington, and the wisecrack went around the capital that McAdoo was "coming to Washington to attend his father-in-law's funeral Wednesday, and his own the next." [45] The *Springfield Republican* pronounced his appearance a "McAdieu." [46] (Six months later, at the Democratic National Convention, though a majority remained pledged to McAdoo, the Democrats could not bring themselves to nominate him and battled through a 108-ballot Donnybrook that left delegates so exhausted and the party so enfeebled that it never swung any Teapot Dome haymaker at the Republicans.)

The scandal, meanwhile, kept spreading so far and so fast that nobody knew what the next day would bring. After Gregory's name had been knocked out for special prosecutor, Strawn's had to be withdrawn when Walsh established that the Continental Bank of Chicago, of which he was counsel and director, was "the Standard Oil of Indiana's bank." [47] Other names were proposed and had to be dropped. "Just think," said Will Rogers. "America has 110 million population, 90 percent of them lawyers, yet we can't find two of them who have not worked at some time or another for an oil company. There has been at least one lawyer for each barrel that ever came out of the ground." [48] The *Literary Digest* asked

> Is oil gaining such a position of dominance in this republic that it thinks it can dictate to both political parties, buy high executive officers of the Government, bend legislation to its own ends, and silence the criticisms of the press? [49]

In the daily disclosures, Senator David I. Walsh, Democrat of Massachusetts, professed to see "the revelation in successful operation of that heretofore intangible thing called by Theodore Roosevelt 'the invisible government' and by Woodrow Wilson 'the invisible empire.' " Senator George Moses, Republican of New Hampshire, said in New York that he could "name a dozen senators spotted with this flood of oil. Those yet unnamed are greater in number. . . ." [50]

In their fight to prevent a public reaction that would sweep them from office, the Republicans had staved off the worst by letting Fall walk the plank. But Walsh, not content with Doheny's admission and convinced that the former secretary had taken money for the Teapot Dome lease too, kept probing into Sinclair's affairs. When Sinclair was slow about returning from Europe, Walsh placed the oilman's lawyer on the stand and wrung from him the admission that Sinclair had given Fall $25,000 in Liberty bonds after Fall left office. Walsh, recalling that Sinclair's secretary had let drop a mention of Liberty bonds for a "Mr. Hayes," [51] began tracing these bonds.

They seemed to have some connection with a mysterious entity incorporated in Canada as the Continental Trading Company. A number of top oil executives appeared to be involved in this outfit, and every one of them, Sinclair included, had suddenly decamped abroad. Then, when Walsh called Will Hays for enlightenment about Sinclair's Liberty bonds, newspapers blossomed with a sensational report that the oilman had donated $1 million worth of Sinclair Consolidated Oil stock to the Republican campaign chest. Taking the stand, Hays launched into a righteous denial of the report as "as false as it is libelous in purpose." Though Walsh introduced evidence that Hays's publicity man, pulling off one of the oldest ruses in the game of politics, had planted the false story so that his boss could deny it, Hays took all morning denying it; and not until late in the session did Walsh get to ask the key question: "Now, Mr. Hays, please tell us what Mr. Sinclair *did* have to do with making up the deficit of the Republican national campaign." [52] At once Republican senators protested that the question was "irrelevant" to the investigation. Toward evening, after long wrangling, votes and adjournments, Hays said, "I don't know, I simply don't know," and slipped off to his duties as moral supervisor of the nation's movies.

The rawest of all Washington rumors had it that a million dollar slush fund had been created by big oilmen to cover the speculation of Harding administration insiders. This and all such rumors were invariably coupled with the name of Attorney General Daugherty, a devious Harding crony still holding office. He boldly turned the FBI on the investigating senators, who found their offices ransacked and their papers rifled as they went about unearthing the details of the corruption. The fact that President Coolidge had appointed special prosecutors to pursue the Teapot Dome case amounted to admission that the attorney general had failed on the job, and Senator Walsh attested that "not one scintilla" of evidence had ever been furnished him by Daugherty's office in all his investigations.[53] Senator Burton K. Wheeler now charged that Daugherty had refrained from enforcing the law not only in the matter of oil leases but also in antitrust, customs, and especially liquor cases; and he hinted darkly that Daugherty had participated in stock market pools. "Everybody knows," he shouted, "that Daugherty was a friend of McLean, Sinclair, Doheny, and other grafters."[54] Amid Republican silence, Wheeler's resolution to investigate the Justice Department passed, 66 to 1.

If Wheeler's investigative style lacked Walsh's cold nose for facts, it made up for any such prosaic deficiencies by its melodramatic flair and wild-swinging, prosecutorial fury. Wheeler's first move was to go to Ohio, where Daugherty's egregious FBI chief, William J. Burns, made a crude attempt to frame him with a woman. But in Columbus, Wheeler persuaded Roxie Stinson, former wife of Daughtery's late confidant Jesse Smith, to appear as his lead-off witness. At forty, Roxie was still slim, still handsome, and what she had to tell of the sordid goings-on behind the imposing Harding facade in the early 1920s was almost more than the nation could stand to hear.

She knew everyone in the "Ohio Gang," as the newspapers now called the men who had flocked to Washington with Harding. She had been the president-elect's dinner partner at one gay party in Marion following his landslide victory. She had been present through innumerable conversations back in Ohio between her former husband and Daugherty. Washington's backstairs gossip became headlines across America as Roxie testified about what Jesse Smith told her when he came to her on his frequent trips back to Ohio. For the first time the nation heard about the little house on H Street, where Daugherty and Smith first lived and connived in the capital; about the "little green house on K Street," where Smith and others met favor-seekers and, before closing deals, let them peek over the stairs at the president of the United States entering for a poker session.[55] Roxie Stinson told of the payoffs, of the suitcases of liquor, the stock certificates, the thousand dollar bills—everything she could remember that Jesse Smith in his boastfulness or anxiety had confided to her, even to the "they" who were out to get him.

It was sensational stuff: the little woman repeating the words of a dead man out of the center of the concentrated fraud and thievery of the Harding years, and the whole nation listening in. Of course, those were preradio days, and America was only figuratively listening and certainly not listening *and watching*, as when the equivalent of the Walsh-Wheeler team, Senator Ervin's committee, carried out a similar but infinitely more enveloping process of "public education" fifty years later. In due course, two of the denizens of the little green house on K Street, Veterans Administrator Forbes and Alien Property Custodian Thomas W. Miller, were sent to jail for defrauding the government while in office. And within the month Wheeler achieved his avowed purpose of forcing Daugherty from office, an achievement for which Republicans proceeded to take credit since it was Coolidge who finally asked for and received the attorney general's resignation. But Wheeler's investigation was never able to nail down the report about the million-dollar slush fund, and some of his later witnesses spun tales out of whole cloth. Wheeler failed in his wider effort to establish that the attorney general, for all his sleazy dealings, was guilty of anything more than lack of zeal in the great Teapot Dome case that was being tried before the American people well in advance of any court action. The closest he came was when Roxie Stinson told of a deal in the fall of 1922 in which five men, friends of Smith and Daugherty whose names were not known to Roxie, made $33 million in two or three days by buying and selling Sinclair oil stocks (both Smith and Daugherty, she said, were "sore" because they had not been cut in).[56]

★

Though the special prosecutors secured indictments of Fall, Doheny, and Sinclair by June 1924, the court dismissed them on a technicality; and to the satisfaction of the Republicans the cases went over to the following year. Everybody around President Coolidge knew that one false step might beat him; yet the ruling Republicans managed through the most damaging of the disclosures to keep control of the situation. In this they were unquestionably aided by the moral climate of the day. The harshest condemnation on the part of the press and the public was reserved, not for those who had defrauded the government, but for those who insisted upon bringing the facts to light. Walsh and Wheeler were castigated by *The New York Tribune* as "the Montana scandalmongers." *The New York Post* termed them "mudgunners." *The New York Times*, a newspaper of Democratic leanings, called them "assassins of character." [57]

Readers echoed these sentiments. Some businessmen, using language occasionally heard after Watergate, said it was unpatriotic to "cast discredit on the government" by criticism. Frederick Lewis Allen wrote:

> A commuter riding daily to New York at this period ob-
> served that on the seven o'clock train there was some indig-
> nation at the scandals, but that on the eight o'clock train
> there was only indignation at their exposure and on the nine
> o'clock train they were not even mentioned.[58]

The most that people seemed willing to say was that politicians were a venal lot who always had their hand out. The fact was that any investigation of the scandal threatened to disturb the *status quo*, if only slightly, and any disturbance of the *status quo* was the last thing that the dominant business class of the country wanted.

Having demonstrated by the deadlocked sterility of their convention that they were incapable of forging a strong alternative to the scandal-stained Republicans, the Democrats nominated for president John W. Davis, an ultraconservative Wall Street lawyer, whose chief virtue seemed to be that his long string of corporate clients happened not to include an oil company. "I am a great believer in business," proclaimed Davis.[59] Accordingly, the ruling elements prevailed in the great trial of the Teapot Dome case before the American people, and the Coolidge version of big-business normalcy was returned to office.

As the years went by, it began to appear that the "mistakes" of 1921–23 had been larger than the friends of normalcy had supposed. Special Prosecutor Owen Roberts and his ornamental partner, former Senator Pomerene, finally got the Teapot Dome and Elk Hills oil leases annulled, but only in 1927, after taking their case all the way to the Supreme Court. They failed utterly to get a conviction of oilman Doheny, prompting Senator George W. Norris, Republican of Nebraska, to say "it seems impossible to convict a million dollars in this country."[60] Sinclair saw the inside of a jail only because he was brought to book for contempt of the Senate after refusing to answer Walsh's questions—and then had his six-months term extended by three more when he was found to have hired twelve Burns detectives to shadow the jury. Fall, whose trial was delayed because of his illness, was then convicted of accepting the bribes the others were declared innocent of giving and sentenced to a year in prison. After all appeals and delays had been exhausted, he went to jail in El Paso in 1931.

Daugherty had the dubious distinction of being the only attorney general to have been twice the subject of investigations while in office and twice indicted afterwards for malfeasance. Brought to trial, he refused to take the stand even when it was known that he had burned the account records of his joint bank account with Jesse Smith. Instead he scribbled this statement:

> Having been personal attorney for Warren G. Harding before he was Senator from Ohio and while he was Senator, and thereafter until his death . . . and having been attorney general of the United States during the time that President Harding served as President. . . . I refuse to testify and answer questions because the answer I might give or make and the testimony I might give might tend to incriminate me.[61]

The audacity of this evasion, gratuitously associating in its self-serving plea the name of the dead president, far surpassed that of Daugherty's cabinet colleague Fall and successfully upset the deliberations of the jury, which after 65 hours reported itself unable to reach a verdict. For the record, it should be said that in the half century since his death no evidence has yet come to light that Harding was involved in any misappropriation of government funds, a finding that cannot be made for his attorney general.

In 1928, another election year, the implacable Walsh returned to the Teapot Dome case and conclusively established what the ruling Republicans had gone to such lengths four years before to conceal—that Sinclair had used his Liberty bonds not only to bribe Fall but to help pay off the Republican campaign deficit at the time when Walsh was hot on the oilman's trial.

First witness called was Fall's son-in-law, Mahlon Everhart. The three-year statute of limitations having expired, Everhart could no longer plead self-incrimination. Faced now with the choice of testifying or being jailed for contempt of the Senate, he told Walsh that in 1922 Sinclair personally handed him $233,000 in Liberty bonds, a payment, he said, for a third interest in the Fall ranch, though he had no papers to prove it. With the new information, Walsh was able to trace the links between the shadowy Continental Trading Company, Sinclair, Fall, and the Republican campaign chest.[62]

The trading company, which certainly would never have been heard of but for Sinclair's political tricks, now emerged as a starkly revealing example of oil-industry morality. Incorporated in Canada with a Toronto petroleum lawyer as president, the company was organized in New York shortly before the Teapot Dome transaction by four oil-company executives—Harry M. Blackmer of the Midwest

Oil Company; James E. O'Neil of the Prairie Oil Co.; Colonel Robert W. Stewart, chairman of the Standard Oil Company of Indiana; and Sinclair of Sinclair Consolidated Oil Company. It was organized for the sole purpose of contracting to buy 33,333,333 barrels of crude oil from Texas Oilman A. E. Humphrey's new Mexia field at $1.50 a barrel. The company then resold the oil to Sinclair's and O'Neil's companies—but at $1.75 a barrel. As now exposed by Walsh, the trading company proved to be nothing but a brutally simple device by the executives to rob their stockholders by diverting to its coffers a nice profit of 25 cents a barrel that otherwise would have gone to their companies. In the year or so before it was closed out and all its papers were destroyed, the Consolidated Trading Co. collected some $2 million which its president (after taking out two percent for himself) invested in Liberty bonds and distributed to the four principals. Having traced the serial numbers of the Liberty bonds, which remained on file beyond destruction, Walsh could pose some sharp questions.

Rather than return and answer his questions about their shares, O'Neil and Blackmer hid out in Europe for the rest of the decade, and the story Colonel Stewart told when he turned up was so unconvincing that stockholders led by John D. Rockefeller, Jr., drove him out of Standard Oil. Of his $757,000 share, Sinclair was shown to have turned over $233,000 to Everhart for Fall.[63] Having now traced an additional $26,000 worth of Sinclair bonds to the Republican National Committee, Walsh subpoenaed former Chairman Hays for an explanation.[64]

Lawyer, congressman, manager of the victorious 1920 campaign, postmaster general, president of the Motion Picture Producers and Distributors of America, and lifelong professional politician, Will Hays never saw fit to mention this particular confrontation in his stately *Memoirs of Will Hays.* Squirming and wriggling like an outraged rabbit, sometimes so rattled that he jumped out of his seat, he was forced to admit that, even as the Teapot Dome scandal began to break, he had appealed to his friend and former client, Harry Sinclair, to help make up the $1,200,000 Republican campaign deficit. Sinclair (in addition to an outright gift of $75,000) had "loaned" him $260,000 in Liberty bonds, later getting back $100,000. The jittery czar of the movie industry now testified that he had tried to use these bonds in a highly unusual way. He and his associates approached a number of wealthy men, potential donors to the cause, and told them that if they would contribute to meet the deficit, they might have Sinclair bonds to the amount of their contributions. Walsh was unable to get any clear answer from Hays as to how long they might keep the bonds—or why, for that matter, the contributors could not simply cash them. This method of concealing a big Sinclair contribution was euphemistically described by Hays as "using the bonds in efforts to raise money for the deficit." [65]

One of the prominent Republicans to whom Hays had peddled these "hot" bonds was Secretary of the Treasury Andrew Mellon, who returned his $50,000 worth, saying he preferred to contribute an equal amount from his own funds. Calling Mellon to the stand, Walsh drew from the "greatest secretary of the treasury since Alexander Hamilton" the admission that he had known that the bonds were from Sinclair, but neither then nor during the presidential prosecutors' investigations had he felt called upon to say anything about it.

In twentieth-century America the politics of campaign contributions is awash in the politics of oil. "Fence" as Senator Thad Carraway's bitter epithet for the campaign chairman who gave Albert Fall a push toward the penitentiary in his rush to conceal that he had solicited and accepted Teapot Dome money for the Republican campaign chest. Of Mellon, whose family control of Gulf Oil made him a petroleum magnate disposing of vastly greater wealth than strivers like Sinclair and Doheny, Carraway added bitingly, "Although he declined to aid in the marketing of the goods . . . [he] handed them back so that the fence could find somebody else who would act for him." [66]

These were harsh words, far too harsh for the ears of an America that battened on the slogan of "two cars in every garage." Business was good, and nobody wanted to rock the boat in 1928. When Tom Walsh allowed his name to be put forward for the Democratic nomination that year, he had to withdraw it because so few came forward in his support. (Not until after the Great Crash shook everything up and, in the hard times of 1933, President-elect Franklin Roosevelt nominated him for attorney general, did Walsh receive recognition for his public services. And then the acknowledgment came too late: Walsh, aged 73, died on the train on his way to the inaugural.)

In 1928, the slanting of government to suit the dominant business interests went on much as before. The nation elected Herbert Hoover as president, and Hoover reappointed as secretary of the treasury the oil-aluminum-banking statesman who was disclosed a few years later to have awarded himself income tax rebates for at least one of his eleven years in office.[67] Meanwhile, the official organization of the nation's oil industry, the American Petroleum Institute, reelected Harry F. Sinclair as its treasurer.[68]

5

From Gasoline Alley to One World

As vastly as the steam engines of the nineteenth century increased the range and speed at which men and goods moved, they were soon surpassed by the time and space-shrinking powers of twentieth-century oil transport. At sea, with oil-driven ships, both war and commerce became global. On the land, oil-powered transport took man through tracts of the earth's surface that steam engines had never penetrated. And in the air, man could now travel quite independently of terrestrial formation.

Both the motor vehicle and the airplane wrote twentieth-century history. As carriers of death, they made two world wars the most widespread and destructive ever seen. As bearers of peaceable trade and commerce, they became instruments of social unification. If in America oil transport changed the national psychology and national manners, its full impact was especially notable in Asia and Africa. Once a bus arrived in an Indian village, to which transport had previously been by animal, the old self-supporting economy gave way in a moment to a new dependence upon objects made thousands of miles away—and villagers became members of a general as well as a local society. In times past, the process of standardization moved as imperceptibly as a glacier. But now it was sudden, universal, and convulsively disturbing. The onset of "one world," made possible by oil-driven machines, was probably the primary event of the twentieth century, energizing the tremendous economic growth of the West and fueling the ferment of the rapidly rising Third World.[1]

Within the United States, the automobile both symbolized and embodied these changes. The historian Allan Nevins wrote:

No other single machine, in all probability, did so much to induce people of provincial mind to begin thinking in national terms; none did so much to knit together different parts of the country; none did more to create a sense of freer and more spacious life.[2]

"Why on earth do you need to study what's changing about this country?" a townsman said to an inquiring sociologist in Muncie, Indiana, in 1925. "I can tell you what's happening in just four letters: A–U–T–O."[3]

John Jacob Astor had 32 of them; the Duke of Portland is supposed to have kept six cars and twelve chauffeurs.[4] In the earliest years it was not the Germans, who had invented it, nor the English, who haughtily held their horses, nor the Americans, whose bad roads kept them back, but the French who gave the automobile its big push ahead. The French of the 1880s and 1890s—*la belle époque*—loved tinkering with cars. It was they who gave the name to the automobile, formed the first auto clubs, and staged the first races, establishing that motor cars were practicable and that the gasoline-fueled ones were the best. The poplar-lined Routes Napoleons, built a century earlier for the quick marches of the first modern military campaigner, ran high dry, and well-metaled across French landscapes. Seventy-five years later, they were too narrow for the swarming traffic, and people like Albert Camus lost their lives in speeding sports cars, which crashed against the white painted boles of the bordering trees. But these roads were made to order for Emile Levasso, who captured the historic 1895 Paris-Bordeaux race by racing the 732 miles unassisted (while exhausting the supply of 22 extra inner tubes with which his backer Albert Michelin had provided him).[5] English toffs and American sports imported Panhards and Citroens, raced them as the French, and put them up in new fangled edifices christened, in French, garages.

By traditions very nearly as old as civilization itself, mounted transport was reserved for the gentleman. Even in America, where the rich owned fast horses and loved to display them on the avenues, these ancient associations persisted, so that when horseless carriages began to be built in greater numbers, everybody supposed that, like the sedans and phaetons and cabriolets they were named after, these new automobiles would belong only to the well-heeled gentry. The early manufacturers, and they were legion, began manufacturing their vehicles for this market. But not Henry Ford.

A maverick of genius, Ford was stubbornly determined to build cars that cost less, not more. Around 1908 he broke with partners and rivals and went his solitary way. His first car had cost $1,200. Experimenting, he produced one in 1910 that sold for only $700, and he sold 700,000 of them. Still unsatisfied, he devised a simple version in 1911 that cost $600. He picked a scrap of vanadium steel off a Florida race course and said, "That is the kind of material we ought to have in our cars." [6] Finally, in 1912, he fixed upon his Model T as the car that cost the least. Then he set up assembly lines to put large numbers of them together and sold the cars dirt cheap—$450. He was fantastically successful. The public, not just the cavaliers, wanted his cars, and he offered them at prices the plebes could afford.

"Nothing has spread socialistic feeling in this country more than the use of the automobile," Woodrow Wilson once said.[7] The car opened lives. The great thing about it was that it took its owner where he wanted when he wanted. It took the city dweller away from the trolley tracks. It took the farm resident out of rustic isolation.

When the automobile came to the American family, all sorts of things happened. The rural home was still the center of life, as it had been since colonial times. The farm family was large because children were an asset when there was no machinery on the premises to do their chores and turn them into an economic liability. But the family was walled in at home by bad roads and the short range of the workhorse. In consequence, when not working long hours in the summer when crops had to be planted, tilled, and harvested, its members spent a lot of time together. They entertained each other or joined with neighbors for the purpose of amusement. One sang; another recited, played the fiddle, or performed card tricks. There were innumerable games of lotto, parchesi, blindman's buff, spin-the-bottle, or post office. Work itself often took the form of play, as in quiltings and cornhuskings.

The Ford in the farmyard changed all that. Ready-made professional entertainment was now to be had for a price in the nearest town or city. Those who got there sat in a darkened movie theatre and drank in images flickering across a screen. The effect, however mechanical the means, was as sensational as the arrival of the first bus for the Indian villagers. The city had always enchanted men. Now, as if by magic, one could be in the city and not of it, through the use of the car. The village fiddler faded into the mists; the movies, the phonograph, and later the radio took his place. Girls no longer learned "accomplishments" with which to amuse boys in their parlors. Instead they danced with them twenty miles from home—and might drive a lot farther before the evening ended. The indrawing influence of isolation upon the farm home was weakened. The family gathered less often around the parlor piano after the day's work was done. The realm of dreams no longer lay over horizons where rails and telegraph wires ran out to infinity, but was well within reach of Henry Ford's runabout.

Of course, farmers drove to town Saturdays for other reasons than to see a picture show. In town stores, they found a wider variety of goods at lower prices than was available back at their crossroads. A casualty of this change in shopping habits was the general store, as national an institution as the bald eagle. Bolts of calico, overalls, hip boots, chamber pots, door knobs, window shades, patent medicines, chicken feed, harness, seeds, staple groceries—just about all lay about in aromatic confusion under its roof. Here countrymen traded chickens for axle grease or rice and complained about the weather, weevils, prices, wheat rust, and politicians. It was marketplace and stoveside forum, where neighbors got their mail, paid their bills, and gave their cracker-barrel opinion on anything under the sun in a kind of never-adjourned town meeting. Now the car put the old-fashioned general store out of business, and with it went the Four Corners Hotel and the traveling salesman who savored its 35-cent chicken dinner. As villages withered and towns grew, manufacturers and wholesalers revised their sales maps. Enlarging their drummers' territories, they sent them out by car instead of train. Though still lonely, the towns where these men called were at least big enough to have Carnegie libraries. Whiling away Kansas winter nights in the 1920s, Thornton Wilder's traveling salesman in *Heaven's My Destination* got as far as *K*, reading the encyclopedia through in successive town libraries.[8]

This was Main Street, and by 1920 its curbs and sidewalks were cluttered with electric light poles, telephone poles, and gasoline pumps for motor cars. When the train pulled into the local station, a handful of Fords and possibly a large Paige were drawn up to meet descending passengers. Though a horse-drawn lumber wagon still creaked down the block, it was a Ford, backing up as if it were shaking to pieces, then recovering with a roar and rattling away, that made the noise and stirred the dust. Facing one another in their stodgy brick and concrete, the Ford garage and the Buick garage upstaged the old stable and feed store down the street. Inside them, old and new cars stood on grease-blackened concrete floors. Tire advertisements filled their windows. As Sinclair Lewis did not fail to note, "Surly young men in khaki union overalls bustled about these vital new places."[9]

In another Middle American scene observed by Lewis in 1920, the up-and-coming Floral Heights real estate development on the outskirts of Zenith City, George F. Babbitt lived "prosperous, extremely married, in a house with a cement driveway and a corrugated iron garage." [10] The first sound to which Babbitt woke in the morning was "the familiar and irritating rattle of someone cranking a Ford: snap-ah-ah, snap-ah-ah, snap-ah-ah." [11] Getting results with the crank in the morning was a special trick, usually learned from another Ford owner, but sometimes through a period of appalling experimentation, which often caused a broken arm. In the favored procedure, the trick was to leave the ignition switch off, step to the front, pull the choke (which was a little wire protruding through the radiator), and give the crank two or three quick upward lifts: snap-ah-ah, snap-ah-ah, snap-ah-ah. Then, whistling hopefully, the driver would go back to his seat and turn on the ignition, step forward to the crank again, and this time, catching it on the downstroke, give it a quick spin with all his strength. If this procedure was followed, E. B. White told *New Yorker* readers, "the engine almost always resounded—first with a few scattered explosions, then with a tumultuous gunfire, which the driver quelled by dashing around to his seat and retarding the throttle."[12]

An old Ford hand, Babbitt would lie abed, cranking with the unseen driver, with him waiting through "a taut eternity" for the roar of the starting engine, with him agonizing as the roar ceased and again began the infernal, patient snap-ah-ah—

> a round, flat sound, a shivering, cold morning sound infuriating and inescapable. Not till the rising voice of the motor told him that the Ford was moving was he released from the panting tension.[13]

Later Babbitt went out to the garage to drive his own Buick to work:

> To Babbitt and most prosperous citizens of Zenith, his motor car was poetry and tragedy, love and heroism. Among the tremendous crises of each day none was more dramatic than starting the engine. It was slow on cold mornings; there was the long, anxious whirr of the starter; and sometimes he had to drip ether into the cocks of the cylinder. . . .[14]

Hours later, Babbitt could hold a luncheon companion's undivided attention with a drop-by-drop chronicle of this almost intravenous resuscitation and fall into lengthy discussion about how much each drop had cost him.

The heart of this motorizing world was "Gasoline Alley," named and peopled in 1918 by the *Chicago Tribune* cartoonist Frank King. An historian of the comic strip evaluated "Gasoline Alley" as "not a piece of life—life itself." [15] It grew out of the circumstance that Middle America, one of the flattest regions on earth, had been laid out in grids. The rural geometry was foursquare, causing traffic generally to flow along angular section lines. The Ptolemy of towns and cities had picked the rectangular block as the defining shape for human habitations. Down the middle of every such block ran an alley. Quite possibly the original blueprints intended these passageways for horse-drawn service vehicles. Behind a good many of the houses backing on these alleys were sheds that might conceivably once have harbored a horse. Dusty in summer, mired in spring and fall, snowdrifted in winter, the alley was the thoroughfare by which the houses on the block were supplied in such essentials as could be hauled through its ruts. Here slithered and heaved the ice wagons and milk carts, the department store delivery vans and the garbage trucks. But by the year the war ended, Henry Ford was selling 700,000 cars a year, and the backyards of every neighborhood were lined with more or less makeshift edifices such as George Babbitt kept his car in. The garage had come to America's alleys.

This was the original trysting place in America's love affair with the automobile, where American males, when they were not earning their living, could be found most often. Few of their houses then had built-in garages. The building that sheltered the car stood well back of the house and was entered either by a newfangled driveway like Babbitt's, or, more commonly, from the alley. The car cradled inside represented in those years a very substantial investment for the Middle American, and he took pride in it. In 1920 every man took pride in the gleaming products of American manufacture, and to the householder his car was his own prize specimen. He never doubted that he must look after it, and since his first car was likely to be secondhand, there was plenty of looking after to do. Early and late, and without fail on holidays, these men met out back of the house in Gasoline Alley—roly-poly Walt Wallet, skinflintly Uncle Avery, bespectacled, derby-hatted Doc, acid-tongued Bill—to patch their tires and mend their flivvers. They talked about the Black Sox and Harding and taxes and all the money some people made by taking a flyer in oil leases. But mostly they talked, as Americans did in those years, about their cars. "If you do a little each day on your car, it beats spending all Saturday afternoon on it," said Avery, chomping on his dead cigar.

"Say, if you fuss with it every day you unearth enough work to keep you going Saturday and Sunday too," said the owlish Doc. Walt, the alley fat man, said, "The only way to keep things up is to spend all day every day at it. And I'm eleven months behind right now." [16]

When Walt drove his first new touring car into the alley, everybody crowded up for a look at the black beauty. "So you traded that other jazz orchestra on this, did you?" said Doc. Walt said, "Say, you ought to hear this baby with the cutout open. She'll rattle all the windows in the block." From the back porch the wives watched intently. "I wanted an enclosed car," said Hazel, "but Doctor is afraid I'll want him to dress up as my chauffeur." [17]

Thanks to Ford and his rivals, the country's cars had far outgrown its roads. The maintenance and construction of roads was a local, township responsibility, often discharged by farmers taking a few days off to fill mud holes in lieu of cash payment of their taxes. As early as 1903, President Roosevelt and William Jennings Bryan spoke up for concrete at a Good Roads convention in St. Louis. Three years later, a first experimental mile of county road paved with concrete was opened outside Detroit. Astonished at "heavy wear of roads by automobiles," *Scientific American* in 1907 reported that motorized traffic near Boston "swept the [gravel] binder from the road and left it in windrows along the roadside." Brick roads, its experts concluded, might prove most satisfactory, "but the cost is prohibitive." [18] The big idea at first was to lift the farmers' wagons out of the mud. Cyclists, of course, favored paving, and, along with state officials, engineers, bicycle manufacturers, a few auto makers such as Packard and Olds (Ford was always too busy churning out Model Ts to bother), and ag-college professors anxious about the social isolation and economic handicaps of farmers—these were the early agitators for improving America's two million miles of unimproved roads. The oil industry's only involvement was some interest in marketing asphalt to city street departments.

But rebuilding a continent's roads cost money, and roads had always been a local affair run by county supervisors. Could anybody imagine local property owners ponying up all the tax money that would be needed to pay for city slickers to wheel at high speeds through their fields and villages? The difficulty was pinpointed in one Gasoline Alley session. "What jars my wool loose is the way they build a good stretch of road and then forget it," growled Bill. "Sure," said Avery, folding up his car blanket, "but think of the taxes to keep it in shape." "Taxes," yelled Doc, who was polishing the windshield. "Avery, you poor sardine, wornout roads cost you more in tires than you pay in taxes. You're so nearsighted you can't see the end of your nose without a telescope." [19]

Myopic or not, the Averys were simply unwilling to finance out of their local real estate taxes roads that they knew would largely be used by strangers. About the only concrete achievement of a noisy campaign for creating a well-marked, well-drained transcontinental Lincoln Highway, on which the entire nation could drive to the San Francisco World's Fair of 1915, was one small concrete patch built in Iowa. The remedy was only partially found in the Federal Aid Roads Act of 1916. This law made road building funds available to states that would raise matching sums and set up state highway departments to administer them. Small as were the first federal grants, the states had trouble raising the matching money. In vain the National Highways Association filled rural mailboxes with brochures picturing heavily laden hayracks rolling smartly over well-laid hardtop. Proponents might plant such signs as "For fishing only" and "Boats cross every half hour" alongside highway mudholes in Ohio,[20] but they lost the referendum just the same.

Suddenly, after the end of the first World War, a way out of the impasse was found. The solution was for those who wanted highways, for those who actually used them, to pay taxes directly for the purpose.

It started in Oregon. No state had greater need "to get out of the mud." [21] Though by 1919 the state had 80,000 motor vehicles, "the conditions of the road," in the words of a Portland legislator, "remain the same—mud in winter and deep dust in summer." [22] After the first Washington funds became available, Oregon raised three times the amount by tripling automobile license fees. Far more was needed. The solution, proposed by the editor of a good-government sheet called *The Oregon Voter* and pushed through the legislature by his friend, the chairman of the newly formed roads committee, was a one-cent tax on gasoline. Their argument was spelled out in the bill's preamble: gasoline was used to propel vehicles over roads, and these heavy vehicles damaged the roads; therefore, a tax on the gasoline consumed by the vehicles in traversing them was a just way to pay for the upkeep of the roads.

The beauty of this solution was that it released the legislature from all pressure to raise what most people then thought of as their *taxes*—namely, the sums they were required to pay upon the assessed valuation of their land and other property. Not only was this quite another sort of levy to be paid by those who actually used the road, but it was possible to specify that this new impost be used specifically for the roads. By directing that all proceeds be paid into a special highway-building fund, New Mexico, one of two other Western states that followed Oregon and enacted a gasoline tax in 1919, did just that. In all of these state legislatures was a desire to tax out-of-state cars that used their roads: the new levy, collected at the pump, accomplished this purpose as neatly as if Oregon, say, had raised barricades at the California border and collected tolls from drivers crossing the state line from the south. Even more important was the insistence that gasoline used off the roads—in tractors and other farm machines—not be taxed.

The Oregon solution proved unexpectedly popular. Even the petroleum industry, later so active in fighting gasoline taxes, failed to bestir itself at the time. Wholesalers acted "cheerfully" to collect the money for the state. The Standard Oil Company of California, which controlled half the Oregon gasoline market, shrugged off the one-cent levy as no more than "nominal"—as not big enough to warrant a squawk.[23] But at the meeting of the American Association of State Highway Officials in Louisville that year, highway commissioners and engineers heard about the new tax from colleagues from the three Western states. It was the answer to everybody's problem. The idea took fire. "Never before in the history of taxation has a major tax been accepted in so short a time," an expert wrote.[24] By 1929 every state in the country imposed a gasoline tax, some of three or four cents a gallon, and collected $431 million in revenue. By then no fewer than 21 states had ceased entirely from tapping general property taxes for roads.

Thus the highway builders were not to be denied. Another federal act in 1921 confirmed the system by which the United States Bureau of Roads in Washington merely approved and inspected roads before reimbursing states for half their cost. But the act also required states to submit to orderly scheduling so that the roads they built were interconnected and did not end up suddenly in cornfields at state lines. This set the stage for the emergence by 1925 and 1926 of uniformly numbered "U.S." highway routes, many of which became as familiar to Americans as their telephone numbers. The old Santa Fe trail lived again in concrete as Highway 66, the great, grease-streaked road that marched over plains and deserts from Chicago to Los Angeles, a thronging passageway for a whole generation seeking lost frontiers. The Lincoln Highway finally achieved existence as the coast-to-coast Highway 30. Highway 20 was the Yellowstone Trail. "U.S.1," hymned in poem and story, was the way to Maine or Florida; and to far western wayfarers from John Steinbeck to Ken Kesey, Highway 101 had the same forming influence in Pacific Coast travel.

Thus it was that in early summer Walt Wallet could stand at the curb, urging his next-door neighbor Doc to join him on a Yellowstone vacation trip and pointing at a flivver laden with suitcases and duffle. Said Walt, "Look, Doc, there goes one of us now—a tent, a frying pan and independence. That bird's only address is North America." [25] From the first, even while Henry Ford was giving his countrymen the most severely practical, stripped-down runabout he could contrive, Americans were slow to think of their cars as mere drive-to-work transport. Much more, the automobile gave to each American who owned one, a heady sense of his own freedom to wheel wherever he pleased, whenever he pleased. His car, even when indistinguishable from millions owned by others, was uniquely his own, garaged behind his own house, lovingly cared for by his own hands, and steered out onto the nation's highways for destinations that only he determined. In the cities he had to vie with rival motorists for space along downtown curbs and watch out for motor cops trailing him when he stepped on the gas. But out in the country he felt free, and being in command of thirty horsepower could be a virile adventure masterfully executed.

With the spread of mass production of cars, life-styles little altered since colonial times went out the window. No sooner had the farm families taken off for town for their fun than city folks went out on the roads. Tin-can tourists, they were called, or auto-bummers, or motor campers. Some pitched their tents along roadsides. More usually the night's stand was the public campground, an institution that became almost universal in the early 1920s in Western towns, though much less so in the guarded East.

The American people—professors, mechanics, doctors, grocers— were seeing their country for the first time. Vast numbers of them were getting back to nature. More than frying pans, they lugged along mosquito netting, tire chains, an icebox, plenty of blankets, and a water bag slung from the front bumper. Some carried their equipment after them in two-wheel trailers. For those who wanted to travel first class, pioneering concerns had already constructed homes on wheels. One such tour trailer of 1924 held two beds and a 12′ × 14′ tent, all for $78.[26] That year the state of Minnesota advertised 1,600 summer hotels and camps for tourists.[27] Sometimes farmers put up travelers whose cars they pulled out of the mud and sent them away with a hearty breakfast in the morning. But construction had already begun on overnight cabins, and the first tourist courts appeared on main roads. Thus the automobile, having delivered the farmer to the city's fleshpots, bore the denizen of the city to the milder joys of the great outdoors. Perhaps this artifact of oil-powered technology was not yet a necessity for existence. But for millions it created a sense of freer and more spacious life.

There could be no question that the gas buggy, putting the public on the roads, vastly increased the mobility of the population. Determined to See America First, a generation of wanderyearlings from the youthful E. B. White in his wonderfully tenacious Model T to Fredric Manfred's rollicking midwestern college boys in their topless Marmon chugged back and forth across the continent. Even before the end of the first World War rovers like Bo Mason, stopping in a Montana hamlet for a bucketful of gasoline from a garageman's drum luring a memorable flight and pursuit in Wallace Stegner's novel, seemed to pursue their American-dream Big Rock Candy Mountain most hotly when hunched at the wheels of their motor cars.

By 1923, there were 20,000 filling stations along the roadways. A single gadget, the self-starter, invented by Charles F. Kettering in 1912, had transformed the automobile from Henry Ford's bucking bronco into an obedient monster that a 95-pound woman could command at whim. This made the enclosed automobile into everybody's amenity, a kind of mobile room-on-the-road. In 1923 *Vogue* said that a lady could camp confidently in a spacious trailer while "a small auto-tent attached to one side of the trailer accomodates the nurse and maid, and the driver sleeps on a car bed slung inside the automobile." [28] *Woman's Home Companion* lectured on motoring manners:

> We have not gone two blocks before our driver is concerned about her gasoline. Back she makes for the garage, or she decides to try her luck along the highway where our eye, that was to be so quick for the green landscape, is diligently trained with hers in search of a red tank. Once her need is filled, she grows doubtful of the gasoline. Like a doctor making a diagnosis, she leans forward, listening for a symptom of bronchitis in the mixture or for the engine skipping a pulse. Yes, before she takes it out again she must have the whole thing overhauled.[29]

The proper lady driver, commented the *Companion's* editor, "takes what comes her way like a good sport—a delay in our return, a make-shift inn for luncheon, or a puncture."

At family breakfast tables, quarrels broke out between adolescents over the use of Dad's Buick that night. Babbitt's son Ted snarled, "I ought to have my own car." [30] Those who drove along Connecticut's Route 10, the "college highway" linking Yale and Smith in Rudy Vallee's time, did. Important lessons in higher education were taught as brash boys and "nice" girls tussled in rumble seats.[31] In Muncie, Indiana, the judge of the juvenile court told investigators in 1927 that the automobile was becoming "a house of prostitution on wheels." Of thirty girls brought before him, nineteen were involved in sexual offenses committed in a car.[32] Texas sociologists, mapping out where patrons at some tourist courts came from, found that most were "couples" trysting from nearby Dallas.[33]

Though half of the gasoline sold in the United States went to business customers, it was still hard to say how far combustion on wheels had yet altered American economic life. When the general store proprietor's son left for the city to seek his fortune, he probably took a train. Though Babbitt had moved to the outskirts of Zenith City, his house in Floral Heights was not so far from "the loop" that he was dependent on his car to get to work. On the contrary, he often took the trolley car downtown, and when he did not, one of his supreme satisfactions was passing it on a narrow street—"a spurt, a tail-chase, nervous speeding between the huge yellow side and the jagged row of parked motors—a rare game and valiant." [34] When eight years later Herbert Hoover ran for president on a slogan (which Babbitt might have written) of "Two cars for every garage," this was taken as a vaunt of affluence rather than a reflection of changing needs. It was already plain that the ambiguity about just what Americans wanted their cars for had doomed the strictly utilitarian Model T. At that point General Motors, stressing styling and comfort in its cars and changing models every year to encourage customers' dissatisfaction with the cars they had, sold half of all new automobiles, and Henry Ford withdrew entirely from the market to design a completely new Model A.[35]

The depression of the 1930s made the nation at large more mobile than ever, and this time by no means for fun. When fifteen million lost their jobs, so many took to the roads that people began to speak of the American highway as the forty-ninth state. You did not need to have much money to be on the road. Gasoline cost as little as ten cents a gallon, and the filling stations were giving away free glasses and soft drinks to boot. The phenomenon of the used car had long since brought even the poorest citizens to car ownership. No farmer, in particular, was too poor to drive some sort of car or truck.

John Steinbeck's highway epic, *The Grapes of Wrath*, dramatized the plight of Oklahoma sharecroppers "dusted out" by drought, low crop prices, and the competition of mechanized farms. By the thousands, such people began trekking west to make a new start in California.[36] They might have journeyed by train. But for all their poverty and misery, the Okies and Arkies of the 1930s possessed mobility. The Joad family owned a 1925 Dodge truck, and of course it was in their minds that they would need its wheels to find work after they got to California. Loading their belongings, they rattled out on to Route 66 to join the great migration.

Before the truck had gone far, the radiator cap began to jiggle up and down, and steam started to whoosh out. Near a small Oklahoma town they spotted a shack by the road with two gas pumps in front of it and, beside a fence, a water faucet and hose. The filling-station man in his T-shirt and cardboard helmet came over:

You folks aim to buy anything? Gasoline or stuff?
Al was out already, unscrewing the steaming radiator with the tips of his fingers, jerking his hands away to escape the spurt when the cap came loose. "Need some gas, mister."
Got any money?
Sure, think we're beggars?
The truculence left the man's face. "Well, that's all right, folks. Help yourself to water. . . . Think any them big new cars stop here? No sir! They go on to them yella-painted company stations in town. They don't stop no place like this. Most folks stop here ain't got nothin'." [37]

The family drew their water and bought their gasoline. They saw the oil barrels, only two of them, inside the shack and the candy counter with stale candies and licorice whips turning brown with age, and they called as they pulled away, "Pretty soon you'll be on the road yourself." [38]

Joads died, and Joads were born on the 2,000-mile journey. The old truck drank oil "like a gopher hole." [39] But with the help of a connecting rod scavenged from a wheelless Dodge in an Arizona wrecking yard, they staggered on like 100,000 other families that got to California by grace of gasoline.[40]

★

"Incredible as it may seem" wrote a petroleum geologist later, "in 1920 we thought we were facing the beginning of the end of crude-oil resources in America, drilling what we thought were our last known structures and frowning—can you imagine it?—upon the rambling motorist who drove into our stations and demanded gasoline." [41]

Far from running out of oil, the nation found and produced so much of the stuff that keeping up with the mushrooming demands of motorists in the 1920s was never an industry problem. Even when the Mexicans, in the throes of revolutionary upheaval, virtually ceased exporting oil to the United States, there was no shortage. The proponents of the depletion allowance sometimes attributed the postwar productive spurt to the extraordinary inducements created by Congress in 1918—and indeed the favors granted them were considerable. Not only was the industry permitted to write off its tax liabilities, but the treasury issued new regulations that permitted oil companies to deduct as "intangible" costs almost all expenses incurred in drilling new wells.[42] A number of major companies ended up paying no taxes at all.

Even so, the greatest factor in the changed picture was the discovery in Texas after 1920 of some of the largest petroleum reserves on earth. The succession of great fields brought in after the first World War, rivaled as they were by rich finds in Oklahoma, Arkansas, and California, soon created an overproduction of oil that became the obsessive preoccupation of the major companies not only in America but the world. No matter where men drilled, Texas yielded up oil. During the decade, there were strikes all along the Gulf Coast, strikes in the Western ranchlands, and strikes in the Eastern cotton fields. By 1925 wildcatters planted the first rigs in the thinly settled counties of the far northern Panhandle.

At that time, the total population of Hutchinson County, near the Oklahoma border, was 883. Little grew there but mesquite. The only habitation was the tiny county seat town of Plemons (population 250). Across the county meandered the Canadian River, without so much as a single bridge over it.

On March 6, 1926, a wildcat blew in with a roar that shook the whole state. Having seen bonanzas just about everywhere else, the eyes of Texas now swiveled north to the Panhandle. The gusher was in a broken, gullied area near Dixon Creek. Excitement was intense. Amarillo, fifty miles to the southwest, overflowed with strangers. In the rocky countryside geologists scurred about as thick as jackrabbits. Lease seekers beat on every ranch house door. In the van were Oklahoma outfits led by the Phillips and Marland companies. Close behind hustled an Oklahoma townsite promoter named A. P. (Pete) Borger. He bought surface rights to a 240-acre tract along Dixon

Creek and began selling 25-foot by 120-foot lots at $1,500 apiece. Overnight these postage-stamp plots sold for twice that price.

The history of an oil boomtown, as Texas had learned since Spindletop, was all too predictable: boom, bust, and one to five years later, "stabilization" again. No community was ever prepared for the eruption; no city was ever big enough to take the excitement, confusion, and disorganization calmly and normally. In east Texas or west, on the Gulf or in the Panhandle, any spot where oil blew in turned straightway into a rip-roaring frontier town. A motley horde of laborers moved in. Living conditions sank to primitive levels. Chaotic intermingling of strangers established a prevailing anonymity that shorted and jammed the ordinary switchboards of social controls. The mania for money seized all comers. The press of a huge floating population loaded with cash and spoiling to spend it created a dependence on commercialized pleasure that rumrunners, gamblers, hustlers, and panderers rushed to provide. And as the town opened wide, other communities, sniffing the odor of sin and hearing the din of dance hall nickelodeons, drew away, or pretended to; and the process of social isolation was completed.

So it was in Beaumont, in Ranger, in Mexia. And so it was in Borger, named for its promoter. In rushed thousands; crude as well as skilled manpower was needed. All the complex machinery of oil production had to be installed from scratch—roads had to be built; pipes, laid; leases, signed. And by petroleum's zany old "law of capture," every leaseholder knew that he had better drill as soon as he had signed, or some one close by would soon be draining the oil out from under him. So drilling crews, pipeline teams, and supply truckers worked night and day.

In Hutchinson County the result was a social cyclone. The meager machinery and institutions of society toppled. The voices of local leaders were submerged, the conserving glue of familiar face-to-face relationships dissolved, and public opinion ceased to be a controlling force. When Pete Borger was asked to donate a lot for a Baptist church, for example, he replied that he would much rather give the $10,000 lot price to keep the church out of town. But he did not inquire much at all about the purposes of those who paid cash for his lots.

The workers and their families pitched their tents and raised their shacks helter-skelter. Five months after its founding, the population was estimated, on the basis of mail deliveries, at 35,000—perhaps 50,000, counting all those living within a ten-mile radius from Dixon Street. Living conditions were bad. So rudimentary was the housing and so extreme the overcrowding that cleanliness was as far away as godliness; privacy became a myth when thousands lived in tents and boxlike "hotels." In the heat of the Panhandle summer, water hauled in by trucks sold for 75 cents a barrel, flies swarmed around open latrines, and garbage putrefied in streets and alleys under the blistering sun. But the Rock Island line was building a $4.5 million branch from Amarillo, and the Santa Fe was starting a spur; by its first anniversary Borger had not only a railroad, but also electric power and light service and a water system. Permanent buildings appeared, and sanitary conditions improved.

In the early days of Borger, according to subsequent report, "over 2,000 women of easy virtue had their home there." [43] They lived principally in rooming houses. The Betty Jane Hotel, Murphy's Dance Hall, Dew Drop Inn, Stagg Billiard and Pool Hall stood, false front by false front, alongside hot dog stands, chili parlors, barbershops, drugstores, a bank, hardware stores, groceries, and other entertainment dumps for the whole two-mile stretch of Dixon Street. In one block, six or seven gambling houses held forth. Stores of legitimate merchants kept busy long past midnight. Liquor joints did a rushing business. A frequent sight was a bootlegger fetching in a fresh supply from his beer wagon in the street. The night sounds of Borger were the roar of gas escaping from nearby wells, the clanging of slot machines, the clinking of glasses, the endless grinding of the player piano, the wail of an ambulance, the loud squabbling of a man and woman hoarsely heedless of who might hear.

Before the oil strike, the whole area got along fine with a single justice of the peace and his constable. After Borger burst into existence, the county sheriff appointed a series of deputies to carry the star and six-gun of legal authority in the oil country. A farmer accustomed to dealing with friends, Sheriff Joe Owensby had no taste for facing down a bunch of drunken roughnecks or quelling a prostitute who had overdosed on heroin and gone on a rampage. But among the tougher types he deputized was Six-Gun Charlie, a convicted felon from Oklahoma. An even more serious disqualification than the murder rap he had fled was the new deputy's addiction to pistol-whipping—handcuffing a drunk and beating him over the head until he fell unconscious. Charlie knew a lot about how beer and whiskey reached Borger, so much in fact that witnesses later testified he raked off $40,000 and used it in Oklahoma City to get his sentence suspended.

The incorporation of Borger as a town, with its own mayor and police, in October 1926, did not particularly restrain conduct. The flouting of liquor and gambling prohibitions went on unabated. Robberies, assaults, and murders continued. In March 1927, after two deputy sheriffs and a policeman had been murdered in the space of two days, the town petitioned Governor Dan Moody to send aid. He sent ten Texas Rangers to "clean up" Borger. They raided dives, poured out liquor, destroyed stills, demolished gambling devices, and, as the official report stated, "no less than one thousand prostitutes left town." [44] The entire town government was forced to quit, and a new slate took over to "enforce the laws."

By April 1927, the tide of population was turning. Those who stayed on began to build houses, churches, schools. But the new town fathers proved unfit to enforce the laws. Streetwalkers still accosted customers, if with somewhat subtler words and gestures. Whorehouses became "hotels," and liquor joints bore the exterior of soft-drink parlors and drugstores. Hijacking, assault, and robbery by no means ceased. Between March 1926, and September 1929, Borger saw twenty slayings. At the September climax an assassin ambushed and killed the district attorney in his garage. Governor Moody thereupon declared martial law, and a second cleanup began.

General Clem Wolters, who had quelled the riotous Mexia field, finally brought authentic law and order into Borger. His first act was to arrest a drunk staggering down the railroad platform just as his troops climbed off the train. The general named a board, which took hundreds of pages of testimony. Out went the sheriff and his deputies and the whole city administration. A Texas Ranger took over as sheriff; the new police chief was a man transferred from a similar assignment at Mexia. On October 29, 1929, martial law was lifted, and Borger became just another Texas town. The Chamber of Commerce proclaimed, "We do not allow poolrooms." [45] The population, according to the 1930 census, had subsided to 6,532.

As Texas oil strikes went, Borger's was not a big one, although it probably lifted the Phillips Company into the rank of major oil producers. By 1928 the state of Texas was producing 250,000 barrels a day and leading all others in output. Such wealth could not help altering the life and outlook of Texas in wider ways than by disrupting communities like Mexia and Borger. One immediate effect was to enrich thousands of landholders across the state. By 1930 almost $200 million was paid annually to farmers, ranchers, and other holders in royalties, rentals, and bonuses. This great inpouring of outside money added enormously to the overall economy and broadened the base of the oil interests in the state.

In many spectacular ways, oil and industries based on oil changed

Texas. Petroleum created something like the Eastern industrial upper class of the nineteenth century—a group of immense wealth, whose rise was aided by provisions of the depletion allowance, which enabled many of them to pay no more into the federal treasury than Rockefeller and Vanderbilt and Carnegie paid in preincome tax days. The Texas new-rich oilman personified ostentatious vulgarity, replacing in sterotype the Eastern robber baron of the earlier generation. The image made an impression around the world more apparent than real—the oilman did not assume that much importance in Texas life.

Unlike the offspring of the Eastern industrialists, the oilman was freed from economic worry and responsibility to pursue whatever form of social disintegration he preferred. H. L. Hunt, for instance, gambled. With an income of $200,000 a day, he hired an M.I.T.-trained mathematician to figure odds on horses and boasted that he made a million betting in one year; he lost $300,000 gambling on a single baseball game. "Just like the oil business," he is reported to have said. Tom Waggoner, whose oil pool was named after his daughter Electra (she kept a closet filled with fur coats and had 350 pairs of shoes), built his $3 million Arlington Downs estate between Fort Worth and Dallas, complete with a 46-million-gallon artificial lake, a million-dollar string of ponies, and, though betting was outlawed in Texas, a racetrack with a 6,000-seat grandstand. The track was used for matched-racing only on "a Southern gentleman basis," [46] until in a kind of valedictory salute the great state of Texas allowed parimutuel betting for the last year of Waggoner's life—and then reimposed its ban as soon as he died. Glenn McCarthy, so independent he eventually went broke rather than incorporate, built Houston's fanciest hotel just so he could have, in its Cork Club, a place to drink with his friends without a care for the state liquor ban. He also maintained a flotilla of planes, in which he could fly his friends to Acapulco for fun. H. Roy Cullen bestowed largesse upon the Houston Symphony, which took care to perform, at every concert he attended, his favorite piece, "Old Black Joe." Cullen later made a present of a $6,000 Cadillac to Joe McCarthy, the Red-hunter. His opinion was duly printed from coast to coast: "I think Senator McCarthy is the greatest man in America." [47]

The oil barons' ethic, in most cases, did not adjust to anything else. Sol Brachman of Waco, who sold them oilfield equipment, said, "Some of them don't realize there was a world before they arrived." [48] There were, as always, important exceptions, especially where beef and cotton money had preceded the new wealth. Those who made it big tended to pursue more wealth, often elsewhere (Sid Richardson and Clint Murchison bought up the New York Central Railroad in a couple of phone calls), enjoy it in the same places as well as their limited cultural vision permitted, and sometimes (Richardson sat in on the Paris parley in early 1952 at which Eisenhower agreed to run) to indulge in presidential politics by writing checks.

The individual oil-rich family, again with important exceptions, tended to remove itself from daily life and politics in Texas, following the characteristic pattern of the northern industrial upper class. It had less influence on the customs, mores, and even social life of Texas than supposed, because it was not fully engaged—great wealth tended to close as many doors as it opened.

In ways, then, oil only reinforced old trends. Thus, the industrialization caused by oil was not quite all it seemed. Oil was extracted wealth, based on land, and thus fitted easily into old patterns of land speculation and development. For many owners of producing wells, it was merely another salable crop, and the great majority of Texas's 5,000 oil-producing landowners in 1928 were small. Oil was extracted by machinery, without much labor; it was hauled to market and sold. The lease of oil lands was similar to the lease of grazing lands or the contract for machine-harvesting of a wheat or cotton crop.

The structure of the oil industry itself, meanwhile, had undergone an important change. By this time, all the large companies of the United States, including the successor Standard firms, had moved in a big way into the production as well as manufacturing and marketing of oil. This meant that all were now "integrated" companies, engaging in all operations from the derrick to the street corner pump. And what that meant for Texas and other states was that the exploration and production of oil were no longer carried on exclusively or even predominantly by a lot of small independent operators wildly competing to get the oil out of the ground before their neighbors did. The major discoveries continued to be made by wildcatters, but by no means all. The big oil companies now had large exploration departments, staffed by keen and experienced geologists, and these men sometimes struck oil before the independents found it. However often, as at Mexia or Borger, a discovery might confound the company geologists, there really was a science to petroleum formation, and year by year the companies made more and more of it. But what with their tremendous requirement for crude-oil supplies for their pipelines, refineries, and far-flung markets, as well as the big sums they felt compelled to invest to meet these requirements, the big companies moved in swiftly after each discovery, buying out the wildcat discoverers and leasing huge tracts on all sides of the discovery well.

There could be but one result: no matter how unexpected a discovery might sometimes be, no matter how feverishly small operators raced for promising leases, no matter how doggedly some of them hung onto valuable properties, and no matter how resourcefully yet smaller numbers of them contrived to develop producing wells in the seemingly endless oil horizons of Texas, the big companies inexorably acquired a larger and larger proportion of the state's oil-producing properties. Those few giants that dominated Texas oil production, Texaco (after 1912) as well as the successor Standard companies, which had now penetrated Texas as Rockefeller had never managed to, were all based outside the state.

This was the most substantial element of change that came with oil to Texas in the 1920s. At first large and small producers alike kept pumping out more oil to keep up with a motorized nation's demand for gasoline and more gasoline. Jim Hogg's Railroad Commission, authorized by legislation in 1919 to keep watch over Texas oil, was far too sensitive to independents' and small leaseholders' impatience with regulatory restraints to fiddle with anything like production controls. But the power of the majors grew steadily. In the early 1920s they used it to keep gasoline prices at levels high enough to provoke senatorial complaints, occasional government action, and antitrust suits. Then, as production in the United States and the world at large kept topping demand, the statesmen of the major oil companies began talking about the importance of "conservation." Most of all they were talking to Texans and to the Oklahoma and Kansas segments of the mid-continent oil industry. They made speeches about the vast quantities of oil prodigally wasted in the ferocious rush to drain each new pool as fast as it was found. Controlling as they now did most of Texas's oil lands, they argued that the kind of anarchy that prevailed at Spindletop and countless other discovery sites thereafter must cease. If instead, they said, wells could be spaced at decently wide intervals at the points where geological surveys showed they could best tap the riches below, in fact if only entire new fields could be thus surveyed and then exploited as "units," then Texas could end the waste that had become a byword in the oil industry ever since the first gusher at Oil Creek. Of course, what these oil statesmen meant by conservation was not precisely the same thing as was meant by Sierra Club members and other defenders of America's natural riches against commercial exploiters. Their concern was that overproduction would drive down prices and profits. And to them "conservation" meant curtailing output to stabilize the market.[49]

By the middle of the decade, the successors of Rockefeller had established such a dominating position in Texas oil production that the small producers, their apprehensions quickened by a drop in crude-oil prices, began to listen to them. The word the major companies used was "prorationing." [50] The idea, anathema to small-time operators, was for every producer to reduce daily output of his wells by a certain proportion. The amount of this reduction would be established by adding up total output of all wells in the field and prorating the reduced output for each according to his share of the former total.

Opportunity arived when the huge new Yates field was brought in in 1926. The major companies held more of the leased acreage than ever before, and for once, since crude oil was in oversupply, they could blanket the small producers. The president of Jersey Standard's Humble Oil Company, W. H. Farish, called a meeting at which the new field was divided into 100-acre "units" and each "unit" assigned a fixed quota irrespective of whether it contained one, two, or ten wells.[51] This effectively reduced the number of wells. The potential of each 100-acre unit was then rated according to the oil its wells produced. The Texas Railroad Commission endorsed and enforced prorationing in the Yates field.

The stage was now set to curtail competition and limit it worldwide. The obvious American leader was the Standard Oil Company of New Jersey. Powerful as it had become in Texas (as Humble Oil), the essential role of this huge corporation was operating as the successor overseas of the old Standard monopoly. Rockefeller's Standard Oil had never held less than a third of the British market and was almost as strong in the rest of Europe. The successor company held onto these markets and as an integrated corporation actively expanded after the war into overseas production—in the East Indies, in Venezuela, Peru, Rumania, and the Middle East. Soon world output, like American output, outstripped demand. Sir Henry Deterding, master of Shell, then the world's biggest oil producer, declared that any intensification of the international oil competition in the face of "softening" prices was the height of futility.[52]

In the late summer of 1927, Deterding invited Walter C. Teagle, president of Jersey Standard, and Sir John Cadman, chairman of Anglo-Persian, the other big British oil combine, to join him for grouse shooting at his castle at Achnacarry in Scotland. On September 27, 1928, the petroleum summit ended in the so-called "as is" agreement.[53] A price war in India ended, and with it the turmoil that had spread to the American and European markets. A line drawn in

Mexico ended rivalry there. The Standard companies of New Jersey and New York obtained recognition as partners in the development of rich Iraqi deposits.

In return, the British insured that Middle Eastern oil would not arrive so suddenly as to overwhelm world markets. No longer would there be the temptation to cut prices, for the partners would trim production to demand. As Deterding wished—and that was why it was called the "as is" agreement—the partners would accept their present division of the world market and expand production jointly. With all the partners assured access to the main sources of supply, the need for duplication of facilities was eased. Each market would be supplied from the nearest source at a world price based on the high-cost Texas Gulf price, thus guaranteeing an extra one-dollar profit to the big international oil companies on all the low-cost petroleum produced in Venezuela, the East Indies, and the Persian Gulf.

Thus was created what fourteen years later the United States Federal Trade Commission called "the international oil cartel." Though Teagle had negotiated it, the big American companies could not openly adhere to the Achnacarry agreement for fear of running afoul of antitrust prosecution. When in 1929 two of them signed a pact with Deterding to restrict Venezuelan output, the Federal Conservation Board in Washington refused approval to what it termed a violation of the antitrust laws.[54] But the majors kept pressing for "conservation" in Texas and Oklahoma and extended voluntary pro-rationing to the new Hobbs field in New Mexico and the Van field in Texas. Then, just after the shares of the ten top oil companies dropped by one-third in the Wall Street stock crash and crude oil prices plummeted to less than 40 percent of their 1926 level, the greatest oil strike in American history exploded in east Texas.

The hero of this hazard was a flop-eared, fast-talking promoter named Columbus Marion Joiner. Dad Joiner, as Rusk County farmers all knew him, was a wildcatter in the wildest Spindletop tradition. Stooped and wizened, at 70 he had lost every dollar he ever made. But he could smell oil a hundred miles away, and against the evidence of geologists and dry wells he said east Texas was loaded with it. He went about among the widows and spinsters cajoling them to keep the faith and renew his leases. He sat with farmers in country stores holding forth on his certainty, shared by no other oilman, that the same Woodbine sand stratum that began near Dallas and farther east had yielded such famous strikes as Mexia, Wortham, and Powell, ran thickest and oiliest beneath their farms.

The big companies scoffed, but when Dad Joiner began drilling his third well, Jersey and Gulf hedged, as was their wont, by taking precautionary leases in the neighborhood. The widow Daisy Bradford gave Dad Joiner a few more days to pony up payments on the drilling site. One or two others spudded wildcats a half dozen miles away. Joiner, strapped for funds, kept going off to sell a few shares in Dallas. A tall, boater-hatted man who visited the drillsite and talked to Joiner by the hour was a land speculator and oil promoter from Arkansas named Haroldson Lafayette Hunt.

On October 5, 1930, Joiner's Daisy Bradford No. 3 blew in before a huge crowd of east Texas farmers. Oil shot high above the derrick. Leota Tucker, the crew's cook, her face and arms splashed by the black rain, shouted, "I'll never wring out another dishrag in my life." [55] "Sixty-eight hundred barrels a day—unbelievable," croaked Dad Joiner.[56] But in a day or two the flow fell, then came in strange spurts. Dad was also worried about title to his 5,000-acre leases. Then the other wildcats struck big. It was just as Dad said—he had hit the Woodbine sand, but apparently on the fringe. The oil companies began drilling too. The old promoter, pressed hard and out of his element with problems of storage and pipeline construction, grew restless. It was the moment the tall man in the straw hat had been waiting for. Hunt paid Joiner $1,335,000 for his rights, just $30,000 of it cash. It was the deal that started H. L. Hunt on his way to a billion-dollar fortune. Dad went off to sell more stock in Dallas and prospect in west Texas.

This huge field was too big for the majors to preempt. There was no stopping the flood. Within a year, east Texas, already found to be by far the biggest field ever opened in America, had produced 109 million barrels from 3,607 wells. But there was already too much oil. The posted price of crude skidded to ten cents a barrel. Both Oklahoma and Texas tried to impose prorationing and hold back the flood. The small producers rebelled, fought. The Texas Railroad Commission forbade all sales of oil not registered at its offices. In reply to this order, small producers began transporting their crude oil across the state line to sell it. As days passed, more and more such "hot oil" poured onto the markets.[57] Down went prices until water cost more than oil—two cents a barrel for crude oil, four cents a gallon for "Eastex" gasoline distilled at the field's ninety-odd small refineries and offered at pumps with a free chicken dinner, a dozen eggs, or a crate of tomatoes with a fill-up.[58] When officials tried to shut down small producers and stop trucks, rioting erupted. Governor Ross Sterling proclaimed martial law.

By then, such troubles in oil were only the Texas manifestations of the greater problems of national and worldwide depression. As Franklin Roosevelt took over in Washington, the banks were closed, 15 million were jobless, and the economy was stagnating. Major oil company heads, led by Teagle and Harry Sinclair, pleaded for federal controls in their industry. The new president's answer to the emergency was the National Recovery Administration. NRA was to rescue all industries stalled by too much output and too little demand. Wheels were to be set spinning again; boilers, relit; assembly lines, rolling again. In one grand start-up, the industries would form committees to write codes orchestrating output according to the tempo of demand. In the hurly-burly, oilmen saw their chance to return to the first World War's "cooperation" with the federal government and enforce from Washington the prorationing that the rebel independents frustrated in the states.

Here the oil interests ran up against Secretary of the Interior Harold L. Ickes.[59] Member of a prosperous Chicago family who had worked for Theodore Roosevelt's Bull Moose candidacy in 1912, Ickes was, with Henry A. Wallace, one of two Progressive Republicans taken into Franklin Roosevelt's cabinet in 1933. Practicing law and fighting the archconservative *Chicago Tribune*'s influence in Illinois affairs, Ickes had steadfastly worked for conservation, protection of public lands and parks, and a better break for the Indians. After backing FDR in 1932, Ickes had hoped to be nominated commissioner of Indian affairs. Instead, when Republican Senators Bronson Cutting and James Couzens turned it down, Roosevelt nominated him for Interior.

Gruff, outspoken, combative to the point of irascibility, Ickes soon made a name in Washington as an administrator who got things done. Roosevelt valued his independence, his hard-bitten honesty, and his readiness to take on all comers either in public controversy or in bureaucratic infighting. As much as any cabinet member, Ickes took on extra assignments. He headed the Public Works Administration, whose task was to create jobs by building bridges, dams, highways, and public buildings, while Harry Hopkins ran the Works Progress Administration, whose priority was to put men to work at almost any sort of project. The press called him "Honest Harold." Stubborn, idiosyncratic, given to outbursts of temper, Ickes went out of his way to court such a reputation and published a book called *Autobiography of a Curmudgeon*. With genuine flair for public invective, he charged that General Hugh Johnson of the NRA was afflicted by "mental saddle sores" and "halitosis of the intellect" and in the 1940 presidential campaign called Wendell Willkie a "barefoot boy from Wall Street."

Ickes had strong political instincts and excellent judgment in almost everything except his own prospects (he thought he might be FDR's successor). Never were these qualities more evident than in his conduct of his cabinet office, which he held throughout Roosevelt's presidency and through six months of Truman's, the longest tenure of Interior on record. It is said that when French promoters were angling in the 1880s to build a canal in Panama, they tried to bribe the American interior secretary of the day in the mistaken notion that he exercised the same political power as a European minister of the interior. Over the years the secretary of the interior in America has become a kind of guardian of the nation's natural resources. Often, though not always, he is a man of the West, where public lands and interest in conservation are keenest. In placing a man like Ickes in the post, Roosevelt was not unmindful that just two years before a former interior secretary had been imprisoned for taking bribes to hand over public-land oil reserves to private oil companies.

This was not to say that Ickes made the New Deal's oil policy. Though Roosevelt, on his third day in office, asked Ickes to find a way to limit oil production, not much came of the meetings the secretary organized. Before long, Roosevelt also made Ickes oil administrator and then took administration of the new petroleum code out from the hands of NRA Administrator Hugh Johnson and gave it over to Ickes. Not much came of that either, if only because the Supreme Court soon struck down NRA and its price-fixing codes for limiting competition within industries.

Ickes always took the position, in the spirit of an old-school conservationist, that oil was a precious national asset that government must ultimately control in the national interest. When Teagle and others came urging price and production controls in 1933, he supported their plea even though it required, as he saw, suspending the Sherman act's prohibition against restraint of trade under the NRA Oil Code. But when the oil companies, after the worst days of the 1933 panic, again backed away from federal regulation, Ickes took up with the small independents. On their behalf, Senator Elmer Thomas, Democrat of Oklahoma, asserted that oil was so basic to the economy and national security that the industry should be declared a public utility and proposed federal control of petroleum production. Ickes backed the bill.

Roosevelt had been number two man in the Navy Department in the first World War, when Secretary Josephus Daniels came out for nationalization of the country's oil resources, and he had pointedly sent the man he still called "Chief" to be ambassador to a Mexican government that ardently wished to nationalize its oil. But Roosevelt, even while egging Ickes on, was listening to other voices, notably that of House Majority Leader Sam Rayburn of Texas. In the end, the president sided with Rayburn, who reflected the views of the oil interests and controlled the votes in Congress. Instead of the Thomas bill, Congress enacted the Connally Hot Oil Act, forbidding interstate oil sales. Then, with Rayburn in firm command, a simple resolution was adopted endorsing an interstate compact drawn up by oil-producing states for implementing prorationing at the state level.[60] Thus the Roosevelt administration, which intervened so forcefully in other fields during the New Deal years, leaned over backward to stay out of oil. The result was to help the oil industry follow its own way in trying to hold down output in the teeth of the huge discoveries of oil in Texas and abroad. In this program, the oil industry was no more and no less successful than the Roosevelt administration was in its program of restoring prosperity and ending unemployment in the United States. For the oil industry, as for the New Deal, it took a war to achieve its goal.

On August 23, 1934, Sir Henry Deterding of Royal Dutch Shell and President Teagle of Standard Oil of New Jersey went to see Harold Ickes, taking with them Stanley Hornbeck, the State Department's expert on the Far East.[61] They wanted to talk about oil and Japan. At that moment, Japanese forces had occupied all of Manchuria, and militarists were talking about the necessity of moving south into China. With only two or three extremely small refineries, Japan had to depend on foreign supplies for all its fuel oil, gasoline, and lubricating oils.

All this the visiting oilmen explained to a fascinated Ickes. Of late, they continued, the Japanese had begun to buy fuel oil for their navy in very large quantities. And the Japanese government had decreed that companies supplying gasoline must maintain at least six months' supply ashore in Japan. The oilmen explained that their two companies and affiliates were almost Japan's sole suppliers, and such demands could mean costly losses to them. They proposed that the United States, Britain, and the Netherlands protest against the six months' requirement and back the protest with a threat to cut off all oil supplies from the outside world.

Though no government wanted to act in 1934—any more than Western European governments wanted to act when Hitler sent troops into the demilitarized Rhineland two years later—Ickes never forgot this conversation. Thus when, three years later, Japan's militarists invaded and seized most of China, Ickes told Roosevelt, "We ought not to ship Japan any essential of war when we know it is to be used against beleaguered China." [62]

Precisely *because* oil was essential to the Japanese militarists, others urged against cutting it off. General George Marshall and Secretary Cordell Hull resolutely opposed any threat to Japan that might bring a war for which the United States was unready. That was in 1939, when the second World War had begun, but Hitler had yet to strike westward. Roosevelt's answer to Ickes was to point out that if he cut off American oil shipments to Japan, the Japanese might seize the Netherlands East Indies for their oil.

Then Hitler launched his panzers against France, and Secretary of War Henry Stimson learned from the army chief at San Francisco that Japan had contracted to buy almost all aviation gasoline available on the West Coast. Ickes, Stimson, and Morgenthau demanded that Roosevelt ban shipment of war materials. The president thereupon issued an order placing scrap metal, oil, and oil products on a list of vital materials that were not to leave the country. But, as Roosevelt allowed the State Department to redraft the order, the restrictions were limited to high-octane gasoline, airplane motor oil, tetraethyl lead, and top-grade scrap. Ickes and Morgenthau protested that the Japanese could still import crude oil and convert it into aviation gasoline. When the Japanese made a deal with the Vichy French to move 6,000 troops into Indochina, Morgenthau noted, "Hull is going to do something about scrap iron—but he won't touch oil." [63] At the end of 1940, scrap shipments were embargoed. But Japanese tankers continued to load huge shipments of fuel oil for their navy at California ports.

Slowly but surely, the United States government stepped up the pressure. Early in 1941, a series of presidential orders extending the licensing system had the effect of cutting off a lot of items for Japan. This piecemeal application was intended to avoid outright provocation. Large oil shipments continued. But the pinch of other shortages helped gradually to persuade various Japanese officials to consider seeking an accommodation with the United States.

What the United States wanted was to keep the World War from spreading to the Pacific. As Washington saw it, American interests in Europe came first. War must be avoided in the Pacific at the same time that Japanese ambitions were checked in China, Indochina, and the Netherlands East Indies and possible threats to Singapore and Australia were fended off. Japanese strategy, on the other hand, was to seek economic and political domination of Southeast Asia and to conclude the "China Incident" satisfactorily while avoiding war, if possible, with America, Britain, or Russia. As great as was the desire for accommodation on both sides, the abstract principles of Hull in the end required the Japanese to renounce their designs on Indochina, the Netherlands Indies and Malaya and to withdraw from China. This was too much for the Japanese military, government, and public opinion. The China Incident had gone too far to be abandoned. And so in April 1941, the Japanese enormously strengthened their position by concluding a neutrality pact with Russia.

Shortly after the German invasion of Russia in late June, the Japanese poised to move in force into Indochina. When Morgenthau and Ickes pressed Roosevelt to ready economic reprisal, Roosevelt launched into a long speech, saying that any American act to cut down on oil shipments would drive Japan to the Netherlands Indies and to war in the Pacific. Ickes responded that it was embarrassing to him as fuel administrator to start rationing gasoline along the East Coast when oil was still going off to Japan. Still temporizing, Roosevelt agreed to tighten oil export regulations and to redefine aviation gasoline to bar shipment of anything higher than a 67-octane rating.

The navy promptly objected that the new limitations on oil shipments would bring a Japanese attack on Malaya and the Netherlands Indies. But on July 24, Roosevelt learned that the French had given in to Japanese demands for suzerainty over Indochina. Convinced that Germany had forced the French to do so, Roosevelt overruled the navy's objections and ordered the freezing of Japanese funds along with the rest. He also permitted further tightening of licensing restrictions that finally ended shipments of oil. Thus by August 1, 1941, the sanctions that Ickes, Morgenthau, and Stimson had urged for more than a year were at last substantially complete.

According to opinion polls, these sanctions had the overwhelming endorsement of the American people. At last, the newspapers proclaimed, the United States was denying to Japan the oil of conquest. The Japanese did indeed feel the bite of sanctions. Though they remained as determined as ever to hold China, they were eager for a *rapprochement* with the United States.

The president still tried to keep peace in the Pacific on American terms. Such a peace, leaving America free to concentrate on the Nazis in Europe, required Japan to break its link with the Axis, maintain the *status quo* in Southeast Asia, and guarantee self-government and independence to all of China. The ultimate negotiations that fall, when Saburo Kurusu was sent as a special emissary to Washington to talk with Hull, were sterile. By then, American wireless intercepts were telling of secret Japanese preparations for an offensive that would strike southward to Hainan, Malaya, and the oil of the Netherlands Indies.

Plan A, as deciphered, called for an overall adjustment in the Pacific. Japan would renounce the Axis and would not extend its "sphere of self-defense." [64] This meant that it would stay out of Indochina, but would remain in China for a "suitable interval" of 25 years.[65] In return, the United States would agree to nondiscrimination in its international trade—that is, resume oil and scrap shipments to Japan. Hull, having already studied it in the intercepts, rejected this plan the moment Kurusu offered it. Plan B called for a *modus vivendi* prolonging the uneasy truce—withdrawal in Southeast Asia "with the exception of Indochina," access for Japan to Netherlands Indies raw materials, lifting of America's oil embargo, and a United States promise to "engage in no activities which might put an obstacle in the way of Japan in her efforts to make peace with China." [66] This would have required a reversal of the whole American policy—an eventuality so unlikely that even as Kurusu proposed it, the Japanese military pushed ahead with their war plans.

Notwithstanding the daily evidences furnished by intercepts, Roosevelt said to Hull in mid-November that a temporary easement might be possible if the United States resumed economic relations— "some oil and rice now, more later"—and Japan agreed to stand still and not carry out the terms of the Axis pact if the United States went to war.[67] In the Atlantic, American destroyers were attacking and being sunk by German U-boats. On December 1, Roosevelt was saying, "It is all in the lap of the gods." [68] With Stimson, Hull, and Marshall, he continued to believe that the Japanese troop and warship movements disclosed by their intercepts were aimed at Southeast Asia. They so believed until December 7. On that day Japanese fleet aircraft launched their assault on Pearl Harbor—and began the first war fought by one power because another cut off its oil.

The second World War, fought on oil, indeed sometimes seemed fought *for* it. Hitler, amassing stocks and driving his industry to synthesize what it could, said, "We must be sure of oil for our machines." [69] Blocked from access to all but Rumanian fields, the Germans sent Rommel racing around the southern flank for the rich oil fields of the Middle East while charging across the Russian Ukraine from the north to lay hold on the oil of the Caucasus. In the Atlantic, German U-boats fanned out to sink so many oil cargoes that the Allies would lose power to keep the war going. "The most anxious moment of the war," Ickes said later, "was when German submarines were taking such a heavy toll of tankers." [70] In the Pacific, having completed their lightning sweep to the Indies oil fields, the Japanese soon began to feel the drain as American submarines opened the counterattack with assaults on the long string of tankers by which the Japanese nourished their fighting power.

In this kind of war, armaments without oil were nothing but scrap. Everything depended on oil. Without it, no guns fired, no tanks rolled, no ships sailed, and no planes flew.

Moving armies overland (at least 60,000 gallons of gasoline were needed daily to keep one armored division fighting), oil also heated billets, ran mobile laundries, helped purify water, and killed tropical bugs. Powering warships and transporting troops at sea, oil also hoisted anchors, lubricated turbines, trained turrets, and passed ammunition. For the air force, besides lifting piston and jet planes to combat, oil shielded gunners in plastic blisters, fitted crews with rayon parachutes, and hardened landing strips with asphalt. As jellied gasoline, spurting from flamethrowers and spattering as napalm, oil was one of the war's deadliest weapons.

The Allies' single greatest advantage was control of 86 percent of the world's oil. The big problem was to get it where it was needed. Piles of oil drums marked every invasion beach from Normandy to Iwo Jima. Across the wide Pacific, one of the most necessary feats was the successful replenishing of American carrier forces in mid-battle; in one five-month period, a force of 34 long gray fleet oilers poured 8¼ million barrels of fuel oil and 14½ million gallons of aviation gasoline into fighting ships at sea—despite submarines, kamikazes, and typhoons. Engineers laid a pipeline 1,800 miles long over the mountains from India into China. Another followed American forces a thousand miles across North Africa. And when General Patton's tanks raced across France in 1944, Texan specialists stayed close behind them, laying pipe at a 50-mile-a-day clip. In the end, the Axis ran out of fuel, immobilized by the devastation of their synthetic oil industry, and the Japanese were marooned on their home islands. The Strategic Bombing Survey called the attacks upon the synthetic war plants "decisive," and said, "It was the Nazis' lack of gasoline, not the loss of plane production, that gave us air superiority." [71] On the other hand, General Marshall could write in his victory report, "No plane has failed to fly, no ship has failed to sail, for lack of oil." [72]

Oil also fought on the home front. It kept tractors and trucks moving, provided an essential ingredient of tires, heated and powered homes and factories, and propelled war workers to their jobs. As early as July 1940, Ickes told Roosevelt that building a crude-oil pipeline from Texas to the East Coast of the United States might be "absolutely necessary" in the event of war.[73] A preview of what this necessity might bring was furnished a year later when the president ordered 30 tankers diverted to carry emergency supplies to beleaguered Britain. It took six days for a tanker carrying 100,000 barrels of crude or refined products to sail from a Gulf of Mexico port to New York or Philadelphia—and when tankers began to run short, even wholesale commandeering of railroad tank cars could not begin to make up the difference. Before long, German submarines began sinking these precious tankers in the Gulf of Mexico, in the Caribbean, off Cape Hatteras, and almost within sight of the Statue of Liberty.

The pipeline project at first ran into some stubborn barriers. Railroads and railroad union opposition persuaded the Georgia legislature to withhold right-of-way permission to pipeline builders. Even Henry Wallace's Board of Economic Warfare tried to veto the plan to build a 24-inch pipeline, the world's biggest, from the edge of the east Texas field to the Philadelphia-New York area because of conflicting demands for the steel. Finally, at Ickes's outraged demand, the government itself built the pipeline, with H. Alton Jones of Cities Service in charge of construction.[74] More than 1,400 miles long, and completed in less than a year, it was dubbed the Big Inch.[75] Every day, it delivered almost 300,000 barrels of crude oil to the eastern seaboard. Later, to transport gasoline and other refined products between Texas and the East Coast, a 20-inch pipeline, inevitably named the Little Inch, was built paralleling the first. Together these pipelines delivered some 379 million barrels of crude and refined products during the war and saved the Atlantic Coast from a fuel famine. They also proved to be a profitable investment. The government got its money back after the war when the companies bought them to ship natural gas (sea transport of oil was still cheaper) from Texas to newly developing industrial and household markets in the Northeast. They still provide the East with a small proportion of the fuel it uses.

For all its strategic importance gasoline was not the first item to be rationed in the second World War. This distinction went to rubber. When the Japanese thrust southward, they not only gained oil for themselves but denied rubber to the rest of the world: their conquest gobbled up 97 percent of the world supply. In the United States, only 660,000 tons had been stockpiled, roughly equivalent to one year's civilian supply. Since military demands were huge, the government decreed a freeze on tires and called upon anyone with more than five for his car to turn them in at a filling station. But sacrifice was not enough; synthetic rubber, manufactured from petroleum was the answer. Yet until plants could be built, the nation had to live off its stockpile, 75 percent of which was reserved for the military. In these straits, the simplest solution was to force civiilan motorists to stop using gasoline—by rationing, since no other limitations were enforceable.

Gasoline rationing began along the East Coast in May 1942, for the immediate reason that fuel ran short there because of the toll Nazi U-boats were taking of tankers lugging oil from the Gulf and the Caribbean. Price Administrator Leon Henderson announced a plan to allocate each motorist in the East from 2½ to 5 gallons a week.

When Bernard Baruch then reported to Roosevelt that the only way to save tires was to limit mileage for the entire nation, the president decreed nationwide gasoline rationing. At the same time, he banned pleasure driving and set a 30-mile-an-hour speed limit on all highways effective December 1, 1942. Every motor vehicle in the United States blossomed with a ration sticker. Owners were issued books of coupons to present at filling stations. An *A* sticker on the front window got the driver the lowest gasoline allocation—four, later three, gallons a week, an amount that the government estimated, at 15 miles to the gallon, would permit 60 miles of driving. An *A*-sticker man's allotment of coupons enabled him to do "necessary" shopping, attend church and funerals, go to the doctor, meet emergencies involving "threat to life, health or property," and make necessary trips connected with family or job.[76] A *B* sticker in the window denoted a driver permitted a supplementary allowance for some sort of essential driving—a war worker, say, driving in a car pool. A *C* sticker authorized still more gasoline for the cardholder's essential activities—a doctor merited a *C*. There was also a *T* sticker for truckers, who could get all the gasoline they needed.

Obviously, *A* cardholders were nobodies. At one point, the government estimated that nearly half of the nation's 20 million cars had *B* or *C* stickers. On this showing, 15 million drove about in essential occupations, though a Gallup Poll showed that of the 45 percent of Americans who drove to work, three-fourths said they could get there another way if they had to. Gasoline tax collections, however, plummeted to half their former levels. Highway deaths fell even more dramatically: where 423 had died in Labor Day weekend motor accidents in 1941, only 169 road deaths were recorded on the same weekend in the following year. Authorities estimated that the highways were being used at only 20 percent of capacity.

The price-control administration, taking a dim view of all pleasure driving, ruled that *A*-sticker motorists could stop for a soda on an essential trip only if this did not "add as much as one foot to the distance traveled in a car for such purpose." [77] In Rochester, New York, price-control investigators stopped those who had driven to a symphony concert and took away their coupon books. In New York City, owners of cars parked in front of night clubs and restaurants lost theirs. Automobile trips of any distance were soon unheard of. To travel on an airplane required a government certificate of priority—and the only passport to Florida was a railroad ticket.

Gasoline rationing led to a Prohibition-style black market. Mobsters peddled counterfeit gasoline coupons to filling station men, who were thus enabled to sell their gasoline for 10 to 25 cents over ceiling prices and yet account for their illegal sales by turning over the fake coupons to the price-control agency. The government tried to stop such tricks by treating the paper on which its coupons were printed with chemicals that changed color under ultraviolet-ray scrutiny. The black marketers then stole the government's paper, sometimes with the help of price-control personnel. Coupons worth five million gallons of gasoline fell into mob hands in Cleveland, twenty millions' worth in Washington. With help from the Federal Bureau of Investigation, the price-control agency won 1,300 convictions for gasoline black-marketing, closed 4,000 filling stations for unlawful activities, and took away ration books from 32,500 motorists for using counterfeit or stolen coupons. Price-control officials said that at least five percent of all gasoline sold was bought with counterfeit coupons—in places like New York and Chicago, the proportion was said to run between 30 and 35 percent.

At times, especially along the East Coast, it was impossible to get any gasoline at all. In the summer of 1942, the pumps literally went dry; most stations closed, and some kept their "out of gas" signs up and sold only to old customers. In New York City, drivers sometimes spotted a tank truck and trailed it in ever-growing procession to its delivery point. When word spreads of a delivery, as many as 350 cars lined up for three-gallon driblets. For the rest, life was a matter of forming car pools and share-the-ride clubs and eking out the life-span of worn-out cars and tires. At a time when forty percent of the vegetables consumed were grown in 20 million Victory Gardens, an estimated ten percent of all war workers took part in car pools. All in all, it was only a fair performance.

The same German submarine campaign that cut off East Coast gasoline compelled the institution of fuel-oil rationing in the icy winter of 1942–43. Already the huge demands generated by the North African invasion, increased use of oil as an industrial fuel, and the diversion of oil to the railroads for diesel fuel had intensified the shortage. The price-control agency issued sheets of coupons, leaving homeowners to figure out their allotments on a complicated formula based on the square-footage in their houses. Simplifying the formula later, the government said the consumer could have two-thirds of what he had used in 1941, a quantity that the price-control agency said would suffice to keep his house warmed to a level of 65 degrees. The Pacific Northwest was hardest hit; firewood and then coal were rationed there in 1943. That year, Fuel Administrator Ickes had advised homeowners to convert to coal; something like ten percent of them changed their furnaces from oil to coal and went back to furnace tending, shoveling coal night and day, only to rise on the coldest mornings and find the fire out.

In the winter of 1944, even coal was in short supply in the eastern United States. With only one-fifth more freight cars, the railroads were obliged to carry more than twice as much freight as in 1939, and neither equipment nor manpower were up to the heavy burden. On top of this came blizzards, leading War Mobilizer James Byrnes to order a nationwide brownout. Neon lights were banned; stores closed at dusk. For the first time, inland areas had to turn out street lights just as coastal cities had since Pearl Harbor. Schools closed for lack of fuel; businesses went on short weeks. Downtown shopping centers in Detroit and Chicago fell empty and dark at night.

As fuel administrator, Harold Ickes worked closely with a Petroleum War Advisory Committee of oil-company chiefs, just as Mark Requa had in 1917. This time the industry achieved a far higher gain in production. In the first World War, America produced only 90 million more barrels of oil per year at the end than it had in 1914; but after the second World War, production had increased by 450 million barrels over 1939. Almost all of this amount, and the greater part of the oil required to wage the second World War, came from Texas, much of it by the Big Inch pipeline.

Ickes, besides trying to boost domestic output, sought to stimulate foreign sources of supply. In the minds of American oilmen, Mexico, lying alongside the same Gulf Coast as Texas, was potentially one of the world's great sources of petroleum. Ickes repeatedly urged Roosevelt to establish government-owned production and refining facilities south of the border, buying out the claims of expropriated American oil companies to clear the way. Later, Secretary of the Navy James Forrestal, who had floated many a major oil company security as a Wall Street investment banker and was assuredly no Josephus Daniels demanding nationalized oil for United States warships, pressed hard in the cabinet for a political settlement with Mexico that would reopen the country's undoubted great petroleum resources to international development.[78] But it was contrary to the interests of Standard Oil of New Jersey, which had suffered expropriation in Mexico in 1938 and desired no encouragement for a possible repetition in Venezuela, where the majors were sinking big money in offshore oil in Lake Maracaibo. Hull and others fought off any deal that might have implied American endorsement of the Mexican government's program of nationalizing foreign-owned oil.

Attention therefore turned to the oil of the Middle East. E. I. de Golyer, assistant deputy administrator on Ickes's staff, reported that the center of the world oil industry was already shifting from the Gulf of Mexico to the Persian Gulf. The British had long held the upper hand in the Middle East, but in 1937 the Standard Oil Company of California obtained a concession to prospect and develop oil in Saudi Arabia. Texaco joined as California Standard's partner in a new Arabian-American Oil Company. The promise of rich petroleum deposits was great, but the risks, especially after the outbreak of the second World War, were even greater. When Rommel's tanks thrust across North Africa, cutting the Mediterranean supply line to Egypt, it raised doubt that the Saudi-Arabian concession could be kept out of Axis hands. When German agents stirred up a revolt in Iran and German parachute troops captured the main Iraqi airfield during an abortive Baghdad coup, the risk grew. Harry D. Collier, president of Standard Oil of California, and W. S. S. Rodgers, chairman of Texaco, sought Ickes's help not only to safeguard their Saudi concession, but also to put up funds to aid in developing it.

At Ickes's request, Roosevelt in early 1943 arranged to extend lend-lease aid to King Ibn Saud's government. As military and cabinet officials grew concerned at depletion of America's own reserves, Ickes also persuaded Roosevelt to set up, under the Reconstruction Finance Corporation, a Petroleum Reserves Corporation to acquire and develop new foreign reserves.[79] Its first venture, Ickes proposed, would be to exploit Saudi Arabian oil for the United States Navy. In August 1943, the PRC undertook to buy the Saudi Arabian properties of the American corporations holding concessions there.

As the tide of war turned slowly in Russia and the Mediterranean, the oil companies' inclination to let government assume the risk of Middle East investment evaporated. California Standard and Texaco dug in their heels. The American Petroleum Institute (after inviting Ickes to address its annual meeting) voted to condemn his program, and the Independent Petroleum Producers Association protested against any government-controlled oil production overseas that might compete with domestic petroleum.

General Rommel's threat to Middle East supply routes having faded, the United States Navy now proposed building a pipeline from the Saudi oil fields to the Mediterranean coast. Ickes was all for this scheme, which involved an outlay bigger and far chancier than the government-funded Big Inch. In February 1944, the Petroleum Reserves Corporation announced agreement with the oil companies. In return for construction of a $160-million pipeline, the companies would earmark a billion barrels of oil for the United States government at a discount of 25 percent from U.S. prices.

This agreement stirred intense opposition in Congress and the oil industry. Although the president himself defended it as vital to the war effort and the future needs of national security, the opposition was strong enough to keep Ickes from implementing the agreement. Senator Edward Moore, Republican of Oklahoma, called the project an "imperialist adventure." [80] In its report on petroleum, the Truman War Investigations Committee urged a policy stressing private enterprise.

And just as Truman was moving into the White House, private companies found a way to embark on the project entirely on their own. The Standard Oil companies of New Jersey and New York, whose participation in the "as is" agreement of 1927 had led them to take the British side against the American contenders for Saudi oil development, switched sides and became the partners of Standard of California and Texaco. The Arabian-American Oil Company was reorganized. Jersey Standard acquired 30 percent of Aramco, Standard Oil of New York 10 percent, and the $450 million the two giants paid for their share provided the money needed to get the pipeline built. The transaction was founded upon estimates that the deserts of Saudi Arabia contained perhaps the world's richest oil reserves and that, in the emerging world of superpowers, British partners in Iraq and Kuwait could not and would not prevent the Americans from developing their Saudi concessions without the by-your-leave required in the days of Achnacarry.

The government's Petroleum Reserves Corporation went out of business, and Ickes himself soon left office. Just as Secretary Daniels had been rebuffed in his efforts to nationalize oil supplies for the navy in the first World War, so Secretary Ickes lost his bid to establish direct federal control over petroleum resources in the second.

In time of war, government and the oil enterprise draw closer together. Each sees the crucial nature of this relationship, and the ties formed are so close that the effects linger long afterward. In the public official, the experience quickens the sense that anything of such surpassing importance ought to be under the central government's control. It was upon this awareness that Winston Churchill acted in 1914 when he put the British government in the oil business by acquiring half ownership of the Anglo-Iranian Oil Company, to assure oil for the Royal Navy's command of the seas. The same perception doubtless animated Roosevelt, Stimson, Knox, and Ickes when they backed formation of the Petroleum Reserves Corporation to expand the United States government's holdings beyond the small Elk Hills and Teapot Dome reserves in 1944.

For industry, the experience leads perforce to other conclusions. It raises the businessman's consciousness of government's power to modify the environment in which oil is produced and sharpens his determination to see that such modifications work to the advantage of his industry and its operations. Out of the close government-industry collaboration in two great wars, even though men like Daniels and Ickes raised important alternatives to the contrary, private enterprise emerged in command while the role of government became, at most, "supplemental and suggestive." [81]

The drawing together of government and the oil industry in the first World War brought an unprecedented and fateful intervention of oil interests in domestic and government affairs. The big oil companies obtained huge tax concessions that helped finance their switch into the direct production of crude oil afterward in the United States. A consequence of this shift was a chronic and wasteful overproduction of petroleum that was never matched by demand until the second World War arrived with its immense requirements to take up the slack. A further consequence, already scented at the Republican National Convention of 1920, was a corruption of the political process and a venality in public office that were laid squalidly bare in the 1924 investigation of the Teapot Dome scandal. The second World War collaboration of government and the oil industry led to an unprecedented and fateful involvement of private oil interests in American foreign policy. The major companies emerged with government backing for their further expansion into the direct production of petroleum *outside* the United States. The consequences, already hinted at in early cold war interventions by the United States in Iran, Greece, and Turkey, were to commit America to a kind of oil colonialism in the Middle East and ultimately to make not only America's allies but America itself dangerously dependent on oil from that volatile region.

The peculiar characteristic of petroleum, as geologists said, was its fugacity. Oil moved, and the only way you could find it for sure was by drilling to see if it was down there. Above ground as below, in the first century after it was brought to the surface, oil made its tremendous impact on the world by reason of its special mobility. The ease with which this new source of light and power moved—and could be moved—bowled over mankind.

Rockefeller, exploiting oil for light, furnished the first clues as to how easy oil was to transport (and, thereby, monopolize). Then the Germans, exploiting oil for power, showed how oil could be harnessed to wheels—and in a few years the fugacity of oil, embodied in machines on land, sea, and air, became a force that flowed into two terrible wars.

In the arts of war, the internal combustion engine had probably already had its day by the end of oil's first century. But in the peaceful pursuits of civilization, a century proved too short a spell for societies and individuals to adapt themselves to its transforming power. The fugacity of oil coursed through the culture, uprooting Americans and others from slow-won moorings in space and time. That the automobile changed the national psychology, as well as its manners and mores, could not be questioned. It took getting used to—traveling so fast, so far, so effortlessly. George Babbitt and Walt Wallet never felt so free as when they took the helm of their motor cars. To them and their families it gave a sense of a more spacious life. Wherever they wheeled, the filling stations followed them—out of the garage, onto the curb, then to the corner, then to the edge of town, and finally out into the country, where hardly anybody lived anymore, but a boy might like to drive. There were 280,000 filling stations in 1939, and such was the fugacity of oil that an American could stop anywhere and say, "Fill 'er up."

6
Burning up the Road—
to Offshore Oil

Is there such a thing as American Character? Nineteenth-century savants thought the answer lay in a linkage to the frontier. But then how did people stay American after 1890, when the frontier disappeared? Professor George Pierson of Yale suggested a few years ago that the answer, already hinted at in the notion of the frontier, was in what he called the "M-factor" in American history. What made Americans different, he said, was not just the wildness of their continent, nor its vast open spaces, nor even its wealth of resources, powerful as these influences had been. Rather, he thought, it was this "M-factor"—the element of movement, migration, mobility.

Americans were always on the move, he pointed out, not only to the frontier but away from it, not only across the Atlantic but within the national borders, from farm to town, from region to region, from city to city. He recalled the nineteenth-century visitor's observation that if the trumpet of doom were to sound, it would surprise two-thirds of all Americans—out on the roads like ants. The freedom to move, whether in mass exodus or in just milling around, was taken as a primordial right. The wandering mania was not only in America's blood but in its very mode of speech:

> "Get going!" "Don't be a stick-in-the-mud." "I don't know where I'm going but I'm on my way." "Anywhere I hang my hat is home, sweet home to me." A man on the road to success is a *comer*, a *go-getter*. "That's going some," we say. A man who is growing old is *slowing up*, and then by and

by he reaches the *end of the trail.* Death itself used to be spoken of as *crossing the divide.*[1]

President John F. Kennedy's promise was to "get the country moving again."

Oil gave tremendous force to the M-factor. When the second World War ended, the entire pattern of the nation's economic and social arrangements was shaped to provide inducements to individuals to keep moving in vaster numbers than ever before. These inducements were substantial. First of all, an automobile owner was required to pay very small taxes on it. Second, the gasoline tax, while higher, went directly to build more roads used by the private car. Third, both federal and state governments subsidized the highway construction program while abandoning support of public transportation. Fourth, the social and environmental costs of automotive growth—highway deaths, traffic snarls, smog, high-speed roads through parks and residential neighborhoods, for instance—were accepted by the community at large. Finally and most important, all political and economic institutions, from the Congress in Washington to the mortgage bank down the street, supported an automobile-dominated organization of urban and suburban development. In short, just about all the resources in the society stood committed to producing automobility, no matter what the constraints.

In 1945, impelled by a population explosion and pent-up war savings, all kinds of people seemed as never before to seek a place to live where they could bring up a family. Industry needed big new markets, and housing policies worked out in Washington transformed both these aspirations into a mighty outward surge from the central cities into the suburbs.

The Federal Housing Administration and, through the G.I. Bill of Rights, the Veterans Administration, were the main instrumentalities. They guaranteed home mortgage loans at such low interest rates that almost any borrower could qualify. The banks leaped to lend, the developers rushed to buy up open tracts on the fringes of the cities, and the builders lined their raw drives and lanes with new houses. The pattern of government lending favored such new houses over the old ones and single-family dwellings over city apartments. And if the law itself did not give the outlying tract development all the breaks, guidelines set by the FHA bureaucracy reinforced the thrust toward the suburbs. The agency conducted itself as if it were a private business. To minimize investment risks, its staff rated all neighborhoods according to prior experiences of repayments, with the result that any area containing older properties was marked so low as to be virtually ineligible for federal funds. By contrast, an ever higher proportion of loans flowed to the new suburban tract houses. By force of such public policies as much as their individual private impulses, 30 million Americans moved out from the cities in the biggest lateral population shift in the nation's history.

Oil lubricated this move and sustained the new life in the outlying neighborhoods. In the next five years, when births rose to record levels, automobile registrations shot up by two-thirds, and the number of oil burners doubled.

From Nassau County, Long Island, to Orange County, California, tank trucks began pulling up in front of tricycle-filled front walks and discharging No. 2 medium oil into underground tanks at thousands and thousands of new tract houses. Older houses might still have coal-burning furnaces, but not the new ranch houses that proliferated around all cities. Though coal was cheaper, oil heat was so much more convenient. The oil company, calculating the size and type of house against daily weather changes, undertook, in return for a year's fuel-supply contract, to keep the tank filled.

Under command of the thermostat in the living room, the oil burner consumed the fuel as needed to keep temperatures at desired level. Certainly, here was a big convenience for everyday living; it seemed fair enough to call this new kind of effortless heating automatic.

The thermostat controlled the temperatures to which oil warmed these new suburban homes, and no young father adding more bedrooms in the "expansion attic" for arriving babies even considered stinting on the heat. Dr. Benjamin Spock, whose *Pocket Book of Baby and Child Care* all young parents read after it appeared in 1946, advised that "it is preferable that he [the infant] not sleep in his parents' room after he is 12 months old." [2] Like Dr. Spock's opinion that "it's fine for each [child] to have a room of his own, if that's possible," [3] the advice was unquestioningly obeyed. And just as the new suburbanites never thought twice about the quantities of energy required to heat separate rooms for their arriving children, so the young couples went ahead and heated their houses to temperatures in which their babies could lie uncovered in their cribs, and they themselves could go about with far lighter clothing, especially underclothing, than their grandparents did—or the English and French did in less severe winters in these same years. Such indulgences, which left their mark in the unencumbered nurture of the suburban young, required expenditures of energy beyond all comparison with the meager coal and kerosene that took off some of the chill in the city.[4]

If heating oil made these prodigiously dispersed dwellings habitable, motor fuel made them viable. While provisions were trucked and children bussed, suburbia was overwhelmingly a world of automobiles. The ritual worship for the motor vehicles in the new suburbs resembled very little the communal celebrations of the old Gasoline Alley—there were no alleys in postwar tract developments; there were not even sidewalks for people to stroll on. Men lavished on their car loving care indeed, though maintenance now meant not so much repairing the vehicle as washing and polishing it. In an annual rite of special toilsomeness (it took all of a Sunday) they "simonized," that is, waxed and burnished it like the Holy Grail. Millions who would not have maintained a shrine in their homes kept a plastic image of the Virgin above the dashboard. Even more draped a talismanic pair of baby's boots over the rearview mirror. Others, in the ambiguously public privacy afforded by such windowed mobility, fitted the car out with liquor, tape player, medicine chest, or other gewgaws of private indulgence that a man liked to have close by where he spent, after all, a sizable portion of his daily life.

All the same, moving to the suburbs often meant that a man had to have a wife as chauffeur. Much was made of these female slaves of the wheel who lived through their husbands, fetching them to and from their places of work and dashing about in Buick station wagons from school and supermarket to golf and bridge at the country club. A valiant effort was made to build up the suburban wife as both glamour queen and housekeeper: the women's magazines did their level best to play up domesticity and the wonderful world of feminine fulfillment in appliance-filled kitchens in children-filled homes amid flower-filled gardens. But more and more, she needed a car of her own and soon took a job to get one. The number of multiple car families multiplied; soon one in three families owned two cars and about 2½ percent owned three cars. Sooner than seemed possible, the children, making the progression from back seats and station-wagon rear decks, took over the drivers' seats—in hardtop convertibles that General Motors triumphantly introduced to the suburbs in 1955.

Throughout these years of the population explosion, automotive growth outstripped the increments of people by three to two. At the height of the suburban boom, the country produced more motor vehicles than housing units. In their classic study of life in Muncie, Indiana, in the 1920s, Robert and Mary Lynd found that people drove their cars mostly for pleasure, or at least for reasons not related to making a living, and often used them little at all in winter.[5] About one-third of automobile trips were made for travel to and from work.

After the second World War an urbanized America not only bought twice as many cars as it did in the 1930s but also drove the cars many more miles. Though 75 percent of all cars then were operated in metropolitan areas, each traveled an average distance each year equal to halfway around the world. Surveys showed that three-fourths of all automobile trips were made for economic reasons, 46 percent of them to and from work.[6] And as ownership and use of private cars rose, public transportation fell.

Fell, that is, or was pushed. For years, companies rigged by General Motors and the big oil firms systematically bought out and scrapped electric transit systems throughout the nation to make new markets for their buses and gasoline. As late as 1945, for instance, thousands of workers commuted to jobs on trolleys operated by a traction company through San Francisco streets and across the Bay Bridge from Oakland and other Bay area communities. In that year, a corporate front for General Motors, Exxon, and the Goodyear Tire Company took over the Bay Transit Company and shortly sold it. Terms of the sale required that the buyers junk the trolley cars and replace them with buses built by General Motors, using only Exxon gasoline and Goodyear tires.[7]

Similarly, Los Angeles had, until the 1940s, the world's largest electric railway network. But in 1940 an outfit controlled by General Motors, Standard of California, and Firestone began to acquire and scrap the interurban system, whose 3,000 trains carried 80 million passengers daily. In December 1944, they took over a downtown trolley company whose tracks the trains used. Soon, as thousands of miles of track and transmission lines were ripped out, the entire metropolitan area was left dependent for public transport on General Motors buses burning Standard of California diesel fuel.[8] In this fashion, the big companies blotted out 100 electric railway systems in 45 cities—including New York, Philadelphia, Baltimore, St. Louis, and Salt Lake City. In 1949, they were convicted of criminal conspiracy. The ringleader, General Motors' treasurer, H. C. Grossman, was fined one dollar, a pretty fair indication that the public at the time thought they were doing their communities a favor. But in the destruction of its efficient electric railway system, Los Angeles lost the indispensable nucleus for the mass transit network it later saw the need for. And, as San Francisco painfully shelled out $4 billion to replace the system only twenty years later, Mayor Joseph Alioto in 1973 denounced the companies for deliberately destroying the mass transit they now took ads, in the cause of energy-crisis conservation, to applaud.

If streetcars disappeared fast, buses proved something less than a substitute. Between 1945 and 1954 the number of mass-transit riders fell by 55 percent—and automobile registrations doubled. Cars carried more and more people to work, and of course there was not room for them all on the streets. Congestion was stupendous. To ease the crush, the nation spent $2 billion on new roads in 1949; $3 billion, in 1950; $4 billion, in 1955. It was clear that something would have to be done, and President Eisenhower proposed a vast, ten-year, $27-billion program of highway building. Existing highways were unsafe, he said, full of traffic delays and a costly impost on the conduct of business. Better roads were also needed for the conduct of the cold war. Modern highways would be highly useful for swift military movements across the country, and "in case of atomic attack on our cities the road net must permit quick evacuation of target areas." [9] He therefore gave to his "grand plan" the name of Interstate Highway and Defense System.[10]

Politicians leaped to salute what turned out to be the largest public works project ever undertaken by man—an enterprise to dwarf the pyramids of Egypt and the Great Wall of China. The plan coincided exactly with the automotive and oil companies' decision to put higher-powered engines and gasoline in the country's cars. It was ecstatically hailed by the highway lobby, a phenomenally broad pressure group that went far beyond the oil industry and its well-placed friends. Included also were rubber, automobile, asphalt, and construction industries; car dealers and renters; trucking and bus concerns; banks and advertising agencies that depended on companies involved; the American Automobile Association; state and local officials who wanted the federal government to pay for new highways in their areas; and labor unions. "Highways and motor vehicles," declaimed the president of the American Association of State Highway Officials, "are truly the keystone of the American way of life." [11]

The president's scheme had been started to help rural districts. Now that Americans had massed in the cities, they should use their new-won leisure to get away, by automobile of course, into the great outdoors. By the Eisenhower years, paid vacations had risen to the point at which all breadwinners could take slightly more than a week off annually, and white-collar workers considerably more than that. Adding in the eight-hour days and long weekends, Americans were in a position to spend 70 times as much of their lives in outdoor recreation as they were before the automobile came on the scene.[12]

The number of visitors to national parks, almost all of them located in the West at a distance from cities, rose from 32 million in 1950 to more than 86 million a decade later.[13] The scale of summertime movement was further suggested by a set of figures from Wisconsin, a state much favored by automobilists from Chicago: no fewer than 43 percent of all fishing permits issued by the state went to vacationing nonresidents.[14]

The motel was another phenomenon of postwar automobility. Like the myriad restaurants that sprang up along the roadsides, it catered to a public that had not patronized the hotel. The first motels were a pa-and-ma sort of enterprise with no more than 10 of 15 units for tired families who wanted only to get off the road for the night before wheeling away again at daybreak. All that was needed to start such a wayside roost was a few thousand dollars and a tract of farmland on the outskirts of town. With Pa acting as room clerk, cashier, and general handyman and with Ma bustling about as maid of all work, operating costs could be kept low. After the war, many couples who had reached retirement age invested their war work savings in a motel. At the height of the boom and with plenty of tourists stopping, they could pay off their indebtedness in three years.[15]

By 1950, motels had become big business; the number shrank while the total number of motel rooms increased. Some banded in cooperative associations that specified standards for membership and offered joint services for reservations. Others emerged in chains, such as Travelodge, Howard Johnson, Holiday Inn. Organized mostly on a franchise basis, these big chains operated under a central authority that furnished some financing and such coordinated managerial and architectural plans that it became possible to eat identically prepared hamburgers, wash in identically sanitized bathrooms, and sleep in identically laundered linens from the Atlantic to the Pacific. Ten years after its founding in 1952, "the nation's host," as the Holiday Inn chain grandly called itself, could boast that there were 500 Holiday Inns; by 1974 there were 1,679, with 264,117 rooms along the nation's highways.[16] By 1964, when even downtown hotels had built garages and added drive-up parking facilities, most of the $11 billion that hotels and motels earned (according to the Bureau of Public Roads) was highway-generated. By 1968, there were 60,500 motels along American highways, and motel earnings, having trebled in five years, reached $6 billion.

★

Thus the Interstate Highway System unquestionably fomented automobility on a continental scale. Indeed, General Lucius Clay's planning committee sold the system to Congress in 1955 as the carrier of long-haul traffic, bypassing downtown areas with only a limited number of feeder highways to link the high-speed, cross-country network with the central cities. To that end, the Clay panel had decided that instead of making construction grants to the states on a fifty-fifty basis, the federal government must take "principal responsibility" and furnish 90 percent of the funds. Congress, after a long wrangle about the method of financing, voted a special federal gasoline tax and directed that all proceeds be paid into a Federal Highway Fund, out of which the Bureau of Public Roads would then dispense funds to the states for freeway construction.

Out of $27 billion spent in the next decade, as it worked out, $15 billion went for building superhighways in urban areas. The Interstate Highway and Defense System was transformed from a high-speed, long-distance network into a blunt instrument for chopping huge gashes through central cities and their environs for concrete spillways carrying the floods of local, commuter traffic in and out of the burgeoning suburbs. After all, most people took only one or two long trips at most each year, and it was in short journeys around their homes and above all in daily commuting to work that their cars racked up most of the mileage. This sort of automobility, far more than the long-distance excursions, generated the gasoline tax revenue that enabled the engineers to build the highways. There was no provision for, and little thought of, social planning. Since Washington had agreed to the ninety-to-ten split in cost apportionment, cities could not resist the temptation to get as many miles as they could out of their state highway departments. The states were happy to join in because inner-city expressways built up the gasoline-tax receipts that enabled them to build the rural portions of the system.

The result was that the interstate routes soon cut massive concrete strips into the downtown areas of every big American city. Far from solving the cities' traffic problems, the new roads created new ones. Besides engulfing downtown areas with commuter automobiles, they devoured living quarters, jammed those displaced into other habitations, and sealed off carless ghetto dwellers in a new and frustrating kind of urban isolation. Thousands were uprooted; whole neighborhoods were blighted. By 1959 General Eisenhower himself questioned the cost of these urban welts, which ran up to $40 million a mile, and warned the road builders that running the interstate system into the cities contravened the law. "The national interest," he said, extended only to long-distance travel.[17]

But the general had gone to a lot of trouble to avoid overcentralization in framing the law, and, in the confusion of contending authorities and pressure groups, the single-minded highway engineers in the state capitals paid no heed to Eisenhower's guidelines. Building went on as scheduled. In this, the bulldozing road builders simply represented the dominant mood of a society whose structural and institutional arrangements had supported the development of the automobile for forty years.

By this time, the automobile had become the chromed, finned vessel of an institutional automobile culture. Technology, though worshipped, was trivialized. The making and fueling of motor cars had become what the economists call "mature" industries. Innovation, such as there was, was manipulated. The marketers were in command.

The aging Edison of this era was Charles F. Kettering, the lanky, inquisitive Ohio farmer's son who back in 1912 had created the gadget that domesticated the automobile—the self-starter. With this invention, Kettering put the woman in the driver's seat.

"I am a wrench and pliers man," Kettering liked to say.[18] He was also a canny General Motors executive who sold Americans comfort and luxury with their automobility and wound up fourteenth (after eight oilmen and General Motors Chairman Alfred Sloan among others) on *Fortune*'s mid-century list of the hundred richest Americans. He was interviewed by the newspapers and honorary-degreed by the universities as the archpriest of a triumphant technology.

Trained as an electrical engineer at Ohio State (class of '04), Kettering was filled with Edison's determination to try everything until he hit on the answer. He talked shop nonstop and worked late into the night. But he also made leaps. His early work in perfecting the electric cash register for the National Cash Register Company suggested the self-starter: a little motor could carry a huge load if the burden was only momentary. Selling his invention and his Delco Company for a pile of General Motors stock, Kettering went right on devising comfort on the road. He helped enclose cars and redesigned the heater to keep Americans on the road at the room temperatures to which they were accustomed. Working with General Motors stylists, he gave cars their chrome plating and a lacquer job that withstood all weathers (and could be put on in two hours instead of two weeks).

The gadgets he touched had a way of turning to gold. Freon, the coolant he developed for General Motors' refrigerator, made such a success of the Frigidaire that many still call all electric iceboxes by that name. Taking a fancy to diesel engines, he set his wrench and pliers to turning the 1894 invention of Rudolf Diesel into a two-cycle machine. "According to theory our diesels don't work," he grinned.[19] Their oil power drove steam engines right off the railroad tracks; later they were used in General Motors buses and trucks. But diesels in Detroit's luxurious cars? Kettering never tried that. It was left for the oil-famished Germans to develop diesel-powered cars—which use half the fuel that conventional automobiles do.

Kettering, who always wanted more power in cars, never forgot an early lesson in how wastefully the internal combustion engine converts gasoline to energy. When his pioneer ignition system was blamed for the knock in early Cadillac engines, he tracked down the noise to the propensity of some of the fuel in the cylinder to explode before the flame touched off by the spark plug reached it. It was another Kettering leap. As a result, General Motors talked to Standard Oil. But years passed, and in the end it was Kettering and his men whose try-try-try-again research found the remedy: adding tetraethyl lead to the gasoline. In 1922, General Motors and Standard of New Jersey jointly formed the Ethyl Corporation to market Kettering's magic antiknock fluid.

Everybody connected with its manufacture knew there was serious danger of lead poisoning. Almost immediately an accident at Standard's Bayway plant in New Jersey sent two dozen workers to the hospital with bad lead poisoning. Five men died. Ethyl was pulled off the market. The U.S. Public Health Service was asked to verify that the stuff could be used if Kettering's safety rules were enforced. After prolonged tests, Surgeon General Hugh Cumming announced, "There are no good grounds for prohibiting sale of ethyl." [20]

From the time it went back into the nation's gasoline tanks in 1924, Kettering's fluid was an immensely profitable product for its two supercorporate owners. Licensed to other oil companies, it was sold as "high test" gasoline for two cents a gallon more than the regular brand—as standard an offering at filling stations as a quart of oil or free air. Eventually, ethyl was not only sold from the premium pumps but added in lesser amounts to the regular brand.

In essence, the ethyl acted upon the gasoline-air mixture in the automobile engine in such a way as to cause all of the fuel in the cylinder to explode simultaneously. This did not only eliminate the knock but also, as Kettering saw, opened the possibilities for a higher compression of the mixture before it exploded. Thus high-test gasoline—so called because on a numbered scale it compares with test fuels containing a high proportion of the hydrocarbon iso-octane—was amenable to much greater compression and could therefore be made to deliver much more power. Unquestionably, because much of the gasoline-air mixture that formerly failed to do its share of the work could now be usefully exploded, this made possible big advances in engine efficiency. In the years before the second World War, for instance, aviation gasoline was refined to much higher octane levels, and high-compression, high-speed, turbocharged airplane engines were designed that produced much greater power. Thus the Liberty aircraft engine of the first World War was only four percent smaller than the Allison engine that drove such second World War planes as the P-38 and the P-40. Yet where the Liberty engine developed 400 horsepower, the Allison, using ethyl gasoline, developed 1,500 horsepower.

As soon as Detroit reconverted to civilian output in 1945, Kettering tried to get the oil industry to change the nature of its gasoline so that automobile manufacturers could put out high-compression engines in cars. He said, "When Mother Nature formed petroleum in the earth, she did not have the automobile in mind any more than the hog intended his bristles for toothbrushes. It is foolish to expect that the best arrangement of molecules in gasoline will be found in crude oil." [21] To this the oilmen and others replied that if Kettering tried raising compression ratios in cars above the conventional 6½ to 1, the engines would run rough and he would have ignition trouble.

Thereupon Kettering built an experimental plant in Detroit to test fuels. When General Motors' postwar Chevrolet came out in 1946, Kettering put his own pilot-model Chevrolet on the road, identical with the other except for an engine of 12½ to 1 compression. On the eve of his retirement at 70 the next year, he reported in a paper to the Society of Automotive Engineers at French Lick, Indiana, that the roughness had been overcome in his high-compression engine and his Chevrolet had outperformed the standard model while keeping the regular ignition system. The American Petroleum Institute gave Kettering its Gold Medal for Distinguished Achievement. "The oil industry, not the automotive industry, should be paying your salary," said the institute's president.[22]

That was the start of the great postwar horsepower race through the crowded highways of America, although the souped-up models did not become standard on the Big Three—Chevrolet, Ford, and

Plymouth—until several years later. Master lines of policy were laid down by General Motors Chairman Sloan, an engineer whose skills were greatest in management and sales. Changing models every year and dinning into consumers' ears their need for "bigger and better cars," General Motors and its imitators (which even included, before his death in 1947, Henry Ford) made car owners somehow dissatisfied with the cars they had and put them in mind to "trade up" for costlier new ones.[23] The stress on styling and annual model change required by the Sloan system wasted $5.06 billion a year during the 1950s, or $700 for each new car.[24]

With the pent-up postwar demand and then the need to fulfill defense contracts during the Korean War, these changes were confined mostly to face-liftings. But in the superstitious ritual of the automobile culture of the 1950s, such innovations as tail fins and two-tone trims were doubtless symbolic. Luxury and styling, the marks of prestige and status, were what sold cars, said the oligopolists of Detroit. By then cars had grown a foot wider, two feet longer. They came equipped with more and more luxurious accessories—automatic transmission, power steering, power brakes, power-opened windows, all at added cost. By 1955, as Detroit saw it, bigger engines were *necessary* to power the heavier, lower, accessory-laden cars. That year Chevrolet dropped its twenty-year-old six-cylinder engine for a 265-cubic inch, eight-cylinder power plant that carried out Kettering's ideas for higher compression and that soon had motorists queuing up at the high-test gasoline pumps.

"The real end which Americans set before them is acceleration," the English critic Lowes Dickinson wrote in 1902. "To be always moving, and always moving faster, that they think is the beatific life." [25] "Acceleration!" was the chant in 1955 as the organs of hired persuasion saluted the arrival of more powerful engines.[26]

Acceleration is a direct function of horsepower. After the war, Detroit's cars had edged up in horsepower, from 90–100 to 120–160 in the three basic makes of car; and the fancier Cadillacs had 250 by 1955. That year, a record eight millions cars were sold in America, and the golden times of motor car merchandising arrived. In 1957, when the engine was increased in size to 185 horsepower and General Motors President Harlow Curtice made speeches hailing economic growth, Chevrolet ads bugled, "This year the hot one's even hotter." Later the Chevy's horsepower rose to 325 and even 400. Ads urged "billing yourself as a Human Cannonball," and driving the 400-horsepower model "like you hate it—it's cheaper than psychiatry." [27]

Buyers could choose from among cars named Stingray, Tiger, Cutlass, Cobra, Co˗˗gar, Marauder, Fury, Charger, Barracuda.

Kettering had said that high-compression engines would save gasoline; and if that was what automobile and oil companies wanted in postwar cars, it might have turned out that way. But "more is better" was the slogan of those years, and little was heard about economy in performance except from Studebaker, which went out of business in 1966. The cars got bigger; the accessories, fancier and costlier. Yet by the end of the decade, 91 percent of domestic American cars were sold with the optional extra of automatic transmission. This convenience alone increased gasoline consumption by as much as 40 percent. The Federal Department of Transportation reported in 1970 that it added approximately seven cents a mile to an owner's costs over the life of his car—three cents for the hardware, four cents for the loss in gasoline mileage.

Over thirteen years Americans bought 13 million Chevrolet Impalas with the big engine, a record that bears comparison with the 15 million Model Ts Ford built over 19 production years; [28] the Model T retailed for $268 and the Impala, with automatic transmission and other widely-chosen options, at an average $2,680. This car, the "low-price" leader of the affluent sixties, needed leaded, high-octane gasoline for its big engine, which contributed heavily to the 82 million tons of pollutants then discharged annually by automobiles. Its acceleration, puffed as a "thrill," was occasionally useful for passing on two-lane country roads; but in crowded and narrow streets, where it logged almost all its miles, it was a positive menace.[29] In 1959, Daniel Patrick Moynihan calculated that one out of three cars built in Detroit wound up with blood on it.[30] In the fifteen years after the horsepower race started, road accidents killed a million people. Automobiles became the chief cause of death for Americans aged 18 to 25.

By 1968 Americans drove a trillion miles a year. The design of their car had evolved from the essential to the sybaritic. In many families teen-agers drove their own cars. The culture and the commerce were described by Tom Wolfe with faithful hyperbole in an essay titled "Kandy Kolored Tangerine Flake Streamline Baby." [31]

Oil as energy facilitated, then dictated accelerating velocity of goods as well as people. The same competition of passenger and freight traffic broke out on the highways that had formerly occurred on the railroads. On the privately owned railroads, freight, of course, had carried the day; on the publicly owned highways of the boomtime years, the nation simply kept pouring more concrete to carry the load of both passenger and freight traffic. By 1956, trucks numbered 16 percent of all registered vehicles; and thereafter, as cars multiplied at record rates, the growth of trucking kept pace.

Railroad trackage needed a freight traffic of a thousand tons per mile per day to be viable in 1960, a criterion by which only 37 percent of the American railroad system could be profitably operated.[32] Trucks rose as short-haul carriers when fast and frequent movements were required by accelerating velocity within an expanding economy. Although railroads continued in 1971 to lead in ton-miles, trucks carried 75 percent of all freight by volume.[33]

Trucks could go door to door. They could avoid the transfer headache with all its cost, delay, inconvenience. Flexibile, they could move when the shipment was ready to go, and deliver the goods when and where they were needed. That was not all. If the truck belonged to the shipper, its operation could be integrated into the manufacturing process, thereby reducing the need for added inventory and eliminating storage. The use of trucks at a construction site illustrated the advantage of being able to get materials to the site directly and in ordered sequence.

Trucks, of course, had their drawbacks—chiefly, their inadequate capacity for moving large quantities of bulk materials and the high cost of long hauls—and for these basic reasons railroads continued to hold first place in long-haul traffic.

In the oil, automotive, and other manufacturing industries, the biggest productivity gains of the 1950s were achieved by putting machines to tasks formerly performed by men. It was the other way around in the trucking industry, where every new machine put another driver on the highways. By the 1950s the Teamsters Union with 1,200,000 truck drivers as members, was already the largest and richest of all American trade unions. And James R. Hoffa, whose ruthless grasp of the centrality of transportation recalled that of John D. Rockefeller in an earlier day, was its master.

As chairman of the Teamsters' big Central States Conference, Jimmy Hoffa stepped up to the union presidency when Dave Beck was sent to prison for embezzlement of union welfare funds in 1958. Son of an Indiana coal miner, without formal education beyond the fourth grade, Hoffa was a product of the same Detroit labor strife of the depressed 1930s that gave Walter Reuther to the American labor movement. But there was a world of difference between these men. The social idealism of the New Deal passed Hoffa by. Five feet five, 170 pounds of mostly muscle, he was a no-holds-barred scrapper who led his first strike (of strawberry loaders) at eighteen. Hoffa fought to survive—and then dominate. "Whatever you can do to me I can do to you, only more," he boasted. "I know where I'm going. . . . I'm no damned angel." [34] Reuther and his men only made the trucks; Hoffa organized the men who drove them; and brawling, browbeating, blustering, bribing, he built up for a time more raw power than the United Auto Workers' president and probably more than any other American labor leader. "I will tell you something about politics," Hoffa said. "There are just two ways to play it. You either make speeches or else you spend dough. We spend lots of dough." [35]

In his rise to teamster power, he won wage rises and improvements in working conditions that gained the lasting loyalty of the drivers. The key to his command lay in the structure of the trucking industry. Trucking was essentially a short-haul business, and the owners and operators were not organized on the same national scale as the union. At no time did teamster strikes compel such public attention as the great stoppages in the auto, steel, and coal industries, which were industrywide and felt throughout the country. But the strikes Hoffa called, invariably local, were effective precisely because it was in local transport that trucking loomed large. And since Jimmy spent the money where local political and industrial decisions were made, the teamsters invariably won.

The truck's ascendancy in the vital short-range dimensions of economic exchange was nearly absolute. Of all shipments destined in 1959 for points less than a hundred miles away, no fewer than 88 percent moved by highway; only 6 percent, by rail.[36]

The impact of oil on postwar America was not limited to ground transport. In the years after 1945 Americans switched from trains to planes as their favored mode of travel between cities. Air freight, though high-cost, also scored big gains because of savings it enabled those who used it to make money elsewhere. Between 1950 and 1970, air-freight shipments rose fivefold. It was possible to ship perishables to market by air that would otherwise have spoiled. Livestock too could be moved to market by air, eliminating the loss in weight incurred when the animals were moved long distance by slower transport. Delivery of machinery and spare parts by air was often found to pay when to do so avoided closing down, waiting, or amassing costly inventories.

★

The manipulation and control of government to serve the oil industry helped give Americans a politics that talked one way and acted another, that made millions distrustful of government's ability to respond, to lead, to act ethically and equitably for the welfare of all.

The effect of the prorationing system put over in depression years was to hold back postwar production and hold up postwar prices. Never again, though new fields opened in Illinois, Utah, Colorado, New Mexico, and North Dakota, did wildcatters bring in such a great discovery as east Texas. As fewer big fields were brought in, more and more old wells were subsidized to keep pumping long after they were largely played out. The effect, since Texas and other big producing states were limiting overall production from month to month, was to keep output down and make fuel cost more than it should have. Texas, for instance, could at any time during the 1950s have produced more than twice its actual output. But the oldest and most marginal wells were exempted, under local political pressures, from all prorationing, whereas the newer and more productive wells were kept under wraps. In fact more than half of Texas's 194,500 wells in 1965 were superfluous. In November of that year, no fewer than 1,500,000 barrels out of the state's production of 2,828,000 barrels of crude oil came in dribs and drabs out of these exempt wells.

The secret of this system was that the buyers of the crude oil taken from these tired old wells liked high crude prices because they too were crude producers. These thousands of marginal wells might indeed have been owned by the state's 20,000 small-time operators, the statistical equivalent of the small farmers who during the depression years received comparable relief by New Deal schemes for curbing agricultural overproduction. But the pipelines that carried the oil away from the small-timers' wellheads belonged almost invariably to one of a half dozen major companies—and of course, the majors produced much or most of the rest of the state's oil. Thanks to the depletion allowance and other special tax treatments the industry had won, they could make more money in the production end of the business than they could by refining and marketing it. They liked the stability of the arrangement, and most of all they liked the stability of prices.

In the quarter century after the prorationing system was put over in 1934, the oil industry experienced only a dozen price changes.[37] This was half as many as had occurred in the preceding twelve years. And when prices did go up after the second World War, they stayed up. Even when demand tapered off, they held firm, thanks to the drastic production cutbacks ordered by state authorities. The majors benefited most by this system, for even after 1949, when their tremendous expansion overseas began paying off, their share of domestic production did not fall below 60 percent. So huge were the sums of money involved that the remaining 40 percent, besides affording outdoor relief to a number of small-time oil producers, helped build up the greatest individual fortunes of mid-century America. H. L. Hunt's income, to cite but one example, was at the time a million dollars a week. In 1951, when the depletion allowance benefit came to an estimated $2.1 billion, 96 percent of the rake-off went to oil companies with assets of $1 million or more.

By that time the cooperation between government and big oil had grown so close that the industry operated in every sense as an insider. The major companies, making their most important postwar moves overseas in the Middle East, worked intimately with the federal government in realigning ownership and markets of Saudi Arabian oil. On the home front, all branches of government lent aid to the industry's program for "stabilizing" production and prices.

Even the vulgarities of a new crop of oil millionaires did not upset these vested ties. On the contrary, the kind of tacit alliance that was an important part of Franklin Roosevelt's coalition of urban and Southern voting blocs easily survived the trust-busting impulses of the later New Deal and emerged as a main force in the Washington of Sam Rayburn and Lyndon Johnson.[38] From the time he raised campaign money for the Democratic congressional campaign committee in 1940, Johnson, ever watchful for the depletion allowance, kept close ties with such "independent" oil operators as Sid Richardson, Roy Cullen, H. L. Hunt, and others. In 1947 the chairman of the Texas Democratic executive committee could say, "The oil industry today is in complete control of State politics and State government." [39] And when Governor Price Daniel ran for the Senate in 1955, he observed publicly that he did not see how anyone could get elected in Texas without the backing of oil money.[40]

From Rockefeller's time the single characterizing trait of the oil industry has been its secretiveness. Compared with oil companies, other American corporations live in goldfish bowls. Practically nothing is know of the sums that Hunt and Cullen gave Lyndon Johnson. There are reports that Sid Richardson pledged a million dollars when Eisenhower said he would run for president. The Rockefellers and Mellons, who no longer participate in the management of the great companies founded by their families, gave substantial sums in each presidential campaign since the 1940s.[41] During hearings on his vice-presidential nomination in 1974 Nelson Rockefeller informed the House Judiciary committee that his family spent more than $17 million on his campaigns over 16 years. Richard Mellon Scaife alone gave $1,067,000 to Nixon's 1972 reelection campaign.[42]

But oil company money in politics remains the most elaborately laundered of all. Lesser men do the errands. When Alton Jones, chairman of Cities Service and one of three oilmen who paid all expenses of President Eisenhower's Gettysburg farm,[43] died in an airplane crash in 1962, a bag stuffed with $85,000 in currency was found in his luggage.[44] The company press officer hastily announced that Jones was an art collector on his way to buy paintings. It was pretty generally understood that he was carrying money for use in California's governorship campaign. After Gulf Oil was fined for making gifts to Nixon and others in 1972, the Securities and Exchange Commission charged that between 1960 and 1973 Gulf Oil had funneled no less than $10 million into political activities through a subsidiary in the Bahamas, a "substantial portion" of which was spent illegally. Back in 1952 oil paid big prices for Republican support of the offshore oil bill, but those were only outsiders trying for the inside.

Inside, the influence is too intimately pervasive to be seen. Oil does not have to reach out before the public eye; it has what it wants. For years Rayburn saw to it that no one who was not "sound" on depletion allowance went on the House Ways and Means Committee. Oil has its senators too, as well placed as Payne and Penrose, as Fall and Gore, were in their day. The key members of the finance committee in these years were Robert Kerr of Oklahoma and Russell Long of Louisiana. Both owned oil wells and Kerr, as a founding owner of the Kerr-McGee Company, was the richest senator of his day.

In the pursuit of oil, the American petroleum industry ended up bringing a quarter of all the country's privately owned land under lease for exploration and exploitation. Prospectors then spread over the public lands of the West, a drive that produced, along with a lot of oil, the Teapot Dome scandal. After that there remained only one sector of the American earth where oil could yet be sought—beneath the shallow waters off the country's coasts.

Nobody supposed that these submerged lands could be exploited as private property—although the first buccaneers who struck oil on

Los Angeles beaches in 1920 were soon found to be surreptitiously "slant drilling" seaward to tap oil located a half mile and more offshore. In putting a stop to this piratical practice, the state of California asserted its ownership. Then the state began granting leases to search for underwater oil as far out as the three-mile limit. Both Standard Oil of California and independent operators entered this new field, and by the late 1930s the state of California had gained some $4 million in royalties on offshore production. In Texas and Louisiana, geologists reported that oil pools as big as Spindletop and other Gulf Coast gushers almost surely existed off the coasts of those states. Interior Secretary Ickes, concerned as guardian of the nation's resources at this new drive to exploit public lands, brought the federal government into the picture. In 1937, he persuaded Senator Gerald P. Nye, Republican of North Dakota, to introduce a resolution affirming that coastal waters were federal domain. Though the measure passed the Senate, it bogged down in the House, where representatives of oil states interposed objections.

The urgency of the second World War forced Washington officials planning for the national interest to take a more searching look at all natural resources. Offshore oil at once became a center of attention. In the Navy Department, talks began for setting aside offshore reserves for the requirements of the fleet. Secretary Ickes urged the president to have the federal government clear its title to coastal waters in the courts.

Among the rising independent oilmen of California was Edwin W. Pauley. Born in Indiana and reared in Alabama, Pauley had arrived in California when his father went into the oil business there. Entering the university at Berkeley, Ed Pauley worked his way through as a sweating oil field roustabout in the summer and a salesman of encyclopedias in termtime. Six feet three and weighing 220 pounds, he not only played tackle for the Golden Bears, but pulled an oar on the varsity crew. After a try at teaching, he joined his father in the oil game, starting on the derrick floor. Hospitalized for nearly a year with a broken neck after a plane crash, Pauley recovered and went into oil leasing. By 1929 he was far enough ahead to organize what became the Petrol Corporation, with assets mostly from bankrupt firms. In the depression years, he not only led price wars as president of California's Independent Petroleum Association, but worked to defeat a Standard Oil-sponsored bill to limit state output and fought off prosecution for selling hot oil in defiance of a voluntary scheme to hold down production. He organized more oil companies and took a flier in Los Angeles real estate.

As shrewd as he was tough, Pauley went into politics, as he said, "to protect and advance my business operations." [46] That was in 1938, when he raised money for Culbert L. Olson's successful race for governor and doubled as treasurer of Democratic Senator Sheridan Downey's campaign. At the time Pauley's affairs were in bad shape. Oil prices were down sharply, his holdings were heavily mortgaged, and all his assets were pledged at the bank. As a way out, Pauley sold all his properties to Signal Oil, a Standard subsidiary.

A cool million of Standard-Signal money in his pockets, Pauley branched out in all directions. The pelican wearing a sweater with the initials *P. D. Q.* became familiar as a symbol of his Petrol Oil Corporation from San Diego to San Francisco as he built up his marketing operations and developed new fields. Now friendly with his old foes at Standard, he also acquired offshore oil rights. In 1940 he took his fund-raising capabilities to Washington, where he handed over to Democratic party Chairman Ed Flynn a substantial contribution from the president of Standard of California, a Republican.

Once on the national scene, Pauley stayed. The big, heavy-fisted, hard-eyed Westerner was no shrinking violet about tackling the Democrats' $750,000 deficit left over from Franklin Roosevelt's third-term campaign. Installed as secretary-treasurer of the party, Pauley was given a free hand. All kinds of enterprises were getting war contracts. Pauley turned on the heat and got results. He ended up wiping out the deficit. At one point he lent the New York State committee $25,000 out of his own pocket. He was soon in and out of FDR's office, insisting that oil was the key to Allied victory, crisscrossing the country until 100 tankers were rounded up to carry the stuff abroad, and visiting England and Russia to check on deliveries. He lent influential support to Ickes's program for building the Big Inch and Little Inch pipelines and helped Ickes find aides from industry. But when Ickes urged in 1944 that the attorney general bring the federal offshore land case to court, Pauley persuaded the president to hold off.

It was a campaign year, and Big Ed was strong for a Roosevelt fourth term. He was also enthusiastic for Truman for vice-president. He said, "We're not nominating the vice-president; we're nominating the next President." [47] On the theory that Vice-President Wallace was too far to the left, Pauley joined Democratic party Chairman Robert Hannegan and city bosses Ed Flynn and Ed Kelly in backing Truman as the new running mate. The chief opposition came from the California delegation, which was red hot for Wallace. Pauley beat down the resistance and won out as his state's national committeeman.

After the convention, Hannegan and Pauley paid a visit to Ickes, who had not only backed Wallace, but sent Roosevelt a wire urging against Truman's nomination. In the interests of unity, they asked Ickes to make some five-minute radio speeches for the ticket. But Pauley had more on his mind. Remaining behind, he brought up the subject of offshore oil. Ickes, ever suspicious, called in Undersecretary Abe Fortas and made a memorandum of the conversation immediately afterward. Pauley, his notes said, had talked with Roosevelt, and Roosevelt had told Pauley to talk with Ickes. Pauley said that he could raise $300,000 from oilmen in California who had interests in offshore oil if they could be "assured" that the federal government would not try to assert title to these lands.

On February 2, 1945, Ickes had another talk with Pauley and made another memorandum. Pauley, his notes said, had told him that he had collected $500,000 for the 1944 presidential campaign, $300,000 of it from California oil interests. Pauley "thought it would be a great mistake to disturb these interests." [48] He told Ickes that he had discussed the offshore question with Roosevelt on "two or three occasions." [49]

Three months later President Roosevelt died, the matter of federal action on offshore oil still unresolved. On April 15, Ickes wrote a third memorandum. Just after the burial of Roosevelt at Hyde Park, Ickes stepped into the observation car of the presidential train. He found Pauley there with Postmaster General Hannegan and Truman's aide, Harry Vaughn. Truman was in his compartment taking a nap. All, wrote Ickes, drifted away except Pauley, "and he had the hardihood to turn to me and ask me what I proposed to do about offshore oil." [50] Ickes said that he had given it to the court. "Shortly President Truman came in and Pauley disappeared." [51]

Actually, the offshore matter was at that point in the hands of Truman and Attorney General Francis Biddle. As almost his last act before leaving office, Biddle filed suit. Three months later the president issued an executive order proclaiming federal domain over the entire continental shelf of the United States. By this time state officials as well as oilmen plunged into the conflict, and a quitclaim bill on all federal rights to offshore land out to the three-mile limit came before Congress. Forty-four state attorneys general wired the House to stand by states rights against a federal "grab." The bill whipped through the House with only eleven dissenting votes.

Ickes suspected that the quitclaim bill was an oil-industry ploy, and he was not the only one. The *St. Louis Post Dispatch* headlined that the bill had been drawn up by the California attorney general and an aide whose fees had been paid partly by the state and partly by oil companies. The newspaper further charged that the Californians had been introduced to House leaders by Big Ed Pauley and that the wires from the 44 attorneys general had been prompted by letters written in Pauley's office. Pauley, the newspaper noted, was financially interested in California offshore oil.

At this point, when the *Post Dispatch* seemed convinced that it had the makings of another Teapot Dome scandal (Paul Y. Anderson, a *Post Dispatch* reporter, broke the 1927 story of the bribe Secretary Fall accepted from California Oilman Edward Doheny), President Truman sent up Pauley's nomination for undersecretary of the navy. The presumption in Washington was that Secretary James A. Forrestal would shortly vacate his office, and Pauley would move up as his successor.

An oilman in charge of the naval oil reserves—this was too much for Ickes. The old curmudgeon went before the Senate Naval Affairs Committee, whose chairman, Charles W. Tobey, a Vermont Republican, had a great name for vigilant probity. Ickes said he was opposed to the nomination. He produced his memorandums of conversations, including Pauley's request, after soliciting campaign funds from California oil interests, for "assurances" that the secretary would not disturb their satisfactory arrangement with the state of California. Reading from the witness stand, Ickes fairly rasped out the concluding sentences: "This is the rawest proposition that has ever been made to me. I don't intend to smear my record on oil at this stage of the game." [52]

The following day Pauley produced in his defense Democratic National Committee records. They showed no more than $25,000 in contributions from California oil interests in four years, a large part of them from Pauley's family. Furious, President Truman defended his nominee against "vicious and unwarranted attacks." [53] He refused to see Ickes. But before Truman could act, Ickes announced his intention to leave the cabinet. In the presence of 300 assembled newsmen, he proudly announced his resignation:

> I do not care to stay in an administration where I am expected to commit perjury for the sake of the party. I do oppose the appointment of Edwin Pauley because he is an active oil man in private business and is proposed for a job that carries responsibility for government oil. He made me a proposition which should disqualify him for public office.[54]

Shortly afterward Truman withdrew the Pauley nomination. But now the offshore issue had been dragged out before public attention and by a nomination that even the *Oil and Gas Journal* said brought back memories of Teapot Dome.[55] Wrangling followed in Congress and state legislatures that lasted seven years. Local officials, especially in California, Louisiana, and Texas, fought for high stakes in oil revenues for state government and party coffers. Oil industry leaders warned that Washington was engaged in an assault upon free enterprise that could spread to other sectors of the economy. Congress held repeated hearings, and the literature and mythology of the "tidelands" grew.[56]

"Tidelands" was the wrong name, since nobody was disputing title to the land between low-tide and high-tide levels. Such inshore terrain remained with the states, although it was almost impossible to find this out by listening to the tirades of state and oil-industry spokesmen. The real question was who was to control the underwater lands beyond tidal limits. "Every state has submerged lands," was the cry, and the partisans of "states rights" claimed title out to the three-mile limit.[57] In Texas and Florida, where experts talked of "historic boundaries" that went back to days when these states were not yet in the Union, the claim extended to three leagues, or roughly 10½ miles.[58] "Yes, more is at stake than land or sands or oysters," cried Representative Richard H. Poff of Virginia. "The sanctity of private property and the lifeblood of our democracy hangs in the balance." [59]

There it remained through 1946, when President Truman vetoed Congressman Poff's quitclaim bill, and through 1947, when the Supreme Court ruled, five to four, that California did not hold jurisdiction over its offshore waters. But there was no stopping the push for oil. By the next year Louisiana had already gone ahead and collected $24 million in rentals, bonuses, and leases from offshore operations. Texas, earmarking its royalties for schools, proceeded to lease to major oil companies nearly 150,000 acres of lands on the continental shelf beyond the three-mile limit. Pressure for congressional action to overrule the Court and hand the "tidelands" to the states mounted. The major oil companies, which had never hidden their preference for dealing with the states, pressed for a settlement—any settlement—that would secure their titles and promise some return on their growing investment.

These first ventures off the Gulf Coast quickly established that offshore oil, at least beyond the coastal shallows, was not a game in which old-time wildcatters could play. Everett de Golyer, the industry's most respected geologist, said that if salt domes occurred offshore with the same frequency found on shore, there should be 10½ billion barrels of oil within 30 miles of the coast.[60] But underwater prospecting was fiendishly expensive. Mobil's operating subsidiary Magnolia put in $7.7 million drilling its first four holes, two of which found oil; and Humble spent $1.2 million building a two-story platform nine miles off the Louisiana coast and even more maintaining 54 men in such an outlandish place. Even big-time independents like Kerr-McGee, facing drilling costs of a million dollars per hole, had to hedge the risk and lighten the financial load by taking in such majors as Phillips and Standard of Indiana as partners.

Meanwhile, as royalties were impounded in California, Louisiana, and Texas, the political battle raged onshore. In 1951, the *Dallas Morning News* charged that "the federal grab of tidelands has clouded title to property all over America." [61] To Senator Blair Moody, Democrat of Michigan, the states' righters' bill was "a scheme that makes Teapot Dome look like a conservation project." [62] Speaker Sam Rayburn, of Texas, shepherded the bill to passage, and President Truman again vetoed it. The tidelands issue, having been stoked up by no fewer than sixteen congressional hearings, grew sizzling in the 1952 presidential campaign. Texas oil millionaires buzzed around General Eisenhower. Roy Cullen endorsed him; Alton Jones of Cities Service golfed with him; Sid Richardson furnished funds that helped seat pro-Eisenhower delegates from Texas in the convention fight that gave Eisenhower the Republican nomination. In a letter to oilman H. Jack Porter, the Texas Republican chairman, Eisenhower came out for awarding title to the tidelands of the states:

> Federal ownership in this case, as in others, is one that is calculated to bring about steady progress toward centralized ownership and control, a trend which I bitterly oppose.[63]

Feelings ran highest in Texas, where the tidelands issue topped all others. When Democratic Candidate Adlai Stevenson came out for federal control in the face of crowds bearing placards "Remember the Alamo and the Tidelands Oil Steal," [64] Governor Allan Shivers announced that he could not support the party's candidate. With the hero born in Denison, Texas, leading the way, the oil of the tidelands had much to do with detaching Texas from its historic allegiance to the Democratic party.

The new administration's ties with members of the oil industry were soon disclosed. Less than a week after taking office, it moved to kill a Justice Department criminal antitrust suit against the seven majors for controlling Middle East output. Eisenhower's oil-business friends such as Alton Jones, George Allen, and Sid Richardson counseled speedy action on the tidelands, and they got it. Within three months of taking office, the new president signed into law an act finally relinquishing to the states all federal claims to submerged lands lying within the three-mile limit. When *The New York Times* denounced "one of the greatest and surely most unjustified giveaways in history," [65] Secretary of the Interior Douglas McKay replied, "All we are doing is giving it back to the people where it belongs." [66]

So ended the long fight over tidelands jurisdiction, which in some ways recalled an earlier struggle when not oil but cotton was king. Then spokesmen debated issues of federal versus state powers while the question on their minds was really the extension cf slavery, just as later men appealed to the cause of states' rights while they were really concerned over extension of concessions to exploit oil.

Where the cotton kingdom lost its fight, however, oil won the right to expand its realm. Today, two decades later, it seems hard to understand all the hullabaloo over a mere strip of land three miles wide except in these terms. The ten-year campaign to hand over the tidelands to the states effectively foreclosed the far more significant question of how the oil of the continental shelf was to be developed. After Harold Ickes bowed out in his fight to keep an oilman out of the Navy Department, nobody in high office remained to pursue the question for public policy: should these valuable oil lands be left for industry to exploit as it had since the days of Colonel Drake, or should the government itself take a hand to develop them as perhaps America's ultimate reserve of an irreplaceable national resource?

In the bickering and shouting over title to the three-mile strip, nobody asked this larger question. Two months after passage of the tidelands law, Congress at the request of the Eisenhower administration enacted the Outer Continental Shelf Act. The measure placed under federal jurisdiction all offshore areas beyond the three-mile limit (or three-league limit in the case of Texas and Louisiana). Secretary McKay was authorized to lease these lands in lots not to exceed 5,760 acres under competitive bidding. Thus, without debate, the crucial question was settled: mineral development of all offshore lands, whether state- or federal-controlled, was ticketed for private hands.

Already it was clear, even in California with its narrow offshore shelf, that the richest oil prizes lay not in the bitterly disputed three-mile strip, but in the federal domain beyond. This much the oilmen had verified during the long delay in settling the ownership dispute. The famous salt domes of the Gulf Coast appeared to be as numerous as expected. Geophysicists had been roaming the shallow seas off Texas and Louisiana, where the continental shelf extended outward for more than 100 miles. Shooting off dynamite charges along the sea surface (and infuriating shrimpers by the destruction they wrought), they traced on their seismographs buried domes all the way out to the continental rim. The salt, comparatively light and plastic, had poked through ancient sediments and bent them upward, forming many pockets that, in turn, trapped the oil formed out of marine organisms buried in these sediments. For the probing "doodlebuggers," these invisible formations stood out rank on rank in domes one to two miles wide and taller than peaks in the Rockies.

Going to sea was a drastically different experience for the oil industry. You could mix oil and water, the first drillers growled, but it was not easy. One rigger said, "In west Texas we operate as dry as horned toads. They bring us down to Louisiana—and there's the ocean!" [67] Pink pelicans flapped past their steel platforms, porpoises sported around their boats, and the crew learned about the marsh-dwelling Cajuns with their picturesque ways of shrimping, shooting muskrats, and grunting over alligator holes to entice the beasts into range of their rifles.

Twisting and smashing the steel work of the new sea rigs, the hurricane of 1949 taught the oil companies a valuable lesson: only the highest type of scientific engineering could cope in such an environment. Shell added two admirals to its payroll. The first rigs of the 1950s were prefabricated monsters built out of yard-thick steel cylinders, decked high enough for waves beneath and held in place by steel piles driven a hundred feet through the sea-bottom muck. Humble's Platform A stood like a giant stork on skinny legs in fifty feet of water off Louisiana. By "whipsocking"—essentially the same technique as the slant drilling of the California beaches—the company drilled no fewer than six wells into a salt dome from this one platform and soon was pumping profitable quantities of oil ashore through an underwater pipe.[68] But platforms, because they were permanent, were almost a total loss if drilling found no oil.

Mobile rigs called jack-ups got around this drawback. They were shallow barges with huge steel caissons running through their sides. When such a craft was underway, these tall cylinders stuck up like grotesque smokestacks. At the drilling site they were dropped until firmly planted on the bottom. Then inch by inch the barge climbed up on its own caissons like a boy shinning up a tree. When the platform was high enough, drilling got under way. Later, after the well had been completed, the barge shinned slowly down its legs, pulled them up out of the mud, and sailed away, leaving only a few piles behind to protect the top of the well casing. At $2 to $4 million apiece, such rigs were so costly that they could be used only for exploratory drilling.

It took the equivalent of a good-sized factory to drill one of these holes—4,000 bags of cement, 80,000 barrels of fresh water, 10,850 barrels of chemicals, two tons of welding rod. Renting the drilling gear alone cost $10,000 a day. For a 12,000-foot well, four concentric steel tubes were necessary. To emplace all this, the 376,000 pounds of cement had to be forced down the drill tube to the bottom, from which point the cement was pumped upward—outside the casing. When the cement set, you had a telescope encased in the earth. Down the hole you poured specially prepared "mud," mainly bentonite weighted with barites, for the drill to turn in. The drill pipe itself came in 30-foot sections, each weighing 500 pounds and each one screwed on as it was needed by giant steel tongs. Every day the bit had to be changed, which meant that the pipe had to be pulled. Up it came in 1,500 pound sections, swinging back on an overhead block like a balloon in the wind. Such a bit change was called "yo-yoing the pipe," or "making a trip." [69] When the bit was two miles down—and the holes drilled were often that deep—it took four to six hours just to take it out and put it back. A steel pole two miles long can veer considerably from the vertical; so the offshore engineers of the late 1950s had to lower a camera and take pictures of compass readings 10,000 feet down to determine the degree and direction of deviation.

This was simply not the kind of prospecting the oilmen were used to. Gone was the wild excitement of bringing in a gusher. Gone was the volcanic blast of surging crude, which crowds rushed to see and smell and hear. In this game, the word of the college boys in the geology department counted for everything. They told you where to drill, and you took star sights and loran and radar readings to make sure you were drilling where they told you to. People told of the company that found out $250,000 too late that it was drilling on another company's plot. Another was a mile down before it learned that it was three miles away from where the geologists said they should drill. They kept going and found a good gas well anyway.

Eeriest of all, the young fellows also told you at what level to look for the strike. As L. F. McCollum, the hard-bitten old Texas operator who was president of Continental Oil, described it:

You drill a well, thousands of feet under the ocean floor, and at a certain place stop and say: this is it. You send down a gun and perforate the well, and suck up water on top of it, and then out comes the oil. Just like those pink-cheeked boys said it would. Goddamn, I tell you it can't be done.[70]

Continental, joined in a syndicate with Atlantic, Tidewater, and Cities Service, was soon the biggest plunger offshore, with 43 wells in 14 fields and a 43-mile pipeline off Louisiana. Three years after Congress passed the tidelands act, 35 companies had spent a billion dollars, leased 2½ million acres off Louisiana, and sent eighty-odd rigs probing in water as deep as 100 feet. They could not dally because the federal leases for which they had paid dear became void after five years if they had produced neither oil nor gas.

Life offshore was all that technology could provide—air-conditioned rooms, color television, steaks and drinks flown in by fleets of helicopters. Drillers got $1,000 a month. Lowest paid roughneck on the rig drew $500 a month—and the routine was to work seven days on and seven days off. A problem nonetheless was labor turnover: the companies found the best help were men who worked small farms near their shore bases when they were not on the job at sea. More and more, however, they subcontracted as much of their operations as possible, and let others worry about finding help.

In the first years in the Gulf, the oil companies' offshore income was only $400 million, less than the total paid to the state and federal governments. The platforms were not only costly but vulnerable. In 1953, Pure Oil lost $1 million on a fire in a blowout. The oil, when found, was costly to get ashore—35 cents a barrel by barge or else a heavy investment in underwater pipe. By 1956 the concessionaires had brought in 14 major fields, each capable of ultimately producing 50 million barrels of oil. On shore, companies would have jumped at the chance of a 10-million-barrel field. Offshore, costs ran so high that nothing less than a 50-million-barrel find promised to pay out. On top of this, the states imposed production limits on the offshore wells, even on federal leases; and this put a damper, especially off Texas, which permitted production only nine or ten days a month. Many of the wells brought in were capped.

Still the exploration went on, and the rigs got bigger and bigger.

Their platforms grew as long as football fields, as high as twenty-story buildings—so big they had to be marked on maps and charts. Some, like Exxon's Platform A off Louisiana's Grand Isle, were man-made islands on legs. Some would pull up their legs and swim to another site. Some had large ships tied up to them to provide power, storage space, living quarters. And some *were* ships, ships of a kind never seen before. Some went down like submarines when they reached their destination, leaving their top decks above water. Others put their legs on the bottom and climbed up their legs until they were out of reach of the highest hurricane waves.[71]

The majors continued to bid record prices for offshore acreage. At three successive sales in New Orleans the federal government took in more than $1 billion for Gulf leases. In 1968 three companies joined to bid $602 million for one tract in the deepwater channel off Santa Barbara, California. Such big outlays in the face of daunting costs were characteristic of huge enterprises with special tax benefits that generated a cash flow so large as to be positively inundating: exploration was a good place to put a lot of money back to work. The industry's explanation was that the majors felt there were few places to look for oil on the mainland any more.

Then in January 1969, a blowout occurred at Union Oil Co.'s Well A–21 in the shallow channel off Santa Barbara. No mishap that could be coped with far out of everybody's eyeshot, this was an accident that took place in a busy harbor lined by thousands of observant and concerned property owners. Even more embarrassing, oil continued to bubble up after the technicians shut off the well. It seemed that the oil-bearing sands were just a few hundred feet down, on the Rincon Structural Trend extending out from shore fields; and the seepage discharged not only from the well itself, but along a line 800 feet eastward from the drilling platform. The people of Santa Barbara rose in arms. Senators demanded an end to offshore drilling. Ten days later, after a huge slick had blackened Santa Barbara's famous beaches, Secretary of the Interior Walter J. Hickel ordered a stop to all drilling and production in the area.

The impact of this spectacular spill roused Americans to the environmental risks posed by offshore oil. Congress stiffened the Outer Continental Shelf Lands Act of 1953 to provide greater protection against such disasters and made offshore operators liable for cleaning up such spills. Union Oil, stanching the flow after some 80,000 barrels had escaped, spent $3.4 million cleaning up the mess on the beaches.

Although Hickel later ordered resumption of offshore drilling at Santa Barbara, there was deep concern in coastal states. Fifty members of Congress asked the Interior Department to defer any explorations for oil in the Atlantic, despite a gas strike by Mobil on a Newfoundland beach that seemed to signal good chances of oil under fishing banks all along the Northeast coast.[72] Five years after the Santa Barbara blow out, a grand total of two rigs drilled for new sites on the Pacific shelf.[73]

Offshore oil operations were thus confined to the Gulf of Mexico. Texas and Louisiana, accustomed to far larger operations ashore, took the oceanic activities as a matter of course. Production from the Gulf yielded the industry what Dr. Richard Howe of Exxon in 1968 called a "low but acceptable" return,[74] and brought the federal government no less than $18 billion in lease bids and royalties. And if all the operations off Louisiana were lumped together, the 2.2 billion barrels pumped ashore after 1948 seemed a respectable enough showing.

But on balance the first two decades of American offshore oil were disappointing. Nobody had struck it rich by the standards of east Texas—or of the Persian Gulf and other foreign waters. Offshore as well as on land, the oil welling up in the world seemed to be coming from elsewhere than the United States. Of the 10 million barrels a day produced from beneath the seas in 1973, the United States accounted for only 1,588,539 barrels, a total that represented a decline for the third straight year. In offshore production the United States stood third, well back of Saudi Arabia and Venezuela (whose oil had for years been largely drawn from beneath the salt-tinged waters of Lake Maracaibo).[75] After drilling disappointments off Alabama and west Florida in 1974, nobody made any claims for the American Gulf waters to compare with those made, for example, for the North Sea.

On the British side of the North Sea, a four-billion-barrel capacity had been assigned to the Forties field scheduled to come into production in late 1975. On the booming Norwegian side, where operations had already begun, more fields were found and an ordinary driller from Texas got $30,000 a year plus whatever was needed to pay all income taxes on it, a free residence in Oslo and schooling for his daughter in Switzerland. On the far side of the Pacific, Indonesian offshore production was coming on fast, but industry eyes were turning toward Communist China. If the deposits in the Gulf of Pohan were anywhere near as big as the *Peking Review* stated,[76] it was conceivable that China might detach Japan from Exxon, not to mention from Russia.

America's energy shortage of the 1970s ran smack into the

nation's ambiguous experience with offshore oil. Suddenly the nation needed all the oil it could squeeze out anywhere. The North Sea finds suggested that offshore was still the coming place for finding oil. Since only the Gulf Coast had been tapped so far, the federal government at once proposed offshore leasing everywhere else—along the entire length of the Atlantic coast from Maine to Florida, and along the Pacific coast from California to Alaska.

Texas and Louisiana, accustomed to far larger operations onshore, might put up with a rash of new docks, pipes, tanks, and refineries on their coasts as a matter of course. But the twenty states in which the oil industry now threatened to come ashore took quite a different view of the prospect. They rose in alarm at the thought of oil-smeared beaches and oil companies tearing up their countrysides in one way or another for money that was destined to bypass them and flow largely to Wall Street and Houston. Besides, the states and cities concerned were physically in a position to thwart operations from their shores.

By yet another irony of oil history, therefore, the states, some of them the oil companies' partners or pawns in the fight for title to the shoreline "tidelands" two decades before, now led in demanding overhaul of the cozy arrangements for offshore tract-leasing between the industry and the Interior Department. California told the Interior Department that its draft assessment of the environmental impact of offshore leasing on that state was superficial and should be completely redrawn. Alaska officials said flatly they would refuse to cooperate unless their state got some of the income. New York called for a carefully controlled, three-stage development program—preliminary studies, then exploratory drilling, and finally restricted production, all monitored and evaluated at every stage by federal, state, and local authorities. This was supervision of a sort oilmen were not used to. Yet if America were to tap its remaining offshore oil, as it must, the system would have to be changed. States, communities, and citizens would have more say—and no doubt federal revenue-sharing would be broadened to include sharing offshore oil income.

How the oil industry would share in the money was also in question. In exploiting the oil of the Outer Continental Shelf, the companies had dealt only with the federal government, and thus been spared the fuss over lease payments to individual farmers and the laborious assembling of acreage to assure that someone else just across the road did not put down a well and tap the oil your men discovered. The tracts the government leased were big enough to contain entire oil fields. Under the system that had grown up, the companies held a virtual monopoly of exploratory information and "nominated" the tracts for leasing. The Interior Department, relying almost entirely on the industry's data and—often erroneous—valuations, then auctioned off the tracts.

Now all this came under review. The 16⅓ percent federal royalty rate was most favorable to the industry—far below the 45 percent that the British government fixed as its share in the companies' North Sea oil production. The auction prices, to be sure, ran high, so high in fact that the majors themselves had long clubbed together in joint bids. Congressional critics chorused that the offshore game was so expensive that only the majors could play. Even when independents joined in combinations, it was beyond their purses. The only way they could get a piece of the action was by so-called farm-out contracts from the majors, which gave them drilling rights and a share of the oil on certain tracts leased by the majors. Senator Adlai Stevenson's proposed government oil corporation for finding and producing oil on federal offshore land would surely loosen things up and at least give independent refiners and distributors an assured source of supply.

With the old system lagging in output and the states back in the picture stronger than ever, changes could be expected. New ways would have to be devised to procure the oil from the continental shelf in the Atlantic and Pacific that, with due safeguards, could supply something like 10 percent of the nation's needs for a limited period starting in 1980.[77]

7

To the Middle East and Back

The overriding obsession of America's foreign policy after 1945 was its cold war confrontation with "international communism." In Europe, in the Middle East, in Korea, in the Third World, the United States strove endlessly for the containment of what was thought to be an aggressive and subverting force controlled from Moscow. Through two decades, the Truman Doctrine, the Marshall Plan, NATO, SEATO, CENTO, military assistance pacts with 42 countries, and open and secret warfare from Iceland to Vietnam were all varying manifestations of this one dominating doctrine.

It in no way detracts from this judgment that long before America became locked in its cold war with Russia, a succession of government and oil company officials had hammered out a world petroleum policy for the nation, which reached the height of its effectiveness at this same time.

The first part of this policy took note that America was both the foremost producer and foremost consumer of oil in the world; the second part looked both to the future needs of the nation and the peculiar structure of the oil industry, which promotes the integration of operations all the way from the oil well to the filling-station pump. In general outline, this policy was to conserve, at higher prices, oil resources within the continental limits of the United States, while pushing production and development of secure supplies at lower prices abroad.

The policy had its origins in the Wilson administration's close collaboration with the oil industry during and after the first World War and was strongly reinforced under Franklin Roosevelt in and

after the second World War. The United States oiled both these
wars; in the second, it supplied some six-sevenths of all the oil the
victors used plus that needed to keep the domestic economy going.
To protect and supplement the American reserves that had been so
severely drained, however, key government officials encouraged the
oil companies to find and develop other sources abroad.

In the earliest years after the first World War this cooperative
policy entailed the expansion of American oil companies with State
and Commerce Department assistance within the Western Hemisphere. Later it required the State Department to assert on behalf
of American companies, against the entrenched resistance of the
British, the doctrine of the Open Door for American oil companies in
the Middle East.[1] Just as it was becoming clear that the Middle East
possessed the world's biggest oil reserves, American companies gained
big concessions there. During the 1920s, Exxon and Mobil had been
admitted to Iraq as part of a cozy arrangement extracted from the
British. But the dramatic new finds in Saudi Arabia and Kuwait were
made by other companies. On the way from a summit conference at
Teheran in the midst of the war, President Roosevelt made time to
pay a visit to Ibn Saud, king of the oil-rich realm of Saudi Arabia.

Like the rest of the vast pool of Middle East oil, the fabulous
wells of Ibn Saud bordered the desert shores of the Persian Gulf—
and never absent from the minds of U.S. policy makers after the
second World War was a document that came to light when the
German Foreign Office papers were captured in 1945. This was a letter
Soviet Foreign Minister Vyacheslav M. Molotov wrote the Germans
in November 1940:

> The territorial ambitions of the Soviet Union lie south of
> Soviet territory in the direction of the Persian Gulf.[2]

Indeed when the fortunes of war made Russia a belligerent instead
on the side of the Western Allies, Russian forces moved south to
occupy northern Iran in 1941. What amounted to a curtain raiser for
the cold war then took place in 1946. The Western Allies provoked
a big debate in the United Nations over the reluctance of the Russians
to withdraw their troops. On the strength of their still mobilized
might—and by compensations in Eastern Europe that Hitler could
never have conceded—they managed to persuade Stalin to pull his
forces back out of Iran.

This victory won, the big oil companies proceeded to make the
most of it. In cooperation with the State Department, they moved

boldly to fit the enormous oil potential of the Persian Gulf into their world production and marketing system. Like Victorian colonialists dividing up Africa at a European high table, the majors set up an international prorationing system for the new Middle Eastern oil. The four companies that had found such vast quanties of oil in Kuwait and Saudi Arabia came to terms with the three big traditional world marketers of oil to make it a seven-way parlay. Standard of California and Texaco, original partners in the Arabian American Oil Company, cut in Exxon for a 30 percent slice and Mobil for 10 percent of the Saudi output.[3] Gulf and British Petroleum agreed to supply Kuwait oil to Royal Dutch–Shell, the third old-timer, and split the profits down the middle.

These deals, which cost millions, were worth billions. They were struck because California Standard, Texaco, and Gulf now stood to have masses of crude oil—but little in the way of outlets to market it; and Exxon, Mobil, and Shell had less crude oil—but did have extensive marketing facilities built around the world by Rockefeller and Deterding and their successors.

The deals ruled out, or at least limited, the possibility for latecomers to fight their way into these world markets; they consolidated the position of the longer-established companies that took their crude oil. Thus was formed the seven-member cartel: Exxon, Mobil, Shell, British Petroleum, Socal, Texaco, and Gulf. It was not exactly a classical cartel, though the U.S. Department of Justice later attacked it as such. The setup simply made it unnecessary to have a cartel. It was a famous arrangement—granted a world of reasonable peace and order.

Breathtaking changes in the nation's foreign affairs were in the making. The United States was stepping forth as a superpower. American arms would guarantee the peace; emergency American aid would help construct the order. Right after Exxon and Mobil were taken into Aramco, Defense Secretary James A. Forrestal recorded in his diary that Secretary of State George Marshall showed him a memo:

> . . . informing the United States government that Britain
> could no longer be the reservoir of financial-military support
> for Greece and Turkey. Marshall said that it was tantamount
> to British abdication from the Middle East with obvious im-
> plications as to their successor. . . .[4]

Within weeks, President Truman called for $400 million emergency aid for Greece and Turkey to keep the Russians from moving into the eastern Mediterranean. Proclaiming the Truman Doctrine, he pledged the United States to resist "international communism" everywhere. But the first big American move of the cold war took place in the Middle East—and in short order the Sixth Fleet took station in the Mediterranean and the air force flew into bases in Libya, Turkey, and Saudi Arabia, where they could help guard Persian Gulf oil.

But the Truman Doctrine was not enough. Important as the Middle East might be to America's future, it was a secondary interest compared with the preservation of Western Europe, which the British retreat now suggested was weaker and more susceptible to Communist infiltration than the Americans had supposed. Only four months after the Greek-Turkish intervention, the American secretary of state proposed the Marshall Plan.[5]

By identifying Western Europe as the critical area for American support, the Marshall Plan reestablished priorities. But it also reinforced the meaning of the Truman Doctrine for the American position in the Middle East. If the purpose of the Truman Doctrine was to enhance opportunities for American exploitation of the Middle East by denying the area to communism, the Marshall Plan promised to help the war-weakened economies of Western Europe by shipping these countries quantities of commodities and other American exports needed for their reconstruction. One of these commodities was oil.

★

Oil was the link between the Truman Doctrine for the Middle East and the Marshall Plan for Europe.

From the time of the industrial revolution, coal had been the staple of Europe's economy. But war left the Continent prostrate; coal was in calamitously short supply. The nations of Western Europe tried by every means, including subsidy, to get coal out of the ground. In the emergency, America shipped in quantities from across the Atlantic. Still, plants stood idle for lack of coal, and hunger spread across Europe in late 1947 and early 1948.

The trouble with coal, in the cold war for which America now girded, was that it was a labor-intensive industry. The Marshall planners, looking for a way to set Europe back on its feet to hold off the Communists, ran up against the hard fact that the miners who had to produce the coal for recovery in Britain and France belonged to Commuinst-led unions. The same situation was feared in the western zones of occupied Germany. For decades, coal had been the sick industry of Britain; and in France, where De Gaulle had nationalized the industry after the war, Interior Minister Jules Moch felt compelled to send tanks into the fields around Lille in November 1947, to force striking miners back down into the pits. From the moment in July of that year when the Russians walked out of the Marshall Plan conference in Paris, battle was joined. The problem was to overcome resistance by large Communist parties in the West, above all in France and Italy. The fight, as Major General William J. Donovan, the United States wartime intelligence chief, said, was "essentially a labor fight—a fight to gain control of the unions." [6] In the coal fields the Communists held an unassailable position.

While officials in Europe faced this intractable problem, others in Washington were busy looking into ways of opening up the Middle East. Forrestal, the leading business voice in the Truman administration, lunched at this time with the chairman of the Senate Commerce Committee, Republican Owen Brewster of Maine:

> I said that Middle East oil was going to be necessary for this country not merely in wartime but in peacetime because if we are going to make the contribution that it seems we should make to the rest of the world in manufactured goods, we shall probably need very greatly increased supplies of fuel.
>
> Brewster said that he had had a long talk with John D. Rockefeller, Jr. . . . . Europe in the next ten years may shift from a coal to an oil economy, and therefore whoever sits on the valve of Middle East oil may control the destiny of Europe.[7]

The key move in the Middle East, once Ickes's plan for government participation in the development of Saudi oil had been thwarted, was the creation of Aramco. True, the deal went against the Open Door doctrine because it meant that only American companies participated in Aramco's exclusive concession for Saudi Arabia. But more important to officials concerned that the United States was depleting its home reserves, it opened the way for Saudi and Kuwait oil to flow under American direction into European markets.

The $400 million that Exxon and Mobil paid for their shares in Aramco was only part of the deal. The companies also joined to build a pipeline to carry Saudi oil 700 miles across the desert to tankers in the Mediterranean. This was the pipeline that Ickes had wanted the United States government to build. Though the companies now went ahead on their own, they still needed all the help they could get from Washington to buy scarce steel pipe. On September 2, 1947, W. S. S. Rodgers, the Texaco chairman, told Forrestal:

> I personally think that it's worth about five or ten times as much in that line as it is in one of those [domestic American] lines, particularly if we are to go ahead with this Marshall Plan and try to do something in Europe. Because a barrel delivered in the Mediterranean is in a way the same as a barrel delivered here in this seaboard.[8]

Thus the project for the American companies to develop Middle East oil in place of their American oil for marketing in Western Europe began to emerge. Some days later Forrestal, having fought off domestic bidders to clinch the pipe for the Middle East line, noted in his diary that at a cabinet meeting

> I took the position that we should not be shipping a barrel of oil out of the United States to Europe. From 1939 to 1946 oil reserves were up about 60 percent in the world while American discoveries added only about 6 percent to ours—the greatest field of untapped oil in the world is the Middle East.[9]

The trans-Arabian pipeline, called Tapline, was triumphantly completed by 1950. But there was another, equally important link to be filled in the emerging system. Tankers were as crucial as pipelines for the transporting of Middle East oil to help save Europe. The British government built up its own tanker corporation to close the gap. The United States government's contribution, decided at an emergency cabinet session in mid-1947, was to declare one hundred 16,500-ton T2 tankers to be war surplus and clear them for sale to foreigners as well as American citizens. Most of these found their way into the hands of the major oil companies, though not without some hanky-panky. A former congressman from Massachusetts organized a transaction by which a number of well-placed Washingtonians (including former Secretary of State Edward R. Stettinius) invested $5,000 apiece and then sold their surplus tanker to Exxon for $2,500,000. The fast-rising Greek shipowner Aristotle Onassis alone bought twenty T2s—with the aid of an $8 million down payment advanced by the National City Bank. In the light of the Truman Doctrine, Greece was a favored ally, and other Greek entrepreneurs were permitted to acquire tankers for the Middle East lifeline to Europe.[10]

As the Marshall Plan was being hammered out, Forrestal consulted frequently with oilmen and other industrialists. One businessman Forrestal saw at that time was Robert McConnell, an industrialist and engineer who had served in various positions in the war and had just been in Germany. Forrestal's diary notes:

> McConnell came in to see me with a vigorous expression of the thesis that it would be a basic mistake to reactivate the coal industry of the Ruhr. He said that an oil economy would produce greater efficiency at lower cost (and would have various political advantages).[11]

Never did these profitable efficiencies and political advantages loom larger than in the winter of 1948. Every day saw the plight of a Europe dependent on Comunist-controlled coal grow worse. The power of mine union bosses to tie up a nation's economy was demonstrated to Washington's discomfort as United Mine Workers President John L. Lewis called a strike and closed down America's coal industry for the fourth time since the war. The day after discussing the possibilities of oil for energizing Europe's recovery, Forrestal noted the way things were going in the United States. Interior Secretary Krug "reported a 50 percent increase in the use of fuel oils since the war," and Attorney General Tom Clark said demand had outrun supply.[12] In a memorandum to Truman, Forrestal said:

> Without Middle East oil the European Recovery Program has a very slim chance of success. The U.S. simply cannot supply that continent and meet the increasing demands here.[13]

By contrast with the coal of Western Europe, the oil of the Middle East was in abundant supply and could be pumped effortlessly and with little labor to the surface in the almost uninhabited desert areas bordering the Persian Gulf. It could be piped to tankers in the Gulf or in Mediterranean ports. It could then be shipped over sea-lanes safeguarded by the United States Navy and delivered at bargain prices to power plants and factories in Europe. Accordingly, a possible changeover to oil took on new significance as a way to promote European recovery.

Of course, there were obstacles to overcome in working out the system. In the rush to get going, some were hastily papered over.

Domestic American oil interests, like all commodity producers, wanted to get in on the Marshall Plan aid. Spokesmen for Texas interests like Tom Connally, ranking Democrat of the Senate Foreign Relations Committee, protested that the new European Cooperation Administration could pay Gulf of Mexico rather than Persian Gulf prices for oil it purchased. For a time, quantities of independent-produced Texas oil found their way to Europe.

The British demanded that Shell and British Petroleum have their fair share; their government, which held a majority interest in the latter, not only wanted to pay at the lower Persian Gulf prices, but to pay, as it always had, in sterling. There was not much question in 1948, however, of who was calling the tune. The Americans were putting up the entire $13 billion for the Marshall Plan; they could and did say how and where funds were spent. To be sure, as part of the price of admission years earlier to the Middle East producers' cartel, the major American companies had accepted the lower Persian Gulf prices for the modest quantities of oil they then pumped from Saudi Arabia and Bahrein. But when domestic American oil interests and their congressional friends demanded that the ECA buy oil at American prices, which were 40 percent higher, the American majors active in the Middle East went right along with the campaign.

In the sequel, the British kept the larger part of their home market for sterling oil, but in the fall of 1949 Exxon's subsidiary in the United Kingdom, Anglo-American, built a huge refinery at Fawley on the Thames and was soon selling Middle East petroleum for dollars to the ECA for the British market. The American companies, supported by timely testimony by Undersecretary of State Dean Acheson, successfully insisted on dollars for all they sold under the Marshall Plan. In the hue and cry over "American" prices for American oil, the American internationals coolly sold their Persian Gulf oil under the Marshall Plan at Gulf of Mexico prices.[14]

So bold a raid on the American taxpayer placed excessive strain on the cooperation of government and oil companies. After repeated protests, the companies in 1949 lowered their Persian Gulf oil price to ECA from $2.22 a barrel to $1.88. Finally, in 1952, the Department of Justice brought suit against the major oil companies for recovery of $66 million in excessive charges they had collected for their Middle East oil.[15] The oil companies fought a delaying action until the next year, when the Eisenhower administration took office and dropped the criminal suit for a civil one that fizzled out harmlessly five years later. By that time all five U.S. majors had gained a strong place in every Western European market as they helped these countries shift the basis of their economies from coal to oil.

So fundamental a transformation required far longer to accomplish than the Marshall Plan's four years. At the same time pipelines had to be laid, ports constructed, and tankers mobilized, the petroleum industry of Europe itself had to be realigned. Up to the second World War, oil in Europe was still thought most valuable for bunkering warships, and comparatively little refinery capacity had been developed in Europe—less than a tenth of what existed in the United States. Now Marshall aid powered what an English expert has called the "petroleum takeoff" in Europe.[16]

In its first 2½ years, ECA authorized countries receiving Marshall Plan funds to purchase $384 million worth of dollar oil from the Middle East. One consequence was that U.S.-owned production in the Middle East grew much more rapidly than nondollar production. A second was that the Middle East displaced the Western Hemisphere as chief source of Europe's oil. Before the Marshall Plan, less than half of Europe's crude oil came from the Middle East; in ECA's first year, the Middle East's share rose to 66 percent and by 1950 it stood at 85 percent. Thus Europe had to a significant degree become dependent on U.S.-produced Middle East oil.

Not only that, ECA backed loans and grants that permitted American companies to build and expand refineries in Europe—in the fall of 1949, the European Marshall Plan Council programmed a five-fold expansion of refinery capacity.[17] Since ECA at the same time refused to finance European-owned refinery projects that might "reduce market outlets for American-owned oil and thus jeopardize American concessions in foreign lands," the lion's share of this expansion went to American companies.[18] In this way, Standard of California and Texaco were enabled to join Exxon and Mobil in selling their Saudi oil in Europe, and Gulf also gained a position in the European market. In 1950, Caltex, the Standard of California–Texaco marketing subsidiary, opened its first refinery in Rotterdam [19]—supplied from the freshly completed trans-Arabian pipeline.[20] During the Marshall Plan years, refinery capacity in Western Europe nearly tripled.[21] By 1954, no fewer than a hundred new European refineries were completed or commissioned—and by 1970, refinery output in Western Europe exceeded that of the United States.

From the Marshall Plan beginnings, there was an important difference in the way Europe used its oil. In the United States, by reason of the prodigious early development of automobile transport, a very high proportion of refinery capacity had always been allocated

to producing gasoline. In Europe, on the other hand, the great bulk
of the oil was processed as fuel and diesel oil—and used to power
the Continent's industrial plants. Thus, as the Marshall Plan term-
inated amidst the Korean War boom of the early 1950s, a new energy
pattern was already set for Western Europe. Almost overnight the
European "workshop of the world" was back in operation at full
blast, powered by oil rather than coal.[22] By 1956, western Europe was
dependent on the Middle East for 30 percent of its energy; by 1970
—notwithstanding subsidies everywhere to encourage coal mining—
for 55 percent. American companies that year held a 40 percent share
of the French petroleum market; the five international American oil
companies were numbered among the ten largest American corporations; and the largest of them, Exxon, was the No. 1 multinational
corporation, deriving 60 percent of its billion-dollar profits from outside the United States.

The combination of Marshall Plan aid, the phenomenally low
cost of producing Middle East oil, and the decision to base values of
Middle East crude oil on Gulf of Mexico prices served to generate
an enormous cash flow for the five big American companies. In the
15 years after the opening of Tapline, U.S. oil interests took more
wealth out of the Middle East than the British took out of their empire
in the entire nineteenth century.[23] In short order, oil became, as
Benjamin Shwadran wrote a few years later, "the decisive factor in
the recovery of Western Europe and the backbone of the NATO
structure." [24]

The oil-producing countries around the Persian Gulf, though
contributing little labor in the bringing of petroleum to the surface,
were sovereign states holding power over the land from which the
oil was pumped. Demanding greater control over management and use
of their oil or a bigger share in the income it produced, they could
upset the working of an arrangement that depended for its success
on reliable deliveries of oil in Europe on terms assuring attractive
profits to private American companies. Nobody in government worried more about the possibilities of such an upset than Defense Secretary Forrestal, who nervously watched the United States extend diplomatic recognition to an Israel carved out of territories that Saudi
Arabia and all other Persian Gulf states, except possibly Iran, considered unalterably Arab.

No American oilman needed to be reminded of how Mexico in
the 1930s had risen up and expropriated all foreign oil properties
within its borders. Big oil companies had gone to great lengths to
make sure that the Mexican government found no outlet in world

markets for its nationalized oil. But they could not prevent the Mexican government thereafter from providing its own people from the sequestrated wells with all the petroleum they required. In Venezuela, the country that had more or less taken Mexico's place as America's chief source of overseas oil in the Western Hemisphere, the companies thenceforth operated in less high-handed and arbitrary fashion. Not only did they build highways, hospitals, schools, and utilities, but they assumed responsibility for the welfare of their local employees and their families. When a postwar revolution toppled the Venezuelan military dictatorship they were used to dealing with and a radical regime came to office, the companies negotiated with the new government a sweeping revision of their concessions. Under its terms the host country was guaranteed a fifty-fifty split of profits from all crude oil pumped from its soil. This agreement took effect in November 1948.[25]

Though Saudi Arabia harbored no political parties to press bothersome demands for greater control of its oil, it did have a monarch who was in constant need of more money to rule in his absolute style. The Saudis heard about Venezuela's favorable new deal, and asked Aramco's officials for a like fifty-fifty split.[26] The company was scheduled to complete its pipeline to the Mediterranean in 1950 and was only beginning to make the big profits the parent companies expected. The oilmen took their problem to the State Department.

At the helm was Dean Acheson, former partner in the Washington law firm of Covington and Burling, whose founder had represented the oil companies before the committee that wrote the original depletion allowance clause in 1918. Strategically as well as commercially, stakes in the Middle East were tremendous: already a nationalist regime in Iran was pressing the British for control of that country's petroleum, and there was no telling when the Russians might begin to meddle again. For Washington it was essential both that the Communists be kept out and that Middle East oil be kept flowing to the reviving economies of Western Europe.

The outcome was the most explicit application yet of the cooperative policy of the State Department and the oil companies. First step in the plan, the "brainchild" of the Acheson-dominated National Security Council, was to have the Saudis adopt a corporation income tax law. Since Saudi Arabia, one of the world's most fiscally primitive nations, did not even have a budget then, let alone an income tax, Washington sent in lawyers from Wall Street to draft a corporation income tax law—and make sure that the law conformed with the tax credit provisions of the U.S. Internal Revenue code.[27] Under the new law, royalties Aramco paid the king were defined as corporation taxes, and at the urging of Acheson's men at State, the U.S. Treasury Department agreed to this. Then, once the law was on the books, the treasury further ruled that under regulation barring double taxation, Aramco would not be required to pay U.S. corporate income taxes on its Saudi revenues, having already paid taxes to the Saudi Arabian government.[28]

Essential to the deal was a renegotiation of Aramco's royalties, most of which were now called taxes. These were increased to a level equal to half the company's expected profits for the year. The amount of the rise just happened to equal the income taxes the company had been paying to the U.S. Treasury. Thus, by a transfer to the Saudis of a sum that would henceforth have to be made up to the U.S. government by its taxpayers, the progressive fifty-fifty profit-split plan was introduced to the Eastern Hemisphere, and the lord of the world's richest oil pools was bound over to the United States as never before: the Saudi monarchy became outspoken in its anticommunism.

This plan was approved in secret session of the National Security Council and carried out without any request for authorization by Congress. A quarter of a century later, when members of the Senate Foreign Relations Committee unearthed details, the source of the king's added income had become too self-evident for comment. In 1949, the year before the plan was adopted, Aramco paid United States taxes of $50 million; in 1950, the tax tab was only $6 million. Thus in one year there was a drop of $44 million in the federal treasury's income from this source. In 1950, Aramco made over exactly $44 million in added payments to the Saudi Arabian government.[29]

"National security" was the reason given for financing, out of the U.S. Treasury, Aramco's 1950 arrangement with the Saudis. The added compensation to the king should have quieted some of the fears for the continued flow of oil. But the oil-producing countries were not the only Middle Eastern lands possessing power to upset the international system. The nonoil-producing lands of the region also had the capacity to disturb the system by their ownership of land and territorial waters traversed by pipelines and tankers. So long as this was true, the cooperative policy of the State Department and oil companies in the Middle East—producing for the profitable markets of Europe while maintaining the fields as a secure reserve—might be thought insufficiently integrated with overall anti-Communist strategy. If the policy and the system had survived a half dozen years of raging Middle Eastern quarrels—between Arabs and Jews, between Egypt and the British overlord, between the Saudis and their neighbors, between nationalists and colonialists—this was in considerable part due to the extreme caution of Premier Stalin.

So it seemed to that redoubtable Cold Warrior John Foster Dulles when he took office in 1953, made a three-week swing through the Middle East, and set down his conclusions in a policy memorandum. The overriding need, in Dulles's judgment, was to strengthen and extend the containment of communism in the Middle East by extending right across the area a kind of eastward projection of NATO that—joined with SEATO on the eastern end—would form an unbroken wall of containment around communism's southern flank.[30]

At the time, Dulles found the British position "rapidly deteriorating," the "Israeli factor" and American ties to Britain and France "millstones round our neck," and the entire region wavering "between outright neutralism and the desire (but also the fear) of being protected by the West." [31] He concluded that "the Arab states will not, at this time, openly join defensive arrangements with the West." [32] As the preliminary to any anti-Communist pact in the area, the United States must work out some sort of accord with the leaders of Egypt's revolution. For "the delicate role the U.S. has to play in this situation," Dulles said, the old Open Door commercial doctrine for oil would need political supplementing:

> It is of utmost importance that U.S. assistance to the area be somewhat increased and the Point IV concept sharpened as to its application. . . . People are beginning to expect improvement and . . . it is in the U.S. interests to provide small amount of economic development funds in certain states . . . primarily for water development.[33]

By far the most important preliminary to a more aggressively anti-Communist policy in the Middle East, however, was a second action not mentioned in Dulles's memorandum. The one country Dulles had not visited on his Middle East trip was Iran, and with reason. For three years, an ultranationalist regime in Teheran led by Mohammed Mossadegh had been locked in a violent dispute with British Petroleum, the company (then called Anglo-Iranian) that held a monopoly on oil production in Iran. Charging that the company was "not in business, but in looting," the Iranian government, backed by a majority of the Majlis and a 99.5 percent popular vote in a plebiscite, had seized all Anglo-Iranian properties.[34] But the cartel of Middle East oil companies had closed ranks, and Iran could find no buyer for its nationalized oil. By the spring of 1953, frustrated in efforts to find any Western company to do business with, Mossadegh was rumored to be negotiating a big loan from the Russians.

At this point the Americans struck decisively in Iran. In a bold coup, the Central Intelligence Agency, headed by Dulles's brother Allen, sent in guns, radios, trucks, armored cars, funds, and tactical direction to overthrow the intransigent Mossadegh and bring back the shah, who had fled some days before to Europe. As the new premier, the Americans installed Mohammed Zahedi, a policeman with a wartime record of collaboration with the Nazis.[35]

It was a big triumph for Dulles. By a single stroke, two of his most important goals had been accomplished. Iran had been saved for the West, so that it was now possible to construct the anti-Communist wall across the Middle East that was his top objective for the area. This new alliance against the Russians would draw together the "northern tier" countries of the region—Turkey, Iran, Iraq, Pakistan—that bordered directly upon the Soviet Union.[36] Strickly speaking, Iraq had no frontier and was, moreover, an Arab state. But on the crest of the Iran triumph, Dulles agreed at British prompting that Iraq should join. The British, who had bases in Iraq, also joined the Baghdad Pact, as the new lineup was called. But the United States, while sponsoring and financing the whole arrangement, stayed out, in deference to the nationalist sensibilities of Egypt and other states.

The second result of the coup in Iran was to consolidate, in the American way, the system by which Persian Gulf oil flowed to the markets of western Europe. That is to say, the outcome conformed to the cooperative State Department-oil company policy for opening Middle East trade doors. Dulles dispatched a special emissary to Teheran, oilman Herbert Hoover, Jr., who proposed to the government a plan for putting Iranian oil back on the world market. In Hoover's wake followed representatives of the major oil companies to negotiate details of the deal. To pave their way, the Department of Justice, at the request of the National Security Council, gave them immunity from antitrust laws with respect to joint production. National security as Dulles interpreted it—keeping Iran out of the hands of the Communists—was given as the reason for the extraordinary exemption that enabled the American companies to get a foot in the Iranian door.

Thus, in place of the old British monopoly, an international consortium was established. Membership now consisted of eight companies. British Petroleum (as Anglo-Iranian was rebaptized) got a 40 percent share, the five American majors divided up another 40 percent share, and the remaining 20 percent was allocated to Anglo-

Dutch Shell and French Petroleum. On the face of it, the new consortium appeared to be identical with the "international oil cartel" described and denounced in a Federal Trade Commission report only two years before. This embarassing oversight was soon corrected. After the contracts were signed, the Justice Department changed its mind about approving the deal. Responding to pressure from the independent oil companies' lobby in Washington, it abruptly announced that no antitrust waiver would be granted unless the consortium was enlarged to include more American companies. To avoid trouble, the five American majors then met and decided to cede five percent of their share (one percent each). Nine small independent companies, only two of which had had any involvement in the Middle East before, wound up as participants in the Iranian bonanza.[37]

An important part of the new deal specified that the consortium would pay income tax instead of royalties to the Iranians. Thus it could be announced with suitable fanfare that the fifty-fifty system that gave half the oil companies' earnings to the host government had spread to Iran. The arrangement was fine for the Iranians and the oil companies. For the U.S. Treasury, it meant losing thenceforth something like $200 million in tax revenues every year from American oil companies operating in the Middle East. But the monarchs of the Persian Gulf, the resurrected shah, as well as the rulers of the deserts to the south, were bound over to the United States as never before: all of them became outspoken in their anticommunism. As Iranian oil again flowed freely to Europe, the U.S. having cracked the British monopoly in Iran, the Iranian government was tied securely to the Western camp.[38]

★

It was an exemplary achievement of businesslike Republican management—decisive and economical. A single timely exercise of American power realigned the stance of Iran and thus of the whole Middle East, all without extravagant expenditure of foreign aid funds on programs far less likely to sway nations to the United States' side.

After the success in Iran, Dulles sought, but with less urgency, accord with Egypt's new nationalist regime. The United States pressed the British to hasten their pullout from their big base at Suez and canvassed a variety of schemes for meeting social needs in the Middle East. Eugene Black of the International Bank came up with the strongest idea, to which both the American and British governments

gave their backing. This was to build a billion-dollar high dam at
Aswan on the Nile and add two million acres to Egypt's six million
acres of cultivated land. After the turn in Iran, however, many in
Washington, including Herbert Hoover, Jr., then undersecretary of
state, viewed the plan as a waste of money. Dulles himself had carefully specified that a "small amount" be provided. So when President
Nasser turned around and bought arms from the Communists, Dulles
told the Egyptian ambassador that the dam deal was off.[39]

The Americans expected that Nasser might hit back by getting
the Russians to finance the dam. Instead, the last British soldier having
just sailed away from his country, the Egyptian chieftain seized the
Suez Canal. This infuriated its British and French owners, whose
prestige, fortune, trade routes, and vital oil supplies were all bound
up in the Suez "lifeline." They launched a military invasion to retake
the canal. The United States wanted no part of such a nakedly
colonialist expedition, which would alienate the Arabs and might
turn the whole Third World toward communism. Washington compelled its allies to stop, and the Russians moved in to halt the in-
vaders. The Suez fiasco brought the end of the British and French
empires and, before long, French withdrawal from the NATO alliance.[40] Within a year, the Baghdad Pact was shattered by a nationalist revolution in Iraq. Soviet Russia did finally undertake the
construction of the Aswan dam, and broke past Dulles's anti-Communist barricade into the Middle East.

The international oil system that had been built for the cold
war proved somewhat more durable and survived Dulles and his
regional anti-Communist pacts. By dint of dextrous adjustments, the
system even learned to live without the Suez "lifeline." Up to the time
the Egyptians blocked it during the 1956 invasion, 70 percent of
Europe's oil had flowed through the Suez Canal. But by the time of
the 1967 Arab-Israel war, when the canal was blocked again, the
system had so far freed itself from dependence on Suez that most
of the Persian Gulf oil was traveling around Africa to market. The
industry built 250,000-ton tankers of such fantastic efficiency that it
became cheaper to transport the oil the long way around.[41]

These were the big oil companies' golden years. Their best-kept
secret still was how little it cost to produce a barrel of Persian Gulf
oil.[42] Not until decades later did it come out that Aramco's cost of production in its huge Ghawar field in Saudi Arabia was no more than

five cents a barrel. Economies were phenomenal: in a land bigger than Texas and Alaska put together, Aramco was the sole concessionaire and had to deal with but one landlord, the king; it put down only 164 wells—and one of them produced more than half of what all the wells in Texas produced. The oil lay close to the surface and close by the sea: in fully mechanized operations, it was piped from wells to shore and through offshore pipelines directly into giant tankers. It was a superbly efficient operation, a triumph of automated technology. Iran, and the smaller oil-producing states of the Gulf were almost equally overflowing: their production costs were perhaps twice as high—ten cents a barrel. Almost anywhere else in the world, and certainly in Texas, the cost was at least a dollar a barrel. Even with royalties and tax payments added on, Persian Gulf oil could be landed in Europe and Japan for far less than prevailing world prices, which were always based on the more expensively produced U.S. oil. Besides the shah, the king, and the sheikhs, the biggest oil companies of Britain, Holland, and France, as well as Greek and Indian tanker magnates, were cut in on the system. The consumer countries of Western Europe and Japan also got their goodly share, since the international oil companies held profits down on the refining and marketing end of their operations— Department of Commerce figures for 1972 [43] showed company profits in Western Europe only $117 million, or 1.7 percent of investment— and these countries found the price attractive enough to buy more oil year after year.

In one of his more oracular interviews, André Malraux, noted man of letters and friend of De Gaulle, once asserted that the United States was "the first country in history to have become the most powerful in the world without having sought it." [44] Nonimperialist as even Malraux might believe the United States to be, colonial history records no grander government-industry design than the system by which American companies produced and sold Persian Gulf oil for the reconstructed nations of Europe and Japan under the nuclear umbrella of Washington's cold war power.

But in economic as in political and social life, nothing stands still. In the words of the social theorist Thomas Mathiesen,[45] whatever is finished is "finished," and the inexorable process of change eventually came to the system built on American oil hegemony.

The beginning of this process may well date from the summer of

1960, when world demand for oil fell off. Russian petroleum flooded the European market, the emergency shortage created by the Suez invasion faded, and oil began to be shipped from nearby sources in Algeria and Libya. At that time, without informing any of the Middle East producing countries, Exxon cut the posted price of its Persian Gulf oil by fourteen cents a barrel.[46] It was presumably the prudently profit-motivated action of a very big commercial enterprise, though some in the Middle East suggested it was also calculated to make a revolutionary regime in Baghdad think twice about revising company concessions in Iraq.

The posted price had long been a peculiarity of the oil business. As previously noted, oil, unlike wheat, copper, and other basic commodities, was not traded on the open market. Instead, the big companies announced "posted prices," the most important of which was that posted at Gulf of Mexico ports. Even the posted prices tended to be mostly mythical because, whether in Texas or Saudi Arabia, subsidiaries like Aramco sold most of their oil to parents like Exxon at much lower prices. The Persian Gulf posted price began to acquire significance when the Saudis won their fifty-fifty deal with Aramco. The host country's revenues thereafter depended on this price, and governments began to fix their expenditures accordingly.

That was the problem. The Exxon action caught the Saudi government just as it was embarking on some costly but necessary development projects. At a single stroke, the country's income was slashed by $30 million for the year 1960–61. Outraged, Sheikh Abdullah Tariki, Saudi minister of petroleum resources, rushed to Baghdad to proclaim solidarity with Iraq against pressures from the West. Other Middle East oil ministers flew into the Iraqi capital, where they were joined by Juan Perez Alfonso, minister of mines and hydrocarbons in the Venezuelan government. He urged the Arabs and Iranians to band together, but it was the angry Saudi who led the move to form an official association.

Tariki and the others may not have thought at once to apply against the oil companies the "divide and rule" tactics that the companies had used effectively against their countries in Mossadegh's day. But they vowed to stick together against any offers of special advantage that might tempt any individual country to break ranks. Thus in September 1960, *they* formed a cartel—the Organization of Petroleum Exporting Countries. Iran, Iraq, Kuwait, and Saudi Arabia joined with Venezuela to press for a larger share of the oil income. In due course, they won the adherence of eleven more oil-producing states to OPEC.[47]

The formation of OPEC was not taken seriously by the majors. President Kennedy, apprised of the development by their lawyer, John J. McCloy, was alarmed mostly that the Russians might exploit the development. He sent McCloy to his brother Robert; McCloy explained to the attorney general that the companies might need the by-your-leave of the antitrust division at some point to act jointly to deal with OPEC.[48] (Kennedy saw no problem.) Actually, the world surplus of oil continued as OPEC members failed to agree on a formula for prorationing to limit output. Venezuela, the largest producer at the time, wanted past levels of production used as a base; Iran favored population; and Saudi Arabia and Kuwait argued that production should be calculated on the basis of proved reserves. On the other side, more American companies entered the international field because of the rising costs of finding and producing oil in the United States, the attractiveness of foreign tax credits on top of depletion allowance benefits, and the seemingly endless demand of Europe and Japan for oil. So rich were the Middle East stakes that some of the recent arrivals, like Continental, soon became majors; and some of the new producing states, like Libya, handed out exploration rights to fifty concessionaires instead of just one. J. Paul Getty, who had wangled rights to Saudi Arabia's half of the narrow neutral zone between that country and Kuwait, was discovered by *Fortune* in 1968 to be the world's richest man.[49]

In these years, the traditionally close cooperation between the oil companies and the State Department fell slack. The prevailing industry attitude seemed to be that the system had been built, and cartel members would run it their way. "We don't recognize this so-called OPEC," said the president of Aramco. "Our dealings are with Saudi Arabia, not with outsiders."[50] Pursuing their own style of diplomacy, the companies never restored the 1960 cutback in the posted price. They conceded a few small technical changes in agreements that added slightly to revenues of individual producing countries.

This overall complacency was only slightly upset by the 1967 Arab-Israeli war, which closed Tapline as well as the Suez Canal for one hundred days. The international oil system bore these buffets without breaking stride. Japanese and German shipyards were turning out supertankers that could ply the oceans without having to run the Middle East gauntlet. And oil companies now had a much handier source of supply to bring into full production: oil of an excellent light grade had been found in Libya, just across the Mediterranean from the chief markets for Middle East oil. Under the rule of a friendly king and the protection of a huge American air base at Wheelus field, Libya quickly built up output to fill the supply lines to over-flowing.[51] Overnight, Europe began taking up to 30 percent of its needs from Libya's much more accessible new fields.

Then came the big change.

In 1969, the pro-Western king of Libya was overthrown in an army coup. Its leader was 27-year-old Colonel Muammar al Qaddafi, anti-Western and anti-Communist—a fanatic Arab nationalist. Under his regime, the United States was forced out of its base almost as un-ceremoniously as the British had been expelled from Suez thirteen years before. Sensing Europe's dependence on Libya's oil, Qaddafi demanded an increase in payments. The oil companies offered trifling changes. Furious, Qaddafi ordered cutbacks in production. "We must show we are masters here," he declared.[52]

One major oil company officer, sure as ever that nobody else could sell Libya's oil, urged Washington to dare Libya to go ahead and nationalize its industry.[53] He did not doubt that the major com-panies, with their spare capacity here and there around the world, would simply step up output elsewhere. That was what they had done when Mossadegh nationalized Iran's oil in 1951—though it is not recorded that Washington issued any dares then or ever.

This, however, was not a time for throwing out challenges. By 1970, Europe and Japan were buying four times more oil than they had a decade earlier, and the world petroleum supply was consider-ably tighter.[54] And the major oil companies were no longer the only firms in the field. In contrast with Iran, where one major had pro-duced all the oil, there were many companies in Libya to deal with. Of the fifty-odd tracts given out, the Seven Sisters, to be sure, held the biggest and best. But other tracts had gone to independent companies, and some of them had made big finds.

And so, when the majors girded for a showdown, Qaddafi did not even call them in. Instead, his government called in the repre-sentative of only one company, Occidental Petroleum. Of all the independents operating in Libya, Occidental was the most vulnerable to a government ultimatum—it had no other source of supply. It could not afford a cutback, much less a shutdown, in production. When the Libyans moved in troops and ordered an immediate 30 percent slash in Occidental's output, the company caved in and accepted a compromise that not only cracked the united oil-company front, but altered the fifty-fifty profit split, which had prevailed in the Middle East for two decades: Occidental agreed to a 30 percent rise in the posted price of its oil and a boost in Libya's share of crude oil from 50 to 58 percent.[55] An incident in the Syrian Desert helped speed the

Libyan outcome. In broad daylight, a bulldozer "accidentally" broke the Tapline, cutting off the daily flow of 500,000 barrels of Saudi oil to the Mediterranean; the Syrian government stonily refused to allow its repair. At this point, the other Libyan oil producers, led by the seven majors, fell into line and accepted Qaddafi's demands. They had been outsmarted, and to the youthful strong man of Libya went by far the greatest victory ever won by an oil-producing country.

What Qaddafi had won, the shah of Iran and the king of Saudi Arabia had to have. The Persian Gulf countries successfully insisted that their share of profits be raised. That brought more leapfrogging: the Libyans insisted on fresh increases to "balance" the new Persian Gulf prices. In the oil capitals of the West there was an apprehensive stir. The market price of Persian Gulf crude, after staying near $1.80 a barrel for more than a decade, was jarred loose from its moorings by OPEC waves. OPEC now loomed as a well-financed, well-coordinated group capable of united and flexible action. When OPEC members, including Libya, merged their demands in 1970, the companies regrouped and sought help. Both the U.S. State and Justice Departments were drawn in as McCloy sought and got an antitrust division letter clearing the way for 26 companies to bargain as one with OPEC.[56]

It is tempting to see in what followed the same pattern that took shape when organized labor emerged as a force in America after the second World War. Once the unions had forced recognition and then industrywide bargaining, it soon became the rule for the two sides to wind up their annual confrontations in a kind of big business-big labor partnership as the unions won wage rises and industry passed them on to the public in the form of higher prices. The February 1971 agreements at Teheran [57] were indeed the most expensive ever made by the companies with producing countries, and the $3 billion rise in oil states' revenues for 1971 (plus benefits promising a further $2 billion yearly through 1975) was accompanied by upward price adjustments for Europe and Japan. And there is no question but that in the next three years both the oil-producing states and the international oil companies enormously increased their incomes by the series of price rises that the Teheran agreements touched off.

The significance of Teheran is not to be described, however, in the accommodating style of American slug-and-hug collective bargaining. At the shah of Iran's insistence, the companies negotiated these terms with the Persian Gulf states on the premise that they would keep the system going at least until 1975. But even before the signatures on the paper were dry, both sides could see that the balance was swinging OPEC's way. Already, the contest was turning into a struggle for control of the oil. Qaddafi, the Libyan radical, made no bones about it. His way was to use troops to enforce production cuts and thus force up prices. The more conservative Persian Gulf states shied away from such practices. They seemed more disposed to boosting their revenues by boosting their output—which left control, and prices, still in company hands.[58]

Then even this divergence within OPEC narrowed. Under the leadership of Saudi Oil Minister Ahmed Zaki Yamani, OPEC in July 1971 demanded that member states share in ownership of the companies operating on their soil. It mattered little that where Qaddafi had screeched "nationalization," Yamani now murmured "participation." [59] The OPEC states could afford to pay for what they took over, and it turned out that their "participation" meant taking a share of the oil for themselves to sell. The companies saw the handwriting on the wall and accepted the reality of having to surrender exclusive control over oil production in the Middle East. Thus, late in 1972, OPEC won its battle: the companies gave the Persian Gulf states a 25 percent interest in existing concessions, with rights to buy back their share in oil, and a timetable by which their share would rise to a controlling 51 percent by 1983.

On the face of it, such terms might suggest that the big oil companies had taken the big producing countries in as partners and that the international system had been prolonged for no less than a decade. But the dynamics of the situation dictated otherwise. OPEC members were fully aware of the companies' success in raising world prices, and they knew all about the emerging energy problems of the United States.

At no time since the grand international system had been devised in the early cold war years had the United States ever taken more than a mere 6 percent of the Middle East's oil. Never had the country drawn upon what Harold Ickes had once been pleased to call its "reserves" in Saudi Arabia. Now, however, what Ickes and Forrestal had foreseen thirty years before had happened: with its prodigious appetite, America had consumed its petroleum resources faster than it located new ones, and neither domestic supplies nor imports from nearby Canada and Venezuela sufficed for its burgeoning demand.

By 1973, the sources that American companies had opened up around the globe were strained to meet the needs of Japan, Europe, and the rest of the world. It was time, the industry agreed, to lift the import controls it had once fought for and to bring oil into the United States from the only place where there was oil enough—the

Middle East.[60] And the only place in the Middle East with the spare capacity equal to the large amounts America would need at expected levels of demand was Saudi Arabia.

At such a conjuncture, Ickes and Forrestal might have sat up in their graves. What they would have seen and heard, however, would have been enough to drop them back at once. The world had changed, and nobody talked about U.S. "reserves" in Saudi Arabia any more. The National Oil Company of Saudi Arabia held a 25 percent share of Aramco and was demanding more. The Tapline had been sabotaged and closed a dozen times in six years.[61] In protest at U.S. backing for Israel in its 1967 quarrel with its Arab neighbors, the Saudi government had taken the step of shutting down oil shipments.

Now, when America for the first time stood in need of substantial amounts of Saudi oil [62] and Aramco approached Saudi Oil Minister Yamani with a program for expanding Saudi output from five to eight million barrels a day, the subject of American support for Israel came up again. Yamani said that without a more evenhanded American policy in the Middle East, there could be no increase in Saudi output. In May, King Faisal himself repeated the warning. But Aramco went ahead with plans to boost output and build a new port and installations to receive the biggest supertankers. By late 1973, the United States was getting 18 percent of its oil imports from the Middle East. United States dependence on Middle East oil was becoming a reality.

At the same time, OPEC was building up for a showdown. The shah took over from the consortium in Iran, Libya sold nationalized oil in Europe, and at $3.07 a barrel the posted price of Persian Gulf oil was fast overtaking the world price. Citing the high prices the companies were getting in Europe and Japan, OPEC demanded that the companies revise the Teheran agreements. Then the Arab-Israeli war of 1973 exploded. At once OPEC unilaterally announced that $5.12 was the new price of Persian Gulf light oil. When Washington then air-lifted emergency arms aid to Israel, the Saudis embargoed all oil shipments to the United States. In January, by an OPEC accord reached in October, the Persian Gulf posted price was raised to $11.65 a barrel.

At the end of 1974, Saudi Arabia, having already assumed 50 percent control of Aramco, announced plans to take over 100 percent ownership of the company. The National Oil Company of Saudi Arabia would thereby become sole possessor of oil produced in the country—and Aramco's founders mere commercial mercenaries marching the Saudi product to market.[63]

Thus the international system built to save Europe ceased to exist, though the oil continued, after the political interruptions of 1973–74, to flow through more or less the same channels to more or less the same markets, with the United States receiving some 16 percent of its imports from Saudi Arabian wells. Whether, how long, and at what price it would continue to do so, however, was up to OPEC. Controlling the production, OPEC now controlled the system, and Saudi Arabia controlled OPEC.

8
Natural Gas— the By-product Bonanza

So rich and so vast is the kingdom of oil that a mere subdivision within it, dealing with a petroleum by-product, has become the nation's fifth largest industry. This realm within a realm is the natural gas business.

Like oil itself, natural gas is a fugacious substance and lends itself to the fluidized operations of twentieth-century commercial science. It can be piped and pumped and moved around literally for thousands of miles, quickly, easily, and economically. In manufacturing, natural gas flows into and inside the plant as both raw material and fuel. The cycle of free-flowing materials is completed when the gas or oil is delivered through pipes and hoses to the ultimate customer. Such elegance and efficiency of handling are practically unmatched in modern technology: both oil and natural gas flow unseen and untouched by human hands from the time they leave the ground until delivered to the ultimate consumer in his car or home. He scarcely needs to lift more than a finger to benefit by the energy he has bought. He needs only, by touching accelerator or thermostat, set fire to it.

Natural gas seems to millions the perfect fuel: clean, cheap, and requiring no storage. Half the prodigious growth in energy use that has taken place in this country since 1945 has come from natural gas—for electric power, for industry, for home heating. Natural gas now heats forty-one million homes—53 percent of our total.

Natural gas is found and produced in the same places where oil is found. It has the same origins, millions of years back, in decayed vegetation and animal life that, buried by earth movements, either decomposed or were distilled by heat into these twin substances.

Both gas and oil accumulated deep in the earth's crust, in porous rock formations, the natural gas commonly appearing as a cap over a pool of oil or else dissolved in the oil. A lid of impervious rock overlies and entraps this accumulation, and not until someone drills a well through can it be determined whether the formation contains predominantly oil or natural gas (or nothing at all).

Thus it is that natural gas is produced by the same people who bring you Exxon and Texaco and Phillips 76 and Shell. On the whole, one does not go prospecting solely and simply to find natural gas. Even after the great postwar gas bonanza, oil remains more valuable, commands a higher price, and generates proportionately more energy as measured in British thermal units. This is not to suggest that discovery of a gas field is not economically interesting to petroleum operators; it is. But if natural gas had to be sought and exploited by and for itself, with oil completely out of the picture, costs might have precluded the industry's development.

The potentialities of natural gas as a fuel have been known for the century and a quarter that Americans have cooked and lit their homes with gas made from coal. In 1825, four years after natural gas was brought to the surface through a 27-foot well in Fredonia, New York, Lafayette noted that the town was lit by this gas and that his meals in the local hotel were prepared over a gas flame.[1] Fredonia Gas and Light Co. was incorporated as America's first natural gas company in 1858. Joe Guffey and Jack Galey, the two Pennsylvania prospectors who brought in the first oil fields in Kansas, Oklahoma, and Texas, later piped natural gas from nearby wells to heat some two hundred homes in Tulsa. This was done in many places in the West and Southwest in early days. Accidents, of course, happened, especially because the natural gas was often odorless. In Casper, Wyoming, Mrs. John Opsahl, a grocer's wife, was blown to her death when she struck a match unaware that gas from a leaking main had already filled her kitchen. Later, utilities mixed natural gas with manufactured, or "town" gas, which had the telltale smell.

But so long as natural gas was found far from large cities and no way existed to pipe it great distances, its commercial possibilities remained small. Even when the gas sometimes contained a fair amount of what oilmen called "light gasoline," or naphtha, there was little demand for it. Indeed, until around 1920 it was something of a calamity when wildcatters drilled for oil and found natural gas instead. So it was set afire like a giant torch right at the wellsite. When wells gushed out oil under great gas pressure, operators effected a rough separation of oil from gas on the spot, and the gas was flared, or burned off. It was dangerous stuff to have around. Rich oil fields in Texas and Oklahoma glowed like furnaces in the night because of the endless burning of gas from one year to the next. In the 1970s, these eerie orange fires of burning natural gas still lit the skies over the Persian Gulf, where no nearby markets existed as yet for its consumption.

Like oil, gas was thought of as a fuel. To this day, the industry that burns most natural gas is the petroleum industry itself. From the very beginning, oil refining required comparatively large amounts of energy, and thrifty management had sound reason to use its own product as far as possible in the manufacturing process. Rockefeller burned heavy oil in his Cleveland refineries. In the Southwest, boilers, furnaces, and retorts were first heated by heavy oil. But by 1926, the giant refineries that Exxon and Mobil built on the Gulf Coast used natural gas for fuel.[2] Both oil and gas were cheap, especially for the big oil companies.

Long before John Diebold coined the word in 1953, the petroleum industry knew and practiced automation. Oil was the first energy-intensive business. The companies employed their cheap energy to reduce human labor to a minimum in their manufacturing operations—to such an extent that the United Oil Workers of America, launched in the depression with the same high hopes as the United Steel Workers, United Auto Workers, and other big CIO industrial unions, never achieved comparable mass membership and bargaining clout.[3] Though the petroleum industry turned out products valued at $22 billion in 1944, the number of workers employed was only one-seventh of those employed in the automobile industry, with production worth roughly the same. Only 1,800 worked in a huge refinery like Exxon's Bayonne operation, where in one day a handful of men turning valves could process enough gasoline to keep 100,000 cars running for a month. Even the men who maintained the plant were not Exxon employees, but workers hired by an outside firm that contracted to perform this service for the company. The same was true in the oil fields, where contractors drilled Exxon's wells and paid the roughnecks and roustabouts. Most oil industry employees were found in distributing and marketing, fields that did not lend themselves to mass organizing. The United Oil Workers languished: membership was 100,000 in 1945; 170,000, thirty years later. The absence of labor's countervailing power meant that the big oil companies gained a kind of ascendancy in their industry beyond anything attained by similar giants in autos, steel, rubber. It was a lot easier, for instance, for the oil companies than for other big outfits to go overseas after 1950. More fully automated, they were not obliged like the others to reckon with a powerful organized labor movement in their plants.

The second important use of natural gas is as raw material in manufacturing. Basically, natural gas is the simplest combination of two elements, hydrogen and carbon, which is called methane. Although the gas contains other, more complex hydrocarbons, methane is the primary ingredient; and this has been fundamental to another and fabulous modern development—the petrochemical industry.[4]

At or near the gas fields of Texas and Louisiana there sprang up a whole complex of manufacturing plants. They owed their existence to the catalytic cracking process that had been devised by the petroleum industry to make gasoline out of petroleum and petroleum products when it became evident that the simple process of distilling would never yield enough gasoline for the needs of the automobile age. Manipulating the hydrogen and carbon molecules on a vast scale as they did, petroleum chemists soon found themselves synthesizing much more than fuels. The gases turned out to be particularly useful building blocks for transmutations. They could be used in certain forms as solvents, and as pure chemicals they were valuable in industrial processes. After further treatment, they emerged as structural materials such as films and fibers, plastics, adhesives, and rubbery products.

By 1964, more than two hundred firms made chemicals from petroleum feedstocks, chiefly from natural gas. Their output accounted for a third of the volume and two-thirds of the value of the 10,000 products made by the U.S. chemical industry. In textiles, such synthetic fibers as dacron, orlon, and nylon had gone far toward replacing wool and cotton. In the burgeoning packaging field, plastics had wrought tremendous changes and were used in innumerable applications in both sheet and molded container form. In building materials, fiber glass panels and plastic-coated aluminum siding came into widespread use. The synthetic rubbers in automobile tires were a petrochemical as were additives for gasoline and lubricating oils. Paints, lacquers, insecticides, refrigerants, aerosol propellants, drugs, anesthetics, toiletries, detergents, and fertilizers were also synthesized from natural gas. By 1972, petrochemicals were a $20 billion industry and Texas's biggest business. All told, petrochemicals consumed about 5 percent of all natural gas produced.

There is a third use for natural gas. Like oil, natural gas as it emerges from the ground is not always of uniform quality. Some has more of the lighter carbon molecules found in gasoline. Some is so richly laced with such molecules that it can be drawn off at the wellhead as wet natural gas, or natural gasoline. With a little processing, it can be sold as automobile fuel. Processing natural gasoline became a minor industry in Texas.

It is also possible, by cooling natural gas to extremely low temperatures, to liquefy it.[5] This reduces its bulk to one six-hundredth of its former state, and eases problems of transporting it long distances and storing it. In 1944 liquefied natural gas received a setback when tanks in which it was stored near the Cleveland waterfront blew up with the loss of 131 lives. Later, French researchers claimed to have overcome the difficulty and in 1970 built two double-hulled tankers to transport LNG, as it was called, at temperatures of $-250°$ Fahrenheit from Algerian gas fields. Brought to Europe and the United States, the stuff was regasified and sold at considerably higher prices for distribution in urban markets.

Synthetic gasoline was something else. After the first World War, Germany faced an energy crisis. It possessed only small amounts of native crude oil, and the country's leaders were alarmed by pessimistic forecasts of dwindling world supplies. They faced fuel shortages of the sort that had spelled military defeat in 1918 and an exhausting drain on the nation's limited foreign exchange.

In these circumstances Germany's largest chemical firm, I. G. Farben, responded resourcefully. Having already pioneered in synthetic drugs and invested in equipment for producing synthetic ammonia and methanol, the company decided to make the heaviest research and development investment in its history in a process for making synthetic gasoline from coal, which was abundant in Germany. Chief of I. G. Farben at the time was Carl Bosch, who had gained the Nobel Prize for synthesizing ammonia.

Making the most of their war-gained experience in using high pressures at high temperatures to handle nitrogen fixation, Bosch and Farben chemists solved the problems of making synthetic gasoline and synthetic rubber. They developed a process called hydrogenation. Their idea was to think of coal as merely a very heavy oil—and to convert it into a light oil by forcing hydrogen into it. With this brute-force chemistry, they found a way to make huge quantities of hydrogen and to drive it, under terrific pressure at high temperature and in the presence of a suitable catalyst, into coal products. This was getting gasoline out of a coal mine. When the chief of research for Exxon, then called Standard Oil Company of New Jersey, was shown the process, he reported, "This matter is the most important which has ever faced the company since the dissolution [decree of 1911]. This means absolutely the independence of Europe in the matter of gasoline supply." [6]

Standard was so impressed that it entered into a cartel with I. G. Farben. Farben agreed to market its new product only in Germany; Standard won assurance of its undiminished share of the German oil market—and Farben obtained by the patent exchange Standard's proprietary formula for ethyl gasoline that enabled the Germans to raise their synthetic gasoline to 100-octane performance. By the same deal, any American tire manufacturer which wanted I. G. Farben's synthetic rubber process, known as buna, would have to go through Standard Oil to get it.

Though hugely expensive, the hydrogenation process overcame Germany's oil shortage. When the Nazis won power in 1933, they struck a deal with I. G. Farben. For their diplomatic and military purposes, the price of the synthetic gasoline was no object if they could only have an assured supply. Too impatient to wait for Farben's chemists to make hydrogenation economic, they froze the process at its existing stage and built twelve high-cost plants that supplied some 85 percent of Germany's aviation gasoline in the second World War.

After the war, American occupiers rushed to grab German missile and nuclear scientists. They paid less heed to the synthetic plants. After all, the West then had plenty of natural gas and oil. I. G. Farben's hydrogenation struck them as impossibly high-cost. While Farben went back to making dyes, drugs, and plastics, a single Frankfurt firm called Lurgi kept alive the high art of German fuel chemistry. As early as 1933, Lurgi had hit upon a process for gasifying brown coal under high pressures and temperatures.[7] Presumably too small to be concerned about, Lurgi slowly improved its process, which came to be used after the war in some 60 small European plants for fortifying manufactured gas. In the late 1960s, an American company, El Paso Natural Gas, acquired rights. By including a methanation stage to bring the product up to U.S. pipeline quality, it hoped to generate a modest 25,000 cubic feet of synthetic gas per day from strip-mined New Mexico coal by 1976.

★

Pipelines are central to the American petroleum industry. They gather the crude oil, funnel it to the refineries, and then carry the oil products to docks, terminals, and delivery points in almost every county of the United States. Even before the Supreme Court broke

up the Standard Oil trust, Congress passed a law in 1904 making pipelines public utilities subject to regulation by the Interstate Commerce
Commission, and senators still demand from time to time that the
companies be stripped of their petroleum pipelines to reduce the
danger of monopoly.

With a technological breakthrough in the 1930s, pipelines became, if possible, even more important to the natural gas industry.
Development of welded pipe capable of withstanding high pressures
made possible the transmission of natural gas as efficiently as oil
through long-distance pipelines. Safety standards were devised, especially for pumping stations in populated areas. Within the decade,
natural gas flowed to such cities as St. Louis, Chicago, and Minne-
apolis.

Unlike crude oil, natural gas did not flow to refineries for processing. Instead, it went directly to the big-city gas companies, which at
first mixed it with their manufactured gas and pumped it through
their mains to consumers in homes, commercial establishments, and
factories. It seemed to work especially well for cooking and heating
water. Praising its efficiency in warming the baby's bottle, *Parents'*
magazine explained, "It may take a split second longer for the burner
to light, and the flame will look softer, more velvety and be somewhat
longer than your present flame."

That was how natural gas entered eastern cities and suburbs,
where something like one-tenth of all householders had already taken
to heating their homes with oil and where natural gas made its first
entry around 1950 as men from the utilities swarmed into kitchens to
bore pilot holes one one-hundredth of an inch bigger to suit the
bigger jet of natural gas. Arriving earlier in the Middle West, natural
gas accomplished far more sweeping changes in the home.

The American male of the 1930s began his winter morning by
stumbling out of bed into the cold, still dark and trotting down to
the basement, where coal dust was thick and fumes rolled up to
choke him as he struggled to get the fire lit in the furnace again.
Throughout the country, eleven of twelve householders still shoveled
coal.

It was not that most of them lacked for money; in 1937, Americans
dished out $400 million for radios—three times what they spent for
heating appliances. One in three already had electric refrigerators.
But neither oil nor gas could compete with coal when it came to costs.
In the days when gas companies offered only manufactured gas, they
gave a special rate for house heating, something like a third of what
they charged for cooking gas. There were few takers. Service charges

were also a cost factor, though some small gas companies sometimes took over servicing without charge as a goodwill measure.

But what the thermostat did for the householder was to save in other ways. People told with envy of the man who started his automatic burner on the first cool day of fall and never poked a finger into the old furnace room all winter. Such a man no longer had a truck chuting its delivery into the coal bin and filling the air with grime just as his wife tried to launder bed sheets in another part of the basement. The thermostat ended the spine-numbing ordeal of dragging heaped ashcans down the icy path to be hauled away in the back alley. With gas heat, there was no more turning out at six in the morning to stoke up, no more 58-degree temperatures at breakfast, 80 degrees at noon, 60 degrees at dinner.

Oil was better, but a lot of the old furnaces converted to oil leaked at the seams and smelled up the house. Gas, on the other hand, was the perfect fuel—it could be switched on or off as easily as electricity, and it was so clean that families began converting basement rooms to playrooms after converting their burners. Natural gas cost 15 percent less than manufactured gas, but somewhat more than coal or oil. After the second World War, coal and oil rose in price. Natural gas, its price held down by federal regulation, became a bargain. People began converting their furnaces, and new homes came with gas heat. Utilities promoted this product heavily with "Gas Heats Best" as a slogan.

By the Natural Gas Act of 1938, Congress placed the natural gas industry under supervision of the Federal Power Commission, the agency set up by the New Deal to regulate power companies. As the FPC took jurisdiction over the gas pipelines, a new kind of industry evolved. The major oil companies that produced most of the country's oil continued to produce, as a by-product, most of the natural gas. But a new group of companies, which before long became giant corporations and household names too, built and operated the natural gas pipelines.

Transmission was their business, and good business it was. Once they had their lines laid—to the Middle West, to the Pacific Coast, and up "pipeline alley" after the second World War to the population centers of the Northeast—they could buy up huge quantities of natural gas for five cents or ten cents per thousand cubic feet in Texas and sell it for twenty-five or thirty cents in New Jersey. Then they could sign long-term (20-year) contracts to sell it to big-city utilities and other industries that had formerly used manufactured gas or coal. Making enormous profits, applying for huge sums for construction, the pipeliners were the darlings of Wall Street. Their underground network grew bigger in size than the U.S. railroad system. And like the railroads of old, they fought for entry into rich markets like Los Angeles. They schemed for control of key feeder lines like Pacific Northwest's link between Canada's fields and the San Francisco and Portland areas.[8] Officers of El Paso Natural Gas, with assets of $1.5 billion, heard with dismay that their telephones had been bugged during merger talks. Tennessee Gas Transmission, biggest of all with assets of $2.4 billion, was charged with bribing Utah politicians to expedite a franchise application.

As volume and profits ballooned, producers as well as distributors began to champ at government fetters. In Washington no lobby was more formidable than the oil lobby—or as it was beginning to be called, the oil and gas lobby. Its friends held the most powerful positions. In 1952, President Eisenhower, a son of Texas by way of Abilene, took office with notable backing from oil interests and with oilmen numbered among his most intimate associates. Presiding over the House of Representatives was Speaker Sam Rayburn of Texas, who had sold Franklin Roosevelt on the industry's pet scheme for self-regulated oil production and allowed nobody on the Ways and Means Committee who was not "sound" on the depletion allowance. A rising force in the Senate was Lyndon B. Johnson of Texas, who made sure that new Senate Finance Committee members took a positive view of oil's special tax benefits.

These men could be counted upon to hold the fort for oil. But none of them, for all their power, were politicians directly involved in the oil business. That distinction was reserved for Robert S. Kerr, who entered the Senate as a Democrat from Oklahoma in 1946. You had to go back to the turn of the century, when the Senate was known as the Millionaires' Club and was filled with figures like Guggenheim (copper) of Colorado, Warren (wool) of Wyoming, Du Pont (explosives) of Delaware, and Elkins (coal) of West Virginia, to find a match for Bob Kerr.

Often called " the uncrowned king of the Senate," [9] Oklahoma's Kerr was founder and principal stockholder of Kerr-McGee, one of the twenty major gas and oil corporations of America. Born in a log cabin in the old Indian Territory, he was the richest man in the United States Senate. One of his first acts upon entering Congress was to introduce a bill to free natural gas producers from federal regulation. He himself stood to profit substantially if, as expected, prices rose when the bill passed. But neither then nor in the rest of his 16 years in Washington did Bob Kerr ever apologize for advancing his own interests in gas and oil. He said, "I represent the farmers of Oklahoma, though I have no large farm interests. I represent the oil business in Oklahoma, because it is Oklahoma's second largest business, And I am in the oil business. I represent the financial interests of Oklahoma, and I am interested in them and they know that and that is the reason they elect me." [10]

A fellow senator said, "Whether you like Bob Kerr or hate his guts, you have to admire him for knowing how to get what he wants." [11] As a young sprout, Kerr stated his ambitions, "A family, to make a million dollars and to be Governor of Oklahoma—in that order." [12] He overachieved. While still studying law in a country judge's office, he married. That was after he had gone to France as an artillery lieutenant in the first World War and spent two years at Oklahoma Baptist University. Having absorbed some oldstyle Western Populist ideas from his father, a supporter of William Jennings Bryan, he liked to recite his father's advice against going out for collage football, "I would rather have written Bryan's Cross of Gold speech to the Democratic Convention of 1896 than have won every athletic contest staged on this earth since Cain and Abel ran their first footrace on the banks of the Euphrates River." [13]

As a small-town lawyer in Enid, Kerr (who was state American Legion commander) got into oil drilling with his brother-in-law on a borrowed shoestring. When oil was discovered in Oklahoma City, he moved to the state capital. Derricks gushed oil in churchyards, along railroad tracks, on the Capitol lawn. But residential areas east of the capital were barred to drilling by ordinance. Frank Phillips, the hard-bitten ex-barber who bossed Phillips Petroleum, sent his treasurer to ask Kerr if anything could be done about some leases he had acquired in the restricted area. Next day Kerr told Phillips he thought that more people would gain than lose by lifting the restriction and that they could probably carry a popular vote opening up the residential neighborhood to drilling. When Kerr agreed to lead the campaign, Phillips asked how much he would charge. Kerr said, "Nothing. But I'd like to do the drilling for you if you win." [14]

They won. Kerr not only obtained contracts to drill on Oklahoma City front yards, but soon was drilling for Phillips in west Texas and the Texas Panhandle. The jobs were worth well above Kerr's target million dollars. In the Texas deals, Phillips, taking oil from the wells, let Kerr have production rights for the natural gas. At the time the gas brought no more than half a cent per thousand cubic feet, but later the price rose and Kerr made a tidy profit. In 1936, Kerr took Phillips's chief geologist, Dale McGee, as his partner. Kerr-McGee, which rapidly became one of the biggest oil-drilling companies in the world, soon branched into all phases of oil and gas production.

Kerr's foray into electioneering also paid off in politics. He managed statewide campaigns, raised money for the Democrats, became Democratic national committeeman for Oklahoma. Then in 1942 he stood for governor and won. Big, rangy, and loud, he was a spellbinder; in 1944, he keynoted the Democratic Convention that nominated Roosevelt for a fourth term. As governor, Kerr wangled interstate support for flood control of the Arkansas River, a project he later expanded into one of the biggest pieces of pork-barrelry of modern times. *Land, Wood and Water* was the title of a book he wrote about it. He loved the Oklahoma plains; and with the help of $1.5 billion in federal funds, the muddy Red River was made navigable for 516 miles from the Mississippi to a point near the Poteau, Oklahoma, ranch, where Kerr kept 4,000 head of Angus cattle and entertained eleven grandchildren in a 356-foot-long ranch house.

In 1948, Kerr ran for the Senate against former Governor Roy Turner. It was a race between two oil millionaires. The state spending limit being $3,000 for senatorial campaigns, Kerr's reported outlays totaled $2,675; Turner's, slightly less. Actually, through dummy committees and other fictions, Kerr poured out more than $1,000,000 (to Turner's $500,000), and Turner was probably right in blaming his narrow defeat on last minute "deluges of money." [15]

In the Senate, Kerr carried himself with the absolute confidence that stemmed from strong Baptist beliefs and self-made wealth. He became a mover and shaker at once. Jovial and courteous, he was a booming and colloquial speaker, a tough and eye-gouging debater, an aggressive infighter who shot from the hip when he heard a rustling in the brush. He was also a hard cloakroom and conference trader. His bill to exempt natural gas producers from FPC regulation gained support in both houses. Ed Pauley, still the influential California oil politician, let it be known that he was in Kerr's camp. When the bill met resistance in the House, Sam Rayburn himself made a speech on the floor to help it through, 176 to 174. But in the Senate, Paul Douglas, Democrat of Illinois, stirred up an inconvenient row on behalf of big-city consumers, whose gas prices were about to be inflated. Though the bill passed, Truman vetoed it, quoting Douglas's arguments.

What Kerr called Truman's "throatcutting" wrecked the senator's hopes of being nominated for president in 1952. He applied himself to the Senate, where he was increasingly respected and feared, and to Kerr-McGee, which had acquired 25 percent of the nation's uranium lands and was on its way to becoming the Atomic Energy Commission's chief supplier. He worked to free offshore oil from federal control, with the boast, "I think most people would agree we [Kerr-McGee] were pioneers in the offshore drilling business." [16] Then the Supreme Court handed down its bombshell 1954 ruling: prices of interstate natural gas were subject to FPC control at the wellhead.

Kerr at once joined Lyndon Johnson in backing a bill to exempt producers from such federal regulations—in essence, it was Kerr's 1951 bill again. Once again, Rayburn swung the House into line. But just when the bill was ready for passage, Francis Case, Republican of South Dakota, stood up dramatically in the Senate to say that a Nebraska lawyer representing the Superior Oil Co. of Texas had tried to bribe him to vote for it. The fellow, Case said, had offered him a $2,500 contribution to his 1956 campaign fund in return for a favorable vote. There was a stir in Washington. Newspapers blazoned headlines. Though Congress passed the bill, President Eisenhower was embarrassed. On the point of standing for reelection, he could not countenance such crudity. He condemned the industry's intervention as "arrogant . . . defiance of acceptable standards of propriety." [17] To Kerr's disgust, he vetoed the natural gas bill.

Shortly afterward, Kerr remarked in the Senate that Eisenhower could not comprehend the nation's fiscal policies "because one cannot do that without brains, and he does not have them." [18] Loyal but hapless, Senator Homer Capehart, Republican of Indiana, rose to protest. Next day Kerr answered Capehart with a deft revision of the *Congressional Record*: "I do not say that the President has no brains at all. I reserve that broad and sweeping accusation for some of my cherished colleagues in this body." [19]

When Lyndon Johnson moved up to the vice-presidency in 1960, he left a vacuum in effective Senate leadership. In such vacuums power goes to those who seek it. Kerr sought it, and even though he held no leadership title, he soon became known as the senator-to-see to get things done. He was, said Rayburn, the "kind of a man who would charge hell with a bucket of water and think he could put it out." [20] Kerr-McGee became the Atomic Energy Commission's number one contractor. "We probably have more in dollars and cents in Ambrosia [N.M.] uranium than all the gold was worth that came out of California and Alaska," boasted Kerr.[21] Yet thanks to the depletion allowance, his company paid no U.S. taxes in 1958, and data later placed in the *Congressional Record* by Senator Douglas suggested that Kerr paid virtually none. Oklahoma also did well. After Kerr headed both the Senate space and public works committees, his state wound up with 10 percent of all federal works projects.

When oilmen sought support for restricting foreign oil imports in 1958, Lyndon Johnson and Kerr drafted an amendment to the Trade Extension Act that led directly to President Eisenhower's proclamation imposing quotas on oil brought in from overseas. Seen in retrospect, this was a turning point for the world's leading oil-producing nation. For an industry that had never resorted to tariff protection, the call for limiting imports was a tellingly defensive move. The reason stated for the new policy was the need to protect the "national security" against an overdependence on foreign oil.

Despite his Baptist faith, Kerr was ruthless in legislative horse-trading. A Kennedy adviser said it was "useless to request help from Kerr unless you were prepared to offer something in return, and if you needed a lot of help ultimately you would pay through the nose." [22] In 1962, Kerr saw to it that the Kennedy administration's medical aid bill was cut to ribbons. Later that year, JFK wanted the Trade Expansion bill passed. Kerr personally piloted the bill through—but only after the administration accepted a "little arrangement," whereby the executive modified oil quotas to cut imports still further and shelved plans to lower the depletion allowance.

Those were Kerr's last oil and gas deals. He died of a heart attack on New Year's Day, 1963.

By then, the natural gas industry was booming. As early as 1947, one observer estimated that natural gas was on its way to displacing 50 million tons of coal each year, or about one-twelfth of that industry's annual production. By the late 1950s all the mining machinery introduced underground and all the giant shovels brought in to strip-mine the Appalachian coalfields could not stem the rush to substitute natural gas for coal. Not only power plants but factories converted to the new wonder fuel. Within the natural gas industry there was the same headlong rush to profit amid confusion about government policies that took place after the Supreme Court split up Standard Oil at the moment the automobile boomed demand for its product.

The issue after the Supreme Court decision of 1954 was essentially the same as that after the Court's decree of 1911—namely, how much government regulation there was going to be. The 1911 verdict was the crowning act in a long struggle waged in the courts by the Roosevelt and Taft administrations. In 1954, the Supreme Court acted because the executive and legislative branches had reached an impasse over how to administer the Natural Gas Act. There was no intention of reshaping business competition as in the Standard Oil decree of 1911.

For the losing side in 1954, the big producing companies' lawyer argued, "They don't believe they are a public utility. They believe they should be permitted to conduct a gas business like they conduct their oil business." [23] On the government side, the pipeliners and their big industrial customers had a special interest in seeing that natural gas producers were not free to raise prices. But this was not so evident at the time. Broader issues were in the forefront. The sudden importance of the natural gas industry was making all concerned with economic stability, President Eisenhower included, more sensitive to its national impact. Prices in an industry whose product now entered millions of small homes were very closely tied to the cost of living. There was also growing concern that so valuable, so exhaustible, and so widely used an energy resource be husbanded for the common good. Thus it was that Associate Justice Sherman Minton invoked the general welfare clause to ratify and expand the powers of the Federal Power Commission to regulate the price of natural gas at the wellhead—that is, to keep it down.

This was more authority than Eisenhower's FPC expected or wanted—and certainly more than it knew what to do with. Caught unprepared, the commission reacted reflexively. It froze natural gas prices as of the date of the Court's decision, forbade all further deliveries without its approval, and began a company-by-company review of rate schedules for the 4,000 assorted operators, large and small, that sold gas for shipment in interstate pipelines. For several years, while waiting to see if Congress would undo the Supreme Court's ruling, the commissioners haggled over definition of the "just and reasonable price" specified. When it became clear that the ruling would stand, the commissioners decided to regulate wellhead gas rates the same way pipeline and other public utility rates are regulated—by setting them just high enough for a company to earn enough to attract new capital.

The commission then found that regulating utilities and regulating gas producers were two different things. A utility is granted a franchise or area monopoly in return for supplying that area with service, and the regulators in turn can compel it to provide the service. But gas producers in the field could not be franchised, because they rarely if ever had an area monopoly (although Phillips had come fairly close to it in the early Texas Panhandle gas fields). The FPC could not force them to drill a well, produce gas from wells they had drilled, or, unless it was produced offshore on federal property, to sell the gas they produced in interstate commerce. More important, gas producers, unlike electric utilities or even gas pipelines, had no uniform cost-and-profit pattern. Oil and gas were often joint products, pumped from the same field and frequently the same well, and it was impossible—or at least the gas producers, who were also oil producers and feared federal regulation of their oil business too, said it was impossible—to allocate the costs with any precision. Costs seemed to vary widely from one producer to the next and from one field to another.

The FPC's company-by-company policy was doomed from the beginning. In the face of a pileup of two thousand unsettled cases it was abandoned in 1961. Taking office as President Kennedy's FPC chairman, Joseph Swidler, a New Dealer who had distinguished himself as a TVA administrator, initiated an "area pricing" policy. It attempted to average the costs to producers in each of six large regions of natural gas production within the nation, establishing a pricing system for each. Swidler's approach cleared up the backlog in short order. It also brought hundreds of settlements, many involving price rollbacks. The new ceiling prices, disregarding individual producer's costs, established average prices for each of the areas. These remained at 1962 levels, and that was the rub. While the low-ceiling policy certainly made good on President Kennedy's promise to assure homeowners a cheap supply of gas for their furnaces and kitchens, it also opened the door wide for industrial users to devour natural gas at giveaway prices.

As a result, the drive to free natural gas from federal regulation let up for a while. After all, though the producers liked Washington's "meddling" no better than before, their oil did not command very high prices then; and they could not complain too much when selling vast quantities of a commodity they had formerly flared off as useless. For their part, the pipeliners prospered—delivering the stuff at FPC-set rates that assured them at least 12 percent profit. By the time natural gas was consumed in all 48 contiguous states, furthermore, increasing numbers in Congress believed that their constituents would benefit by regulated prices. For, above all, it was the consumers, industrial even more than residential, who made a good thing out of the Supreme Court's decision. Between 1950 and 1957, as the pipelines were completed, consumption rose by 10 percent each year; between 1957 and 1962, as the system was consolidated, home use of natural gas rose 5.7 percent and industrial use 4.8 percent annually.

After that came still another surge—in the years between 1962 and 1968 when prices rose not at all and American industry gorged on cheap natural gas.[24]

Neither then nor later was there any such thing as a national energy policy, nor any notion then that the country had need of one. Certainly, the Federal Power Commission was not charged with seeing to any balanced use of various energy resources, and it lacked inclination even to keep check on how much of the natural gas supply the nation was using up. Under the system the Court ordered and under the bargain-basement prices the commission set, the nation's energy binge turned into a natural gas binge.

Through the rush to gas in the 1960s, whole regions (southern California) and whole industries (cement) shifted to buying gas for factory fuel. Industrial use between 1962 and 1968 rose faster (4.6 percent annually) then home use (2.7 percent) each year. Half of all natural gas produced went to industrial plants, two-thirds of it as boiler fuel; and 18 percent went to electric utilities, almost all as boiler fuel.[25] The surge was particularly headlong in California, where Pacific Gas and Electric controlled the pipeline company formed to bring in Canadian gas and dictated allocations to the industrial sector, including its own power plants. By 1968, a third of all natural gas used in industry was burned on the West Coast, mainly California.

It was price that caused industries and electric utilities to make the fuel switch. But another inducement to burn natural gas arose late in the 1960s, when many communities became concerned about the quality of the air in their cities. And of fossil fuels, natural gas polluted the atmosphere far less than either coal or oil. In January 1964, the Board of Supervisors of Los Angeles County banned the burning of high-sulfur fuels, with the result that all industrial fuel consumed in the area thenceforth was natural gas. Obviously, atmospheric pollution was a big pro' lem in Los Angeles, as in a number of other large cities. The Clean Air Act of 1965, the first national victory for the fast-growing environmental movement, meant that between 1965 and 1972, almost 400 utilities switched their boilers from coal; and many of them began burning natural gas. In such cities as Chicago and New York, utilities like Commonwealth Edison and Consolidated Edison were able not only to save money, but to score points with environmentalist critics.[26]

A hole in the nation's regulatory fences widened the flood of natural gas. That which was produced and sold within the same state had never been subject to federal regulation; gas producers who sold locally could ask whatever prices they could get. Producers were, of course, glad to sell all the natural gas they could in these "free" markets. Though it usually cost more, intrastate gas, as it was called, was still a great bargain and in plentiful supply. Almost all natural gas produced in Ohio, Kentucky, and Illinois was sold directly to local industries. In Texas and Louisiana, the top gas-producing states, utilities burned nothing but intrastate gas under their boilers. Corporations, attracted by the abundant and assured supplies of cheap energy, built plants in Texas that burned intrastate gas. The petrochemical industry, using natural gas for both fuel and raw materials, grew to great size in the Southwest. Half of the 43.5 percent increase in industrial consumption of natural gas that took place between 1962 and 1968 was the result of intrastate sales. By 1971, 40 percent of all natural gas produced was sold outside the framework of federal regulation as intrastate gas. In that year, 90 percent of all gas produced from new wells was sold as intrastate gas, almost all of it to power plants and industries rather than for household consumption.[27]

Uncontrolled and unmonitored as it was, this consumption could lead to but one outcome: the natural gas shortage of 1973–74. A few industry spokesmen had warned of impending danger. But nobody said that the 1954 Supreme Court ruling had made natural gas too attractive to the wrong users. Only when gas companies began curtailing service to customers and refusing to accept new accounts in 22 states were government and industry spokesmen alike willing to say that natural gas had been widely misused and overused in industry and by utilities. Reflecting the changing priorities, Lee White, chairman of the FPC from 1966 to 1969, said, "It's a national scandal when a utility uses gas as a boiler fuel." [28] Then Frank Ikard, president of the American Petroleum Institute, said that "setting an unrealistic price" for gas "encouraged the [uneconomic] use of gas. It was not the kind of decision that would do anything but have the disastrous result of discouraging the development of new supplies." [29]

Developing new supplies was an industry function, of course, and it was the industry's pitch that the nation had been caught short because the price had been kept too low to lure producers into going out and finding more natural gas. That pitch presumed two things: first, that there really was a shortage, and second, that if prices had been higher, producers would really have gone out and ransacked the continental United States for supplies in a significantly different way.

The industry had been providing the figures on production and reserves, and these looked pretty good right up to 1968. You had to take the industry's word for it because through one hundred years and two wars in which national survival had depended upon an assured flow of oil, the United States government had somehow never started keeping tabs on supplies. The industry's figures were particularly hard to interpret with respect to reserves. When reserves were reported falling in 1968, some FPC officials characterized the warnings as industry's pressure tactics for higher prices. The next year a cabinet task force headed by Treasury Secretary George Shultz, taking its statistics as usual from the oil companies, reached conclusions about national self-sufficiency displeasing to industry leaders. Professor Philip Areeda of Harvard Law School, who served as the task force's staff director, said, "One high [company] official told me he regretted having given us the optimistic-pessimistic data as distinct from the pessimistic-pessimistic data. In other words he had drawersful of data. . . ." [30] In 1973, James S. Halverson, chief of the Federal Trade Commission's economic section, told a Senate committee there had been "serious underreporting of reserves" by natural gas producers.[31]

Beyond dispute was the fact that between 1956 and 1971 the number of natural gas wells in the United States dropped by half, and exploratory drilling fell off by 50 percent. In 1958, 930 wells were completed; a decade later, only 429. Companies came to a belated recognition of exploration costs, which put a damper on such operations. Although the chances of finding gas at deeper levels might be three times as great, drilling at such depths was also three to ten times costlier. From the late 1950s the drilling industry—Senator Kerr's money-maker—was caught in a cost squeeze. By 1968 one authority spoke of the "death agony of the drilling contractors." [32] Between 1957 and 1963 at least 450 drilling firms dropped out of business. Some seven or eight hundred survived, but the number of drilling rigs in the United States fell from 2,400 to 1,800 by 1974.

One reason for the drop was the fact that no big oil field had been discovered in the continental United States since the mid-1950s. It was growing hard, even with the fancy techniques of pumping water and gas underground to force out more oil by what were called secondary-recovery methods, to bring in as much new oil every year as was taken out.

With natural gas it was still harder; oilmen could not say, "We'll drill here for gas, there for oil"; most drilling was for both. The companies talked about how nearly impossible it was to measure the allocation of costs. But there was a way—by measuring each of the products in terms of heat content—British thermal units. A BTU is defined as the amount of heat necessary to raise the temperature of one pound of water by one degree Fahrenheit. Since gas and oil are both mixtures of hydrocarbons, they can readily be measured in BTUs. One barrel of petroleum liquid contains between five and six million BTUs, and 1,000 cubic feet of natural gas contains about a million BTUs. Between five and six times as much of joint costs were, therefore, assigned to a barrel of oil as to a thousand cubic feet of natural gas.

Oil mixed with gas in other ways. Since gas helped keep up pressure in an oil field, the longer a producer could postpone taking out gas, the more oil he would get out of it. Such a consideration led in turn to the political heart of the matter. Though natural gas was regulated on a cost basis, oil was not. Corporation accountants preferred, therefore, to say their company's efforts had been directed to looking for gas, statements that the FPC had good reason to question.

As the thrust for oil in the United States lost its dynamic, a diminishing proportion of the gas produced came from oil wells. By 1973 perhaps 25 percent of the gas came from oil wells, the rest from wells that produced only gas.[33] Yet, if natural gas were still basically a by-product of the multinational oil giants, gas production inside the United States was bound to suffer by the oil industry's decision to shift the bulk of its investment overseas during these years. What domestic efforts the industry made at exploration and development after the 1950s were offshore—and offshore work went very slowly.[34] The California continental shelf, which proved to be narrow, produced oil, but little natural gas. The Gulf Coast, on the other hand, offered extensive opportunities for exploration as far out as 100 to 150 miles. But offshore prospecting was such an expensive game that only the giants could play—and delay seemed the name of their game. Legal tangles, technical troubles, the heavy cost of underwater drilling slowed them. They clubbed together to bid for leases. They cut back on exploration. They made committee decisions. So deliberate was their deepwater progress that *Newsweek* called it "sedate." Gas was less profitable to exploit than oil, and even less so while regulation limited what they could get for it.

Though the majors found oil, what they found the most of was natural gas. After Exxon's Square 1 field at Grand Isle, Louisiana began producing oil at a profit, the companies stopped capping their gas holes, laid pipes from shore, and began sending the gas to market. The first wells drilled offshore were on state territory and hence not subject to federal supervision. But the bulk of Gulf natural gas—ironically, for those who had fought so hard to pass the tidelands bill and avert federal control—was found beyond the three-mile limit off Louisiana. There the federal government held title, and FPC price-setting authority prevailed. The oil companies began signing long-term contracts for delivering the gas to interstate pipeliners, and by 1972 no less than 15.8 percent of the natural gas marketed in interstate commerce and 10 percent of all natural gas consumed in the United States flowed from offshore wells. Even more than with oil, the future of United States natural gas lay offshore.[35] Given the economics of the petroleum industry, this was bad news for gas users.

If one takes into account industrial gorging on natural gas on the one side and the producers' diehard resistance to federal price controls on the other, it was inevitable that the energy crisis of the 1970s cropped up first as a natural gas shortage. By 1969, when output of natural gas rose only 2.5 percent, pipeline companies and utilities already felt the pinch. They continued to supply homeowners, but began limiting new accounts. Prevented from installing gas heat in new houses, New Jersey developers equipped them with electric heating and raised prices from $500 to $750 to cover the added expense. Gas companies also began curtailing service to industrial customers. Contracts with industries, besides delivering gas for about 50 percent less than householders paid, provided that service could be interrupted or shut off in hours of peak use. Now service was cut for days at a time. In 1970, Pittsburgh Plate Glass's glass division plants were cut 25 times. A Michigan beet sugar processing company that switched to natural gas in 1969 found itself shut off four days that year and ten days the next year and the following year was told that it would be shut off all winter. Some factories in these straits fell back on oil, but not all. In 1972, when many midwestern factories shut down, sales of natural gas to industry ended their breakneck rise and tumbled back 12 percent. Some schools also closed. In Paola, Kansas, the local natural gas company chose to stop servicing the town's elementary school for three weeks; on the last day of school before Christmas vacation, the temperature in the classrooms dropped to 42 degrees.

In the 1973–74 energy crunch, President Nixon called for cutbacks across the board. It was not possible to restrict natural gas supplies to homeowners because pressure in the pipeline had to be maintained or shut off, so that the householder either got to use what he wanted or got nothing. But according to industry estimates, residential users voluntarily lowered house temperatures and cut their consumption of natural gas by 4.2 percent. Industry users were asked to use 25 percent less fuel, and according to the American Gas Association, factories also used 4.2 percent less in 1973.[36]

Although the nation went through the 1973–74 winter without

adopting an overall program for balanced energy use, there was new awareness of the dangers of overusing so irreplaceable a resource as natural gas. "Until recently," admitted Joe B. Browder of the San Francisco Environmental Policy Center, "all of us were approaching the problem from the point of view of what was gumming up the environment, not of energy flows." [37] Now the Environmental Protection Agency, which had pressured utilities and industries to shift from coal to meet its pure-air requirements, went back to such companies as Consolidated Edison to urge them to switch from natural gas to oil. Scarcity of gas and the reordering of environmental priorities combined to shift 70 utilities away from natural gas by the end of 1970.[38]

The basic Nixon administration policy, with gas as with oil, was to cope with the shortage through rationing by price. This, of course, was what the producers, who had contributed $5 million to Nixon's 1972 reelection fund, had pushed for all along. Most economists also urged that letting gas prices float free would quickly bring supply back in line with demand, on the one hand rising to end the "free ride" enjoyed by industry users for two decades, and on the other offering inducements to producers to look for new sources of supply. But members of Congress were in no mood, after oil prices and profits skied, to give the same companies another windfall in natural gas. For the opposition Democrats, Senator Adlai Stevenson, Jr., of Illinois said, "The industry claims that present regulations are unworkable. The consumers consider total deregulation unthinkable." [39]

In these circumstances, John F. Nassikas, the New Hampshire lawyer who became Nixon's FPC chairman in 1969, worked to encourage exploration for new sources by putting higher ceilings on newly discovered gas. A kind of two-tier pricing system seemed to be taking shape in 1972 as the commission widened its definition of new gas to include most of that produced in southern Louisiana. In 1975, the commission set a new national ceiling price of 52 cents on all new gas and on all other gas covered by long-term contracts as these contracts expired.

The average three-bedroom house uses about 185,000 cubic feet of natural gas for a year's cooking and heating, and for nearly two decades following the 1954 Court decision the American householder paid about $185, or one dollar per thousand cubic feet, for this supply. New York City paid $1.88, mainly because it cost so much more to pipe its utilities, electricity as well as gas, under metropolitan streets. Of this price 20 cents went to the producer in the field, 22 cents to the pipeline for transport from Texas, and the remainder went to the distributor, Consolidated Edison. The impact on mass-consumer prices of rises granted by the FPC to producers still would be cushioned by the large quantities of natural gas committed under long-standing contracts for delivery at much lower prices. But prices were on the way up. In gas, as in oil, the era of cheap energy had ended.[40] Never again would there be natural gas to burn without limit. In the summer of 1975, appreciably more Americans cooled their living spaces with energy generated without resort to natural gas, and the steel industry went back to stoking its furnaces with coal, not gas. Even the fabrication of articles from natural gas showed signs of diminishing as shoppers turned away from Corfam, DDT, and certain kinds of detergents. Though oil remained enthroned, there was even a rustle of older royalty as in summer temperatures many Americans rediscovered garments made of a quaint old, nonsynthetic fiber called cotton.

PART THREE

Downstream

9
End of the Oil Ride

From the founding of Jamestown on, the history of the United States has been the story of growth. The most influential textbook of our history, by Samuel Eliot Morison and Henry Commager, bears the title *Growth of the American Republic*.[1] It was always the manifest destiny of the dynamic American people to expand across their empty continent, and their unquestioned conviction as they won their way West was that they must lay hands freely upon its riches to do so. For by the authority of their Puritan Bible, man was lord of the nature he subdued. Americans could do with nature what they pleased. They were justified in the exploitation of its bounty. In the freebooting exercise of such beliefs, they leveled its seemingly endless forests, gouged out its seemingly bottomless mineral mountains, and drained its seemingly limitless underseas of oil. Going on to triumph in two great twentieth-century wars, they proceeded to add to their prosperity by expanding overseas for yet more economic growth. American military-industrial power, founded ultimately upon energy derived from the nation's stocks of oil, spread-eagled the world.

Three-quarters of the way through the twentieth century, the age of petroleum is approaching its end. The bountiful American earth has long ceased to gush oil in quantities unmatched anywhere else on earth. Domestic output of both oil and natural gas are falling, and the gross national product, sacred indicator of growth, has been declining. Expansion of the national economy continues to be sought because neither government nor private enterprise knows any other way to maintain employment and profits. But the rate of "growth" (inflation mocks its reality) is only sustained—and the insatiable appetite of Americans for petroleum appeased—by increasing imports of foreign oil. For a superpower, as experience has now taught, this presents grave problems. Can America be held for ransom by oil? Can it continue to live by compulsive growth when being browbeaten, blackmailed, and perhaps bankrupted by Arab sheikhs are the consequences? Can it tolerate being asked by that new monopolist and old-time client of the CIA, the shah of Iran, "Why should I let you waste my oil?" [2] These are questions, many Americans might say, that a great nation like theirs ought not to be asked, let alone expected to answer. Yet when after years of divisive Asian war, racial conflict, and generational strife, the very sinews of United States power fall subject to foreign control, the institutions and leadership of the nation begin to come under question. Rich and prosperous though the country is, the monetary system hemorrhages dollars, and the domestic economy is racked by double-digit inflation. Under the stress of such forces, the national will itself is sapped by self-doubts.

Back of the pervasive malaise and the anxiety that seem to gnaw at us in our growth-oriented and high-consumption society in the 1970s are new and unsettling recognitions. Among these none could be more unhinging than the rising sense that, just possibly, mankind is pushing at the limits of the capacity of the world we live in. America, the land of plenty, is having to learn to live in an increasingly energy-short—and possibly commodity-short—world.

The point at which we began to be open to such profoundly un-American thoughts may well have been, ironically, the moment of our greatest technological triumph: when astronauts in the summer of 1969 first walked in space. Then television enabled us all, while marveling at the sight of Neil Armstrong stepping across the moon, to behold over his shoulder the world we inhabit. We saw, as Armstrong exclaimed, that it was beautiful. It was blue, not green, cloud-shrouded—and not really very big at all. It was, as 300 million viewers saw in a flash, finite. This tremendous perception—like the realization in Columbus's time that the earth was round—changed forever the way we mortals looked at our planet and ourselves. We saw ourselves as sojourners on a spaceship of limited size and limited facilities.

So transforming an insight takes a lot of getting used to, especially for a nation that had subdued its continent and its world and had at that moment planted a first foot in space. That same year, for example, the energy crisis was slipping up on an America unaware. "In 1969, when I came to Washington," Henry Kissinger has since remarked, "I remember a study on the energy problem which proceeded from the assumption that there would always be an energy surplus. It wasn't conceivable that there would be a shortage of energy." [3] Everybody knew how oil shortages had been disproved in the 1920s, again in the late 1930s, and roundly refuted once more after the second World War.

But now James Akins, the State Department's leading oil expert, could announce, "This time the wolf is here." [4] And Professor Kenneth Boulding could publish completely revised assumptions about how America must manage its resources. The principles of the wide-open economy of the past, said Boulding,[5] were those of a "cowboy economy"—reckless and exploitative and prodigal. The closed economy of the future, he suggested, must be a "spaceship economy"—in which the earth had become a single spaceship, without unlimited reservoirs of anything, either for extraction or pollution. In the spaceman economy, he said, success would be measured not by high productivity or gross national product, but by the state of the earth's limited capital stock (including, of course, people). The voice of ecological economics was heard in the land: Congress adopted such conservation measures as the Clean Air Act of 1970. And alongside the president's Council of Economic Advisers, set up in 1946 to help direct the nation's economic growth, was added a Council on Environmental Quality to make sure that conservation was considered in whatever was done.

In the Great Depression of the 1930s, the capitalist countries had to face the problem of unemployment. They met it by programming economic growth, and so vast and untrammeled was the growth that it carried through the greatest of all wars and the longest of all booms. In the postwar years economic growth eased social tensions as the multiplying national wealth provided jobs and higher incomes for increasing labor forces. In the Great Inflation of the 1970s, the United States and other developed countries had to face the problem created by such an overextended expansion. Committed to economic growth, we prolonged our prosperity by continuing to expand overseas. But an ever-increasing inflation was the price. The underlying industrial structure was geared to the lavish use of oil and natural gas that at home grew steadily scarcer. Trying to achieve full employment simply by increasing total monetary demand under these conditions only aggravated the problem of inflation and sent real standards of living into frightening decline. Citizens' discontent intensified, and world monetary and trade dislocations worsened. The cost of living rose in

1974 more steeply than in any year since 1946. The 1974 United States trade deficit of $3 billion, surpassed only by that of 1972, was entirely due to having to send $17 billion overseas to pay the drastically increased price for imported oil. America thus approached the time when it could no longer avoid facing the deeper problem created by the excess of growth: how to adjust to life in an increasingly energy-short world. The United States could not live by growth—yet could not live without it.

Things were mixed up. Americans had been spending too much, going too fast, living too high; and the bills were now coming in from the credit card companies. Though debt in the United States now stood at $2½ trillion, people kept hoping against hope that the extraordinary period of growth experienced since 1945 could somehow continue. Unready to acknowledge the threat of world depression and more war in the Middle East, everybody was looking for painless solutions and hoping to get back to where we were before, with cheap gasoline and 96 fancy models to choose from.

But there was not going to be any going back.

A high standard of living (if not quite 96 models to choose from) may be attained by a combination of any two of three basic factors: capital, manpower, and the minerals-energy complex of resources.[6] Socialism hands over control of resources to labor, the so-called dictatorship of the proletariat. Long ago, the United States, and most Western countries, becoming modern societies by substituting energy and material resources for human and animal labor, took the capitalist way. By applying ever greater amounts of capital to the exploitation of nonrenewable energy and material resources in industry and agriculture, the United States achieved unparalleled affluence for its individual citizens. As the system worked out in competition with socialism, not only the owners of capital but also labor, the subordinated element in the triad, benefited. The worker, his productivity being high, was well paid. Being paid well, he was also important—integral to the scheme, in fact—as a consumer.

This system was at first based entirely upon local resources. Such resources quickly became depleted or inadequate. A wider search started, culminating in the quarter-century expansion after 1945, when virtually the whole globe was brought into play to provide the system's needs. That period has now passed; the nations that provided the additional energy resources have rudely jacked up prices fivefold in three years.

For the United States and its high-consumption system, change is now in order. It is not just that the shiekhs of the OPEC have taken over from the companies as capitalists of their energy and owners of most of the world's oil. The whole scheme of oil-based prosperity has been upset. For when energy costs mount, labor ceases to benefit, expecially when the cost of money is also high. Then productivity begins to decline, as it did for the first recorded time in the United States in 1974. At that point, the whole system lapses into decline, signaling the end to the long boom and a halt in economic growth.

Does the halt spell an end to economic growth? At least a pause is inevitable, a recession, as the economy enters a period of restructuring. In the outcome, America might well see a rebalancing of the three forces, a sequel in which capital begins to be poured in vastly greater amounts than ever before into activities that require more labor—into health, education, and welfare, for instance. The source and supplier of this capital, as it has been for many years in Europe, must be the government. Then we shall have what the economists call a "service" economy, with more and more of us working for the government and other "nonprofit" agencies. There is also the chance that American society, cutting loose from its dependence upon oil and gas, may find substitutes that will enable it, after the readjustment, to resume economic growth based on abundant but new forms of energy. More likely, after a confused period of applying brakes, stepping on the gas, and stripping some gears, it will hit upon a combination of service programs and growth. Two things are sure: the age of cheap oil is over, and there will be unavoidable pain and turmoil while the nation restructures its economy.

For more than a year after the Arabs cut off their oil, the United States struggled to take the measure of the changing situation. The price of oil stayed high, and the country continued to import more oil than ever. While President Ford, a conservative with Herbert Hooverish instincts against government "interference," tried to coax people into voluntary fuel saving, a kind of national debate broke out on the country's energy predicament. Under the charter of former President Nixon's "Project Independence," the federal government amassed its own oil data. Private institutes and citizens' groups leaped in to study and propose. By the end of 1974, the newspaper-reading public had heard what had to be done from such outfits as the Ford Foundation's $4-million Energy Policy Project, the businessmen's Committee for Economic Development, and the huge new entity that mushroomed within government itself, the Federal Energy Administration.[7]

In various ways all said the same thing: if the United States were to avoid another oil embargo and gasoline shortage, the country would have to drastically change its habits of energy consumption. In the next five or ten years, the only way to reduce dependence upon unreliable (that is, Arab) oil was to conserve not only oil but all sources of energy. To organize the necessary measures over the long haul, the nation must establish an across-the-board energy policy and immediately start building up its own energy resources, of which oil was but one. All studies drummed on the huge savings to be gained if the nation would conserve its motor fuel—just bringing the American car's gasoline-consumption performance to those of European and Japanese automobiles would increase its energy efficiency by 40 percent and save the entire 6½ million barrels of oil that had to be brought in daily from abroad in 1974. If, moreover, individuals could be encouraged to insulate homes, especially the homes of the poor, and if office and apartment buildings could tighten up their standards of heating, cooling, and insulating, a further 40 percent energy saving could be achieved. Establishing nationwide lighting standards to save on electricity generated in oil-fired plants and requiring energy-use labeling on all appliances would save still more. Industry, as energy's largest user, could also save by new efficiencies, though of all the different sectors, it seemed quickest to discipline wasteful habits as the cost of fuel shot up.

All such remedies called for "making the system run better." All who proposed them tended to see the answer to the nation's energy problem in what the Ford Foundation group called a "technical fix." [8] Technology and science, which had got the country into the crisis, could be used to get us out of it.

Underlying these prescriptions was the belief that America could change its energy-wasting ways without giving up growth. Growth was the American gospel, the secular religion of the American industrial society. It had become, as Daniel Bell said, "the source of individual motivation, the foundation of political solidarity, and the basis for mobilizing the society for any common purpose." [9] What was once the outcome of largely unconcerted market processes had become the expressed goal of government policy, of the national will. It was not hard to see why. Growth was the ground of every citizen's hope of bettering his lot.

The new conservators conceded that the United States was still well endowed with natural resources. But to go on using up oil as prodigally as America had since 1945, with the rate of growth doubling every fifteen years, would amount to stealing from our grandchildren. Each generation had to act as trustee for the next, or there would be no next generation. Social costs would be ruinous, and troubles with other nations would get worse. Rather than go on as before, then, the new conservators urged looking at growth in a new way. Energy growth, it was suggested, should be differentiated and set apart from overall economic growth. Do this, and you could project a substantially lower rate of energy growth without overly interfering with the growth of general economic activity that Americans had come to expect.

From 1850 to 1950, the gross national product rose at a rate nearly twice that of energy growth, and no particularly bad effects were felt. Only since 1945, when energy was employed so intensively in manufacturing and transport, did energy growth speed up to a rate equaling that of the economy in general.[10] That should now be seen as a passing and abnormal outburst. That was a time when America was uniquely powerful and expanding onto all the continents of the globe. But now the nation must readjust: the United States could and should return to the earlier pattern and for the rest of the century cut its energy growth rate—by half, the Ford Foundation group said; by nearly half, the businessmen of the CED suggested. This could be accomplished by a "technical fix," by stepping up efficiencies. Energy-saving technologies would play a big part, both at the point where energy was processed and where it was actually used. Measures should be adopted not only to save energy, but to save the energy-minded consumer money.

By the end of 1974, just about everybody knew more or less what this meant: though other big savings were possible in fueling homes and industry, nearly half the petroleum consumed in the United States in 1973 went into its motor vehicles. Oil for transport, gas for cars—that was the obvious place to cut.

But gas in the tank was what made America go—and who wanted to tamper with the nation's very bloodstream, to arrest the nation's heartbeat? Not, certainly, Gerald Ford, a man from the automobile state of Michigan.

Of all the courses urged upon the new president in 1974, the one that appealed to him most emerged from the FEA report. As a government document, this report zeroed in on the overriding national interest in fighting free of the growing dependence on "insecure" Arab oil. Though many other options were presented, its pages bore down hardest on obtaining maximum possible oil production from strictly

American sources. Boiled down, what FEA Chief Frank Zarb, a former treasury official, urged was a policy of getting American oil at any price.

Even for purposes of national security, this was a bold ploy. All year, Congress and the citizenry had filled the air with loud protests at the high prices charged by the oil countries and oil companies. Now the administration, in the name of independence, proposed to set oil prices even higher than OPEC's. Such a proposal might be music to the ears of oilmen. It might even console Ford's hard-pressed friends in the automobile industry if all oil products, and not just gasoline, had to bear the brunt of such price inflation. It could hardly please anybody else. But Jerry Ford, an appointed president facing a heavily Democratic Congress, bought it.

The strategy was to put through a protective tariff and came straight out of the old probusiness book written in McKinley, Harding, and Hoover days, artfully adapted to make use of a reform conveniently handed Ford by his Democratic predecessors. Thanks to measures enacted in New and Fair Deal times, power to set tariffs had been taken out of the hands of Congress and entrusted to the executive. Now, as Zarb proposed, the president could simply decree an oil tariff so high that the price of oil inside the United States must rise above the OPEC-set world price. Having thus acted, the administration could then sit back and "let market forces prevail." With such a price for inducement, the industry would increase supply; and under the deterrent of such high cost, demand would throttle back. The administration, removing controls and piously rejecting all calls to intervene, would keep hands off. And the nation, by reason of tariff-boosting intervention, would have the gasoline rationing Ford said he wanted no part of—rationing, in reality, by price. The need for importing foreign oil would melt away, oil industry profits would be stabilized, and the United States energy budget would be brought into some sort of balance.

Of course, the choices were not that simple and contrary forces were at work. For one thing, it was not necessary and probably not desirable to close out all imports of oil. More important, accepting high prices at once would not fetch out significantly more domestically produced oil for years. One of the biggest disappointments after oil prices first shot up in 1973 was the failure of domestic sources to respond. Just before the Arabs imposed their embargo, the National Petroleum Council trumpeted that without undue strain, the industry could boost stateside output a million barrels a day if asked.[11] Yet domestic production not only failed to rise in 1974, but it fell back. The FEA report acknowledged, "Between 1974 and 1977, there is little that can prevent domestic production from declining or at best remaining constant." [12]

The great leap forward provoked by high oil prices would come after 1978, when the Alaska pipeline went into operation. Opening up the big new field in Alaska and new offshore discoveries north of the Arctic Circle would lift Alaska past Texas as the nation's number one oil-producing state. New discoveries offshore in the Gulf of Mexico and off California, as well as some in the Atlantic and the Gulf of Alaska, could be expected to add still more to U.S. oil supplies by 1985. Under the stimulus of high prices, the industry might go to great lengths to develop and apply new techniques of recovering oil from old mainland fields. And coal and nuclear power might come into their own.

In pointing to such possibilities, the FEA report lifted the debate beyond the level of what to do about oil when its supplies were vanishing and posed the decision for the nation in terms of how it might turn to other sources of energy. In the administration's scheme, the alternative source was coal. Coal was the nation's insurance policy. Even after years of neglect, it provided half the fuel consumed by industry. By converting about one hundred electricity-generating boilers from oil and natural gas to coal by 1980, the country could save nearly a million barrels of oil a day and a smaller but still important amount of natural gas. Oil and gas heat might also be banned in all homes and buildings built henceforth in the United States. The effect would be to force a turn to electric heating. At first thought, this might seem a backward step, since about 60 percent of energy efficiency is lost in generating and transmitting electricity, which is thus a much less efficient way of heating than burning oil or gas on the spot.

But the FEA's reasoning was that the United States had 800 years' supply of coal—and "only about ten years of proven oil and gas reserves." [13] Oil and natural gas were simply too precious to be burned under boilers, and burning coal to make electricity was the only substitute available for imported oil until nuclear power began coming on line at some future time.

Thus coal, which, after the nation's biggest bcom, was still producing at about 1943 levels, was ticketed for a comeback. As an energy source it was dirty, and the Environmental Protection Agency was calling for "scrubbers" at utility plants to clean out the worst sulfur-oxide pollutants before the smoke went up the stacks.[14] Then the president vetoed the Democrats' strip mining control bill, and vast deposits in the West were opened to unregulated exploitation.

If coal should begin replacing imported oil, it would be just in time because, as Senator Abraham Ribicoff, Democrat of Connecticut, said, there were "no alternative energy technologies to bail us out." [15] Certainly nuclear power was not ready, thirty years after the dawn of the atomic age, to provide the United States with a major substitute for oil. Although the Atomic Energy Commission had forecast that in 1975 nuclear reactors would be supplying 12 percent of the country's electricity, the program lagged; and as late as 1973, nuclear plants provided about as much of total U.S. energy needs as wood.

Delays in licensing and construction of reactors reflected deeper difficulties. Technical and labor problems, many of them safety-related, enforced higher and higher costs. Operating snags rather than opposition from environmental and local groups were the major cause of delay, contrary to what the AEC and the nuclear industry said. Power-generating economies in the 55 plants operating in 1974 were not impressive—and it had to be remembered that, even if they were, their power would still have to go out over the existing transmission lines, which account for about half the cost of electricity as delivered to the user.

Safety was a continuing headache.[16] Though the industry met with no catastrophes, small accidents occurred disturbingly often. In 1966, an accident knocked out the Enrico Fermi reactor near Detroit when a piece of metal tore loose, blocked the flow of molten sodium coolant, and caused a uranium meltdown of such proportions that no one could get in to examine the core for more than a year.[17]

Disposing of radioactive wastes remained a problem. At the Hanford, Washington, facility, high-level wastes had been escaping for 20 years—in 1973 alone, 150,000 gallons escaped in leaks.[18] There was a scheme to contain the long-lived cesium 89 and strontium 90 in vitreous bottles designed to last forever. But the quantities kept mounting, and nobody knew a place big enough and remote enough to keep them safely forever. Only recently, the authorities entertained a proposal from the Aerospace Corporation for compacting radioactive wastes into copper spheres weighing 11,000 pounds each and hurling them into orbit around the sun like other planets.[19] But no one had an answer for the question, What if the rockets blew up on the pad?

Even if reactors were found to operate safely, there were still unsolved problems of safeguarding nuclear materials against theft and sabotage. Devising answers only raised the price of nuclear power. Federal insurance, fail-safe systems, uranium enrichment, and waste disposal might properly have been accounted part of this price. Operating difficulties alone raised plant costs to $600 a kilowatt of installed capacity, four times the sum projected back in 1965.[20] Though a high proportion of these costs were paid by the taxpayer in the form of financial subsidies, nuclear plants also enjoyed a considerable energy subsidy. There are data suggesting that uranium enrichment alone, for military and peaceful purposes, consumes about 3 percent of all electricity used in the United States, or something like half the 4 to 6 percent of total U.S. energy generated in 1973 by nuclear plants.[21] Almost everything that runs, from passenger cars to electric toasters, enjoys some sort of energy subsidy, of course. But taking into account energy expended in mining, concentrating, enriching, storing, cooling, and in all other processes on the way to the actual generation of electricity, nuclear power still appears to to use up, by comparison with power made by burning coal, oil, or gas, a goodly proportion of the energy it produces, as much as 12 percent according to some sources.[22]

Before Congress finally abolished it in 1974, the AEC came up with a nuclear reactor that requires virtually no outlays for fuel at all. A machine of such surpassing efficiency would not only yank costs back down to something like their post-Hiroshima promise, but could also in a single stroke achieve the goals of Project Independence for freeing the U.S. from energy dependence upon the Arabs or anyone else. In 1975 the biggest part of the government's Research and Development money (some $473 million) was being expended to develop this marvelous machine—the so-called breeder reactor.[23]

The machine, as its name implies, breeds its own fuel. In such a reactor the working fuel is plutonium and the more abundant form of natural uranium—U-238. When the plutonium fissions to produce power, some of its liberated neutrons also ram into the nuclei of otherwise unfissionable U-238 and cause more fissionable material, including plutonium, to form. In this way, new fuel is "bred" to keep the reactor running without resort to outside supplies.

Though an experimental breeder is already operating in France, the first commercial fast breeder is not slated to go on line in the United States until 1990. One reason for such deliberateness was that as such reactors were now designed, there was a chance that an accidental power surge could reduce the density of the sodium coolant, fill the chamber with fast neutrons, and, inducing another power surge, bring on an uncontrolled chain reaction and explosion.[24] A second restraint upon the speed of breeder development was the baleful properties of its fuel. Plutonium, an artificial element manufactured since 1943 for use in nuclear bombs, is the most dangerous substance known to man, 250,000 times more lethal than cyanide by weight. Five grams would be enough to kill 20 million human beings.

In 1969, the costliest industrial fire in U.S. history broke out in a nuclear weapons plant near Denver—triggered by plutonium. A program for establishing commercial breeder reactors would inevitably involve trucking plutonium back and forth across the highways of the nation. Dr. Edward Teller, father of the H-bomb and no foe of nuclear power, said in 1967, "I do not like the hazard involved. Although I believe it is possible to analyze and see the immediate consequences of an accident, I do not believe it is possible to analyze and foresee the secondary consequences, where one or two or five percent of this plutonium will find itself and how it will get mixed up with some other material. . . ." [25]

Controlling a thermonuclear reaction—harnessing fusion—for the peaceful purposes of generating electricity would be incomparably harder. So the H-bomb builders discovered long ago in both America and Russia. Starting in the early 1950s, they tried to contain the fusion of hydrogen inside invisible "bottles" formed by powerful magnetic fields.[26] It seemed the only way—certainly no known metal could have walled in materials heated to temperatures equaling those inside the sun. But nobody knew very much about plasma physics, or what goes on inside the sun and other stars. Beyond the three earthly states of matter—solid, liquid, gas—was this fantastic fourth state that substances enter when brought to extremely high temperatures. It was the state of plasma, which differed from the gaseous state in that all electrons had been torn loose from their atoms by the force of high-speed collisions in the intensified heat. Since the free electrons all had negative charges and their nuclei were left with positive charges, it seemed as certain as the laws of physics that the plasma could be contained by magnetic fields.

But the scientists were groping into the unknown; theoretical as well as experimental confirmation of this certainty eluded them for years. It was not until the mid-1960s that the first fleeting thermonuclear reactions were achieved in laboratories. Then the Russians announced that they had broken the barrier. By instituting a different arrangement of magnetic systems in a device called Tokamak (meaning "large current"), they had caused particles to fuse for as long as a billionth of a second. Thereafter, Americans built a Tokamaklike machine at Princeton that produced temperatures of about 25 million degrees centigrade with plasma densities of about 100 trillion particles per cubic centimeter. Years passed; progress was slow.

In 1968, the Russians took another tack. Academician Nikolai Basov, who had shared the Nobel Prize with two Americans for discovering lasers, demonstrated that a laser beam could be used to start a fusion reaction. His approach eliminated the whole problem of containment. He dropped a pellet of frozen hydrogen into a relatively simple spherical vessel made of metal alloy and filled with molten lithium to absorb heat. Midway in its descent the pellet was hit by a powerful, short pulse of laser light through a small porthole in the sphere, setting off a small thermonuclear reaction. Later, pellets were injected at a rate of two or three a second, and a steady stream of microexplosions took place like a string of miniature flaring suns. But even when the Russians tried beefing up the pulse with mirrors and tried peppering the target pellet with as many as 27 beams at once, they fell short of producing even as much energy as it took to run the lasers. No one yet knew enough about lasers to deliver the bolt of power—a billion times the output of the Grand Coulee Dam— needed to set off a large enough fusion reaction.[27]

The most promising approach remained Tokamak. Biggest U.S. funding ($57 million) in 1974 went to the construction of a much larger machine at Princeton that Harold P. Furth, project director, said would "come close" to proving the scientific feasibility of fusion.[28] Beyond this essential first step lay staggering engineering problems—countering radioactivity so fierce that in a deuterium-tritium reaction, for instance, it could reduce most metals in the machine to chalk. Transmuting atoms deep within metal walls, neutrons could also cause the material to swell. Such problems, said Professor David Rose of M.I.T., could be as difficult as plasma containment itself.[29] As an alternative source of energy for America, the Project Independence report shoved fusion into the twenty-first century, not worth discussing in the country's current plight.[30]

By the 1974 Energy Reorganization Act, Congress abolished the AEC and replaced it with an Energy Research and Development Agency to explore all, not just nuclear, technologies. A Nuclear Regulation Commission was also established to regulate, not promote, the nuclear industry.

The new legislation marked the starting point for a national energy policy that would bring together all sources of power in a drive to free the United States from dependence upon foreign oil. But the most optimistic projection by the Ford administration was that it would take ten years before new energy technologies were available to make the nation self-sufficient.

Thus the first priority for America was to cut back the growth of energy use over the intervening decade—by developing a 20-miles-per-gallon car, more efficient space heating, and energy economies in industrial machinery and home appliances. But that, with all it signified for American habits and even life-styles, was only a starter. It would be necessary to launch the greatest technological undertaking since the Manhattan Project and the moon-landing program—a $20-billion investment in bringing on all sorts of alternative energy sources.

On this Congress and president were in agreement: probably "several" new supply technologies would be needed by 1985.[31] New sources of electric power, which would not be dependent upon either unreliable Arab oil or marginal American oil, indeed would not be dependent upon fossil fuels of any kind—those were what the United States would require to hold its leading place in the world. Great changes were coming, and some might come in sight soon. Dr. Alvin Weinberg, the distinguished scientist who headed the FEA's Office of Research and Development, said that by 1985 the United States would have to have under development a whole new personal system of transportation powered by something radically different from the accustomed essence of Gasoline Alley. Research toward achieving this, he said, should begin at once.[32]

America's technological cupboard would not have been so distressingly bare if certain decisions in the nation's recent history had gone another way. Back in the early 1950s, the Paley commission made its celebrated report to President Truman on America's resources. Its most important recommendation, adopted by Truman as part of his cold war policy, was that the nation should amass stockpiles of strategic materials against future eventualities. The United States accumulated large stockpiles of coal, cotton, grain, and various metals that insured it against the crippling impact of sudden shortages. But these stockpiles also tied up capital, and it seemed rational later to sell them off without replenishing them, an action that even made the country seem more prosperous—rather like a family that seems to have more spending money when it has let its insurance lapse. By the 1970s, Americans knew better: the Ford administration said that at a minimum the country should stockpile enough oil to tide it over the worst pinch of a new embargo.[33]

Sizing up energy prospects in 1952 for the next quarter century, the Paley commission warily called oil's future "the great enigma." [34] But even if crude production should flag, it said, by 1975 the United States would be manufacturing synthetic oil in substantial quantities from coal.[35] After all, the Germans had shown that this could be done: the success of German scientists in producing gasoline by the hydrogenation of coal was what kept Hitler's air force flying through all the blockades of the second World War. After the war, U.S. officials hunted out German synthetic-gasoline factories the same way they sought Nazi missile pads. In short order, the U.S. Bureau of Mines funded a Consolidation Coal Co. test plant in West Virginia to exploit and improve the German process. Few doubted in those confident years that what the Germans could do the Americans could do better. But a little-noticed decision changed everything. The plant was not well managed, and oil interests successfully pressured the Eisenhower administration into cutting off funds.[36] It was, John F. O'Leary, former chief of the Bureau of Mines, said later, "the most serious error in energy policy made in the postwar years." [37]

So in 1975, the time of the once-appointed takeoff for synthetic gasoline, the United States had to go back to where it left off in the 1950s. The task would be costly and slow, but it was well within the capabilities of the world's leader in technology. Essentially, the liquefaction of coal involves mixing crushed coal with an oil solvent and heating it up under pressures of 1,000 pounds per square inch; when it begins to melt, it is forced into a hydrogen-filled chamber. This was what the Germans called hydrogenation; and if the process is carried far enough, gasoline is produced. Of course, producing gasoline in the amount gobbled up by American motor vehicles would require fantastic quantities of coal. Yet the United States does have the coal and could probably build several billion-dollar synthetic gasoline plants in as little as two years if it made up its mind to.[38] Strategically significant they certainly would be; and at OPEC prices, not to mention those proposed by the Ford administration, they might well be at least marginally economic.

Synthesizing gas from coal would not be quite so prodigal an exercise. After all, coal was the principal source of the manufactured gas Americans used for cooking and lighting until the 1930s, when natural gas flooded the markets. Here again the Germans were in the forefront. Lacking natural gas supplies, they kept working at better ways of synthesizing gas from coal. The Lurgi Company of Frankfurt developed a process for gasifying brown coal that held its own commercially in Europe even after the second World War. When natural gas grew scarce in the United States, interest in the Lurgi progress quickened. To bring the Lurgi gas up to natural gas standards, it was necessary to double its heating value. Raising temperatures to 4,000 degrees Fahrenheit, researchers introduced nickel and iron as catalysts to coax out maximum amounts of methane, the chief ingredient of natural gas. El Paso Natural Gas Co. was sufficiently impressed to plan a Lurgi plant incorporating these advances in New Mexico in 1976. According to the National Petroleum Council, 28 such gas-from-coal plants, capable of supplying as much as 10 percent of the gas consumed in the United States, could be built by 1985.[39]

Environmental problems in large-scale liquefaction or gasification of coal were nothing like so awkward as those posed by the other source of synthetic oil—oil shale. For decades, Americans had talked about boiling oil out of the big shale deposits of Colorado, Utah, and Wyoming. These strange rocks were known to be capable of yielding up to two trillion barrels of oil—many times the country's reserves of the regular stuff. Several companies had already staked out claims, and one began building a small processing plant. But in 1974, one group pulled out, protesting that capital costs had grown prohibitive, and the other venture was cut back to pilot-plant size. Under environmental regulations, wastes—which would be mountainous—had to be disposed of. Underground processing, which might avoid this problem, had not even been tried. Most serious of all, the water required for large-scale operations would exceed the amount available from the upper Colorado River. The FEA listed only token output expectable from the shale oil country by 1985.[40]

In the search for new sources of power, one of the major alternatives might be moving in stages from an economy based on the hydrocarbons—oil, natural gas, and coal—to a pure hydrogen economy. Hydrogen is as inexhaustible as the oceans, almost as energetic pound-for-pound as petroleum; and as a fuel is practically pollution-free. As an energy source, it comes in two forms, liquid and gas. A laboratory curiosity until recently, liquid hydrogen now powers missiles and, only slightly adapted, fueled a Volkswagen and a Gremlin that finished first and second in a National Clean Air Race staged in Detroit in 1972. In its gaseous state, hydrogen has been mixed with natural gas and also piped pure through existing mains to cook meals on existing stoves and heat houses via existing gas burners. In short, hydrogen in either form is extraordinarily substitutable for oil and natural gas in their most familiar uses.[41]

Of course, there is a catch: a complete technology of procurement must be created if hydrogen were to rescue the future of the free-wheeling car and the freestanding house in America.

The liquid hydrogen on which the UCLA and Brigham Young University students drove to victory in the 1972 auto race cost $10,000 a gallon. New processes and new industries would have to come into being if hydrogen were ever to fuel the daily trips to work, to shop, to school. The age-old high school experiment of passing an electric current through a glass of water to break its molecules into hydrogen and oxygen would have to be turned into the world's biggest system of electrolysis by a process enormously more efficient than any yet seen. The sea itself would have to provide the water. The demand for electric power might be such as to drain half the juice out of such nuclear stations as the utilities might finally get into operation.

Anticipating such problems, a National Academy of Sciences panel suggested that if the sea provides the water for the extraction of hydrogen, it might as well furnish the power too. Both the electrolysis and the electricity to run it could be generated at the same giant installation built to float on the warm waters off Florida. A thermal seapower plant would exploit the 35 degree differential between the toasty Gulf Stream waters and the cold current beneath by drawing the surface water down through a hollow shaft. In the same shaft would be heat exchangers filled with the same Freon liquid that absorbs heat in household refrigerators. The heat so absorbed would be used to drive turbines that generated electricity, and this electricity would then be used to electrolyze the water to make quantities of liquid hydrogen on the spot.

Even if liquid hydrogen were produced in quantity at low prices, its characteristics would compel some modification in motor transport. Energetic as hydrogen may be in proportion to its weight, its low density makes it only a third as efficient a fuel as oil in terms of volume. It would take a 50-gallon tank of liquid hydrogen to get the same automobile mileage as a 20-gallon tank of gasoline. Hydrogen also has an incorrigible tendency to escape and would have to be dispensed in bottles that fit into cars like cassettes into tape decks; even then, a car left standing a week would have lost an appreciable amount of fuel. Research performed for the National Space and Aeronautics Administration suggests that the first commercial use for liquid hydrogen fuel might be in jetliners: because it is lighter than fossil fuels, it could boost payload efficiency in planes once they were modified to make room in their wings for the bulkier tanks required for liquid hydrogen.

Comparatively minor modification in gas pipelines and burners would be needed for industry and homeowners to use hydrogen fuel in its gaseous state. It could also be piped to local power plants to generate electricity, either through conventional steam turbines or very possibly in large fuel cells. No more serviceable fuel has emerged in two decades' space-program experience with fuel cells than hydrogen. Though such cells, which generate electricity by the chemical reaction between hydrogen and oxygen, have yet to develop high enough efficiency to challenge existing energy systems, this could change if the fuel cell were to be fueled directly with mass-produced hydrogen. The whole energy-wasting step of transmitting electricity would then be bypassed. The way would be opened to the home-sized fuel cell performing on the premises all the functions now provided by electricity transmitted from a central power station. In the words of Dr. Bruce Netschert, of the National Energy Institute, such a hydrogen-fueled cell would "at one stroke make central electric power generation for home use obsolete." [42] Utilities, threatened by this prospect, favor large fuel cells that could function at local stations as part of their present system. ERDA funding priorities could determine the outcome. With big federal outlays, hydrogen could become a significant secondary energy source in ten years' time. If nuclear power continues to hang fire, hydrogen could become an alternative energy resource. Before the turn of the century, the country could move into a "hydrogen economy."

Almost as versatile an energy source for a nation short of fuel is methanol. Most people think of methanol either as the wood alcohol killer that the unwary drank in Prohibition days, or as the fancy fuel that powers the superspecialized racing machines at the Indianapolis speedway. In fact, this long-known alcohol, which has two-thirds of the heat potential of gasoline, can be used right now to replace or mix with oil in existing oil-burning equipment—electricity-generating plants, home furnaces, and automobile engines. A car, for example, will run all right with 15 to 30 percent methanol added to its gasoline fuel; if every American car did so, there would be no need to import any oil at all.

Such notions are out of the question, however, because at the moment our methanol is made from the scarcest of all hydrocarbons, natural gas. But methanol can be made from coal or, better yet, from renewable sources of energy—from farm and city wastes, from garbage and sawdust and logging scraps and the heaps of lignin discarded at paper mills. Scientists, especially European scientists, believe that methanol presents enough advantages to justify substantial research and development aimed at reducing the cost of production from such sources. If OPEC should cut off all oil, countries like Germany and Sweden that produce none of their own would be compelled to turn to such substitute fuels if they wanted to keep their cars and trucks going. This they did in the second World War, when they turned even some food grains into alcohols as fuel for road transport. And if indeed Americans and other passengers on Planet Earth are moving toward a truly recycled economy, all kinds of organic materials that are now thrown away could be reprocessed into methanol. Besides being extractable from sources that are constantly renewed, methanol has another big advantage—it is far less polluting than any of the fossil fuels.[43]

Another major alternative technology for the future is sun power. In our everyday energy budget, every kilocalorie we expend comes from the sun. But we use the sun's energy only indirectly. Processed as farm crops, it sustains us as food. Stored as fossil fuels, this energy, when released, warms us and drives our machines. Men also use the sun's energy indirectly when mariners set sails in the wind, when farmers rig windmills to pump water, when engineers think to harness thermal sea power off Florida for the manufacture of electricity. But so far, we have lagged in directly harnessed solar power.

Of course northerners have always taken care to build their houses with a southern exposure; and the cat dozing in the sunny doorway of a barn seems to know all about direct solar energy. The catch is that the sun's rays arrive in so diffuse a form and at such low temperatures that putting them to practical use has proved all but impossible. Yet in the United States and such other countries as Israel and Japan, there has been progress. A few years ago, the distinguished sun scientist Farrington Daniels remarked, "In 1938 I would have said solar energy would have come first—before atomic energy." [44]

In the peaceful uses of energy, it may yet. The most positive statement that one can make is that the sun still shines: ultimately, there can be no energy shortage because all energy comes from the sun—and Spaceship Earth receives this beneficence in unending quantities. Solar energy has a lot going for it. Whereas our fossil fuel supplies are shrinking and insecure, solar power is abundant and renewable. And when nuclear energy is so painfully slow reaching the point where we can safely harness it, solar energy holds the promise of being not only harmless to handle, but environmentally more benign than any other source of power. Solar energy, the FEA report noted, "is increasingly viewed by segments of the public as the long-range solution to our energy problems." [45]

Before passing the 1974 Solar Energy, Housing and Community Development Act, Congress reviewed the prospects and found them moderately promising. Two Arizona scientists put forward their plan to cover 20 miles of the desert with ingenious nonreflecting mirrors that would catch and concentrate enough solar energy to drive giant turbines capable of producing a million kilowatts of electricity. University of Houston researchers proposed an even bigger array of concentrators that could follow the sun's movement and trap enough heat to manufacture large quantities of hydrogen by electrolysis.[46] But how, others asked, could the United States put its trust in any system that ran only when the sun shone? To meet this difficulty, a Boston scientist urged building a solar-energy-processing plant on a milewide platform in space and beaming the concentrated energy to giant receptors on the ground.[47]

Most friends of the sun urged starting small and only trying to supplement existing energy systems at first. Thus it was established that heating and cooling houses and perhaps shopping centers would be solar energy's first significant task in America. For this technology already existed. Hundreds of thousands of Japanese homes got their hot water from rooftop solar collectors. Absorbing the sun's rays, collectors atop some 71 U.S. homes transmitted the trapped heat to tanks of water or beds of pebbles, whence it was piped to rooms below. In experimental projects funded by the National Science Foundation, four U.S. schools got about 20 percent of their heat from various types of rooftop collectors.[48]

The most ardent solar powerists wanted to see the Department of Housing and Urban Development get behind a mass production program at once to simplify construction of small-home solar systems, drive down costs, and show people in houses down their streets what the sun could already do for people who feel trapped by utility bills. They argued that rooftop collectors could help run air-conditioning units as well as heating systems and thus add an important energy efficiency in the South and Southwest, where such systems were expected to be adopted first.

Even under a more modest ERDA program, a few quick engineering changes could halve the costs of a rooftop collector outfit for small homes. These could lower to $1,000 the price of a 5,000-gallon water tank capable of storing four days' heat at temperatures never lower than 100 degrees Fahrenheit; the whole system, including auxiliary heating facilities for protracted cloudy periods, would then cost $3,500 to $6,000 and increase carrying costs for a householder's mortgage by from $300 to $550 a year.[49] Since the fuel is free, these added amortization costs could fairly be compared with the bills for heating and cooling by conventional fuels. No higher than the cost of electric heating in many states, they were close to competitive with natural gas and fuel oil after the price rises of 1973–74. More research and development should boost the heat-storing capacities of rooftop collectors to a minimum 200 degrees Fahrenheit, alter their design to fit better into the way houses are built, and reduce the maintenance problems that have plagued all early models. If, starting in 1978, half the new houses put up in the United States were outfitted with such rooftop systems, then in twelve years' time, 8.4 million dwellings, mostly in the South and Southwest, would be heated and cooled by solar energy—at a saving of 3½ million barrels of oil a day or their equivalent. With at least four oil companies, led by Exxon, dabbling in this market, it is at least possible that a few years hence people once urged to put a tiger in their tank may be invited to keep one on their roof.

If such small-home plants caught on, total-energy systems might next be developed for shopping centers and small office buildings, using parabolic concentrators to provide steam from turbine plants to heat and cool the buildings. Further along, some sun worshippers see total solar take-over in the twenty-first century. One has already calculated that the combined rooftop areas of the United States, if utilized to the fullest extent, could provide just enough room for massed collectors channeling the nation's entire energy needs from the beneficent sun. At that point, when presumably every structure in the United States would be thatched to the skies with sun-catching poles and dishes, the supposedly immaculate energy of the sun would impose its own pollution upon the American environment—visual pollution.

One other alternative source of energy for America is the natural heat of the earth. The source of this heat is the earth's molten center; and enough of it is caught in pockets quite near the surface, called geothermal reservoirs, to furnish all the energy man can use if only he finds ways to harness it. Geothermal power is most readily tapped in regions of tectonic activity—of earthquakes, volcanoes, geysers—such as Iceland, New Zealand, California.[50] The Italians have used geothermal steam for power since 1904; New Zealanders have been making electricity geothermally since 1950. Reykjavik, the capital of Iceland, now belies its name, which means "city of smoke"—all its 40,000 inhabitants live in chimneyless houses warmed by steam piped (at almost no cost) from nearby hot springs. At one end of the Pacific Coast's zone of tectonic activity, the local college in Klamath

Falls, Oregon, saves 75 per cent by heating its buildings with hot water piped from underground (while universities elsewhere stagger under fuel-bill hikes); and at the other end, in Baja California, a 285,000-watt plant uses steam from subterranean sources to generate power for the city of Mexicali.

The West, dotted with hot springs, is America's most promising geothermal country, and the hottest prospects are along the San Andreas Fault. In the Geysers field in central California, a Union Oil subsidiary profitably pipes steam to a new utility plant that uses it to generate 290,000 watts of electricity for San Francisco. A recent Signal Oil strike considerably enlarged part of the Bay area's power requirements. Farther south there were disappointments. Promoters who thought to tap the terrific pressures in the Imperial Valley and Salton Sea areas to provide power for Los Angeles and San Diego brought up water so briny that it caked the pipe—and even a thin film of silicon can ruin the efficiency of any heat-exchanger system. But others took big leases to drill near Tucson in hopes of hitting a shallow sizzler, and in the Sierras, near Lake Tahoe, one prospector offered to bring up heat to help the state highway department keep California's mountain passes clear of snow.

In some ways, geothermal prospecting was like the oil search in Texas before Spindletop. Everything depended on hitting steam or at least hot water, and drilling was so costly that only the shallowest strikes paid off. There might be few such places, and even they could soon be depleted. Los Alamos scientists have shown that more energy could be extracted from dry rock. On the shoulder of an old New Mexico volcano, they drilled one hole, fracturing the metamorphic rock below. Then they drilled a second a kilometer away and forced water down it. Percolating through the fracture below, the water shot out the first hole piping hot. It was only an experiment at shallow depth, and the idea was that the water boiling up would be run through a heat exchanger for creating electric power, then recycled through the earth to bring up energy again.

In principle, energy from the earth can be developed anywhere in this way, according to John Banwell, the UN's New Zealand-born expert. Oil wells are now drilled to 20 kilometers, he points out, and encounter great heat. You could drill right under the UN's Manhattan headquarters, Banwell says, and, with possibly a few more wells sunk over on Long Island, fetch up enough geothermal energy to heat New York City.

Banwell is quick to add that there are problems, and different problems, at every site. Much still remains to be learned about tapping the pent-up heat. Though geothermal sources, as at the Geysers in California, can be harnessed to make electricity sooner than more conventional power supplies can be developed, much remains to be done before this technology can add notably to United States energy supplies. Potentially, an Interior Department panel reported in 1972, "geothermal resources can have an enormous impact on supplying the nation's need for energy and augmenting the supply of water." [51] But the FEA's report noted little chance of significant output before 1985 at the earliest.

The United States, to maintain its position as world leader, would be investing its estimated $379 billion to $474 billion capital outlays for energy over the next ten years to build up not one but several technologies as alternatives to oil. And, by one form of rationing or another, the nation would be reducing its consumption of oil.

The best estimate was that a ten percent cut in energy use would end the dependence on overseas oil. In an economy as huge and rich as that of the United States, this would amount, as one European said, to no more than "a penalty of inconvenience and minor difficulty—not much sacrifice." [52] The technocrats talked as if the whole thing could be carried off as a mere "technical fix." And it might appear that by all accounts a nation as continentally provisioned and productive as the United States, whose imports and exports amounted to little more than ten percent of its total economic activity, could adjust almost automatically to getting along without Middle East oil.

Not so. Cutting back meant a big change for America, a conscious shift in policy and, probably, purpose. During and after the second World War, the country mechanized its farms in a change that shifted an estimated ten million Americans into the cities; but a booming economy provided jobs and income for all. In the late 1960s, when the nation completed its massive aerospace program, a million Americans lost their jobs; but in those same years, the number of jobs rose from 65 to 70 million and the country as a whole was hardly conscious of what happened. This time, however, the decision had to be made in the midst of a severe recession that made its impact upon employment, especially in the nation's number one industry, automotive manufacturing, painfully noticeable.

The change was already underway, and the meanings resonated far beyond the dandy little prescriptions for a "technical fix." Oil was not just another commodity—it had worked its way into the mainstream of American life, both public and private. When it flowed, America flowed with it—to prosperity on the home front and hegemony in the world. Oil fueled the cold war and made immense profits from it, displacing coal in Europe, mobilizing NATO, fomenting the industrial boom that drew Europe and Japan into fateful dependence upon the wells of the Persian Gulf. In time, oil delivered America, in a swift passage from strength to weakness, to its energy crisis.

For the United States, the nation that rode to world primacy on oil, was caught short by its dependence upon petroleum as an energy resource. Nuclear plants were not yet ready to provide the country with the power to move about and dominate in the style to which it was accustomed. Coal, significantly controlled by oil, was not ready to fill the nation's energy gap, though it was the nearest chance of help. The so-called alternative sources of energy, though deserving the most urgent attentions of the nation, needed many more years before they could bail out America. Oil and natural gas could be reamed out of remaining sources on the outlying margins of the nation, in the Far North and far out at sea. But did people really want to rob the next generation of all that was left to keep power-steered, air-conditioned, automatic-transmissioned gas guzzlers going? At the least, Americans might want the United States government to manage their ultimate petroleum reserves, which belonged, as it happened, to the nation.

★

The choice, as put before the American people, could not be put simply or even mainly in terms of slowing down to 55 miles an hour or trading for a smaller car. But if people could see the choice as a challenge to America's international leadership, they would line up fast not only for conserving energy, but for a larger program of putting America's and the world's energy supply back in balance.

In the aftermath of World War victory Secretary of State George Marshall offered a big plan of economic interdependence at a moment when the country was on the point of settling back into its old peacetime pursuits and preoccupations. Over four years, he said, the United States should invest $13 billion to enable shattered Europe to rebuild its economy free of Communist control, so that it was fit to resume its role as all the world's trading partner. American goods would find markets, and American labor would have jobs. To show the Russians (and Europeans) America's resolve, Marshall got President Truman to put through the peacetime draft.

In the 1970s, though the Russians were still in the picture, the adversary was the Arabs; and the Europeans, who felt that past United States policy had helped make them dependent on Middle East oil, were not even sure they wanted to follow an American lead. Not only that, since Marshall mustered the nation in 1947, American morale and self-confidence had undergone a severe impairment. The people seemed to have lost verve.

But in important ways the situation in 1975 was remarkably like that when Marshall proposed his big plan a quarter century earlier. Now, as then, everybody feared the coming of a depression. Now, as then, political leadership was the key. Now, as then, one party controlled the White House and the other, Congress, only then it was the other way around—a Democratic president and a Republican Congress. In 1947 both sides had to make tremendous accommodations to achieve the consensus they called bipartisanship. The Democrats had to throw New Dealism overboard, along with Henry Wallace and his alluring ideas for peace with Russia; and the Republicans, accepting Truman's leadership, had to conduct themselves with such political restraint that they lost their chance to regain the presidency the following year. This time the Republican administration would have to forego its preference for market economics and intervene both to curb demand and to ensure environmental safeguards that would make it all the harder for its business friends to produce more oil, gas, coal, and nuclear power. The congressional Democrats, besides having to risk the political consequences of added unemployment caused by the shift away from the old policies of maximum economic growth, would not relish building up Jerry Ford's chances for reelection in 1976.

In Henry Kissinger, Ford had a secretary of state who sought to assert United States leadership in the world oil crisis. In a major Chicago address, Kissinger proposed creation of an International Energy Agency in which oil-consuming countries, led by the United States, would make up to $25 billion available to members hardpressed to pay the stiff new oil prices, and the establishment of another credit at the International Monetary Fund to help underdeveloped countries such as India tide over until the IEA nations, bargaining with the oil-producing states, brought oil prices down to reasonable levels.[53] To show America's resolve in resisting Arab attempts to use oil to sway the political policies of oil-consuming states (and swing the Europeans behind America's leadership), Kissinger said that the United States must slash oil imports a million barrels a day in 1975 and a further million barrels a day by 1977.

But Ford, viscerally conservative even when outspending every previous peacetime president, could not establish the needed consensus. He tailored his energy program to the needs of the oil industry when it was no longer automatic to identify oil interests with the national interest. Once when oil and petroleum products were prominent among U.S. exports, higher prices for oil may have been thought to the nation's advantage. Then something was to be said perhaps for the output-curbing arrangements, international agreements, and information compacts that tended to keep supplies more limited and prices higher than they might have been. And since these goods had to be bought for dollars, they contributed to the willingness of other countries to buy dollars and thus strengthened the purchasing power of the nation's currency.

But now the tables were turned. The nation was an importer, not an exporter, both of oil and other raw materials—and could not allow national interest to be defined by a range of narrow self-interest groups. High prices might still benefit the big oil companies as well as the sheikhs of OPEC. But they hurt a large part of the American economy, not excepting the automobile industry; and the need now was for something the nation had never had before: a comprehensive energy policy in which oil was just one of the sources—one of the scarcer ones.

In this wider outlook, oil was at a disadvantage. The depletion allowance, having failed to get out more oil when oil was needed, was on its way out. The foreign tax subsidies that had lured the industry on its overseas spree had also seen their day. The only prices still federally controlled in early 1975 were oil prices, and the companies had not succeeded in their drive to get Congress to "deregulate" natural gas prices, which lagged behind other petroleum industry prices because they were uniquely subject to statutory regulation. With its enveloping sectional power and wealth, the Oil Kingdom in the Southwest had sometimes been compared with the Cotton Kingdom in the South before it. But foreign oil now outgushed Gulf of Mexico oil; Canadians instead of Texans ruled over Exxon; and as plenipotentiaries in Washington, Russell Long and Wilbur Mills were nothing like the wielders of power that Rayburn and Johnson, or for that matter, Calhoun and Polk, once were.

The foreign oil, moreover, from which the industry still drew most of its profits in 1974, was not only exorbitantly expensive but intolerably uncertain in supply. As never before, the international politics of oil determined its economics; and its military impact, in the growing likelihood of another war in the Middle East, overhung its politics. In the fighting of 1973, the Soviet Union had backed the

Arab embargo, and the United States had gone to a nuclear alert against the Russians. Now, as the two superpowers rushed to rearm the combatants, it was not too much to speak of the possibility of Armageddon itself.

For Americans the issues of the 1970s were economic—recession, inflation, energy—and their resolution had to be political. In the modern polity, measures would have to bring relief not only or even chiefly to special interests, but to wider groups—to workers and small taxpayers, to middle-class consumers and welfare families. When deepening recession finally drove Ford to action in 1975, he swung completely around from his cautious, indirect ways of countering inflation to pour giant sums of federal money into the faltering economy. But the prospective $52 billion deficit in his budget appalled him, and he thought he could offset his antirecession outlays by simultaneously instituting a strategy for solving the long-term energy problem through pushing U.S. oil prices even higher than OPEC prices. The stiff oil taxes that would boost prices and force conservation would also bring in $30 billion dollars in new revenues that one way or another ought to help him hold down the huge budget deficit.

This was, at best, a hope. He was obliged to say that much of this revenue would be channeled into income tax adjustments that might enable poorer citizens as well as state and local governments to pay the higher fuel prices. But the effect of such oil levies in terms of early relief from either recession or inflation was self-defeating. Higher prices hurt consumers in the pocketbook and aggravated inflation just when the goal was recovery from the economic slump. Congress demurred.

While the United States delayed, other oil-consumer nations protected themselves as best they could. As the result of the oil-producing states' price coup, world monetary and trade balances were in turmoil. By the end of 1974, OPEC holdings of other nations' currencies topped $50 billion; by 1980, they stand to surpass $250 billion, or far more than the total value of all U.S. investments overseas. With such fantastic incomes, the oil-producing states began investing their funds in the only places they could—in the developed countries of Europe and North America. The greatest threat of these transfers, greater even than the effect of high oil prices in slashing buying power within the consumer countries, was the threat to the very foundations of modern capitalist societies—their interdependent banking systems. The OPEC countries could only hope to spend a fraction of their petrodollars, as they were called, on imports from the advanced countries; the remaining sums they held in the form of short-term deposits and treasury notes in the United States and Europe.

These holdings, the Arabs knew, must be placed in countries that were least likely to default. A nation such as Italy, in 1974 running a balance-of-trade deficit of a billion dollars a month, was most in need of petrodollars, but was also least likely to receive them. At some point, Italy's ability to borrow for further financing of its deficit would end, and when that happened a bank panic would ensue. If Italian banks defaulted on outstanding loans, the result would not be limited to Italy, because with prevailing financial interdependence one country's collapse could be transmitted overnight into bank panics in other countries. Precisely this had happened in the Great Depression with the failure of the Vienna Kreditanstalt bank in 1930. Inability of either Austria or Germany to meet payments on reparations debts then led to financial breakdowns in both London and Paris, with world repercussions that rolled on to play their part in the closing of all American banks in March 1933.

Under Secretary of State Kissinger's prodding, eleven consumer nations agreed to put up a $25 billion "safety net" fund to help any hard-pressed member ward off such a disaster. Kissinger also proposed internationalizing the administration's proposed high-price policy by setting a "common floor price" for imported oil among the member nations.[54] Only in this way, he said suavely, could those who must make high-risk investments in new oil and in alternative energy resources be assured that they would not be priced out of markets by Persian Gulf states that could produce oil, if they wished, for 20 cents a barrel. It was a measure of how far the world had changed since Marshall proposed his 1947 recovery plan that the Europeans, far from leaping to accept Kissinger's offer, murmured that the program looked like exchanging American for Arab control of prices. It was also a measure of how far the Europeans had come back that Kissinger was now asking them, in his scheme for reducing everybody's dependence upon OPEC oil, to come in as partners in new United States energy ventures and, in exchange for a pro rata share of ownership, profits, and fuel, to put up a substantial part of the $500 billion capital he thought would be needed over the next ten years.

★

In the 1930s, Henry Wallace, Walter Lippmann, and others contended that America must choose. As they put it then, the choice was between becoming an exporting or a moneylending nation; but in the larger sense the choice was between isolation and internationalism, between independence and interdependence. Though the nation threw itself into the second World War, the issue was not settled until after V-J Day, when, under the new challenge of the cold war, the United States chose the international way and became leader of, and banker to, the world.

The question of the 1930s was rephrased forty years later when the choice for the nation, it seemed, was whether to depend on foreign oil or so restructure its domestic economy as to reduce this dependence.

For too long the choice had been delayed: the United States was an immensely rich country, with vast resources and institutional strengths that had already permitted years of postponement after the country first became a net importer of oil in 1950. Committed to economic growth, we prolonged our prosperity by continuing expansion overseas. But an ever-increasing inflation was the price. The underlying structure was geared to the lavish use of oil and natural gas; and now the embargo, the raising of oil prices, and the world recession they triggered laid this structural weakness bare.

Unwillingly, an America spaced out by oil—by cars and superhighways, by the rush to the suburbs—faced up slowly, slowly to the change. Habits would have to be adjusted, if not life-styles; people were driving smaller cars now and would have to drive them less. They might have to restrict the use of the automobile as entertainment and cut down on driving to work as well. They would also have to lower their thermostats, recycle their beercans and aerosols, and count their BTUs and kilowatts. They might have to pay some heed to the shah's unsolicited advice to stop using oil as a combustible ("It is a sin to use the noble product to heat houses and light electric bulbs"[55]) and use it only as a material. For the United States would have to cut its overall energy growth rate until economic growth itself was jeopardized—as it plainly was in 1975.

In the midst of the steepest economic downturn since the 1930s, Congress would not allow oil prices to soar. Laid-off workers needed gasoline for their cars. Angry householders wailed that their oil-swollen utility bills already rose higher than their monthly mortgage payments. And to top it all, there was the prospect of a Middle East war that would cut off everybody's oil. When President Ford proposed oil tariffs that promised more unemployment and spurned oil price controls that promised less inflation, he forfeited his chance of ending either the budgetary or energy deficit. Though Henry Kissinger talked of a "grand design" by which technology, "America's greatest resource," would make the United States once more the world's leading energy exporter by the end of the century, prospects that the United States could rally the world as it rallied Europe in 1947 were dim.

Yet now, as then, unity was an essential to the action called for, and both the leaders and the led would have to see this and what all could gain from it. For this the country and its friends, caught in a recessionary slide, might have to look to the next administration coming to power in 1976. But the action was already in the works. For between our declining reserves and the Arabs' demands and prices, oil's days of dominance are numbered. Its dethronement, inevitable before the end of this century, is brought nearer by events. War in the Middle East could bring that day still nearer.

Sooner rather than later, king oil may be relegated to Persian Gulf exile while the United States and other nations regroup and rebuild new sources of power. Redirecting their technology and capital to rely less upon scarce or uncertain supplies of oil and gas and more upon reliable, more abundant, and renewable energy sources, they may make government a central animator and agent. Emergence of a Federal Energy Administration that operates as well as supervises power resources is as historically inevitable as was TVA. Some members of Congress want the government to take over importing oil. Though the tyrannosaurish oil companies may have to scale down their size, appetite, and quasi-sovereign multinationality, they may well adapt and survive. Among the new enterprises springing up to supply energy, some may be of mixed government-private financing, some cooperative, some nonprofit, and some of course capitalized for profit. New Rockefellers may strike it rich geothermally; new Ketterings may put hydrogen on wheels.

The new approaches to energy, however, may be marked by a wider participation than the multinationals ever permitted. People may count for more. There may be a more democratic share for the worker. An important, possibly crucial, element in these endeavors may be the participation of large numbers of university-trained scientists, technicians, and other professionals who have shown little taste for working for big corporations. As C. P. Snow has never ceased to say, it is at its highest levels that American education is most certainly preeminent. From these quarters, as the age of petroleum fades, may come the talents and skills that will replenish and restore American leadership. In such ways independence may lead on after 1976 to a new order of interdependence.

Bibliographical Essay

Historians have neglected the everyday world of work and its humble technologies for the gaudier goings-on of high politics and statecraft. This judgment of Daniel Boorstin—and his indefatigable example—spurred me in attempting this history of oil in America to look beyond the accepted interpretations and beyond the business-school studies that have filled part of the gap in our understanding of oil's role in industrial society. I want to enumerate some of the books that meant most to me in this search.

Though I do not share Dan Boorstin's genial admiration for the freebooters who liquidated our oil, I know of no better overview of how petroleum first flowed into American life than the high-spirited pages on the Pennsylvania oil rush in his *The National Experience* (1973). Older surveys of the nation's past pause at oil only for a brief, usually withering glance at Rockefeller and at Teapot Dome, and then hurry on to the summits of war, peace, and presidential successions. Even the standard economic histories that I consulted gave less than adequate attention to the business that supplies the industrial heart's blood of our nation. A good picture of how we get and use our oil is given in a work that analyzes many industries, *The Structure of American Industry*, edited by Walter Adams (revised 1971). Its essay on "The Petroleum Industry," by Thomas G. Moore, is indispensable.

For the history of oil, the authoritative work is *The History of the American Petroleum Industry*, produced in two volumes (1955 and 1963) by Harold Williamson and his colleagues at the Northwestern University School of Business. It is comprehensive but not critical. The same may be said for the well-researched, company-sponsored histories of Jersey Standard, California Standard, Indiana Standard, Texaco, Shell, Humble, and Gulf, all of which I consulted with profit. Several of these, like the bulky *Growth of Integrated Oil Companies* (1954), whose principal author J. C. McLean became president of Continental Oil, were prepared at the Harvard Business School. More useful, because more critical, was De Chazeau and Kahn's *Intergration and Competition in the Petroleum Industry* (1959). Of many valuable publications from university presses in the Southwest I made good use of J. Stanley Clark's *The Oil Century* (1959), Carl Rister's *Oil! Titan of the Southwest* (1949), and Gerald Forbes's *Flush Production* (1942).

Although journalism produces profiles aplenty of oilmen, oil is a field wanting in good biographies. The archives of Standard Oil were opened for Professor Allan Nevins's *Study in Power: John D. Rockefeller* (1953), and I drew again and again upon this carefully researched and elegantly written two-volume life of oil's greatest figure. It is the portrait of a master builder in business and philanthropy: Standard Oil's political activities, or rather those of which documentary evidence was found in the archives, are left to an appendix in Volume II. It is a biography without rivals, though Paul Frankel's 1966 study of the Italian oil master Mattei, made without any such documentation, is in some ways much more penetrating. There are no biographies of such oil barons as Requa and Ickes, Archbold and Flagler, Sinclair and Doheny, and those of Deterding and Teagle, Ernest Thompson and H. L. Hunt I found less than revealing.

On government-industry relations, Robert Engler made excellent use of congressional committee transcripts in a work of permanent value, *The Politics of Oil* (1961). But legislative documents must be used with care: I found congressional committee data often laden with inquisitorial prejudice and often distorted by pressures seen and unseen. An old difficulty, that up-to-date information about oil is so largely in industry hands, is now being remedied as the Federal Energy Administration and other government offices, under pressure of the energy shortage, begin to amass their own data.

On the broadest aspects of government-industry relations, John Ise's *United States Oil Policy* (1926) is an important and still valuable appraisal; Eugene V. Rostow's *An Oil Policy for America* (1948) is a cold war statement; and Gerald Nash's *United States Oil Policy, 1890–1964* is a rigorously documented and judiciously balanced analysis. The approach and conclusions of the latter work influenced me at several points in this book.

Here, by chapter, are further comments on sources.

Chapter 1.———The basic information about America's tremendous reliance on oil and gas for energy comes from government sources. Important among these are the Office of Emergency Preparedness's *The Potential for Energy Conservation* (1972) and the Council on Environmental Quality's *Energy and the Environment* (1973). M. A. Adelman's *The World Petroleum Market* (1972), though famous for having forecast the fall of oil prices just before they quintupled, demonstrates incontrovertibly what the oil companies were long at such pains to conceal, that Saudi oil is produced at a cost of less than five cents a barrel. In *Competition, Ltd.* (1972) Fred Allvine, Senator Henry Jackson's petroleum expert, did a good job of showing how the big sources of oil profit changed from refining to pipelining and then to production, first at home and then overseas. But in *Highway Robbery* (1975) he goes overboard in arguing the switch to marketing as the new source of oil profits in the 1970s. That the majors passed along at the gasoline pumps the price boosts conceded to OPEC governments we all know firsthand; but exactly how they did so is still not clear and may not be so until well after their divorce from these governments becomes final, a matter that could take weeks—or years.

Chapter 2.———Richest sources of early Pennsylvania oil lore are McLaurin's *Sketches in Crude Oil* (1896) and *The Derrick's Handbook of Petroleum* (1898), and best use of them is made in Giddens's *Pennsylvania Petroleum* (1947). Ida Tarbell's *History of the Standard Oil Company* (1904), made out by intervening generations to be a screeching assault on John D. and all his works and ways, reads uncommonly well and sensibly after 70 years. But, like nearly everything published about oil, her book speaks for an interest—in this case the interest of small Pennsylvania oil producers ruined by Rockefeller, among whom was her father. Williamson and Daum's first volume, *The Age of Illumination* (1959), amply traces the kerosene business's growth; and Nevins's biography, written after the caustic appraisals of Flynn, *God's Gold* (1932), Josephson, *The Robber Barons* (1934), and Myers, *The Great American Fortunes* (1930), authoritatively marshals and judges the evidence on the social value of trust-building, giving Rockefeller the benefit of the doubt. Chester

Destler's *Roger Sherman and the Independent Oilmen* (1967) presents unassailable evidence of Rockefeller's early favors from the railroads. Of the economic retrospects on the trust-building years, the
sharpest and clearest is still Cochran and Miller's *The Age of Enterprise* (1942).

Chapter 3.——Governor Jim Hogg, leading Texas through farm
strikes and rail riots into oil wealth, is seen picturesquely in Gambrell's
"James Hogg, Statesman or Demagogue?" and decorously in Cotner's
James Stephen Hogg (1959). Good details of Hogg's early political
wars are to be found in a 1907 University of Chicago master's thesis
by R. H. Morrison. Boyce House's article "Spindletop" in the *Southwestern Historical Quarterly* (1946) and Clark and Halbouty's *Spindletop* (1952) provide rich color on early oil-drilling feats. W. L.
Mellon's privately printed memoir *Judge Mellon's Sons* (1948) is indispensable for understanding the rise of Gulf and Texaco after the
Spindletop oil strike.

For Deterding's ideas about oil, I gained best understanding from
the writings of Paul Frankel, whose brief but well-judged *Essentials
of Petroleum* (1946) is a work of enduring value. I drew the materials
on the origins of the filling station from a scattering of sources. Nash's
U. S. Oil Policy 1890–1964 suggests the changing relations of government and oil between the breakup of Standard Oil in 1911 and the close
collaboration of 1917–18. Though I turned to government records and
newspapers of the day for the 1918 enactment of the depletion allowance, an industry account—Lichtblau and Spriggs's *The Oil Depletion
Issue* (1959)—was helpful. Nash also has a good outline of the depletion clause's evolution.

Chapter 4.——There may never have been a congressional inquiry as well conducted as Senator Walsh's Teapot Dome investigation, the record of which is established in *Leases upon Naval Oil Reserves* (1924, 1928). Of contemporary accounts, Allen's *Only Yesterday* (1931) is still eye-opening. Among academic studies, Bates's
Origins of Teapot Dome (1963) stresses its place in conservationist
history, but in "Teapot Dome and the Election of 1924" (1955) he
puts the affair in starkest political context. David Stretton's "Behind
Teapot Dome" (1957) has insights about Fall (Stretton has written an
unpublished biography of Fall), and Bert Noggle's *Teapot Dome*
(1962) has helpful details; but the fullest picture available of Harding
and his administration is to be found in Russell's *The Shadow of
Blooming Grove* (1968), and I made repeated use of it.

Chapter 5.————On the influence of the oil-driven automobile, Nevins and Hill's *Ford, the Man, the Times, the Company* (1954) is essential. I also relied on Flink's *America Adopts the Automobile* (1970) and Rae's *The American Automobile* (1965), a volume in the social history series edited by Boorstin; but for what the car did to daily life and habits, I turned most often to David Cohn's affable *Combustion on Wheels* (1944). Scholarly interpretations that yielded insights were Norman Moline's *Mobility and the Small Town* (1971) and Kenneth Jackson's imaginative essay "The Crabgrass Frontier" (1973). John G. Burnham ably spelled out in "The Gasoline Tax and the Automobile Revolution" (1961) how roads were financed and built for the proliferating artifacts of Detroit.

The enveloping impact of oil in the Southwest is vividly exemplified in J. K. Johnson's monograph on the boom town of Borger (1940); in John Bainbridge's *New Yorker* pieces on Texas millionaires (collected in *The Super Americans,* 1961); in the journalism of Hart Stillwell and Ronnie Dugger; and in sundry local histories, notably Fehrenbach's *Lone Star* (1968). The story of the east Texas extravaganza is suitably narrated in Clark and Halbouty's *The Last Boom* (1972). The industry's devices for coping with the glut are tellingly identified and analyzed in Nash's *U.S. Oil Policy, 1890–1964* (1968).

The federal government's equivocating and finally pro-industry role, well traced by Nash, is authoritatively reflected in *The Secret Diary of Harold Ickes* (1953). Oil's dominating force in events leading up to Pearl Harbor is to be seen in the Ickes and Morgenthau diaries as well as the memoirs of Stimson and Hull, and is well summarized in Blum's *Roosevelt and Morgenthau* (1971).

Chapter 6.————In America 53 percent of all oil energy has been expended in motion, compared with only 28 percent among Europeans. In his seminal essay on "The M-Factor in American History" (1962) George W. Pierson singles out movement as the preeminent American trait; he nails the thesis down in *The Moving American* (1973). Supporting evidence is to be found in Helen Leavitt's trenchant study of the interstate highway system *Superhighway-Superhoax* (1970) and in John Burby's indignant *The Great American Motion Sickness* (1971). Lawrence White's *The Automobile Industry since 1945* (1971) zeroes in doggedly on the motorcar economy, but also worth consulting are Alfred P. Sloan's *My Years with General Motors* (1964), Kennedy's *The Automobile Industry* (1941), and John Jerome's *The Death of the Automobile* (1972). On truck transport the authority is Wilfred Owen's *Strategy for Mobility* (1964).

T. A. Boyd's *Professional Amateur* (1957) is the best available life of Charles Kettering, the pied piper of oil-induced motion.

On postwar oil politics in and out of Washington, Engler's *The Politics of Oil* (1961) ranges furthest, but in the 1970s further studies of Rayburn and Johnson seem called for. Here Ickes's disclosures, in the absence of a final volume of his *Secret Diary* (after his death his widow, sensitive about personal references, excised so much from the manuscript that the publisher declined to publish the emasculated result), rest on newspaper accounts of his Senate Naval Affairs committee testimony against Pauley. On the Tidelands fight, Engler's account is the best, though Bartley's *The Tidelands Oil Controversy* (1953) is a valuable monograph. For later developments in offshore oil, I drew upon government reports, trade journals, and press accounts.

Chapter 7.————Literature on Middle East oil is copious, and still largely British. For the formulation of policy, I searched in the Forrestal and Dulles papers, including the invaluable interviews in the Dulles Oral History Project. On aspects relating to Marshall Plan, Truman Doctrine, and NATO policy, Schwadran's *Middle East Oil and the Great Powers* (1955) was helpful. So were Leeman's *The Price of Oil in the Middle East* (1962) and Schaffer's *The Oil Import Program of the United States* (1968). Richard Neustadt's *Alliance Politics* (1970) and Hugh Thomas's *Suez* (1966) are the most penetrating studies of the 1956 Suez affair. Leonard Mosley's *Power Play* (1973) and Ray Vicker's *Kingdom of Oil* (1974) are useful for interviews with many of the principal figures in Middle East oil. An excellently informed source that stresses Libya's part in changing the picture is James Akins's *Foreign Affairs* article (1973), and Michael Tanzer's *The Political Economy of International Oil* (1969), though centered on the underdeveloped countries, is full of wide-ranging perceptions. For no Middle East country is there a clinically factual analysis to compare with Lieuwen's *Oil in Venezuela* (1955). But events in this region move too fast for scholarly detachment.

Chapter 8.————Engler's *The Politics of Oil* (1961) has good detail on the legislative brawling that went with natural gas's arrival as a big new force in the nation's economy. Of many monographic studies I consulted, Paul McAvoy's "The Regulation Induced Shortage of Natural Gas" (1971) is representative, an economist's rigorous analysis that reaches the industry's conclusion that federal controls are bad and should be done away with. For comprehension of all viewpoints, I turned also to congressional reports, newspapers, and periodicals. Petrochemicals are an important part of the picture, and Hahn's *The Petrochemical Industry* (1970) and Wendland's *Petrochemicals* (1969) are both worth consulting. From the stormy days of Senator Kerr natural gas has been a tremendously political subject, not yet adequately appraised. Public policy is in flux.

Chapter 9.————Important sources for analyzing present and future oil policies were the various studies made in the energy crisis of 1973–74. The Ford Foundation Energy Policy committee's report *A Time to Choose* (1974) was technocratic and somewhat radical, whereas the Committee for Economic Development's *Achieving Energy Independence* (1974) was the more thoroughly hedged statement of business activists. To me the most consequential was the Federal Energy Agency's massive *Project Independence Report* (1974) with its prodigious assemblage of collateral documents: out of this vast rockpile the Ford Administration proceeds to quarry its energy program.

On alternative sources of energy, Beck and Rawlings's *Coal, the Captive Giant* (1971) makes the point that oil already owns the one most available. Harry Caudill's *Night Comes to the Cumberlands* (1963) eloquently warns that the human cost of coal comes high. The human and environmental costs of nuclear energy are also the subject of many books, among which Sheldon Novick's *The Careless Atom* (1969) is well worth a look. A European inquiry into alternatives, the OECD report, *Energy Prospects to 1985* (1974), contains more positive assessments. With new developments daily outdating earlier roundups, I found Wilson Clark's *Energy for Survival* (1974), though bearing down hardest in favor of solar power, a fresh and wide-ranging handbook on alternative energy possibilities.

Notes

Note: For full bibliographical information about the sources cited in Notes, see Bibliography.

CHAPTER 1 (pp. 3–18)

1. Strunsky, *The Living Tradition*, p. 172.
2. Automobile use data, see Public Roads Administration, *Highway Statistics*, 1945, pp. 18, 30, 34; Dept. of Transportation, *Highway Statistics*, 1970, pp. 4, 55; and *Nationwide Personal Transportation Study*, #2, 1972, p. 3; #7, 1972, p. 3; #8, 1973, pp. 3, 9; #9, 1973, p. 4; #10, 1974, pp. 9–10, 21, 67; #11, 1974, pp. 9, 50. *Automobile Facts and Figures*, Dec. 1941, p. 3; Dec. 1945, p. 8; Jan. 1949, p. 8; 1973–74, p. 30. Office of Emergency Preparedness, *Potential for Energy Conservation*, p. 13. *Nilson Report*, May 1972, p. 3. American Automobile Association, *Gas Watchers' Guide*, 1975, pp. 4 ff.
3. *New York Times*, Nov. 8, 1973, p. 1. © 1973 The New York Times Company. Reprinted by permission. See also *Environment*, Apr. 1971, pp. 1–19.
4. *Time*, Jan. 14, 1974, pp. 15–16. Reprinted by permission from TIME, The Weekly Newsmagazine; Copyright Time Inc. See also *New York Times*, Nov. 10, 11, 13, and 24, 1973; *Time*, Nov. 12 (p. 107–10), Dec. 3 (pp. 29 ff.) and Dec. 10 (pp. 33–4), 1973.
5. *New York Times*, Feb. 19, 1974.
6. Information from George Young, Port of New York Authority, Dec. 10, 1974. *New York Times*, May 13, 1974. For other details of gasoline shortage behavior, see *New York Times*, Jan. 10, 14, 16, 27 and Feb. 5 and 10, 1974; *Time*, Feb. 4 (p. 37), 11 (p. 27–8) and 18 (pp. 29 ff.), 1974.
7. *Time*, Feb. 13, 1967. Reprinted by permission from TIME, The Weekly

Newsmagazine; Copyright Time Inc.; see also *National Observer*, Aug. 27, 1962.

8. On Mellon and income taxes, see White, *Puritan in Babylon*, p. 333; Schlesinger, *The Crisis of the Old Order*, p. 63; *D.A.B. Supplement*, 2, p. 222; *New Republic*, May 29, 1935.

9. Senate Subcommittee, *Multinational Corporations and U.S. Foreign Policy*, Part IV, dated Jan. 28, 1974; *New York Times*, Jan. 30, 1974, p. 1. See also *New York Times*, Jan. 25, 1974.

10. Federal Trade Commission, *The International Oil Cartel*, 1952, pp. 1 ff.

11. *New York Times*, Jan. 25, 1974. See also De Chazeau and Kahn, pp. 547–51; *New York Times*, Jan. 3, Feb. 25, and Mar. 5, 1974.

12. *New York Times*, July 15 and Aug. 31, 1973. See also Luttwak and Laqueur, p. 33.

13. Marvin and Bernard Kalb, *Kissinger*, p. 453. Little, Brown and Company.

14. Ibid., p. 474.

15. Ibid., p. 478.

16. Ibid., pp. 489–90. See also *New York Times*, Nov. 25, 1973, IV, p. 3; *Time*, July 1, 1974, p. 33.

17. *New York Times*, Nov. 25, 1973, IV, p. 3. © 1973 The New York Times Company. Reprinted by permission.

18. *New York Times*, Mar. 17, 1974.

CHAPTE 2 (pp. 21–50)

1. On bitumen and petroleum in antiquity, see R. J. Forbes, pp. 31, 42, 79. See also Forbes in *Bitumen*.

2. Herrmann, p. 122.

3. Boorstin, p. 42.

4. Ibid., p. 44.

5. Cited by Giddens, *Pennsylvania Petroleum*, p. 66.

6. Ibid.

7. On "right of capture" legalisms, see Williamson and Daum, I, p. 763.

8. McLaurin, p. 79.

9. Flynn, pp. 38–9. See also Nevins, I, p. 53. Nevins, I; pp. 44 ff. See also Flynn, pp. 38–9.

10. For the Sherman well anecdote, see McLaurin, p. 116. See also Williamson and Daum, I, p. 93.

11. Flynn, p. 239.

12. For the Chicago fire details, see Musham, pp. 69, 151; Cromie, p. 2.

13. Cochran and Miller, p. 135.

14. Tarbell, I, pp. 44–5.

15. Destler, pp. 15–21. See also Charles Francis Adams, p. 94.

16. Nevins, I, p. 89. From *A Study in Power: John D. Rockefeller*. Reprinted by permission of Charles Scribner's Sons. See also Flynn, pp.

145–6, 223, and *Report of the Special Committee on Railroads Appointed Feb. 28, 1879, to Investigate Alleged Abuses in the Management of Railroads Chartered by the State of New York, A. B. Hepburn chairman* (hereafter referred to as *Hepburn Committee Report*), 5 vols., Albany, 1880, I, pp. 119 ff.

17. Tarbell, I, p. 49.
18. Nevins, I, p. 100.
19. Flynn, p. 160.
20. Williamson and Daum, I, pp. 346, 354.
21. Tarbell, I, pp. 105–6.
22. Flynn, p. 148.
23. Nevins, I, pp. 95 ff.
24. Tarbell, I, pp. 47, 48, 50, 68, 100, 238. Nevins, I, p. 325.
25. *Oil, Paint and Drug Reporter*, June 4, 1879. See also *Hepburn Committee Report*, I, p. 45.
26. Williamson and Daum, I, p. 643.
27. Ibid., I, p. 644. Josephson, p. 268.
29. Flynn, p. v. See also Samuel Hays, pp. 4 ff.
30. Nevins, I, p. 311.
31. Ibid., p. 312.
32. Ibid., p. 305.
33. Ibid., p. 314.
34. Ibid., II, pp. 131, 472.
35. *Hepburn Committee Report*, IV, pp. 3709 ff. See also Flynn, p. 220.
36. *Hepburn Committee Report*, II, p. 1669.
37. *Hepburn Committee Report*, III, p. 2666.
38. *Hepburn Committee Report*, I, p. 394.
39. *Hepburn Committee Report*, I, p. 709.
40. *Hepburn Committee Report*, III, pp. 2617, 2665.
41. *Hepburn Committee Report*, I, pp. 40–1.
42. Nevins, II, pp. 467, 471.
43. Ibid., I, p. 309.
44. For details on Foraker, see Nevins, II, Appendix, pp. 467 ff. Information came from letters filched from Standard Oil files and bought by W. R. Hearst and published in his New York paper in 1906 campaign. See also *D.A.B.* VI, p. 503; Adams, *Incredible Era*, p. 27; and Russell, *Shadow of Blooming Grove*, p. 191. It was Foraker's disgrace that enabled Harding to get into the Senate.
45. Nevins, II, pp. 469–70.
46. Lloyd's article in *Atlantic Monthly*, Sept. 1881, first put Rockefeller into national perspective.
47. Hacker and Hendrick, p. 282.
48. *Congressional Record*, XXI, Pt. III, 2731.
49. Flynn, pp. 371–3. See also Nevins, II, pp. 356 ff.
50. Nevins, II, p. 379. See also Hamilton, pp. 41–2; Thorelli, pp. 122 ff.

CHAPTER 3 (pp. 51–79)

1. Texas rail strike, see Morrison, pp. 2 ff.
2. Gambrell, pp. 338 ff.
3. Morrison, p. 29.
4. Gambrell, pp. 338 ff.
5. Morrison, p. 8.
6. Gambrell, pp. 338 ff.
7. Ibid. Said by Richardson, p. 266, to be Hogg's strongest oath.
8. Hogg's *Addresses and State Papers*, pp. 395, 487 ff.
9. Clark and Halbouty, *Spindletop*, pp. 107 ff.
10. Ibid.
11. House, "Spindletop," pp. 36 ff. Quoted by permission of the Texas State Historical Association from Boyce House, "Spindletop," *Southwestern Historical Quarterly*, L (July, 1946), 39–40.
12. Thompson, p. 22.
13. Cotner, p. 520. See also Clara Lewis in Webb, II, p. 139.
14. Harvey O'Connor, *Mellon's Millions*, p. 94. See also Mellon, p. 260; Spratt, p. 274; Marquis James, pp. 6 ff.
15. Mellon, p. 260.
16. Ibid., p. 272.
17. Ibid., p. 273. See also FTC report on *Pipeline Transmission*, p. xxvii; Cockenboo, pp. 3, 42.
18. On Magnolia ownership data, see *Pipeline Transmission*, p. 343. See also *The Price of Gasoline* in 1915, p. 23.
19. Harvey O'Connor, *Mellon's Millions*, p. 101.
21. Frankel, *Essentials of Petroleum*, p. 90. Reprinted by permission of Frank Cass & Co. Ltd. See also Davenport and Cooke, p. 15.
22. *Horseless Age*, Jan. 1896, p. 8.
23. Robert E. Wilson, p. 11.
24. Marquis James, p. 35.
25. On the various garages, see *Horseless Age*, May 1, 1912, p. 751.
26. *Horseless Age*, Feb. 14. 1912, p. 365.
27. For material in this paragraph, see *Horseless Age*, May 1, 1912, p. 751.
28. For material in this paragraph, see *Horseless Age*, May 1, 1912, p. 754; May 6, 1914, p. 716.
29. *Horseless Age*, Jan. 8, 1913.
30. Ibid., May 7, 1913, p. 857.
31. *Public Affairs Information Service*, Oct. 12, 1915; also Sept. 1916.
32. On Seattle and Cleveland reports, see *Public Affairs Information Service*, Dec. 1916.
33. Giddens, *Standard Oil Co. (Indiana)*, pp. 79–80.
34. Thompson, p. 61.
35. McLean and Haigh, pp. 268–9.
36. Gerald Nash, p. 9.

37. Ibid., p. 24.

38. Ibid., p. 30.

39. On the 1913 and 1916 depletion allowance, see Lichtblau and Spriggs, p. 29. See also *Legislative History of Depletion Allowances*, p. 1; De Chazeau and Kahn, p. 154.

40. *Revenue Act of 1918—To Provide Revenue for War Purposes: Hearings*, p. 94. See also Gerald Nash, 34–5; Lichtblau and Spriggs, p. 32.

41. *To Provide Revenue for War Purposes*, p. 356.

42. Ibid., pp. 363 f.

43. Ibid., p. 360.

44. Ibid., pp. 433–7.

45. *Senate Report No. 617* (1918), p. 6.

46. *To Provide Revenue for War Purposes*, pp. 89–90.

47. Lichtblau and Spriggs, p. 35. See also Gerald Nash, pp. 34–5; 85–6.

48. Harvey O'Connor, *Mellon's Millions*, p. 152.

49. *New York Times*, Oct. 19, 1918. *New York Times*, Dec. 24, 1918, p. 1, analyzes the tax act without mention of depletion allowance.

50. *Oil and Gas Journal*, Dec. 20, 1918, p. 3.

CHAPTER 4 (pp. 80–102)

1. Kornitzer, pp. 128, 157, 191.

2. Ibid.

3. Hicks, pp. 50, 77.

4. *Congressional Quarterly*, "Dollar Politics," p. 64.

5. White, *Masks in a Pageant*, p. 404.

6. Hagedorn, p. 385. See also Russell, *The Shadow of Blooming Grove*, p. 385; *New York Times*, Mar. 20 and 28, 1924.

7. *New York Times*, Mar. 2, 1924, p. 38. © 1924 The New York Times Company. Reprinted by permission.

8. Russell, *The Shadow of Blooming Grove*, p. 380

9. *New York Times*, Aug. 6, 1923.

10. Adams, *Incredible Era*, p. 152; Russell, *The Shadow of Blooming Grove*, p. 558.

11. Hoover, p. 49.

12. White, in Noggle, p. 61.

13. Fall biographical details are in an unpublished life by D. H. Stratton, cited by Russell, *The Shadow of Blooming Grove*, p. 26.

14. Russell, *The Shadow of Blooming Grove*, p. 436, as told by Hoke Donithen, who was present.

15. *Reminiscences of Albert Davis Lasker*, pp. 66–7. See also Russell, *The Shadow of Blooming Grove*, pp. 501–2.

16. *Reminiscences of Albert Davis Lasker*, pp. 66–7.

17. For Walsh biographical details, see Sullivan, VI, p. 278; also Bates in *Montana Magazine of History*, I, p. 23; also O'Keane, pp. 5, 50.

18. *Leases upon Naval Oil Reserves, Hearings, 1924.*
19. For the material on Hays, see *Leases 1924*, pp. 2900 ff.
20. McLean, pp. 217, 253, 278–81.
21. Ibid., p. 278.
22. Stratton, pp. 385 ff.
23. *Leases 1924*, p. 1429.
24. Ibid., p. 1453.
25. Ibid.
26. Ibid.
27. On the Florida details, see McLean, p. 281.
28. Russell, *The Shadow of Blooming Grove*, p. 613.
29. *Leases 1924*, p. 1695.
30. Ibid.
31. Frank Kent in *Baltimore Sun*, Jan. 23, 1924.
32. *Leases 1924*, pp. 1713, 1749.
33. Bruce Bliven in *New Republic*, Feb. 13, 1924.
34. *Leases 1924*, p. 1771.
35. Ibid.
36. Ibid.
37. Ibid., pp. 1961–2. See also Russell, *The Shadow of Blooming Grove*, pp. 615–6.
38. *Baltimore Sun*, Jan. 27, 1924.
39. Ibid., Jan. 17, 1924.
40. Ibid., Feb. 25, 1924. See also Bates in *American Historical Review*, pp. 303 ff.
41. *New York Times*, Jan. 31, 1924, p. 2.
42. *Baltimore Sun*, Jan. 27, 1924.
43. Russell, *The Shadow of Blooming Grove*, p. 615. See also William Hard in *Nation*, Feb. 6, 1924, p. 133.
44. *Leases 1924*, pp. 1771, 1940.
45. Bates in *American Historical Review*, pp. 303 f.
46. *Boston Transcript*, cited by Noggle, p. 102.
47. *Baltimore Sun*, Feb. 15, 1924.
48. *New York Times*, Mar. 2, 1924, IX, p. 2. © 1924 The New York Times Company. Reprinted by permission.
49. *Literary Digest*, LXXX, 9, Mar. 1, 1924, pp. 8–9.
50. Ibid.
51. *Leases 1924*, p. 1727.
52. Ibid., p. 2900.
53. Russell, *The Shadow of Blooming Grove*, p. 617.
54. *Baltimore Sun*, Feb. 20, 1924.
55. Ibid., Mar. 13 and 19, 1924; *New York Times*, Mar. 14, 1929. See also Russell, *The Shadow of Blooming Grove*, p. 618.
56. *New York Times*, Mar. 27, 1927.
57. Allen, *Only Yesterday*, Harper & Row, Publishers, pp. 178–9.
58. Ibid., p. 157.

59. Abele, p. 24.
60. Allen, p. 144.
61. Ibid.; see also Russell, *The Shadow of Blooming Grove*, p. 620.
62. For Walsh interrogation of Everhart, see *Leases 1928*, pp. 1, 5, 52.
63. On the interrogation of Consolidated men, see *Leases 1928*, pp. 95, 101–2, 145, 147, 165. See also *Investigation of Actions of Consolidated Trading Co.*, passim; Fosdick, p. 22.
64. On the interrogation of Hays, see *Leases 1928*, p. 52.
65. See Allen, pp. 164, 169; see also Russell, *The Shadow of Blooming Grove*, p. 636.
66. Ibid.
67. Smith, p. 295; Lundberg, p. 167; Schlesinger, p. 63.
68. On Sinclair's API reelection on the day he went to trial for tampering with the jury hearing his case, see Jonathan Daniels, p. 116.

CHAPTER 5 (pp. 103–140)

1. On oil and geography, see Robert Byron, "The Story of Oil," *Geographic Magazine*, 16 (Jan. 1941), pp. 182 ff; Major R. A. Walker, "Oil, a Precis for Armchair Strategists," *Army Quarterly*, Vol. 82, No. 1 (April 1961), pp. 95 ff.
2. Nevins and Hill, p. 380. See also Frank Donovan, p. 162.
3. Lynds, p. 251.
4. On Astor cars, see Flink, p. 57. On Portland cars, see Bird, p. 86.
5. Jacques Ickx, "The Great Automobile Race of 1895," *Scientific American*, 226:5, pp. 102–11 (May 1972).
6. Burlingame, p. 66; Nevins and Hill, pp. 466, 469.
7. David Cohn, p. 155. See also Nevins and Hill, p. 380.
8. *Heaven's My Destination*, pp. 13, 126.
9. *Main Street*, p. 40. Reprinted by permission of Harcourt Brace Jovanovich, Inc.
10. *Babbitt*, pp. 22, 23. Reprinted by permission of Harcourt Brace Jovanovich, Inc.
11. Ibid.
12. "Farewell My Lovely," in *Second Tree from the Corner*, p. 34.
13. *Babbitt*, p. 24.
14. Ibid.
15. Waugh, p. 241
16. King, unpaged.
17. Ibid.
18. *Scientific American*, July 6, 1907; also Mar. 29, 1909.
19. King, unpaged. Reprinted by permission of the Chicago Tribune-New York News Syndicate, Inc. All rights reserved.
20. Claudy, "Good Roads v. Mud Holes," p. 3.

21. Burnham, in *Mississippi Valley Historical Review*, pp. 435 ff. See also S. B. Warner, pp. 4, 37, 180.
22. Ibid.
23. Burnham, p. 435. See also Gerald White, p. 506.
24. Burnham, p. 435.
25. King, unpaged.
26. *Outlook*, May 28, 1924.
27. *Atlantic Monthly*, Aug. 1923, p. 278. See also F. E. Brimmer, pp. 15 ff.
28. *Vogue*, Apr. 1923, quoted in Brimmer, p. 47. See also *Vogue*, Jan. 15, 1923.
29. Margaret Emerson Bailey, "Motoring Manners," in *Woman's Home Companion*, May 1923, p. 50.
30. *Babbitt*, p. 23.
31. Alix K. Shulman, "War in the Back Seat," *Atlantic*, July 1972, pp. 50–55.
32. Lynds, pp. 113–4.
33. Cohn, p. 225.
34. *Babbitt*, p. 23.
35. Kennedy, p. 189.
36. Steinbeck, p. 170. From *Grapes of Wrath* by John Steinbeck, copyright 1939 by John Steinbeck. Reprinted by permission of The Viking Press, Inc.
37. Steinbeck, p. 241.
38. Ibid.
39. Ibid.
40. Clawson, in *California Historical Society Quarterly*, pp. 145, 155.
41. Warner Clark, in *Southwest Review*, p. 1.
42. Lichtblau and Spriggs, p. 23; see also De Chazeau and Kahn, p. 154.
43. Johnson, in *Studies in Sociology*, pp. 1–10. See also Lona Shaver in Webb, I, p. 192; Rister, p. 276.
44. Johnson, in *Studies in Sociology*, pp. 1–10.
45. Ibid.
46. Bainbridge, pp. 35, 100, 265, 271, 282. See also Fehrenbach, pp. 620 ff., 666; *New York Times*, Nov. 30, 1974, p. 1; *Esquire*, 67:64–8 (Jan. 1967).
47. Bainbridge, pp. 35, 100, 265, 271, 282.
48. Ibid.
49. On "unit" production as "conservation," see De Chazeau and Kahn, pp. 145 ff. See also Clark and Halbouty, *Last Boom*, p. 149; Warner Clark, in *Southwest Review*, pp. 1–21.
50. De Chazeau and Kahn, pp. 145 ff.; Clark and Halbouty, *Last Boom*, p. 149.
51. See note 50 for sources.
52. Frankel, *Essentials of Petroleum*, pp. 91–4; Roberts, p. 336; Frankel, *Mattei*, p. 84; Gerald Nash, p. 102.
53. On the as-is agreement and the "cartel," see *New York Times*, Oct. 9

and 20, 1928; Harvey O'Connor, in *World Crisis in Oil*, p. 88; Federal Trade Commission, *The International Petroleum Cartel*, p. 125. This authoritative Washington report, made public despite vigorous efforts to suppress it, is based largely upon information brought out some years earlier by a Swedish parliamentary inquiry.

54. Lieuwen, p. 56.
55. Clark and Halbouty, *The Last Boom*, pp. 3 ff., 92, 141, 162, 164. See also Gerald Nash, pp. 117–20; Ickes, *Secret Diary*, I, pp. 13 ff., 142.
56. See note 55 for sources.
57. See note 55 for sources.
58. See note 55 for sources.
59. On Ickes biographical details, see Schlesinger, pp. 471–2; Nash, pp. 147–9; Ickes, *Autobiography of a Curmudgeon*.
60. On the interstate oil compact, see Gerald Nash, pp. 151–2; Mooney, pp. 79 ff.
61. On the Deterding-Teagle visit, see Ickes, *Secret Diary*, I, pp. 192 f.
62. Ibid., I, p. 96.
63. Blum, *Roosevelt and Morgenthau*, pp. 392 ff.; Ickes, *Secret Diary*, I, pp. 132, 236, 273, 297, 330, 339.
64. Blum, pp. 406, 410; Ickes, *Secret Diary*, III, pp. 532, 545–6, 551, 553, 567, 580, 583, 591, 628 ff., 659.
65. See note 64 for sources.
66. See note 64 for sources.
67. Ickes, *Secret Diary*, III, pp. 628 ff., 659; Blum, *Roosevelt and Morgenthau*, p. 415.
68. See note 67 for sources.
69. Ickes, *An Oil Policy*, p. 6.
70. Ibid.
71. Snyder, p. 321.
72. Marshall quoted by Editors of *Look*, p. 21. See also *General Marshall's Report*.
73. Ickes, *Secret Diary*, III, pp. 580, 597; see also Lingemann, p. 238.
74. On W. Alton Jones's role, see J. S. Clark, *The Oil Century*, p. 136; Clark and Halbouty, p. 267.
75. For Big Inch details, see Gerald Nash, pp. 163–5; Ickes, *Secret Diary*, III, p. 617; Clark and Halbouty, *The Last Boom*, pp. 266–71. See also F. B. Dow, "The Role of Petroleum Pipelines in the War," *Annals*, CCXXX, Nov. 1943, pp. 93–100.
76. Lingemann, pp. 235–9; Perrett, pp. 133, 239. For other rationing details, see Lingemann, pp. 241–3, 252, 266.
77. See note 76 for sources.
78. For the Forrestal role in Mexico, see Forrestal Diaries.
79. For the Petroleum Reserves Corp. details, see Gerald Nash, pp. 171–2; Schwadran, p. 310; *New York Times*, Feb. 4 and 6, 1944.
80. Gerald Nash, p. 175; Issawi and Yeganeh, p. 54.
81. *Letters of Franklin K. Lane*, p. 315.

CHAPTER 6 (pp. 141–172)

1. Pierson, in *American Quarterly*, pp. 275 ff. Copyright, 1962, Trustees of the University of Pennsylvania. Reprinted by permission of the University of Pennsylvania.
2. Spock, pp. 164–5.
3. Ibid.
4. Potter, pp. 194–8.
5. Lynds, p. 251.
6. Rae, *Road and Car in American Life*, p. 112.
7. Senate Subcommittee on Antitrust, *American Ground Transportation*, pp. 30–5.
8. Ibid.
9. *New York Times*, Feb. 23, 1955, p. 1. © 1955 The New York Times Company. Reprinted by permission.
10. Ibid.
11. Leavitt, pp. 1, 27 f., 47.
12. Clawson and Knetsch, p. 26.
13. *Statistical Abstract 1964*, p. 202.
14. Clawson, *Statistics on Outdoor Recreation*, p. 99.
15. On pa-ma motels, see Dean, in *Urban Land*, p. 3.
16. Rae, *Road and Car*, p. 105; Communication from Holiday Inns, Inc., Sept. 1974. See also *Highways and Economic and Social Changes*, p. 12.
17. Gelfand, p. 344. See also *New York Times*, Oct. 15, 1972.
18. *New York Times*, Nov. 26, 1958. Jerome, p. 263. © 1958 The New York Times Company. Reprinted by permission.
19. Boyd, *Professional Amateur*, p. 159. About Freon, Communication from R. W. Smith, Frigidaire, Feb. 1975.
20. Rosamund Young, p. 162.
21. Levine, p. 95.
22. Rosamund Young, pp. 162, 189.
23. Lawrence White, p. 259. See also Sloan, p. 5; Burby, p. 22.
24. For cost of annual model changes, see F.M. Fisher et al. in *Journal of Political Economy*. See also *Nation*, Jan. 20, 1962, p. 50; *Consumers Union Report*, Feb. 1961, p. 90 and Apr. 1961, p. 176; Lawrence White, p. 263.
25. Dickinson, p. 106.
26. Jerome, p. 15.
27. Lawrence White, p. 217.
28. Jerome, pp. 28, 158, 164.
29. Ibid.
30. Moynihan, in *Public Interest*, Spring 1966, p. 10.
31. Tom Wolfe, *The Kandy Kolored Tangerine Flake Streamline Baby*, pp. 65 ff.

32. Owen, *Strategy for Mobility,* p. 96.
33. Rae, *Road and Car,* p. 112.
34. R. C. and E. D. James, pp. 45 ff. See also Leiter, p. 39; Hoffa, pp. 1 ff.; Mollenhoff, pp. 66 ff.; Hutchinson, pp. 253 ff.
35. Widick, p. 152.
36. *Highways and Economic and Social Changes,* pp. 12, 50, 59, 63, 65. See also Owen, *Strategy for Mobility,* pp. 96, 116; Rae, *Road and Car,* pp. 52, 109.
37. De Chazeau and Kahn, pp. 152, 164. See also Gerald Nash, pp. 128 ff.; *Fortune,* April 1965, p. 113.
38. On Rayburn and Johnson as brokers, see Gerald Nash, pp. 151–2; Bolling, p. 200; Dorough, pp. 236, 484; Valton Young, p. 77. See also Don Hinga, "Texas Squire," in *Southwest Review,* Vol. 29, Summer 1944, pp. 471–80.
39. Stilwell, pp. 314 ff.
40. Dugger, in *Atlantic,* pp. 66 ff.
41. Herbert Alexander, pp. 47, 139; *New York Times,* Oct. 7, 1974, p. 35 and Nov. 15, 1974, p. 37. Communication from Herbert Alexander, Mar. 11, 1975.
42. See note 41 for sources.
43. Pearson and Anderson, p. 432.
44. *New York Times,* Mar. 2 (p. 15) and Mar. 3 (p. 45), 1962; *New York Herald Tribune,* Mar. 3, 1963, p. 3. For Gulf Oil and the SEC, see *New York Times,* Mar. 11, 1975, p. 1, and *Time,* Mar. 24, 1975, p. 54.
45. *Fortune,* March 1959, pp. 136–8; Courtesy of Fortune Magazine. See also *Time,* Jan. 27, 1967, pp. 22–3; Harter, p. 208; *Esquire,* 67:64–8 (Jan. 1967); *New Republic,* Feb. 24, 1958; *Harpers,* Mar. 1957, pp. 68–74; Kilman and Wright, p. 22; *Commonweal,* 67:142–4 (Nov. 8, 1957).
46. *Collier's,* July 20, 1946, pp. 23 ff. See also *St. Louis Post Dispatch,* Oct. 19, 1945 and Jan. 31, 1946; *New York Times,* Feb. 6, 1946, p. 1; *Current Biography,* 1945, pp. 457–9; *Newsweek,* 27:30, Feb. 18, 1946 and Nov. 5, 1945, pp. 76–7; *New Republic,* 114:173 (Feb. 11, 1946) and 114:251 (Feb. 18, 1946); *Time,* Mar. 18, 1946, pp. 22–3. Ickes, *Secret Diary,* III, pp. 624–5, 628–9.
47. *Collier's,* July 20, 1946, pp. 23 ff.
48. *New York Times,* Feb. 6, 1946; © 1946 The New York Times Company. Reprinted by permission. *St. Louis Post Dispatch,* Feb. 6, 1946.
49. See note 48 for sources.
50. *St. Louis Post Dispatch,* Feb. 6, 1946; *New York Times,* Feb. 6, 1946.
51. See note 50 for sources.
52. *St. Louis Post Dispatch,* Feb. 6, 1946; *New York Times,* Feb. 6, 1946.
53. *New York Times,* Feb. 5, 1946; © 1946 The New York Times. Reprinted by permission. *PM,* Feb. 21, 1946, p. 3.
54. Gerald Nash, p. 183.
55. *Oil and Gas Journal,* Feb. 16, 1946, p. 78.

56. Gerald Nash, pp. 182–3; *New Republic,* Feb. 18, 1946; *Current History,* March 1946, pp. 227–31.

57. See note 56 for sources.

58. See note 56 for sources.

59. Engler, p. 86.

60. Nash, p. 171.

61. Quoted by Ickes in *New Republic,* Mar. 26, 1951, p. 17.

62. Bartley, p. 226.

63. *New York Times,* Oct. 14, 1952. © 1952 The New York Times Company. Reprinted by permission.

64. Engler, p. 358.

65. *New York Times,* Apr. 29 and May 24, 1953. © 1953 The New York Times Company. Reprinted by permission.

66. Engler, pp. 358–9.

67. *Time,* July 5, 1954, p. 46. Reprinted by permission from TIME, The Weekly Newsmagazine; Copyright Time Inc. See also *Business Week,* Apr. 10, 1954, pp. 68–70.

68. *Saturday Evening Post,* Dec. 11, 1948, pp. 36–7. See also *Saturday Evening Post,* May 28, 1955, pp. 38–9; Clawson and Held, *Federal Lands,* p. 101.

69. *Reader's Digest,* 71:119–26.

70. *Fortune,* 54:115–22 (Dec. 1956). Courtesy of Fortune Magazine.

71. On Platform A, see *Business Week,* Mar. 24, 1962, pp. 30–31; Feb. 13, 1965, p. 36; and Nov. 23, 1965, p. 34; *U.S. News,* Mar. 26, 1962.

72. *Business Week,* Oct. 26, 1968, p. 182; *Science,* 164:530–2, May 2, 1969; *Americana Annual 1970,* p. 22; *Britannica Annual, 1970,* p. 277.

73. *Oil and Gas Journal,* May 6, 1974, p. 123.

74. *U.S. News,* 65:66–8 (Aug. 5, 1968).

75. On offshore data and rig dispersion, see *Oil and Gas Journal,* May 6, 1974, pp. 123 ff.; *U.S. News,* 65:66–8 (Aug. 5, 1968).

76. *Oil and Gas Journal,* Jan. 27, 1975, p. 93 quotes *Peking Review.* See also *Offshore,* Sept. 1974, p. 64; *Oil and Gas Journal,* Jan. 6, 1975; and *New York Times,* Jan. 6 and May 12, 1975.

77. Gladwyn Hill, "Offshore Oil, Changes in Leases Likely," *New York Times,* Feb. 15, 1975, p. 58. See also *Oil and Gas Journal,* Jan. 20, 1975, p. 36; *New York Times,* Feb. 26, 1975, p. 53, and Mar. 9, 1975, IV, p. 5.

CHAPTER 7 (pp. 173–196)

1. On the cooperative State Department-oil company policy, see Gerald Nash, pp. vii, 230, 249. See also Ise, pp. 1 ff.; Rostow, p. 27; Ickes, *Secret Diary,* III, pp. 503–4; Forrestal Diaries, IV, Feb. 24, 1947 (Forrestal Papers); Senate Foreign Relations Subcommittee, *Multinational Corporations and U.S. Foreign Policy,* Pt. V, p. 65; Engler, pp. 182–229.

2. For the Molotov letter, see National Archives, T–120, Doc. No. 273, Reel No. 241 (microfilm). See also *New York Times,* Jan. 22, p. 1, and Jan. 23, 1948, p. 18. Quoted in George V. Allen speech at conference of university officials, Washington, Apr. 18, 1956 (Dulles Papers).

3. *New York Times,* Dec. 29, 1945; *International Petroleum Cartel,* pp. 72 ff; Engler, p. 202; *Business Week,* Oct. 25, 1969, p. 87.

4. Forrestal Diaries, IV, Feb. 24, 1947.

5. Joseph Jones, p. 195.

6. William J. Donovan, in Columbia talk, Feb. 10–12, 1949. For labor events, Pelling, pp. 252–4; Arnot, III, pp. 180–2; Werth, pp. 380–90; Beever, pp. 26–7.

7. Forrestal Diaries, IV, May 2, 1947.

8. Transcript of Rodgers-Forrestal telephone conversation, Sept. 2, 1947, in Forrestal Papers.

9. Forrestal Diaries, IV, Oct. 9, 1947.

10. On the procurement of tankers, see Forrestal Diaries, IV, Jun. 2, 1947. See also *New York Times,* Mar. 13 and 30, Apr. 12 and Aug. 12, 1951; *Fortune,* Oct. 1954, pp. 124 ff.; *Time,* Aug. 6, 1956, pp. 55 ff.; Frischauer, pp. 87, 107, 129.

11. Forrestal Diaries, IV, Jan. 6, 1948.

12. Forrestal Diaries, IV, Jan. 16, 1948.

13. "Memorandum to the President," in Forrestal Papers, Feb. 6, 1948.

14. On Texas and British pressure on ECA prices see *New York Times,* Feb. 13 and 22, Mar. 8 and 12, Aug. 7, Oct. 26, Dec. 20 and 21, 1949; Jan. 4 and 6, Feb. 1 and 2 (Acheson testimony) and 18 and 19, Mar. 7, Jun. 1 (Fawley), 1950. See also *International Petroleum Cartel,* p. 15.

15. On the ECA suit on oil prices, see *New York Times,* Aug. 11, 1950 and Aug. 23, 1952. See also Walter Levy address to National Petroleum Council, July 28, 1949, cited by Kolko, *Limits of Power,* p. 447; Schaffer, pp. 13 ff.; Leeman, p. 143.

16. Tugendhat, in *Institute of Petroleum Review,* p. 60.

17. *New York Times,* Oct. 28, 1949, p. 41.

18. Dr. Oscar Bransky of ECA quoted by Shaffer, p. 13.

19. *New York Times,* May 13, 1949.

20. *New York Times,* Oct. 7, 1949, p. 1.

21. Penrose, p. 183. See also *New York Times,* Dec. 30, 1951, III, p. 1; *British Petroleum Statistical Review* for 1957, 1964, 1971; *International Petroleum Encyclopedia* 1972, pp. 20 ff., 294.

22. *British Petroleum Statistical Review* 1964, p. 13. See also Moore, "The Petroleum Industry," p. 117 (U.S. patterns); *OEEC Statistical Bulletin,* Nov. 1950, p. 22; also *OEEC General Statistics,* Jan. 1960, pp. xxxii–xxxiii (for coal statistics). See also UN, *Growth of World Industry,* 1938–61, p. 158; UN, *World Energy Supplies,* 1951–4, Series J, Mar. 1957, pp. 3 ff.; 1955–8, p. 7; 1959–63, p. 3; 1964–66, p. 3;

1966–9, p. 3. Also, OECD, *Energy Policy, Problems and Objectives*, p. 160.

23. J. A. Hobson, pp. 52, 62; C. K. Hobson, pp. ix, 111, 128, 134, 140, 144, 199–200; Lenin, p. 70, cites Otto Jeidel, *Relationship of German Banks to Industry* (Leipzig, 1905), on British overseas oil income.

24. Schwadran, p. 444.

25. On Mexico and Venezuela, see Cline, p. 229; Lieuwen, p. 50.

26. *New York Times*, Apr. 1, 1948, p. 37.

27. On the Saudi tax law, see *Multinational Corporations*, Part IV, p. 83. See also *New York Times*, Jan. 30, 1974, p. 1. Mosley, pp. 188–97, cites testimony of Pres. F. A. Davies of Aramco before Senate Joint Hearings, *Emergency Oil Lift Program and Related Oil Problems*, 85th Congress, 1957.

28. *Multinational Corporations*, IV, p. 3; *New York Times*, Jan. 30, 1974.

29. See note 28 for sources.

30. See J. F. Dulles speech to governors' conference, Washington, D.C., May 2, 1955 (Dulles Papers).

31. J. F. Dulles memorandum, "Conclusions on Trip," Near East trip 5/9–5/29, 1953, Conference dossiers (Dulles Papers).

32. Ibid.

33. Ibid.

34. Longrigg, pp. 159 ff; Loy Henderson interview, Oral History Project (Dulles Papers).

35. On the coup in Iran, see Wise and Ross, p. 129; Copeland, pp. 135 f.; Loy Henderson interview.

36. On the northern tier pact, see LaFeber, p. 157; Longrigg, pp. 159 ff.; Schurr and Homan, p. 115; Loy Henderson interview.

37. On the consortium formed in Iran, see *New York Times*, Jan. 15, 1974; Engler, p. 69. Mosley, pp. 196, 230–1.

38. See note 37 for sources.

39. On the Aswan Dam deal, see interviews of Eugene Black, Dwight Eisenhower, George Humphrey, and Herbert Hoover, Jr., Oral History Project (Dulles Papers).

40. On the Suez affair, see J. F. Dulles, Speech to Latin American ambassadors, Aug. 7, 1956; Statement of U.S. Position, London Maritime Conference, Aug. 16, 1956; Statement, Aug. 20, 1956; Statement to Press, White House, Sept. 16, 1956 (Dulles Papers). See also Neustadt, p. 26; Eisenhower, *Waging Peace*, p. 98; Thomas, pp. 130–5; Canadian Institute of International Affairs, *International Journal*, Winter 1964–5, p. 92.

41. On tankers without Suez "lifeline," see *New Yorker*, May 13 and 20, 1974; W. H. Forbis, *Japan Today* (New York: Harper, 1975).

42. On the cost of Persian Gulf oil production, see Adelman, *World Petroleum Market*, pp. 48, 80, 288; Adelman in *Foreign Policy*, Winter 1972–3, pp. 78 f.; Schurr and Homan, p. 13; Engler, p. 68; *New York Times*, Apr. 17, 1973, p. 26.

43. *Multinational Corporations*, IV, p. 76.
44. Malraux in *New York Times*, July 29, 1974. © 1974 The New York Times Company. Reprinted by permission.
45. Mathiesen, p. 13.
46. Akins, pp. 469 f.; *New York Times*, Apr. 17, 1973, p. 2.
47. On the formation of OPEC, see *New York Times*, Apr. 17, 1973, p. 26; Mosley, p. 292.
48. On U.S. antitrust and OPEC, see *Multinational Corporations*, V, p. 255; testimony of McCloy, Feb. 6, 1974, V, p. 105.
49. *Fortune*, May 1968, p. 156.
50. Braun quoted by Mosley, p. 293.
51. On Libyan oil negotiations, see *New York Times*, Sept. 13, 23, 24, 28, and 29, Oct. 9 and 13, and Nov. 2, 1969; Apr. 17, 1973, p. 26. Mosley, p. 353.
52. Qaddafi quoted by Mosley, p. 356.
53. Akins, pp. 471 f.
54. *ECE Region in Figures*, pp. 346–7, 343–4, 306–7.
55. On Libya and Occidental see *Multinational Corporations*, V, pp. 79 ff., 343; *New York Times*, Nov. 2, 1970; Mosley, pp. 155, 357.
56. *Multinational Corporations*, V, p. 260; *New York Times*, Apr. 17, 1973; Akins, p. 470.
57. On the 1971 Teheran agreements, see *Multinational Corporations*, V, p. 75; *New York Times*, Apr. 17, 1973.
58. On the changes after Teheran, see *Multinational Corporations*, V, p. 61; Akins, pp. 473–6.
59. *Multinational Corporations*, V, p. 77; *New York Times*, May 2, 1971, IV, p. 5; Dec. 8, 1971, p. 1; Oct. 6, 1972, p. 1; Apr. 17, 1973, p. 26; Vicker, p. 227.
60. On U.S. need for Middle Eastern oil, see *New York Times*, Apr. 17, 1973, p. 26.
61. On Tapline sabotage, see *Multinational Corporations*, VI, p. 343.
62. On U.S. dependence on Saudi oil, see *New York Times*, Apr. 20, 1973, p. 7; July 9, 15, 20 (p. 39), 31 (p. 2), 1973; Oct. 14, 1973, p. 66; *Fortune*, Feb. 1971; July 1974; *Commentary*, Oct. 1973, p. 37; *Oil and Gas Journal*, Oct. 15, 1973; Interview, James Akins, Sept. 1974.
63. On the Saudi takeover of Aramco, see *Multinational Corporations*, V, pp. 230–1.

CHAPTER 8 (pp. 197–218)

1. *New York Times*, Aug. 8, 1955; *New York Herald Tribune*, Sept. 13, 1959.
2. Larson and Porter, p. 215; Hahn, p. 22.
3. On the oil workers' union strength, see Harvey O'Connor, *History*, pp. 2, 46, 96, 115; Larson and Porter, p. 215; *Time*, Jan. 28, 1957; *Chris-*

tian Science Monitor, Sept. 3, 1959; *Standard Oil of California Bulletin*, Apr. 1958, p. 2.

4. On petrochemicals, see "The Petrochemical Revolution," in *Petroleum Gazette*, Dec. 1964, pp. 116–9; Hahn, p. 23; Wendland, pp. 92, 93, 145, 155, 223, 246; *New York Times*, Jan. 6, 1974.

5. On liquid natural gas, see *New York Times*, Oct. 21, 1944, p. 19; Mar. 19, 1972, *Fortune*, Nov. 1969; *Washington Monthly*, Feb. 1973, pp. 7–13.

6. Sasuly, p. 143.

7. On the second World War and the Lurgi process, see Engler, pp. 100–101; O'Connor, *The Oil Barons*, pp. 461–5; *Fortune*, Nov. 1973, p. 129; *New York Times*, Jun. 19, 1974, p. 45.

8. On the rise of the pipeline companies, see *Fortune*, June 1965, p. 22.

9. Attributed to Senator Douglas in *New York Times*, Jan. 2, 1963. © 1963 The New York Times Company. Reprinted by permission.

10. *Time*, Feb. 13, 1967. Reprinted by permission from TIME, The Weekly Newsmagazine; Copyright Time Inc. See also *National Observer*, Aug. 27, 1962.

11. *New York Times*, Jan. 2, 1963, p. 1.

12. *New York Times*, Jan. 11, 1963. © 1963 The New York Times Company. Reprinted by permission. See also McReynolds, pp. 383 ff.

13. Paul Niven, *CBS News*, Aug. 12, 1962. See also *New York Times*, Apr. 5, 1951; Oct. 10, 1962.

14. *Time*, Sept. 4, 1950; Feb. 18, 1952; Nov. 8, 1959. Reprinted by permission from TIME, The Weekly Newsmagazine; Copyright Time Inc. See also McReynolds, pp. 383 ff; *Fortune*, Mar. 1959; *St. Louis Post Dispatch*, Jun. 19, 1948 and Oct. 15, 1949; *Time*, Apr. 21, 1943; *New York Daily News*, Apr. 25, 1951; *New York Herald Tribune*, Oct. 10, 1951; Ernie Pyle in *New York World Telegram*, May 13, 1939.

15. *New York Times*, Oct. 23, 1948; *Time*, July 2, 1954; *Life*, Aug. 16, 1963. Kerr wrote *Land, Wood and Water*, ed. by Malvina Stephenson and Tris Coffin, introduction by Senator Lyndon B. Johnson, in 1960. See also D. A. McGee, "Evolution into Total Energy," Newcomen Society, 1971, p. 15.

16. *Time*, Nov. 5, 1958. Reprinted by permission from TIME, The Weekly Newsmagazine; Copyright Time Inc. *New York Post*, Feb. 2, 1952. See also Huitt in *Public Administration and Policy Formation*, pp. 54 ff.; McGee, Newcomen Society, p. 15.

17. Quoted in Huitt, in *Public Administration and Policy Formation*, pp. 54 ff.

18. *Time*, Jan. 11, 1963. Reprinted by permission from TIME, The Weekly Newsmagazine; Copyright Time Inc.

19. *Time*, Jan. 11, 1963; and *Congressional Record*.

20. *Washington Post*, Jan. 2, 1963.

21. *Time*, Nov. 5, 1958. See also *New York Times*, Oct. 10, 1962.

22. *New York Times*, Feb. 10, 1974, p. 42; Feb. 12, 1958; July 12, 1962;

Jan. 2, 1963; June 8, 1964; Apr. 8 and 17, 1967. *Wall Street Journal,* Oct. 30, 1962; *New York Herald Tribune,* Feb. 14, 1958, and Apr. 8 and Sept. 3, 1962; *New York Post,* Aug. 14, 1962; *New York World Telegram,* Aug. 28, 1962; *Washington Star,* Dec. 24, 1962; Drew Pearson, in *Washington Post,* Dec. 31, 1960; Jack Anderson, in *Washington Post,* Feb. 12, 1967; *Time,* July 2, 1962; Jan. 19 and Feb. 13, 1967; May 15 and June 22, 1968. See also Senator Paul Douglas in *Congressional Record,* Vol. 190, 24396 (Dec. 12, 1963); 25033 (Dec. 16, 1963); Vol. 110, 554 (Jan. 16, 1964); Vol. 112, 5702 (Mar. 14, 1966).

23. Hawkins, p. 21. See also Gerald Nash, pp. 232 f.; Crenshaw, in *Law and Contemporary Problems,* p. 336; Troxel, in *Journal of Law and Public Utility Economics,* p. 20.

24. On the Supreme Court decision aftermath, see *Fortune,* Nov. 1972, pp. 108–11, 185–6; Hawkins, pp. v. 2–5, 35–7; Brown, pp. 1–17, 90–112; Balestra, pp. 1–5, 49–50; *Gas Facts 1972,* pp. 24, 76. Adelman, *Supply and Price of Natural Gas,* pp. 22, 76.

25. *Fortune,* Nov. 1972; Hawkins, pp. 220–1; Bureau of Mines, *Minerals Yearbook 1971,* p. 771; *Gas Facts 1973,* p. 76. Breyer and McAvoy, in *Harvard Law Review,* p. 977. McAvoy, in *Journal of Law and Economics,* p. 196.

26. On the environment and natural gas, see McAvoy, p. 196. See also *New York Times,* Feb. 10, 1974, p. 42.

27. On intrastate sales, see *Senate Subcommittee on Antitrust and Monopoly,* Committee on the Judiciary, 1973 Hearings: *The Natural Gas Industry* (Swidler), p. 185; (Nassikas), p. 32; (Lee White), p. 512. See also *Fortune,* Nov. 1972, p. 109; *Christian Science Monitor,* Jun. 22, 1973; and *Minerals Yearbook 1971,* p. 771.

28. *New York Times,* Feb. 10, 1974, p. 42. © 1974 The New York Times Company. Reprinted by permission.

29. Ibid.

30. Ibid.

31. *Natural Gas Industry,* p. 155.

32. *Fortune,* Nov. 1969, cites Prof. Steele of University of Houston. Courtesy of Fortune Magazine. See also *Wall Street Journal,* Oct. 15, 1963; *New York Times,* Dec. 3 and 10, 1973.

33. Nassikas, in *Natural Gas Industry,* p. 43.

34. Ross, in Brown, p. 98.

35. On natural gas from offshore, see Nassikas, in *Natural Gas Industry,* pp. 46, 118. Communication from Win L. Webb, FPC, Jul. 26, 1974 about 15.8 percent from offshore.

36. On the "energy crisis" shortages, see *New York Times,* Mar. 19, 1972; *Wall Street Journal,* Jan. 2, 1970; *Time,* Dec. 13, 1973, and Jan. 7, 1974, p. 40. See also Nassikas in *Natural Gas Industry,* p. 43; *Gas Facts 1973,* pp. 65, 73.

37. *New York Times,* Feb. 10, 1974, p. 42.

38. Communication from Joseph Padgett, Environmental Protection Agency, July 25, 1974.
39. *New York Times*, Feb. 10, 1974, p. 42.
40. On higher natural gas prices, see *New York Times*, Dec. 10, 1973; Mar. 19, 1972; and Jun. 22, 1974. See also *Progressive*, Mar. 1974, p. 23; Nassikas, in *Natural Gas Industry*, p. 44.

CHAPTER 9 (pp. 221–250)

1. S. E. Morison and H. S. Commager, *Growth of the American Republic* (New York: Oxford, 1962), p. 1.
2. *New York Times Magazine*, May 26, 1974, p. 39. © 1974 The New York Times Company. Reprinted by permission.
3. Kissinger quoted by James Reston, *New York Times*, Oct. 13, 1974, p. 34. © 1974 by The New York Times Company. Reprinted by permission.
4. Akins, in *Foreign Affairs*, p. 462.
5. "The Economics of the Coming Spaceship Earth," in *Environmental Quality in a Growing Economy*, ed. by Henry Jarrett (Baltimore: Johns Hopkins Press, 1966). See also *New York Times*, Dec. 9, 1973.
6. For the modern economic triad, see C. R. Cosman, memo for Brookings Institution, "Technological Society—Materials and Energy: A Look Ahead," 1974.
7. Federal Energy Administration, *Project Independence Report*; Energy Policy Project of the Ford Foundation, *Final Report: A Time to Choose, America's Energy Future*; Committee for Economic Development, *Achieving Energy Independence*. See also Richard Gardner, *The World Food and Energy Crises*.
8. *A Time To Choose*, p. 45.
9. Daniel Bell, in *Public Interest*, p. 42.
10. On separating energy growth from economic growth, see *Time to Choose*, pp. 17, 131 ff., 493 ff.; Bernard A. Gelb, "Energy and GNP," in *Monthly Business Review*, The Conference Board, Apr. 1973. See also Schurr and Netschert, pp. 155 f.
11. *Oil and Gas Journal*, July 30, 1973, p. 78. See also *New York Times*, Apr. 12, 1974.
12. *FEA Report*, p. 5.
13. Ibid., p. 17.
14. *Business Week*, Aug. 31, 1974, pp. 81–2; Oct. 26, 1974, pp. 66–77.
15. Ribicoff, in *New York Times*, Dec. 5, 1974. © 1974 The New York Times Company. Reprinted by permission.
16. On delays and safety problems in reactors, see *Science*, 182 (Dec. 14, 1973), p. 1112; 185 (Oct. 11, 1974), pp. 83, 125. See also *Safety of Nuclear Power Reactors (Light water-cooled) and Related Facilities*, *Wash–1250*, pp. 1–6 ff.

17. Novick, p. 147; Paul and Anne Ehrlich, p. 72.
18. Novick, pp. 145–6; Paul and Anne Ehrlich, p. 61. See Lee Dye, "Thousands Perilled by Nuclear Waste," *Los Angeles Times,* July 5, 1973, cited by Wilson Clark, p. 309.
19. William Hines, "Sun Eyed as Atomic Dump," *Chicago Sun-Times,* Jan. 1972, cited by Wilson Clark, p. 310.
20. Communication from Sheldon Novick, Jan. 1975.
21. *Environment,* Mar. 1974, p. 5.
22. Peter Chapman, "The Ins and Outs of Nuclear Power," *New Scientist,* Dec. 19, 1974, p. 867. Communications from J. A. Griffin of AEC, Dec. 1974, and R. S. Carlsmith of Oak Ridge National Laboratory, Mar. 1975.
23. *FEA Report,* pp. 436–7; Science, 182, Dec. 21, 1973, p. 1236.
24. Wilson Clark, p. 293. Personal communication, Ann Michaels, Oct. 29, 1974.
25. Teller paper at American Nuclear Society, in *Nuclear News,* Aug. 1967, cited by Wilson Clark, p. 294.
26. Alexander, in *Fortune,* Jun. 1970.
27. On lasers in fusion, see Lawrence Lessing, "Lasers Blast a Shortcut to the Ultimate," *Fortune,* May 1974, p. 221; *Science,* 177, Sept. 29, 1972, p. 1180; *Fortune,* Dec. 1974, p. 149. *New York Times,* Apr. 23 and 24, 1975.
28. Furth, in *Energy Digest,* Vol. I, No. 15 (Nov, 26, 1971), p. 171, cited by Wilson Clark, p. 315.
29. Rose quoted by Alexander in *Fortune.*
30. *FEA Report,* p. 435.
31. Ibid., p. 438.
32. Weinberg in *New York Times,* Dec. 10, 1974.
33. On stockpiling, see *Resources for Freedom,* I, p. 3.
34. Ibid., I, p. 107; IV, p. 5.
35. Ibid., IV, pp. 5, 77.
36. *New York Times,* Feb. 10, 1974, p. 42; *Christian Science Monitor,* Jan. 22, 1973; Senate Subcommittee on Antitrust and Monopoly, Committee on the Judiciary, 1973 Hearings: *The Natural Gas Industry,* p. 189.
37. O'Leary quoted in *New York Times,* Apr. 17, 1973, p. 26. © 1974 The New York Times Company. Reprinted by permission.
38. *Science,* 180, Jun. 15, 1973, p. 1127.
39. On the liquefaction and gasification of coal, see *Science,* 179, Jan. 5, 1973, p. 56; "U.S. Energy Outlook, an interim report by the National Petroleum Council," 1972, pp. 17, 44, cited by Wilson Clark, p. 258.
40. On shale problems, see *FEA Report,* pp. 6, 28; Wilson Clark, pp. 262 ff.; *New York Times,* Oct. 5 and Nov. 3, 1974.
41. On hydrogen as fuel, see *Science,* 174, Oct. 22, 1971, pp. 367; 180, Jun. 29, 1973, pp. 1325 ff. See also *Saturday Evening Post,* Spring 1972, pp. 54 ff.; *Fortune,* Nov. 1972, pp. 138 ff.; *Scientific American,* Jan. 1973, pp. 13 ff.; *Baltimore Sunday Sun,* Oct. 21, 1972; *New York*

Times, Apr. 18, 1973, p. 21, and Aug. 6, 1973; Wilson Clark, pp. 340, 347.

42. Netschert, in *Energy Conversion Digest,* Vol. 9, No. 7, cited by Wilson Clark, p. 228.

43. *Science,* 182, Dec. 28, 1973, p. 1299; 186 Nov. 9, 1974, p. 785; *New York Times,* Dec. 31, 1973 and Dec. 1, 1974; OECD, *Energy Prospects to 1985,* I, 21, 143.

44. Daniels, ed., *Solar Energy Research,* p. 1. See also *New York Times,* Jan. 22, 1974.

45. *FEA Report,* p. 440.

46. On the Arizona and Houston scientists, see Wilson Clark, pp. 408 ff.; *Technology Review,* Dec. 1973, pp. 31–43.

47. Peter Glaser, in *Science,* 162, Nov. 22, 1968, p. 857.

48. On solar heating and cooling houses, see *Science,* 177, Sept. 22, 1972, p. 1088; *New Scientist,* Mar. 30, 1972, p. 895; *Science,* 162, May 14, 1973, p. 660; *New York Times,* Apr. 18, 1973, pp. 1, 21; Jan. 22, 1974; May 19, 1974; CQ, *Energy Crisis in America,* 55; *Science,* 186, Nov. 1974, p. 811; Shurcliff, pp. 3 ff.; Wilson Clark, p. 578.

49. *Technology Review,* Dec. 1973, pp. 31–43.

50. *New York Times,* Apr. 6, 1974, and Feb. 22, 1974; Wilson Clark, pp. 327, 330.

51. Interior Department report cited by Wilson Clark, p. 330.

52. Peter Odell in *New Society,* Nov. 21, 1974, p. 492. See also *New York Times,* Dec. 5, 1974. © 1974 The New York Times Company. Reprinted by permission.

53. Department of State Press Release No. 500, Chicago, Nov. 14, 1974.

54. Department of State Press Release No. 42, National Press Club address, Feb. 3, 1975. See also *New York Times,* Feb. 4 and 6, 1975.

55. *New York Times,* Oct. 2, 1974. © 1974 The New York Times Company. Reprinted by permission.

Bibliography

MANUSCRIPT COLLECTIONS
Dulles Papers (Princeton University, Princeton, N.J.)
Forrestal Papers (Princeton University, Princeton, N.J.)
Lehman Papers (Columbia University, New York, N.Y.)

GOVERNMENT PUBLICATIONS
Atomic Energy Commission. *The Safety of Nuclear Power Reactors (Light water-cooled) and Related Facilities.* Wash-1250. 1973.
   The Nuclear Industry 1974. Wash-1174–74.
   Proposed Final Environmental Statement: Liquid Metal Fast Breeder Reactor Program. Wash-1535. Dec. 1974.
Bureau of Mines. *Minerals Yearbook.*
Bureau of Public Roads. *Highways and Economic and Social Changes.* 1964.
Cabinet Task Force. *The Oil Import Question.* 1970.
Congress:
   Congressional Record.
   Joint Committee on Internal Revenue Taxation.
   Staff data. *Legislative History of Depletion Allowances.* 82nd Congress, 1st session, March 1950 (for use of House Ways and Means Committee).
   Subcommittee on Tax Policy, Joint Commission on the Economic Report. *Federal Tax Policy for Economic Growth and Stability.* 84th Congress, 1st session. Nov. 5, 1955.
   House Select Committee on Small Business. *The Third World Petroleum Congress.* 82nd Congress, 2nd session. 1952.
   ———. *Effects of Foreign Oil Imports on Domestic Producers.* Hearings.
   ———. *Small Business Problems Created by Oil Imports.* Hearings. 88th Congress, 1st session. 1962.
   House Subcommittee on Activities of Regulating Agencies of the Perma-

nent Select Committee on Small Business. *Energy Requirements of the Federal Government.* Hearings. 93rd Congress, 2nd session. 1974.

House Ways and Means Committee. *Revenue Act of 1918.* Hearings, Pt. I. 65th Congress, 1st session. 1918.

——. *Percentage Depletion and the Option on Intangible Costs.* Hearings. 77th Congress, Mar. 23–24, Apr. 16–17, 1942 (reprinted by the General Depletion Committee for the Petroleum Industry).

Senate Committee on Finance. *To Provide Revenue for War Purposes.* Hearings, on HR 12863. 65th Congress, 2nd session. 1918.

——. *Report No. 617,* to accompany HR 12863, Revenue Act of 1918. 65th Congress, 3rd session. Dec. 6, 1918.

——. *Report, Mr. Simmons: Revenue Bill for 1918,* Pt. I. 65th Congress, 3rd session. 1919.

Senate Interior Committee. *Energy Policy Alternatives.* Hearings, serial no. 92–30, June 7, 1972. 93rd Congress, 1st session. 1972.

——. *U.S. Energy Resources, a Review as of 1972.* Committee print, Serial No. 93–20. 93rd Congress, 2nd session. 1974.

Senate Committee on Public Lands and Surveys. *Leases upon Naval Oil Reserves.* Hearings. 68th Congress, 3rd session. 1924.

——. *Leases upon Naval Oil Reserves.* Hearings. 70th Congress, 1st session. 1924.

——. *Leases upon Naval Oil Reserves.* Hearings. 70th Congress, 1st session. 1928.

——. *Investigation of Actions of Continental Trading Co.,* Report 1236. 70th Congress, 1st session. 1928.

Senate Committee on Public Works. *Air Quality and Automobile Emission Control.* Summary Report prepared by Coordinating Committee on Air Quality Studies of National Academy of Sciences. Serial No. 93–24. 93rd Congress, 2nd session. Sept. 1974.

Senate Subcommittee on Antitrust and Monopoly, Committee on the Judiciary. *The National Gas Industry.* Hearings. 93rd Congress, 1st session. June 26–28, 1973.

——. *American Ground Transportation,* a report by Bradford C. Snell. 93rd Congress, 2nd session. 1974 (27–540 0).

Senate Subcommittee on Investigations, Committee on Government Operations. *Current Energy Shortage Oversight series.* Hearings. 93rd Congress, 2nd session. April 1974.

Senate Subcommittee on Multinational Corporations, Committee on Foreign Relations. *Multinational Corporations and United States Foreign Policy. Hearings.* 93rd Congress, 1st and 2nd sessions. Jan. 1974.

Council on Environmental Quality. *Energy and the Environment: Electric Power,* August, 1973.

Department of Commerce. *Statistical Abstract of the United States.*

Department of Housing and Urban Development. *The Costs of Sprawl.* Executive summary prepared by Real Estate Research Corp. for Council on Environmental Quality, Department of Housing and Urban Development, and Environmental Protection Agency, April, 1974.

Department of Interior. *United States Energy Through the Year 2000.* Report by Walter G. Dupres, Jr., and James A. West. December 1972.

Department of Transportation. *Highway Statistics,* 1970.

——. *National Personal Transportation Study,* Reports 1–11: April 1972–Dec. 1974.

Federal Energy Administration. *Project Independence Report.* Nov. 1974.

Federal Trade Commission:

    Pipeline Transportation of Petroleum. A report. 1916.

    The Price of Gasoline in 1915. A report. 1917.

    Advance in the Price of Petroleum Products. A report. 1920.

    The Petroleum Industry: Prices, Profits and Competition. A report. 1928.

    International Petroleum Cartel. A report to the Subcommittee on Monopoly, Select Committee on Small Business. 82nd Congress, 2nd session. 1952.

Fuel Administration. *Final Report of the U.S. Fuel Administrator, 1917–19* by Mark L. Requa. 1921.

National Archives. T–120, Doc. No. 273, Reel No. 241 (microfilm, State Dept.-Foreign Office Field Team, Office of German Foreign Ministry to German Embassy, Moscow. Collection entitled "Personal Files of Ambassador von der Schulenburg, 1: Conversation between Foreign Minister Ribbentrop and Molotov on Nov. 12, 1940."

Office of Emergency Preparedness. *The Potential for Energy Conservation.* 1972.

President. *Economic Report of the President, 1960.*

President's Materials Policy Commission. *Resources for Freedom.* June 1952.

Public Roads Administration. *Highway Statistics.* 1945.

Temporary National Economic Committee:

    Monograph No. 27. *The Structure of Industry* by W. L. Thorp. 1940.

    Monograph No. 31. *Patents and Free Enterprise* by Walton Hamilton. 1940.

    Monograph No. 39. *Control of the Petroleum Industry by Major Oil Companies* by Roy C. Cook. 1941.

BOOKS, ARTICLES AND INDIVIDUAL MANUSCRIPTS

Abele, Jules. *In the Time of Silent Cal.* New York: Putnam, 1969.

Adams, Charles Francis, Jr. *Chapters of Erie and Other Essays.* Boston: Field, Osgood and Co., 1871.

Adams, Frederic Upham. *The Waters Pierce Case in Texas.* St. Louis: Skinner and Kennedy, 1908.

Adams, Samuel Hopkins. *The Incredible Era.* Boston: Houghton Mifflin, 1939.

Adelman, M. A. *The Supply and Price of Natural Gas.* Oxford: Blackwell, 1962.

———. "The World Oil Outlook." In *Natural Resources and International Development,* edited by Marion Clawson. Baltimore: John Hopkins Press, 1964.

———. *The World Petroleum Market.* Baltimore: Johns Hopkins Press, 1972.

Akins, James E. "Oil: This Time the Wolf Is Here." *Foreign Affairs.* April 1973.

Alexander, Herbert E. *Money in Politics.* Washington, D.C.: Public Affairs Press, 1972.

Alexander, Tom. "The Hot New Promise of Thermonuclear Power." *Fortune.* June 1970.

Allen, Frederick Lewis. *Only Yesterday.* New York: Harper, 1931.

Allvine, Fred C., and James M. Patterson. *Competition, Ltd.* Bloomington, Ind.: University of Indiana Press, 1972.

———. *Highway Robbery, an Analysis of the Gasoline Crisis.* Bloomington, Ind.: University of Indiana Press, 1974.

Anderson, Rudolph E. *The Story of the American Automobile.* Washington, D.C.: Public Affairs Press, 1950.

Arnot, H. Page. *The Miners.* London: Allen and Unwin, 1961.

Asbury, Herbert, *The Golden Flood.* New York: Knopf, 1942.

Automobile Manufacturers Association. *Automobiles of America.* 2nd ed. Detroit: Wayne State University, 1968.

Bainbridge, John. *The Super Americans.* Garden City, N.Y.: Doubleday, 1961.

Balestra, Pietro. *The Demand for Natural Gas in the U.S.* Amsterdam: North Holland Pub., 1967.

Banwell, John, and Tsvi Meidav. "Geothermal Energy for the Future." Paper presented at meeting of the American Association for the Advancement of Science. Philadelphia, Dec. 1971.

Barber, James D. *The Presidential Character.* Englewood Cliffs, N.J.: Prentice-Hall, 1972.

Barnard, Harry. *Independent Man, the Life of Senator James Couzens.* New York: Scribner's, 1958.

Bartley, E. R. *The Tidelands Oil Controversy.* Austin, Tex.: University of Texas Press, 1953.

Bates, J. Leonard. *Origins of Teapot Dome, 1902–21.* Urbana, Ill.: University of Illinois Press, 1963.

———. "Teapot Dome Scandal and the Election of 1924," *American Historical Review,* LX, 2 (Jan. 1955).

Beard, Charles and Mary. *The Rise of American Civilization.* Rev. ed. New York: Macmillan, 1956.

Beaton, Kendall. *Enterprise in Oil: A History of Shell in the United States.* New York: Appleton-Century-Crofts, 1957.

Beck, Lawrence D., and Stuart L. Rawlings. *Coal, the Captive Giant.* Washington, D.C.: Public Affairs Press, 1971.

Beever, R. Collin. *European Unity and the Trade Union Movement.* Leyden: A. W. Sythoff, 1960.

Bell, Daniel. "The Public Household," *The Public Interest.* No. 37, Fall 1974, p. 42.

Biddle, Francis. *In Brief Authority.* Garden City, N.Y.: Doubleday, 1962.

Bird, Anthony. *Roads and Vehicles.* London: Longmans, 1969.

Black, Percy. *The Service Station Dealer, a Motivation Study.* Dow Chemical, 1959.

Blair, John M. *Economic Concentration.* New York: Harcourt Brace Jovanovich, 1972.

Blanchard, Arthur H. "The Highway Engineer in Public Life." Address delivered Feb. 11, 1915, at Engineers Society of Pennsylvania. Pamphlet.

Blum, John M. *From the Morgenthau Diaries, 1928–38.* Boston: Houghton Mifflin, 1959.

——. *Roosevelt and Morgenthau.* Boston: Houghton Mifflin, 1970.

Boatright, Mody C. *Folklore of the Oil Industry.* Dallas: S.M.U., 1963.

——. and William A. Owens, *Tales from the Derrick Floor.* Garden City, N.Y.: Doubleday, 1970.

Bolling, Richard. *Power in the House.* New York: Dutton, 1968.

Boorstin, Daniel J. *The American Experience: The Democratic Experience.* New York: Random House, 1973.

Boulding, Kenneth. "The Economics of the Coming Spaceship Earth." In *Environmental Quality in a Growing Economy,* ed. by Henry Jarrett. Baltimore: Johns Hopkins Press, 1966.

Bowden, Robert D. *Boies Penrose, Symbol of an Era.* New York: Greenberg, 1937.

Bowser Company, S. F. "Where Filling Stations Came From." Ft. Wayne, Ind.: no date. Pamphlet.

Boyd, T. A. *Gasoline, What Everyone Should Know About It.* New York: Stokes, 1925.

——. *Professional Amateur, a Biography of Charles F. Kettering.* New York: Dutton, 1957.

Breyer, Stephen, and Paul W. McAvoy. "The Natural Gas Shortage and the Regulation of Natural Gas Users," *Harvard Law Review,* 86, No. 6 (April 1973).

Brimmer, F. E. *Autocamping.* Cincinnati: Stewart Kidd Co., 1923.

Brookings Institution. *Cooperative Approaches to the Energy Problem.* Washington, D.C.: Brookings, 1974.

Brooks, Michael. *Oil and Foreign Policy.* London: Lawrence and Wishart, 1949.

Brown, Keith C., ed. *The Regulation of the Natural Gas Producing Industry.* Baltimore: Johns Hopkins Press, 1972.

Burby, John. *The Great American Motion Sickness.* Boston: Little Brown, 1971.

Burlingame, Roger. *Henry Ford.* New York: Knopf, 1955.

Burnham, John G. "The Gasoline Tax and the Automobile Revolution." *Mississippi Valley Historical Review,* XLVIII, No. 3 (Dec. 1961).

Burrell, G. A. *Gasoline and How to Use It.* Boston: Oil Statistical Society, 1916.

Campbell, John C., et al. *Energy, the Imperative for a Trilateral Approach.* New York: Trilateral Commission, 1974.

Caudill, Harry. *Night Comes to the Cumberlands.* Boston: Little, Brown, 1963.

Caudill, William W. *A Bucket of Oil: The Humanistic Approach to Building Design for Energy Conservation.* Boston: Cahners, 1974.

Citizens Research Foundation Study #24. *Money/Politics* by Richard T. Stout. Princeton, N. J.: Citizens Research Foundation, 1974.

Clark, James A. *Three Stars for the Colonel.* New York: Random House, 1954.

——. and Michael T. Halbouty. *The Last Boom.* New York: Random House, 1972.

——. *Spindletop.* New York: Random House, 1952.

Clark, J. Stanley. *The Oil Century.* Norman, Okla.: University of Oklahoma Press, 1958.

Clark, Warner. "Midas' Black Gold," *Southwest Review,* Vol. 16 (Autumn 1930).

Clark, Wilson. *Energy for Survival.* Garden City, N.Y.: Anchor Books, 1974.

Claudy, C. H. "Good Roads v. Mud Holes." Washington, D.C.: National Highway Association, Feb. 22, 1916. Pamphlet.

——. "Motor Vehicles and Good Roads Everywhere." Washington, D.C.: National Highway Association, Jan. 28, 1916. Pamphlet.

Clawson, Marion. *Statistics of Outdoor Recreation.* Washington, D.C.: Resources for the Future, 1958.

——. "What It Means To Be a Californian," *California Historical Society Quarterly,* XXIV, No. 2 (June 1945).

——. and Burnell Held. *The Federal Lands.* Baltimore: Johns Hopkins Press, 1957.

——. and Jack L. Knetsch. *Economics of Outdoor Recreation.* Baltimore: Johns Hopkins Press, 1966.

Cline, Howard F. *The United States and Mexico.* Cambridge, Mass.: Harvard University Press, 1953.

Cochran, T. C., and William Miller. *The Age of Enterprise.* New York: Macmillan, 1942.

Cockenboo, Leslie, Jr. *Crude Oil Pipelines and Competition in the Industry.* Cambridge, Mass.: Harvard University Press, 1955.

Cohn, David. *Combustion on Wheels.* Boston: Houghton Mifflin, 1944.

Cole, Arthur H. *Business Enterprise in Its Social Setting.* Cambridge, Mass.: Harvard University Press, 1959.

Committee for Economic Development. *Achieving Energy Independence.* New York: C.E.D., Dec. 1974.

Congressional Quarterly. *Dollar Politics.* Washington, D.C.: CQ Service, Sept. 1974.

———. *Energy Crisis in America.* Washington, D.C.: CQ Service, 1973.

Copeland, Miles. *The Game of Nations.* London: Weidenfeld and Nicolson, 1969.

Cotner, Robert C., ed. *Addresses and State Papers of James Stephen Hogg.* Austin, Tex.: University of Texas Press, 1951.

Cotner, Robert C. *James Stephen Hogg.* Austin, Tex.: University of Texas Press, 1959.

Council of Economic Priorities. *Leased and Lost.* New York: May 1974.

Crenshaw, Charles. "Regulation of Natural Gas," *Law and Contemporary Problems,* XIX, Fall 1954, 336–52.

Croly, Herbert. *Marcus Alonzo Hanna.* New York: Macmillan, 1912.

Cromie, Robert. *The Great Chicago Fire.* New York: McGraw-Hill, 1958.

Daniels, Farrington. *Direct Use of the Sun's Energy.* New York: Ballantine paperback, 1974 (orig. 1964).

Daniels, Farrington, ed. *Solar Energy Research.* Madison, Wis.: University of Wisconsin Press, 1955.

Daniels, Jonathan. *Time Between the Wars.* Garden City, N.Y.: Doubleday, 1966.

Davenport, E. H., and S. R. Cooke. *The Oil Trusts and Anglo-American Relations.* London: Macmillan, 1923.

Dean, Edwin B., 'Practicalities of Motel Development," *Urban Land,* Vol. 19, No. 10, Nov. 1960, p. 3.

De Chazeau, Melvin G., and Alfred E. Kahn. *Integration and Competition in the Petroleum Industry.* New Haven, Conn.: Yale University Press, 1959.

Delaisi, Francis. *Oil, Its Influence on Politics.* London: Allen and Unwin, 1922.

The Derrick's Handbook of Petroleum, 1859–1898. Oil City, Pa.: Derrick Publishing Co., 1898.

Destler, C. M. *Roger Sherman and the Independent Oilmen.* Ithaca, N. Y.: Cornell University Press, 1967.

Dickinson, G. Lowes, *A Modern Symposium.* New York: McClure, Phillips, 1905.

Dictionary of American Biography. New York: Scribner's, 1934.

Dolson, Hildegarde. *The Great Oildorado.* New York: Random House, 1959.

Donovan, Frank. *Wheels for a Nation.* New York: Crowell, 1965.

Donovan, William J. Talk before Columbia College *Forum on Democracy,* Feb. 10–12, 1949. Pamphlet (mimeographed).

Dorough, C. Dwight. *Mr. Sam.* New York: Random House, 1962.

Douglas, Paul. *In Our Times.* New York: Harcourt, Brace and World, 1969.

Dugger, Ronnie, "Oil and Politics," *Atlantic,* 224:66–78 (Sept. 1969).

Economic Commission for Europe. *The ECE Region in Figures.* New York: United Nations, 1973.

Editors of *Look. Oil for Victory.* New York: Whittlesey House, 1944.

Ehrlich, Paul and Anne. *The End of Affluence*. New York: Ballantine paperback, 1974.

Eisenhower, Dwight D. *Waging Peace*. Garden City, N.Y.: Doubleday, 1964.

Energy Policy Committee of the Ford Foundation. *A Time to Choose: America's Energy Future*. Cambridge, Mass.: Ballinger Publ., 1974.

Engler, Robert. *The Politics of Oil*. Chicago: University of Chicago, paperback, 1967 (orig. 1961).

Enos, John Lawrence. *Petroleum Progress and Profits: A History of Process Innovation*. Cambridge, Mass.: M.I.T. Press, 1962.

Evans, Rowland, and Robert Novak. *Lyndon B. Johnson, the Exercise of Power*. New York: New American Library, 1966.

Faulkner, H. U. *American Economic History*. Rev. ed. New York: Harper, 1960.

Fehrenbach, T. R. *Lone Star: A History of Texas and the Texans*. New York: Macmillan, 1968.

Feikema, Feike. *The Primitive*. Garden City, N.Y.: Doubleday, 1949.

Feis, Herbert. *Petroleum and American Foreign Policy*. Stanford, Calif.: Food Research Institute, March 1944.

Fisher, F. M., Zvi Griliches, and Carl Kaysen, "The Cost of Automobile Model Changes Since 1949," in *Journal of Political Economy*, 70:433–450.

First National City Bank of New York, Petroleum Dept. "Petroleum in the Eastern Hemisphere. 1959. Pamphlet.

Flannery, M. J., and D. H. Jaffee. *Economic Implications of Electronic Money Transfers*. Lexington, Mass.: Lexington Books, 1973.

Fleming, Harold M. *Gasoline Prices and Competition*. New York: Appleton-Century-Crofts, 1966.

Flink, James J. *America Adopts the Automobile, 1895–1910*. Cambridge, Mass.: M.I.T. Press, 1970.

Flynn, John T. *God's Gold, the Story of Rockefeller and His Times*. New York: Harcourt Brace Jovanovich, 1932.

Fontaine, Pierre. *Le guerre froide du petrole*. Paris: Editions je sers, 1957.

Foraker, Julia. *I Would Live It Again*. New York: Harper, 1932.

Foraste, Paul. "Depletion in the Oil Industry." Master's thesis, New York University, 1943.

Forbes, Gerald, *Flush Production*, Norman, Okla.: University of Oklahoma, 1942.

Forbes, R. J. *Bitumen and Petroleum in Antiquity*. Leiden: E. J. Brill, 1936.

——. "Fifteen Centuries of Bitumen," *Bitumen*, Jan.–June 1937.

Forbis, William H. *Japan Today*. New York: Harper, 1975.

Fosdick, Raymond. *John D. Rockefeller, Jr., a Portrait*. New York: Harper, 1956.

Frankel, Paul H. *The Essentials of Petroleum*. London: Frank Cass, 1961 (orig. 1946).

——. *Mattei, Oil and Power Politics*. London: Faber and Faber, 1966.

Freeman, S. David. *Energy, the New Era*. New York: Vintage paperback, 1974.

Frischauer, Willi. *Onassis*. New York: Meredith Press, 1968.

Gambrell, Herbert. "James Stephen Hogg, Statesman or Demagogue?" *Southwest Review*, XIII.

Gardner, Richard N. *World Food and Energy Crises*. Rensselaerville, N.Y.: Institute on Man and Science, 1974.

Garraty, John. *The American Nation*. New York: Harper, 1966.

Gelfand, Mark I. "A Nation of Cities: the Federal Government's Response to the Challenge of Urban America, 1933–60." Unpublished Ph.D. dissertation, Columbia University, 1972.

Gibb, George S., and Evelyn H. Knowlton. *The Resurgent Years: History of Standard Oil Co. (New Jersey)*, Vol. II. New York: Harper, 1956.

Giddens, Paul H. *Pennsylvania Petroleum 1750–1852*. Titusville, Pa.: Pennsylvania Historical and Museum Commission, 1947.

———. *Standard Oil Company (Indiana), Oil Pioneer of the Middle West*. New York: Appleton-Century-Crofts, 1955.

Glasscock, C. B. *Gasoline Age*. Indianapolis: Bobbs Merrill, 1937.

Goldman, Eric. *The Crucial Decade and After*. New York: Vintage paperback, 1960.

Gordon, Mitchell. *Sick Cities*. New York: Macmillan, 1963.

Gruen, Victor. *The Heart of Our Cities*. New York: Simon and Schuster, 1964.

Hacker, Louis M., and B. B. Hendrick. *The United States Since 1865*. New York: F. S. Crofts, 1932.

Hagedorn, Herman. *Life of Leonard Wood*. New York: Harper, 1931.

Hahn, A. V. *The Petrochemical Industry*. New York: McGraw-Hill, 1970.

Hamilton, Walton. *The Politics of Industry*. New York: Knopf, 1957.

Hammond, Allen L., William D. Metz, and Thomas H. Maugh II. *Energy and the Future*. Washington, D.C.: American Association for the Advancement of Science, 1973.

Harper, Jack, and John Newburn. *Odd Texas*. Dallas: Banks, Upshaw and Co., 1936.

Harter, Harry. *East Texas Oil Parade*. San Antonio: Naylor Co., 1934.

Hawkins, Clark A. *The Field Price Regulation of Natural Gas*. Tallahassee, Fla.: Florida State University Press, 1969.

Hays, Samuel P. *The Response to Industrialism, 1885–1914*. Chicago: University of Chicago Press, 1957.

Hays, Will. *Memoirs of Will Hays*. Garden City, N.Y.: Doubleday, 1955.

Hendrick, Burton. *Age of Big Business* New Haven: Yale University Press, 1919.

Herrmann, Paul. *The Traces of Man*. New York: Harper, 1954.

Hewins, Ralph. *Mr. Five Per Cent*. London: Hutchinson, 1957.

Hicks, John D. *Republican Ascendancy*. New York: Harper, 1960.

Hidy, Ralph W. and Muriel E. *Pioneering in Big Business, History of*

Standard Oil Co. (New Jersey), 1882–1911. New York: Harper, 1956.

Hilton, George W., and J. Due. *The Electric Interurban Railways in America.* Sanford, Calif.: Stanford University Press, 1960.

Hobson, C. K. *Export of Capital.* London: Constable, 1914.

Hobson, J. A. *Imperialism.* London: Allen and Unwin, 1902.

Hoffa, James R. *Trials of Jimmy Hoffa.* Chicago: Regnery, 1970.

Hoffman, E. J. *Overall Efficiencies of Nuclear Power.* Laramie, Wyo.: Natural Resources Institute, University of Wyoming, Dec. 1971.

Hoffman, Paul. *Peace Can Be Won.* Garden City, N.Y.: Doubleday, 1950.

Hofstadter, Richard. *The Age of Reform.* New York: Knopf, 1955.

Hoover, Herbert. *Memoirs, II.* Garden City, N.Y.: Doubleday, 1952.

House, Boyce. *Oil Boom.* Caldwell, Idaho: Caxton, 1941.

——. "Spindletop," *Southwestern Historical Quarterly,* L, 1 (July 1946).

Huitt, Ralph K. "National Regulation of the Gas Industry." In *Public Administration and Policy Formation,* ed. by Emmette S. Record. Austin, Tex.: University of Texas Press, 1956.

Hurewitz, J. C. *Middle East Dilemmas.* New York: Harper, 1953.

Hutchinson, John. *The Imperfect Union.* New York: Dutton, 1970.

Ickes, Harold L. "Address before the American Petroleum Institute." 1934. Pamphlet.

——. *Autobiography of a Curmudgeon.* New York: Reynal and Hitchcock, 1943.

——. *Fightin' Oil.* New York: Knopf, 1943.

——. "An Oil Policy, an Open Letter to Members of Congress." May 30, 1947. Pamphlet.

——. *Secret Diary of Harold Ickes.* 3 vols. New York: Simon and Schuster, 1953.

Illich, Ivan. *Energy and Equity.* New York: Harper Perennial Library paperback, 1974.

Ise, John. *United States Oil Policy.* New Haven: Yale University Press, 1926.

Issawi, Charles, and Mohammed Yeganeh. *Economics of Middle Eastern Oil.* New York: Praeger, 1962.

Jackson, Kenneth T. "The Crabgrass Frontier." In *The Urban Experience,* ed. by R. A. Mohl and J. F. Richardson. Belmont, Cal.: Wadsworth, 1973.

James, Marquis. *The Texaco Story.* New York: written for the Texas Company, 1953.

James, Ralph C. and E. D. *Hoffa and the Teamsters.* Princeton, N.J.: Van Nostrand, 1965.

Jerome, John. *The Death of the Automobile, 1955–70.* New York: Norton, 1972.

Johnson, Arthur Menzies. *Development of American Petroleum Pipe Lines, 1862–1906.* Ithaca, N. Y.: Cornell University Press, 1956.

Johnson, J. K. "Borger, the Natural History of an Oil Boom Town," *Studies in Sociology* (S.M.U.), Vol. 4, Nos. 1–2, 1940.

Jones, C. L. *Service Station Management.* New York: Van Nostrand, 1922.

Jones, Joseph. *Fifteen Weeks.* New York: Viking Harbinger paperback, 1964.

Josephson, Matthew. *The Robber Barons.* New York: Harcourt Brace paperback, 1960 (original 1934).

Kahn, Alfred E. "The Depletion Allowance in the Context of Cartelization," *American Economic Review,* LIV, No. 4, June 1964.

Kalb, Marvin and Bernard. *Kissinger.* Boston: Little, Brown, 1974.

Keats, John. *The Insolent Chariots.* Philadelphia: Lippincott, 1960.

Kennedy, E. D. *The Automobile Industry.* New York: Reynal and Hitchcock, 1941.

Kerr, Robert S. *Land, Wood and Water.* New York: Fleet Publ. Co., 1960.

Kerr, W. S. *John Sherman, His Life and Public Service.* Boston: Sherman, France Co., 1908.

Kilman, Ed, and Theon Wright. *Hugh Roy Cullen.* Englewood Cliffs, N.J.: Prentice-Hall, 1954.

King, Frank. *Gasoline Alley.* Chicago: Reilly and Lee, 1929.

Knowles, Ruth. *The Great Gamblers.* New York: McGraw-Hill, 1959.

Kogan, Herman, and Robert Cromie. *The Great Fire, Chicago 1871.* New York: Putnam, 1971.

Kolko, Gabriel and Joyce. *The Limits of Power.* New York: Harper, 1972.

Kolko, Gabriel, *The Triumph of Conservatism, 1900–1916.* Chicago: Quadrangle paperback, 1967 (orig. 1963).

Kornitzer, Bela. *The Real Nixon, an Intimate Biography.* Chicago: Rand McNally, 1960.

Labatut, Jean, and W. J. Lane, eds. *Highways in our National Life.* Princeton, N.J.: Princeton University Press, 1950.

LaFeber, Walter. *America, Russia and the Cold War.* New York: Wiley, 1966.

LaFollette, Fola and Bella. *Robert M. LaFollette.* New York: Macmillan, 1953.

Lane, Anne W., ed. *The Letters of Franklin K. Lane.* Boston: Houghton Mifflin, 1922.

Larson, Henrietta M., and K. W. Porter. *History of Humble Oil and Refining Co.,* New York: Harper, 1959.

Lasker, Albert. *The Lasker Story as He Told It.* Chicago: Advertising Age, 1953.

——. *Reminiscences of Albert Davis Lasker.* Columbia University Oral History Research Office, n.d.

Leavitt, Helen. *Superhighway-Superhoax.* Garden City, N.Y.: Doubleday, 1970.

Lebkicher, Roy et al. *Aramco Handbook,* Arabian American Oil Co., 1960.

Leeman, Wayne. *The Price of Middle East Oil.* Ithaca, N.Y.: Cornell University Press, 1962.

Leiter, Robert D. *The Teamsters Union.* New York: Bookman Associates, 1957.

Lenin, V. I. *Imperialism.* New York: International Publishers, 1939.

Lester, Francis E. "Road Building in Santa Ana County, N.M." 1914. Pamphlet.

Leuchtenburg, William E. *The Perils of Prosperity, 1914–22.* Chicago: University of Chicago Press, 1958.

Levine, Sigmund A. *Kettering, Inventor.* New York: Dodd, Mead, 1960.

Levy, Walter J. "World Oil Cooperation or International Chaos," *Foreign Affairs,* July 1974.

Lewis, Richard S., and Bernard I. Spinrad, eds. *The Energy Crisis.* Chicago: Bulletin of the Atomic Scientists, 1972.

Lewis, Sinclair. *Babbitt.* New York: Harcourt Brace, 1922.

———. *Main Street.* New York: Signet paperback (orig. 1920).

Lichtblau, John H., and Dillard P. Spriggs. *The Oil Depletion Issue.* New York: Petroleum Industry Research Foundation, 1959.

Lieuwen, Edwin. *Oil in Venezuela.* Berkeley: University of California Press, 1955.

Lincoln Highway Association. *The Lincoln Highway, Story of a Crusade That Made Transportation History.* New York: Dodd, Mead, 1935.

Lingemann, Richard. *Don't You Know There's a War On? 1941–45.* New York: Putnam, 1970.

Link, Arthur S. *American Epoch.* New York: Knopf, 1955.

Liss, Sheldon B. *The Canal.* Notre Dame, Ind.: University of Notre Dame Press, 1967.

Lloyd, Henry Demarest. "The Story of a Great Monopoly," *Atlantic Monthly,* March 1881.

Longrigg, Stephen H. *Oil in the Middle East.* New York: Oxford University Press, 1961.

Lundberg, Ferdinand. *The Rich and the Superrich.* New York: Lyle Stuart, 1968.

Luttwak, Edward N., and Walter Laqueur, "Kissinger and the Yom Kippur War," *Commentary,* Sept. 1974, pp. 33 ff.

Lynd, Robert S. and Helen. *Middletown.* New York: Harcourt Brace, 1929.

McAvoy, Paul W. "The Regulation Induced Shortage of Natural Gas," *Journal of Law and Economics,* 14, No. 1 (April 1971).

McGee, D. A., "Evolution into Total Energy," Address to Newcomen Society, 1971.

McKie, James W. *The Regulation of Natural Gas.* Washington, D.C.: Public Affairs Press, 1957.

McLaurin, John J. *Sketches in Crude Oil.* Harrisburg, Pa.: by the author, 1896.

McLean, Evalyn Walsh. *Father Struck It Rich.* Boston: Little, Brown, 1936.

McLean, John C., and Robert William Haigh. *The Growth of Integrated Oil Companies.* Cambridge, Mass.: Harvard Grad. School of Business Division of Research, 1954.

McReynolds, Edwin C. *Oklahoma, a History of the Sooner State.* Norman, Okla.: University of Oklahoma Press, 1954.

Mallison, Sam. *The Great Wildcatter, Mike Benedum.* Charleston, W. Va.: Education Foundation of West Virginia, 1953.

Mathiesen, Thomas. *The Politics of Abolition.* New York: Wiley, 1974.

Maxim, Hiram. *Horseless Carriage Days.* New York: Harper, 1937.

Maybee, Rolland Harper. *Railroad Competition and the Oil Trade, 1885–1873.* Mount Pleasant, Mich.: The Extension Press, 1940.

Medvin, Norman. *The Energy Cartel.* New York: Vintage paperback, 1974.

Mellon, William Larimer. *Judge Mellon's Sons.* Privately printed, 1948.

Mendelson, H. G. *Gasoline Facts.* Bradford, Pa.: National Tank Auditing Service, 1926.

Miller, John A. *Fares Please!* New York: Appleton-Century, 1941.

Miller, Max. *Speak to the Earth.* New York: Appleton-Century-Crofts, 1955.

Miller, Roger L. *The Economics of Energy.* New York: Morrow, 1974.

Millis, Walter, ed. *The Forrestal Diaries.* New York: Viking, 1951.

Moline, Norman T. *Mobility and the Small Town, 1900–30.* Chicago: University of Chicago Geography Dept. Research Paper No. 132, 1971.

Mollenhoff, Clark R. *Tentacles of Power.* Cleveland: World, 1965.

Mooney, Booth. *Roosevelt and Rayburn.* Philadelphia: Lippincott. 1971.

Moore, Thomas G. "The Petroleum Industry." In *The Structure of American Industry*, 4th ed., ed. by W. G. Adams. New York: Macmillan, 1971.

Morison, S. E., and Henry Steele Commager. *Growth of the American Republic.* New York: Oxford, 1962 (rev.).

Morrison, Robert H. "The Railroad Commission of Texas." Master's Thesis, University of Chicago, 1907.

Mosley, Leonard. *Power Play.* New York: Random House, 1973.

Moynihan, Daniel P. "The War Against the Automobile," *The Public Interest*, No. 3, Spring 1966.

Mumford, Lewis. *The City in History.* New York: Harcourt Brace, 1961.

———. *From the Ground Up.* New York: Harcourt Brace paperback, 1965.

Musham, H. A. "The Great Chicago Fire, Oct. 8–10, 1871," in *Papers in Illinois History and Transactions for the Year 1940*, Springfield, Ill.

Nash, Don E., et al. *Energy Under the Oceans*, Norman, Okla.: University of Oklahoma Press, 1973.

Nash, Gerald D. *United States Oil Policy, 1890–1964.* Pittsburgh: University of Pittsburgh Press, 1968.

National Academy of Sciences. *Report by the Committee on Motor Vehicle Emissions.* Washington, D.C.: N.A.S., Feb. 15, 1973.

National Academy of Sciences Committee on Resources and Man. *Resources and Man. A report.* San Francisco: W. H. Freeman, 1969.

Neuner, Edward J. *The Natural Gas Industry.* Norman, Okla.: University of Oklahoma Press, 1960 .

Neustadt, Richard. *Alliance Politics.* New York: Columbia University Press, 1970.

Nevins, Allan. *A Study in Power: John D. Rockerfeller.* 2 vols. New York: Scribner's, 1953.

——. and Frank Hill. *Ford, the Man, the Times, the Company*. New York: Scribner's, 1954.

——. et al. *Energy and Man, a Symposium*. New York: Appleton-Century-Croft, 1963.

Noggle, Bert. *Teapot Dome*. Baton Rouge, La.: Press of Louisiana State University, 1962.

North, Douglass C., and R. L. Miller. *The Economics of Public Issues*. New York: Harper, 1971.

Novick, Sheldon. *The Careless Atom*. Boston: Houghton Mifflin, 1969.

O'Connor, Harvey. *History of the Oil Workers International Union*. Denver: OWIU-CIO, 1950.

——. *Mellon's Millions*. New York: John Day, 1933.

——. *World Crisis in Oil*. London: Elek Books, 1962.

O'Connor, Richard. *The Oil Barons*. Boston: Little, Brown, 1964.

Odell, Peter. *Oil and World Power, a Geographical Interpretation*. Harmondsworth, Eng.: Penguin, 1970.

Odum, Howard T. "Energy, Ecology and Economics." Stockholm: Royal Swedish Academy of Sciences paper, 1973.

Oil and Gas Journal. *Petroleum Panorama: Centennial Issue, Jan. 29, 1859*. Tulsa, Okla.: Petroleum Publ. Co., 1959.

Oil Workers International Union. "So You're a Member of the OWIU." Denver: OWIU/CIO, 1945. Pamphlet.

O'Keane, Josephine. *Thomas J. Walsh, a Senator from Montana*. Francistown, N.H.: Marshall Jones Co., 1955.

Organization for Economic Cooperation and Development. *Energy Policy, Problems and Objectives*. Paris, 1966.

——. *Energy Prospects to 1985*, 2 vols. Paris: 1974.

Orski, C. K. "The Potential for Fuel Conservation: The Case of the Automobile," in *OECD Observer*, 68:13–18 (Feb. 1974).

Owen, Wilfred. *The Accessible City*. Washington, D.C.: Brookings Institution, 1972.

——. *Strategy for Mobility*. Washington, D.C.: Brookings Institution, 1964.

——. and Ezra Bowen. *Wheels*. New York, Time/Life Books, 1967.

Pearson, Drew, and Jack Anderson. *The Case Against Congress*. New York: Simon and Schuster, 1968.

Pelling, Henry. *History of British Trade Unionism*. London: Macmillan, 1966.

Penrose, Edith. *The Large International Firm in Developing Countries: The International Petroleum Inlustry*. London: Allen and Unwin, 1968.

Perrett, Geoffrey. *Days of Sadness, Years of Triumph*. New York: Coward, McCann and Geoghegan, 1973.

Philby, H. St. John. *Arabian Jubilee*. London: Hale, 1952.

Pierson, George W. "The M-Factor in American History," *American Quarterly*, Summer 1962.

——. *The Moving American*. New York, Knopf, 1973.

Potter, David M. *People of Plenty.* Chicago: University of Chicago Press, 1954.

Rae, John B. *The American Automobile.* Chicago: University of Chicago Press, 1965.

——. *Road and Car in American Life.* Cambridge, Mass.: M.I.T. Press, 1971.

Richardson, Rupert N. *Texas, the Lone Star State.* Englewood Cliffs, N.J.: Prentice-Hall, 1958.

Ridgeway, James. *The Last Play.* New York: Dutton, 1973.

Rister, Carl C. *Oil! Titan of the Southwest.* Norman, Okla.: University of Oklahoma Press, 1949.

Roberts, Glyn. *The Most Powerful Man in the World, the Life of Sir Henri Deterding.* New York: Covici, Friede, 1938.

Rocks, Lawrence, and Richard P. Runyon. *The Energy Crisis.* New York: Crown, 1972.

Rostow, Eugene V. *An Oil Policy for America.* New Haven: Yale University Press, 1948.

Rothschild, Emma. *Paradise Lost, the Decline of the Auto-Industrial Age.* New York: Random House, 1973.

Rukuyser, Muriel. *U.S. 1.* New York: Covici, Friede, 1938.

Russell, Francis. *The Great Interlude.* New York: McGraw-Hill, 1964.

——. *The Shadow of Blooming Grove: Warren G. Harding and His Times.* New York: McGraw-Hill, 1968.

Sasuly, Richard. *IG Farben.* New York: Boni and Gaer, 1947.

Schaffer, Edward A. *Oil Import Program of the United States.* New York: Praeger, 1968.

Schlesinger, Arthur, Jr. *The Crisis of the Old Order.* Boston: Houghton Mifflin, 1957.

Schriftgiesser, Karl. *This Was Normalcy.* Boston: Atlantic/Little, Brown, 1948.

Schurr, Sam, and Bruce Netschert. *Energy in the American Economy, 1850–1975.* Baltimore: Johns Hopkins Press, 1960.

Schurr, Sam, and P. T. Homan. *Middle Eastern Oil and the Modern World.* New York: American Elsevier, 1971.

Schwadran, Benjamin. *Middle East Oil and the Great Powers.* New York: Praeger, 1955.

Sharfman, I. L. *The Interstate Commerce Commission.* 3 vols. New York: Commonwealth Fund, 1931.

Shurcliff, W. A. *Solar Heated Homes, a Brief Survey.* San Diego, Calif.: Solar Energy Digest, 1974.

Sinclair, Andrew. *The Available Man.* New York: Macmillan, 1965.

Sloan, Alfred P. *My Years With General Motors.* Garden City, N.Y.: Doubleday, 1964.

Smith, Arthur D. H. *Men Who Run America.* Indianapolis: Bobbs Merrill, 1936.

Snyder, Louis. *The War, 1939–45*. New York: Julian Messner, 1961.

Spock, Benjamin. *The Common Sense Book of Baby and Child Care*. New York: Duell, Sloan & Pearce, 1957.

Spratt, John S. *The Road to Spindletop*. Austin, Tex.: University of Texas Press, 1955.

Steele, Henry. "Public Policy Problems of the Domestic Crude Oil Industry," *American Economic Review*, LIV (March 1964).

Stegner, Wallace. *Big Rock Candy Mountain*. New York: Hill & Wang, 1969 (orig. 1938).

Steinbeck, John. *The Grapes of Wrath*. New York: Viking, 1939.

Stern, Philip M. *The Great Treasury Raid*. New York: Random House, 1964.

———. *The Rape of the Taxpayer*. New York: Random House, 1973.

Stewart, George. *U.S. 40*. Boston: Houghton, Mifflin, 1953.

Stilwell, Hart. "Texas," in *Our Sovereign States*, edited by Robert Allen. New York: Vanguard, 1949.

Stocking, George W. *Middle East Oil*. Nashville, Tenn.: Vanderbilt University Press, 1970.

———. *The Oil Industry and the Competitive System*. Boston: Houghton, Mifflin, 1925.

Stratton, David H. "Behind Teapot Dome: Some Personal Insights," *Business History Review*, 31, Winter 1957.

Strunsky, Simeon. *The Living Tradition*. New York: Doubleday Doran, 1939.

Sullivan, Mark. *Our Times*. New York: Scribner, 1935.

Symonds, Edward. "Eastern Hemisphere Petroleum." New York: First National City Bank, 1963. Pamphlet.

———. "Oil Advances in the Eastern Hemisphere." New York: First National City Bank, 1962. Pamphlet.

———. *Oil in the National Balance*. New York: First National City Bank, 1965. Pamphlet.

Tait, Samuel W., Jr. *The Wildcatters*. Princeton, N.J.: Princeton University Press, 1946.

Tanzer, Michael. *The Political Economy of International Oil and the Underdeveloped Countries*. Boston: Beacon, 1969.

Tarbell, Ida M. *History of the Standard Oil Company*. New York: McClure, Phillips and Co., 1904.

Texas Corp. "Report of Stockholders Investigating Committee." Jan. 25, 1934. Pamphlet.

Texas Midcontinent Oil and Gas Association. "Seventy-four Facts About Texas Oil and Gas." Dallas: TMOGA, 1974. Pamphlet.

Theobald, P. K., S. P. Schweinfurth, and D. C. Duncan. *Energy Resources of the U.S.*, U.S. Geological Survey Circular 650, Washington, D.C.: 1972.

Thistlethwaite, Frank. *The Great Experiment*. Cambridge, Eng.: Cambridge University Press, 1955.

Thomas, Hugh. *Suez*. New York: Harper, 1966.

Thompson, Craig. *Since Spindletop*. Pittsburgh: Gulf Oil, 1951.

Thorelli, Hans B. *The Federal Antitrust Policy*. Baltimore: John Hopkins Press, 1955.

Tinkle, Lon. *Mr. DE, a Biography of E. L. De Golyer*. Boston: Little, Brown, 1970.

Train, Calvin J. *The Inside Facts About Trading Stamps*. Annandale, Va.: J and J Publ. Co., Nov. 1964.

Troxel, C. Emory. "Regulation of Interstate Movements of Natural Gas," *Journal of Law and Public Utility Economics*, XII, Feb. 1937.

Tucker, Robert W. "Oil: the Issue of American Intervention," *Commentary*, Jan. 1975, pp. 21–23.

Tugendhat, Christopher. *Oil, the Biggest Business*. New York: Putnam, 1968.

Tugendhat, George. "An Outsider's View of the Oil Industry," *Institute of Petroleum Review*, Feb. 1967.

United Nations. *Growth of World Industry, 1938–61*. New York, 1963.

Vicker, Ray. *Kingdom of Oil, the Middle East*. New York: Scribner's, 1974.

Wall, Bennett H., and G. S. Gibb. *Teagle of Jersey Standard*. New Orleans: Tulane University, 1974.

Walters, Everett. *J. B. Foraker*. Columbus, Ohio: State Archaeological and Historical Society, 1948.

Warner, C. A. "Texas the Oil Industry," *Southwestern Quarterly*, July 1946.

Warner, Sam Bass. *The Urban Wilderness*. New York: Harper, 1972.

Waugh, Coulton. *The Comics*. New York: Macmillan, 1947.

Webb, Walter P., ed. *Handbook of Texas*. Austin, Tex.: Texas Historical Association, 1952.

Wecter, Dixon. *The Hero in America*. New York: Scribner's, 1941.

Welty, Earl M., and Frank J. Taylor. *The Black Bonanza*. New York: McGraw-Hill, 1950.

Wendland, Ray T. *Petrochemicals*. Garden City, N.Y.: Doubleday, 1969.

Werner, M. R. *Privileged Characters*. New York: McBride, 1935.

———. and John Starr. *Teapot Dome*. New York: Viking, 1959.

Werth, Alexander. *France, 1940–55*. New York: Holt, 1956.

Wheeler, Burton K. *Yankee from the West*. Garden City, N.Y.: Doubleday, 1962.

White, E. B. *The Second Tree from the Corner*. New York: Harper, 1936.

White, Gerald T. *Formative Years in the Far West: A History of Standard Oil Company of California and Predecessors Through 1919*. New York: Appleton-Century-Crofts, 1962.

White, Lawrence. *The Automobile Industry Since 1945*. Cambridge, Mass.: Harvard University Press, 1971.

White, William Allen. *The Autobiography of William Allen White*. New York: Macmillan, 1946.

———. *Masks in a Pageant*. New York: Macmillan, 1928.

———. *Puritan in Babylon*. New York: Macmillan, 1938.

Widick, B. J. *Labor Today*. Boston: Houghton, Mifflin, 1964.

Wilder, Thornton. *Heaven's My Destination.* London: Longmans, 1934.

Williamson, Harold F., and Arnold E. Daum. *The American Petroleum Industry: The Age of Illumination, 1855–99.* Evanston, Ill.: Northwestern University Press, 1959.

Williamson, Harold F., R. L. Andreano, A. E. Daum, and G. C. Klose. *The American Petroleum Industry: The Age of Energy, 1899–1959.* Evanston, Ill.: Northwestern University Press, 1963.

Wilson, Kemmons. "The Holiday Inn Story." Memphis, Tenn.: Holiday Inns, 1972. Pamphlet.

Wilson, Robert E. "Pioneers in Oil Cracking." Address to Newcomen Society, Oct. 20, 1946.

Wise, David, and Thomas B. Ross. *The Invisible Government.* New York: Random House, 1954.

Wolfe, Tom. *The Kandy Kolored Tangerine Flake Streamline Baby.* New York: Farrar, Straus, 1965.

Woodward, C. Vann. *Origins of the New South.* Baton Rouge, La.: Louisiana State University Press, 1951.

Young, Rosamund. *Boss Ket.* New York: David McKay, 1961.

Young, Valton J. *The Speaker's Agent.* New York: Vantage, 1956.

SERIAL PUBLICATIONS
Air Conditioning, Heating and Ventilating
American Economic Review
American City
American Historical Review
American Mercury
American Quarterly
American Speech
Annals of the American Academy of Political and Social Sciences
Army Quarterly
Association for Arts Bulletin
Atlantic
Automobile
Automobile Facts and Figures
Baltimore Sun
Better Homes and Gardens
Bitumen
British Petroleum Statistical Review of the World Oil Industry
Business History Review
Business Week
California Historical Society Quarterly
Chicago Sun-Times
Christian Century
Christian Science Monitor
Collier's
Commentary

Commonweal
Congressional Digest
Consumers Union Reports
Current Biography
Current History
Encyclopedia Americana Annual
Encyclopedia Britannica Annual
Energy Memo, Petroleum Dept., National City Bank of New York
Engineering Bulletin (Purdue University)
Environment
Esquire
Facts on File
Foreign Policy
Foreign Affairs
Fortune
Forum
Gas Facts
Gas Heat
Geographic Magazine (London)
Geothermics
Harvard Law Review
Horseless Age
International Journal, Canadian Institute of International Affairs
International Monetary Fund, Annual Reports
International Oil Worker
International Petroleum Encyclopedia
Journal of Law and Economics
Journal of the American Society of Engineering Contractors
Journal of Law and Public Utility Economics
Journal of Popular Culture
Lamp, The
Law and Contemporary Problems
Life
Literary Digest
Los Angeles Times
Mississippi Valley Historical Review
Monthly Business Review, the Conference Board
Montana Magazine of History
Motor
Motor Age
Motor World
Nation
National Geographic
National Observer
National Petroleum News
Natural History

Nature
New Republic
New Scientist
New York
New York Daily News
New York Herald Tribune
New York Post
New York Review
New York Times, The
New York University Law Review
New York World Telegram
New Scientist
New Yorker
Newsweek
Nilson Report
Ohio State Archeological and Historical Quarterly
OECD Observer (Paris)
OEEC General Statistical Bulletin (Paris)
OEEC General Statistics (Paris)
Oil, Paint and Drug Reporter
Oil and Gas Journal
Outlook
Papers in Illinois History and Transactions for the Year
Parents Magazine
Peking Review
People and Taxes
Petroleum Gazette
Philadelphia Inquirer
PM
Proceedings, National Conventions of the Oil Workers International Union
Population Bulletin
Progressive
Public Affairs Information Service
Public Interest
Ramparts
Reader's Digest
Reporter, The
Resources
St. Louis Post Dispatch
Saturday Evening Post
Science
Scientific American
Sierra Club Bulletin
Sohioan
Southwest Review
Southwestern Historical Quarterly

Standard Oil of California Bulletin
Studies in Sociology (S.M.U.)
Technology Review
Texas Business Review
Time
Trip
Truth
United States News
Urban Land
Vital Speeches
Wall Street Journal
Washington Monthly
Washington Post
Washington Star
Woman's Home Companion
Yale Review

Index